11/06

HOLOCAUST IN THE UKRAINE

D1028397

The Library of Holocaust Testimonies

Editors: Antony Polonsky, Martin Gilbert CBE, Aubrey Newman,
Raphael F. Scharf, Ben Helfgott MBE

Under the auspices of the Yad Vashem Committee of the Board of
Deputies of British Jews and the Centre for Holocaust Studies,
University of Leicester

HOLOCAUST IN THE UKRAINE

Editor
BORIS ZABARKO

Translator
MARINA GUBA

VALLENTINE MITCHELL
LONDON • PORTLAND, OR

First published in 2005 in Great Britain by
VALLENTINE MITCHELL & CO. LTD
Premier House, Suite 314
112–114 Station Road, Edgware, Middlesex HA8 7BJ

and in the United States of America by
VALLENTINE MITCHELL
c/o ISBS, 920 NE 58th Avenue, Suite 300,
Portland, OR 97213-3786

Website http://www.vmbooks.com

British Library Cataloguing in Publication Data:

A catalogue record for this book is available
from the British Library

ISBN 0 85303 612 8 (cloth)
ISBN 0 85303 524 5 (paper)

Library of Congress Cataloguing in Publication Data:

A catalog record for this book is available
from the Library of Congress

Printed in Great Britain by
CPI Bath

Contents

Contents   vii

Acknowledgement

The publication of this book was made possible by a donation from the Gotlieb family and the Yad Vashem UK Foundation in memory of Bella Seivenfeld.

The Library of Holocaust Testimonies

It is greatly to the credit of Frank Cass that this series of survivors' testimonies is being published in Britain. The need for such a series has been long apparent in a country where many survivors made their homes.

Since the end of the war in 1945 the terrible events of the Nazi destruction of European Jewry have cast a pall over our time. Six million Jews were murdered within a short period; the few survivors have had to carry in their memories whatever remains of the knowledge of Jewish life in more than a dozen countries, in several thousand towns, in tens of thousands of villages, and in innumerable families. The precious gift of recollection has been the sole memorial for millions of people whose lives were suddenly and brutally cut off.

For many years, individual survivors have published their testimonies. But many more have been reluctant to do so, often because they could not believe that they would find a publisher for their efforts.

In my own work over the past two decades I have been approached by many survivors who had set down their memories in writing, but who did not know how to have them published. I also realized, as I read many dozens of such accounts, how important each account was, in its own way, in recounting aspects of the story that had not been told before, and adding to our understanding of the wide range of human suffering, struggle and aspiration.

With so many people and so many places involved, including many hundreds of camps, it was inevitable that the historians and students of the Holocaust should find it difficult at times to grasp the scale and range of events. The publication of memiors is therefore an indispensable part of the extension of knowledge, and of public awareness of the crimes that were committed against a whole people.

Sir Martin Gilbert
Merton College, Oxford

Introduction

The Book of Memories of the Holocaust survivors was published in 1999 when the Ukraine marked the fifty-fifth anniversary of its liberation from the Nazi invaders.[1] For the Jewish people the liberation, followed by the victory over Fascism, meant deliverance from total annihilation. However, the reality of those days determined not only scenes of rejoicing and triumph. What the soldiers entering the occupied territories of the Ukraine and the ghettos, witnessed was beyond any human comprehension.

Vassily Grossman, the writer, influenced by everything he had seen, wrote in his essay 'Ukraine with no Jews':

> There are no Jews left in Ukraine ... Silence ... Stillness ... The people murderously killed ... Everyone is killed, many hundreds of thousands – a million Jews in Ukraine. This is not a death at war, when armed and fighting ... This is a murder of people, a murder of the home, family, book, and faith ... This is the annihilation of the nation that had been a neighbour to the Ukrainians for hundreds of years, sharing work, joy and sadness on one land. In every place, big or small, in every little town there was murder and mayhem. Where there were a hundred Jews in a city, all hundred were killed, and not a single one left; when there were 55,000 in a big city, then all 55,000 were killed and not a single one was missed. The registers of death had all Jews met by Germans in Ukraine listed.[2]

What the Nazis, along with their collaborators, did to 1.5 million Jews in the Ukraine and 4.5 million Jews in Germany, Austria, France, Holland, Poland, Hungary, Romania, Yugoslavia, Czechoslovakia, Belgium, Norway, Denmark, Lithuania, Estonia, Latvia, Byelorussia and Russia was called the Holocaust. There had never been another tragedy equal in scope to the Holocaust in the history of mankind. One cannot overestimate the tragic consequences of it to world Jewry. Its demographic and cultural centre in Central and Eastern Europe was destroyed, taken off the face of the planet – numerous families and communities, most renowned centres for Jewish culture and education, a complete society with a specific colourful way of life. Everything was gone, and

the process of the numerical and psychological recovery of world
Jewry had not yet begun. This was the ruin of Jewish civilization
and a tragedy for humanity.

The fate of all captured European nations was horrendous, but
with the monstrous consequences of the Jewish Holocaust it pales in
comparision: the Jewish nation was doomed to vanish. Elie Wiesel,
the writer and Nobel Prize winner, described this tragic situation as
follows: 'Not all of the Nazi victims were Jews, but all Jews were the
Nazi victims.'[3] And this is the fundamental difference between the
Holocaust victims and the victims of a military conflict. It is not the
human suffering that differs but the murderous intentions. The
Holocaust was a directed and intentional destruction of European
Jewry, part of Germany's political policy, with the ultimate goal of
completely relieving the world from Jews. Its objective was not a
change in, or even assimilation of, the Jewish people, as it was once
put forward by naïve dreamers of the Enlightenment era, but its
complete and final annihilation.

As Mikhail Gefter – a well-known Russian thinker, historian and
philosopher, and the President of the Holocaust Research and
Academic Center – wrote:

> *Endlosung*: the Final Solution. It was the final solution for Jews
> by the crossing out of all the living; it was the final solution for
> the Germans by making the 'master race' eternal; it was the
> final solution for the world by turning other nations into a
> hierarchy of outcasts … And finally, the Holocaust is present
> everywhere. It is found in the burning of all and everything, a
> crematorium for the living, a pagan sacrificial ritual, the return
> of a New European civilization from the edge of losing itself,
> the breaking of its imperative progress; the ashes reminding
> people of their indestructible 'beginning' and their quite realistic
> End (in the near future). Generally speaking it is a spiritual
> experience, which is directly and indirectly present in all issues
> that the world is currently concerned with.[4]

This is why the Holocaust is more than just a component of European
history: it is a world history phenomenon. Many scholars, represent-
ing various schools and movements, have tried to rethink this
phenomenon and place it in some causal-investigatory and logical
context. They were told to erase the uniqueness of the catastrophe in
order to locate it within the normal course of human history, as noted
by Jean Marie Cardinal Lustiger, Archbishop of Paris during an international symposium, 'The Silence of God During the Shoah' (Tel-Aviv,
1995). Without this it is impossible to relate rationally to the events of

the past. But all these attempts have suffered from extreme contradictions and they have been very immature, even as regards their methodology.

Although Holocaust issues have been covered in hundreds and thousands of research topics, documentary works and memoirs published worldwide – as well as international research conferences and symposia and dozens of anti-Fascist movies – it is enough to mention just a few, such as *The Night in Fog* (France), *This Could Have Happened to Us* (the UK), *Mein Kampf* and *The Life of Adolf Hitler* (Germany), *The Nuremberg Trial* and *Schindler's List* (USA), *Korczak* (Poland). There have also been major documentaries, such as *The Shoah* by Claude Lanzmann, *The Common Fascism* by Michael Romm, and many more. And yet, for many of us, the word 'Holocaust' had been unknown until recently and the phenomenon remains in many aspects unknown even today. It can be barely explained and it does not fall within the framework of human perceptions.

For a very long time, the tragedy of the Jews during the Second World War was a forbidden topic, not only in the USSR, countries in the socialist bloc or the two Germanys (much has been recently published about it), but even in the USA and the UK. I do not even mention France, with its 'Vichy Complex' still being problematical. I would like to remind readers that it was only in 1995 – fifty-three years after the Parisian Jews were deported to Germany – that Jacques Chirac, President of France, publicly and finally said what his predecessor could not. Having admitted that it is difficult to return to old times that have been a disgrace to the history of his country, the President found courage to admit that the:

criminal insanity of the aggressor was backed by French citizens and French state … France, a country of the Public Agreement [Chirac is referring to the famous treatise by Jean Jacques Rousseau], and in historically being a shelter to many dissidents, this time made an incorrigible mistake: it gave its own citizens into the hands of their killers.

To be fair, we would like to note that notwithstanding the complete mutual understanding between Hitler and Pétain with reference to the 'Final Solution', three-quarters of French Jews survived only as a result of the support of the best people in the country.

The Germans were not alone in taking part in Jewish genocide: there were also the Austrians, Hungarians, French, Belgians, Poles, Greeks, Croatians, Romanians, Czechs, Russians, Ukrainians, Byelorussian, Lithuanians, Estonians, Latvians …

The governments of the anti-Hitler coalition were aware of what was going on in the occupied territories. The US Immigration Service denied immigration permits to many thousands of European Jews although they knew well about the unimaginable discrimination practised against the Jews by the Nazis. Swiss banks received huge profits as a result of the murder of Jews, and the Vatican helped the fascists in hiding looted gold.

The non-Jewish world has avoided the topic of the Holocaust for a long time, due to its terror of facing it, and also because this topic implies guilt – real or imaginary – for what happened. (This was noted back in 1968 by Emil Fackenheim, a well-known Jewish theologian, in his book *On Christianity After the Holocaust*.)

Many indisputable facts prove the words of Eli Wiesel concerning the Allies who 'condemned Jews to death well in advance'. The Church was silent when its position should have been stated aloud. A legendary quotation from a sermon by Martin Niemoeller, a German Lutheran pastor, is still relevant today:

> First they came for the Communists, but I was not a Communist so I did not speak out. Then they came for the Socialists and the Trade Unionists, but I was neither, so I did not speak out. Then they came for the Jews, but I was not a Jew, so I did not speak out. And when they came for me, there was no one left to speak out for me.[5]

During the Second World War two fighting parties, as well as the Church, did practically nothing to save Jews from total annihilation. Calming down the world public, Winston Churchill wrote in an article published on 14 November 1941 in the *Jewish Chronicle*: 'nobody is more suffering in this war than Jews. I am confident that when the day of Victory comes, the suffering of Jewish people and its role in the fight against Fascism will not be forgotten.' But six million Jews burned in the flame of the Holocaust, having not lived long enough to witness the victory of the Allies over Nazi Germany.

Historical responsibility is a paradoxical thing. Those who accept it are relieved from it, by this fact alone. Those who do not accept it do not feel it and deny it, become accomplices. And if nobody takes the responsibility for the crime, it keeps repeating itself.

The tragedy of the *Shoah* (and the atrocities seen by soldiers during the liberation of Auschwitz and other death camps) caused a real shock throughout the West, as well as much confusion, but a few years later these were lost in the shadow of the Cold War and the ideological struggle between East and West.

In the last three decades of the twentieth century, the topic of the Nazi crimes and atrocities, as well as the responsibility of representatives from other nations for what had happened, was again drawn from the archives. Perhaps, as the researchers note, this was the result of the activities of the Jewish Center of Documents of the Union of Jews Persecuted by the Nazis, headed by Simon Wiesenthal, as well as the Yad Vashem Holocaust and Resistance Memorial Museum and the International Institute for Research into Issues of the Genocide, among others. Over the course of recent years, the issue of the Holocaust has been transformed into one of the major topics of Western historiography, and a focus for extensive discussions throughout the world.

The International Conference on the Holocaust, which took place in Stockholm in January 2000, became the cornerstone event that confirmed the place of the Jewish catastrophe in the collective memory of the people of the world.

But even in the most fundamental research of Western scholars, the Holocaust in the occupied territories of the Ukraine, Byelorussia, Russia and other former Soviet republics, has not been designated as a separate sub-topic. Analysing their works on the German occupation of the Ukraine, Dieter Paul, a German historian, noted that although Jews were the major victims of the Nazi occupiers and that an extensive literature has been dedicated to their terrible fate, 'the history of the Holocaust in Ukraine has not been written as yet ... The description of the events of those years is still very episodic. And even the mass slaughter of civilians in Babi Yar has not been described in detail yet.'[6]

When it comes to the study of the Holocaust in the USSR, this topic was not of any research interest until recently. It was silenced by all possible means, and not a single textbook, nor the single multi-volume edition of the history of the USSR and Ukraine, which covers both original research mentioned and documentary collections, mentions the catastrophe suffered by Soviet Jews who unwillingly found themselves in the territories occupied by the Germans.

The science of history and historiography was used for the purposes of the continuous process of oblivion rather than preservation of the memory. Yevgeny Yevtushenko wrote, 'Babi Yar was a crime of Fascism. But our silence of many years about somebody else's crime has become a crime in itself. Concealment becomes murder as well, the murder of memory.'[7]

At the presentation of the three-volume *Holocaust Encyclopaedia*, prepared by scholars from the USA, Germany, and Israel, which took place in Vienna, I asked one of the editors, Professor Julian Schoeps, 'Why is there so little material in the *Encyclopaedia* covering the *Shoah* of the Ukrainian Jewry in the years of the war?'

'But you've written so little or almost nothing about it,' he said, and I couldn't help but agree with his answer. And the reason was not only the inaccessible archives. The anti-Semitism of the Soviet period served for a long time as an obstacle to understanding the Holocaust.

There were the testimonies and memoirs of those who survived the catastrophe in ghettos, labour and death camps, of those who fought in partisan detachments, and of those who survived using other names and documents, as well as of those who saved the survivors from death, and of those who saw it all, lived through this and knew all the truth about the horrible years of the occupation and genocide. We were even able to read *The Black Book*, prepared by such editors as Vassily Grossman and Ilya Erenburg in Russian or Ukrainian almost half a century after its first pages were written.[8]

And only in recent years – with an irreparably big delay – we joined in a third noble and humanistic work for commemorating the testimonies of these people. It has been the work of enthusiasts at foundations established in Kiev: 'In Memory of the Nazi Victims in the Ukraine' and 'In Memory of Babi Yar', the Kharkov Regional Historical and Memorial Research Centre 'Drobitzky Yar', the International Memorial Foundation 'Yanovsky Camp' (Lvov), and the All-Ukrainian Association of Jewish Former Prisoners of Ghettos and Camps. It is also the work of organizations, societies and unions of Jewish provenance, including former prisoners of the Nazis in Kharkov, Chernovtsy, Odessa, Kirovograd, Dniepropetrovsk, Poltava, Mogilev-Podolsky, Slavuta and many other cities and towns. The geographical spread of the places grows with every year. Together with Israeli and American researchers we have collected unique testimonies and memoirs from Jews and non-Jews, participants and witnesses of those unforgettable tragic and heroic events.

The importance and value of the collected materials have been growing with every passing year. Soon we will not have an opportunity to communicate with living witnesses of those times, whose knowledge can help us fill the gaps that still exist in our recent history.

Their recollections (in a situation when contemporary documents are not available and many archives related to the Holocaust are still closed) are an indispensable source of information. Until recently the major argument supporting the fact of the Holocaust was based mostly on the testimonies and recollections of the surviving victims. The discussions in research and social circles evolved around them; they became objects of political speculation by nationalist and anti-Semitic groups.

Those who try to deny the fact of the Holocaust (they call themselves 'revisionists', a traditional academic term, although this remains a self-designation only), do not accept, indeed categorically deny, the victims' testimonies. Thus David Cole, the most well-known and uncompromising American 'revisionist', says that we cannot trust the memory of the old witnesses and it is very difficult to separate recollections from imaginative fiction, and especially fiction continuously repeated by people over time, one after another. He explained his ideas as follows:

> Until the 1970s, the Auschwitz survivors were unanimous in saying, for example, that the gas chambers in Birkenau were masked with big birch trees that surrounded these hideous buildings. But recently declassified photographs taken from the air in those days show that there were no birch trees at all. Everything was clear and open. It means that witnesses lied. And now the very same people keep saying that everything was open, and blame Americans and British fighters who had not bombed the chambers since they were clearly visible. How can it be possible to believe them?

He also says that the fact that Ivan Demyanyuk was found not guilty by the Israeli Supreme Court is another proof that the testimonies of the witnesses cannot be regarded as reliable on this issue.

Indeed, the human memory is an imperfect instrument: it voluntarily keeps some facts, events and episodes while missing others – which are sometimes just as important. In this collection we have included recollections of different people who today live far one from another, but who during the war were at the very same place. And we have tried to show how each of them tells his or her story differently. The actual facts, as a rule, are not distorted, although whole details, logic of events, emphasis and numerical data differ. And this, among all other factors, depends on the personality of a witness, their upbringing, their system of values, intellect, education, background, etc.

There is yet another peculiarity of the witness testimonies. This is the inclination of the narrator to look at the past through the eyes of the present, and to depict the events in the past not exactly the way they actually were at that moment in time but through their current perception, over half a century later. The current (unfortunately delayed-in-time) witnesses offer more than a simple look back in time, but they provide a contemporary view, and this may offer a strikingly deep and unexpectedly penetrating look into the complexity of relations between historical events and the present day.

Not all testimonies are exact, some are vague, and everything that has resurfaced in the memory may be presented with the veil of imagination drawn unconsciously over the facts. Myths and stereotypes that have dominated society for a long while also surface. The witnesses have lived through so much suffering and horror (loss of family and friends, killings, starvation, cold, diseases and continuous fear, which is not over even today), through so much inhumanity, shock and spiritual agony, that this could not but affect their emotions. Sometimes these emotions overshadow the truth, which in any instance is very subjective, and we cannot exclude the chance of subconscious distortions of the truth that are as harmful as conscious lies. All these circumstances cannot be excluded when discussing this issue with those who try to deny the Holocaust. And although personal recollections are not a history, and the true history and current understanding emerged only much later, it is impossible to understand the past and present in full and precise detail without them.

The objective of this book is not to relate historical facts and data (they are reflected in extensive scholarly research – see Bibliography), but to relate a story of the inhumane experiencies of people who were destined to die but managed to win through. 'I will not die, but will live,' as it is written in a psalm; this has become Man's answer in the face of death. A man and the catastrophe are the focal points of the book, as well as the intersection of life and death, good and evil, sin and guilt, cowardice and courage, hatred and mutual assistance, meanness and forgiveness, disappointment and faith, despair and hope, treachery and self-sacrifice, suffering and the decision to survive against all odds, crime and punishment, murderers and victims, the indifferent and the righteous.

The idea of preparing a book of recollections of the former prisoners from concentration camps and ghettos appeared after my participation in a project of collecting audio and video testimonies from Holocaust survivors in the Ukraine, organized in 1994 by the Documentation Center of Yale University. The project was carried out in collaboration with the Holocaust Memorial Museum in Washington, DC, and Israeli Beit Lohamei haGhettaot (the Ghetto Fighters' House). It was embarrassing and shameful that the witness testimonies of our compatriots who survived the Holocaust were collected and published not by us, its participants and witnesses, and not our scholars, but by foreigners. But we thank them all for the chance to save and preserve at least a portion of the collective memory of our people! It is shameful that our country does not have any national memorial, a museum of the Holocaust. There is not even a Babi Yar Museum in Kiev, although similar museums have been established in numerous countries of the world. The major research centres in this country are not actively interested in this topic, even though we still have the largest accumulations of archive documents, and at the sites of tragedies there are still a lot of eyewitnesses and survivors of those tragic events: instead, the research takes place in Israel, the USA, Germany and other countries. This book is the result of years of work. The majority of recollections published here show some of the typical characteristics of the Holocaust of Ukrainian Jewry, which, together with Dr Pinchas Agmon, the Director of the Russian Department of the Beit Lohamei haGhettaot, we have tried to establish. The article entitled 'The Trial by the Holocaust' was published in the *Chadashot* newspaper, and includes the following:

> All witnesses and survivors remember clearly and in detail the day of the German invasion and all share a similar view: the attack of Nazi Germany on the USSR was a shock to them, albeit the Seond World War had already lasted for two years in Europe. The fast advances of the Nazi troops and the falling apart of the Red Army efforts resulted in panic and mass fleeing. Attempts to evacuate were undertaken in those territories that were more distant from the front, and included evacuation of civilians and industrial enterprises into the internal areas of the USSR. And many Jews were able to become included in this mass evacuation. There are no exact data on the migration of population and that is why the number of Jews who were saved due to leaving the area is not established.[9]

The Jews faced a dilemma due to the fast invasion of the Germans: whether to abandon all they owned and leave, or to take a chance and stay behind. The majority of witnesses speak about these doubts. The news of the violent suppression of the Jewish revolt in Polish ghettos had not been published in the media because of the Molotov–Ribbentrop Pact. The news of Jewish suffering in Poland was spread only by the refugees who had come to the regions of the liberated Western Ukraine and kept moving on towards the inner regions of the the Ukraine. Jews of the older generation relied on their recollections of the German occupation of Ukraine in 1918, saying that the Germans were a cultured and educated nation, and that they wouldn't hurt Jews. Another argument for staying behind was the desire to preserve the integrity of families. This was why the major part of the Jewish population did not even try to get evacuated. Those witnesses who tried to flee described how they were caught off-guard by the German army as it advanced. They all were forced to return to their places of residence.

Because of the sudden Nazi aggression, the Soviet authorities announced immediate total mobilization of all men. As a result women, old people and children were the sole representatives of most families. Later on, the Germans captured most of the men who had been mobilized. The Nazi policy of selecting Jews from among the prisoners of war and isolating them resulted in many of them trying to escape while hiding their ethnic background by all possible means. In the atmosphere of complete chaos reigning in those days, many indeed managed to escape from imprisonment. The majority of them returned to their families but then, under the threat of being caught and put into the ghettos that the German authorities had begun establishing throughout the area, many of them went into hiding in the forests in hope of joining partisan detachments. Many of them had to hide their true Jewish identity, since Jews were not accepted in every partisan unit.

It is common historical knowledge that the period preceding the 'Final Solution of the Jewish Question' included systematic mass killings of the Jewish population by the special killing squads of the German army carried out in the occupied territories of the USSR. 'Murder' as an abstract term simplifies a wide range of experiences of different people. But each of the survivors who provided us with their testimonies had his or her own detailed definition of the act. From their point of view, the acts of murder is a unique and very personal event in the life of each of them. Many witnesses described various cases of death based on their own experience and information that they had received from people around them. For example, in Zhitomir, where mass murders began earlier than in other places (because the town was very close to the border), we heard a story from witnesses of how the victims would dig trenches in the forest clearing out of the town. They would be killed there and their bodies thrown into the trenches. Only a few people survived this slaughter. A witness, who was thirteen years old, described in detail their walk towards the execution point along the streets filled with people, in the daytime; as well as the killing of all her family before her eyes. Later she described her escape into her parents' empty house, her life with Ukrainian neighbours who were hiding her, and then much suffering until she achieved liberation. All these horrific details add visible and sensible shape to the words 'mass murder'.

This model of mass murder in Zhitomir was then replicated in towns and villages in which the numbers of the Jewish population had been traditionally very high: Berdychev, Vinnitsa, Kamenka in the Cherkassy oblast, and many other towns, cities and villages in the Ukraine.

Introduction

We recorded a testimony from an accidental visitor to the place of a former concentration camp in Pechera who, without any preliminary preparation, standing in front of the video camera, choking on tears, described all he lived through. He told us about the killing of his whole family in the town of Litichev, and the night when, as a thirteen-year-old boy, wounded, he crawled out of the trenches, from under the dead bodies.

The situation in Babi Yar, when all Jews of the city were summoned for 'deportation' to another place of residence, when in fact they were being taken to the place of their mass execution, was repeated in Kharkov. There, the Jews were ordered to gather in large wooden barracks at the edge of the city, halfway towards the trenches where they would be killed in Drobitzky Yar. In Kharkov we heard a detailed story from witnesses about how the exhaust gases were used in special gas vans for mass killings.

The Romanian authorities in Transnistria selected another method of mass murder for the Jews of Tulchin. They were ordered to leave their houses and the entire group of old people, women and children was marched in the cold across a swampy area for a couple of days until they and Pechera reached the place later called 'the death camp'. There were no mass killings here but a lot of people died *en route* from cold, hunger and disease.

In all testimonies local residents are mentioned as participants in pogroms, robbing, abusing, and killing Jews under the supervision of the Nazis. In smaller towns victims knew the names of their murderers well, as they were frequently their neighbours. But only a few witnesses agreed to name them. In one exceptional case, a survivor from Zhitomir gave the names of all the killers and told us that she had submitted an official plea to the officials who investigate cases of military criminals and their collaborators. The desire for vengeance for all the humiliation and the death of her family overcame all her fears and, recognizing the risk she was taking, she testified against ten criminals, some of whom were sentenced to death. In order to protect her, local authorities allocated armed guards.

Each testimony included a description of a ghetto, but in every place it had a different 'colouring' depending on local conditions. In any case, the Ukrainian Jewish definition of 'ghetto' has nothing in common with that of Polish Jews. Based on the witnesses' words, the ghetto was any place in which the Germans concentrated Jews in order to decide on their fate later. Streets of towns were named to show where Jews were sent to be killed, and the others sent to slave labour. (Professionals and workers were more fortunate: the Germans needed them, and their liquidation was postponed for some time.) The barracks on the edge of

Kharkov – from where the Jews were taken to Drobitzky Yar to be killed – was also called 'ghetto' by witnesses.

A difference in the understanding of the word 'ghetto' by Ukrainian and Polish Jews originated first of all from the policy of annihilation of Jews by the Nazi occupiers. In the Ukraine, starting with the first days of the occupation, the Nazis immediately began intensive shootings of Jews. A place in which to concentrate the Jewish population, called the ghetto, was in fact only a temporary form of imprisonment before their final liquidation, which was progressing rapidly. That was why the authorities did not see any necessity to create authorities to run this population such as *Judenräte*[10] or Jewish police, and there were no conditions for setting up a Jewish autonomy among others, as in the Polish ghetto. Another fact was that the role of the Jewish community in Jewish life in the Ukraine as it was in Poland had been destroyed and disappeared before the war, during the Soviet rule, whereas it was still important in Poland. As a result, under the circumstances of the Holocaust in the Ukraine, being a part of the community had no significant meaning and each family had to face its fate on its own.

One of the most common ways to survive was to travel around and hide one's identity. Many witnesses and survivors told us the story of their wanderings throughout the Ukraine, hiding in forests, stables and dairy farms, and asking farmers to let them spend the night indoors during the coldest months. All these stories and lives were different and yet at the same time had many similarities. The testimonies showed that there were many farmers who showed compassion towards the people who roamed the countryside, giving shelter to a mother and an orphan for the night, sharing a piece of bread and wishing to save them. There were farmers who would take these people in and give them some work on their farmsteads, in places from which all men had been mobilized to the war. And there were farmers who would recognize visitors as Jews and yet, risking their lives, would hide them and save them.

I would like specifically to note the lives of the children. Many of our witnesses were born in the 1920s, and during the Holocaust they were in their early teens. Some of them survived all trials. Thus two girls who escaped from Babi Yar saw with their own eyes the death of families and relatives, and hid for some time with their Ukrainian neighbours. Then they made a long and painful journey to the front, to the east, until they reached Kharkov, liberated by the Soviet army almost after two years. One of the witnesses was thirteen years old when the war began. His family, who lived in Cherkassy, could not leave as his mother was ill, and his little sister was only seven years old. They decided that the boy should try to save his own life at least. The parting was tragic, and the boy ventured into the unknown. He eventually found some shelter and survived. When the war was over he did not know anything about the fate of his mother, who had died, or about his sister, who had survived. They met again later, by a miracle. Another witness, a Ukrainian woman, was a teacher in an orphanage and, risking her life, she hid seven Jewish orphans there. All these testimonies prove that the topic of the fate of Jewish children in the Ukraine who survived during the Holocaust needs to be addressed separately.

One way for young Jewish men and women to survive was to join partisans. Unlike those who were hiding in order to save themselves, being a part of the partisan detachment also meant the additional opportunity to fight the enemy, satisfying the desire for vengeance. When mass killings of the Jewish population began, younger Jews would leave for the forests to join the partisans. There are no exact numbers for Jews who were part of partisan units in the Ukraine. Based on the testimonies of many Jewish partisans and from archived lists of partisans that have recently become accessible, it is clear that their number was significantly higher than that noted in official Soviet documents.[11]

The events of the Holocaust in the Ukraine have left an everlasting shadow over the lives of the survivors; they left all their family and friends, and came through a heavy ordeal and suffering, both physical and emotional, each of them in his or her own manner. Each made a major effort to return to normal life in the hard conditions after the victory, which made survivors use all their physical and emotional strength. In this respect, those who survived the Holocaust were no different from all the other Soviet people who had to fight post-war disintegration and losses. They were an integral part of Soviet society. Moreover, the official policy of the authorities emphasized the unity of all citizens under the Fascist occupation and actively created obstacles to describing the specific fates of Jews in the Holocaust by all means they had at their disposal. Jews understood this ideological prohibition and accepted it for the sake of their own safety; many were hiding their Jewish roots.

The echo of this public process received both explicit and implicit expression at the personal level in the testimonies of the survivors of the Holocaust.

New testimonies of Jews who survived the Nazi genocide, gathered and published recently in the Ukraine and abroad (see Bibliography), and especially the testimonies gathered in 1996–98 by

Holocaust in the Ukraine

the Foundation for Historical Video Documents of the Shoah Survivors, add to and correct our knowledge about the Holocaust in the Ukraine. The Foundation's unprecedented survey also tells us more of the complex relationship between Jews, the local populations and the Germans, and allows us to fill in many gaps in the history of the Second World War.

It is possible to follow the specifics of the Nazi genocide in more detail by taking a look at the various occupied territories in the Ukraine: the *Reichskommisariat* Ukraine, the Galicia District, and the so-called military zone of Transnistria and the Transcarpathian Region. It also allows us to learn more about the daily life and struggle for survival in the ghettos and death camps.

The picture of the relationship between the occupiers, Jews and local residents built up by the witnesses is more complex than that reflected in the official historiography, and even in those recollections that had been published prior to the era of Glasnost.

The Ukrainian population also suffered enormous losses during the years of the occupation but not all of them could find strength to protest about the killing of Jews – their neighbours, friends, colleagues at work and in study, and sometimes even relatives. The indifferent did not take part in murder, but neither did they take part in saving. They stood aside. Hiding their disappointment, the writers of the recollections sometimes find explanations for such behaviour. But I would like to recall the words of Dante: 'The most horrible place in the inferno is assigned to those who, during times of major moral crisis, preferred to stand aside.'

The testimonies of the witnesses and participants, as well as the documents and media of those years, confirm that, without the collaboration of the local population, the Nazis would not have 'succeeded' so well in the realization of their human hatred programme of the 'Final Solution'. The collaborators pinned their hopes and built their plans on the expectation of victory for Fascist Germany. They included local policemen, who were used by the Germans to organize the pogroms, robberies and murders of the Jewish population. They performed these function not only in their native Ukraine, but also in the ghettos of Poland, Byelorussia and Lithuania, as well as serving as guards in the concentration camps.[12] They employed anti-Semitic propaganda, used the Ukrainian National Army to kill Jews, and finally relied on treachery and denouncing Jews. Schumakher, a former chief of the security service in Kiev, giving testimony after the war, noted that his service received so much information about Jews hiding in the city that his employees did not have enough time to respond to everything. This is a part of our dramatic history. And God forbid it may ever be repeated.

Introduction

That is why we are reminding modern society about what happened. And we would also like to express special gratitude towards those Ukrainians, Russians, Byelorussians, Poles and others, who, surrounded by asea of hatred and indifference, notwithstanding all dangers and hard ordeals, these people did all possible to help and save people who had become outcasts in their own land.

It is an accepted fact that an absolute majority of Jews (and this is also frequently mentioned in the book) who managed to escape and survive on the territories occupied by the Germans are indebted to their compatriots – Ukrainians, Russians and others. There are hundreds and thousands of cases established where, under the threat of terror and repression from the Fascists and their collaborators, these people risked their own the lives and lives of their families and came to the rescue of Jews. They demonstrated compassion and kindness, warned about Jewish pogroms and planned killings, and advised Jews who had escaped from ghettos and were roaming across the villages which roads they should take, helping direct them to partisans, and to cross to Transnistria, where the situation for Jews was safer. They also brought food into the ghettos, hid Jews in their houses, prepared false documents, and so on and so forth. Even in this horrible time they stood up for the honour and dignity of their people.

Until recently it has not been common to recall these people, maybe because the courage of these people admonished the passive with the proof that even in the darkness of the Holocaust a person could have remained decent and honest.

Perhaps for the first time ever, some survivors speak of 'good Germans', those who were not hostile towards Jews and were sometimes even benevolent. When, on 22 July 1941, the Germans entered Shargorod (in the Vinnitsa oblast), half of our house was taken by a *Wehmacht* officer. My grandparents, my seventeen-year-old uncle, my mum with my younger brother in her arms (he was born twenty days before the war), and I (I was five and a half years old then) tried to stay unnoticed by him. My mum was young and very beautiful and in order to seem older and less attractive she wore black. A few times, the officer would start talking about life, saying that he was a Communist, and looking at the books on our shelves. (Before the Germans took over, we had thrown all books by Lenin and Stalin into the river as well as records with a speech by Stalin on the Sixth Extraordinary Congress of the Soviets, although the photographs of my father and my older uncle were still on the walls. They had both been enlisted in the army; my father was missing in action, and my uncle got burned alive in a tank when liberating Budapest. My grandpa said that they had died before the war, but I think the

Germans understood everything pretty well.) When the German troops left Shargorod at night and went towards the east the Germans officer left bread, tinned meat and money for us in his room. I do not write about this under the influence of the film *Schindler's List*. Not all Germans took part in ruthless acts of brutality; there were many instances when they kept loyal to human values and saved Jews.

The necessity of restoring the truth after the collective loss of historical memory is especially important in our difficult times when aggressive nationalism, neo-Nazism, extremism, xenophobia, racism and intolerance are common everywhere. These – as well as 'ethnic cleansing' and anti-Semitism – are diseases that manifest the darkest sides of human nature.

This book had to appear so that people could read about where hatred and animosity could lead. We cannot forget about our past (no matter how horrible and 'inconvenient' it might be) since, as George Santayana, a famous American philosopher, wrote, 'Those who do not remember the past are condemned to relive it.'

The Holocaust is more than just a Jewish phenomenon; representatives of many nations and countries play a role in its understanding and in overcoming its consequences, especially the Germans.

During the meeting between former Ukrainian and Polish ghetto and concentration camp prisoners and members of a German charity, Maximillian-Kolbe-Werke, the family of Margret and Werner Müller spoke of the feelings they now experienced. We met in Warsaw, a city that stands out as a symbol of the tragedy and triumph of the Jewish Resistance. They said:

> We have six million killed Jews standing in between us. We are personally not guilty of this murder since we were children then but this incomprehensible crime fills us with feelings of deep sadness and shame. And although it is not easy for us to face the crime committed by the Germans, we believe it is our duty not to forget what happened. This is a part of our history and there is a responsibility we take to accept it. Together with the house of our parents, we inherited the history of the house.

Not carrying the burden of personal guilt for actions in which they never took part, but having inherited the hard legacy of their grandfathers and fathers, the Müllers – along with their friends and colleagues – continued carrying the burden of the memory on their shoulders and the responsibility to ensure that the historical memory reached each and every Jew. They believe it is important, so that today and in the future the possibility of crimes against humanity, or racial, ethnic, political persecutions, or the restoration of Fascism in any form, or anti-Semitism or extremism will not be possible anywhere.

In order for this agreement to happen between the Germans and the Nazis' victims (which, as the Müllers say, has become their life's work), they participate in campaigns to assist former ghetto and concentration camp prisoners, establish contacts, and publish in German promotional materials about three survivors of Babi Yar. As a result, you can read testimonies of Raissa Maistrenko, Vassily Mikhailovsky and Ruvim Shtein, as well as the collection *Fragt uns, wir sind die letzen* [Ask us, for we are the last ones]. They helped find a family of the former German officer who saved the life of one of our witnesses during the war (see the testimony of Petr Rabtsevich). They responded to the idea of creating a book of recollections of the former ghetto prisoners who survived the Holocaust in the Ukraine with much interest and attention, and they assisted in putting it together. The writers and the editor are deeply grateful for this.

I consider it my pleasant duty to acknowledge and express deep gratitude and appreciation to the authors of those testimonies who found the strength to return to their tragic past and once again, perhaps for the final time, to face up to their experience of great suffering. We thank them for telling the current generations the stories in their own manner (the testimonies were barely corrected stylistically), these stories of the Holocaust, and of the ways to warn the world against its repetition. I would like to acknowledge all those who helped me to do this. To be honest, the years of work this book demanded drained a lot of emotional strength and anguish from me, since each testimony brings up deep personal recollections of that most horrendous time in our lives.

I would like to acknowledge the Conference on Jewish Material Claims against Germany, the American Jewish Joint Distribution Committee and the Judaic Institute in Kiev for support and assistance in the publication of this book. May it become a memorial to the victims of the Holocaust.

DR BORIS ZABARKO
November 2004
A former prisoner of the Shargorod Ghetto, director of the Institute for Social and Communal Workers, senior researcher at the Institute of World Economies and Foreign Relations of the National Academy of Sciences of the Ukraine.

NOTES

1. I. M. Levitas, *The Book of Memories: Babi Yar* (Kiev, 1999).
2. V. Grossman, *The Ukraine without Jews: On Jewish Themes. Selected Works in Two Volumes*, Vol. 2 (Jerusalem: The Aliyah Library, 1990), pp. 35–8.
3. Elie Wiesel.
4. Mikhail Gefter, *The Echo of the Holocaust and the Russian Jewish Question* (Moscow, 1995).
5. Martin Niemoeller.
6. Paul Dieter, 'The Nazi Occupation of Ukraine in 1941–1944 as Reflected in Works of Western Scholars', *Ukrainian Historical Journal*, 5 (1994), p. 130.
7. Yevgeny Yevtusheko,
8. V. Grossman and I. Erenburg (eds), *The Black Book: On the Murderous Commonplace Slaughter of Jews by the German Occupiers in the Territories of the Soviet Union and in the Death Camps of Poland During the War, 1941–1945* (Jerusalem, 1980; 2nd edn, Vilnius, 1993). For more information, see Ilya Altman, *The Destiny of the Black Book. An Unknown Black Book: Testimonies of the Witnesses to the Shoah of the Soviet Jews (1941–1944)* (Jerusalem/Moscow, 1993), pp. 16–28.
9. No. 1, 1996.
10. *Judenräte* were Jewish councils set up to oversee the ghettos.
11. See, for more information, S. Yelissavetsky, *Half a Century of Oblivion: Jews in the Resistance and Partisan Movements in the Ukraine (1941–1944)* (Kiev, 1998).
12. See Gritsak Yaroslav, 'The Participation of Ukrainians in Anti-Jewish Action During the Second World War', *Lvov*, 8 (1996), p. 61.

Translator's Comments
and Notes

In some instances the choice of ethnic/authentic words is preserved to reflect the cultural and specific notions of the authentic narratives. A few examples are as follows:

Russian:

Aunt/uncle	Title used for any grown-up (female or male, respectively) by children as opposed to uncle and aunts who are in fact their parents' siblings
Grandma/grandpa	As above
Great Patriotic War	A name for the Second World War commonly used and acknowledged on the territory of the former Soviet Union
NKVD	Internal affairs service, later known as the KGB
Oblast	Region (a territorial unit); each oblast contained smaller administrative units, known as *districts*
Oympiad	A contest traditionally held for schoolchildren
OSOAVIAKHIM	Soviet People's Society of Support for Aviation and Navy
-schina	Suffix signifying the area including, but not limited to, the oblast (frequently with surrounding area); for example *Vinnitschina* – an area including and adjoining the Vinnitsa oblast
SMERSH	[Death to Spies] – special military divisions of the NKVD with the purpose of screening and investigating people to avoid penetration of spies/security/etc. during Second World War

Sovkhoz/kolkhoz   Collective farm formations started by the Soviet regime (Soviet and Collective Farm, respectively, the former being smaller in size and number of farmers employed). Many collectives were preserved during the German occupation as a form of agricultural organization, along with their structure and name

Vlasov   As in 'Vlasov's men': military formations of General Vlasov, who formed a national committee and created the Russkaya Osvoboditelnaia Armiia (ROA) [Russian Liberation Army] in 1943, supported by the Germans

GERMAN:

Fritz   Common address towards any German, either by children or adults, during the Second World War

HEBREW:

Kaddish/Eimolerachamim   Jewish mourning prayers

1. The memory of these people warms my heart

Clara Akselrod (Daks) (b. 1935)

I was born on 29 January 1935, in the village of Gorokholino, Bogorodchany district, Stanislav (Ivano-Frankovsk) oblast. Yuda Mendelevich and Hanna Abramovna Daks, my parents, worked on a farm. When Nazis occupied our village, we were in it, and stayed there some time longer. But then my parents decided to move to Stanislav, and stay with my father's relatives. They believed it would be safer in town since it had become a common thing for the windows in Jewish houses to be shattered at night and for the people to be robbed.

However, a few days after our arrival in Stanislav, together with our relatives and along with a few thousand Jews of the city and its environs, we were resettled to the Stanislav ghetto, where we had lived until 1943.

Living in the ghetto people suffered a lot from hunger, cold and various diseases. Because of malnutrition, cold and fear, like many other children, I was ill most of the time; I could not walk, was losing my vision and generally was very weak.

My parents were often forced to do slave labour, including cleaning streets and road construction. Every day was marked by the fear of death. People were dying from hunger and suffering and there were many children among the victims. Those seriously ill or weak were taken out in groups to the Jewish cemetery, where pits had been already prepared. They were shot there. Many of our relatives perished in the ghetto; fifty-two of them.

Life was getting harder with each and every day. Every day the Germans were taking out large groups of people and shooting them. My father was frequently beaten during the work – he was not very healthy and could not keep up with the norm they required. My parents realized that if we stayed in the ghetto any longer, we would all die.

Only because my father knew one of the *polizei* who was guarding the ghetto were we able to flee from this hell, though with great difficulty. But when we got out of the ghetto, we did not know where to go: dangers were abundant everywhere. We decided to return to our village at night. We went to the forest, and spent the day in it. The following we reached the house of Yosif Mikhailovich Petrash, a local priest. My parents considered him the most trust-worthy of all the people they knew. Before the war, my father had been very close with him, and knew how honest and decent he was. The priest greeted us, glad to see us alive. He put us into a separate room, locking it with a key, so that even his maid would not know that we had returned, and so that the news would not spread across the village. It was all very dangerous for him and for all members of his family who were helping us as well.

The Petrash family was indeed taking a great risk: the German garrison was stationed in the village. When a German officer got a room next door to the priest's house, our presence there grew even more dangerous than before. Then the priest called for a deacon he trusted, told him about us and asked him to lodge us at a farmstead in the forest.

At night the deacon came together with his son, and we left on horses, with food given for his family and us. At night we reached the farmstead. The farmer, together with my father, dug a pit under the dairy barn, and we were hiding there for some time. Once a day we were given food. But when the farmers did not have any-thing to eat themselves, we ate some very thin soup made from potato peelings. When even this was gone, my father and the farmer would secretly go to Yosif Mikhailovich, and he gave them some food.

Having stayed in the dark pit for some time, I started to grow blind. My parents were very worried and decided to seek the advice of Yosif Mikhailovich. They decided that I should go to another village where nobody knew me, and try to get a job as a shepherd. The priest's wife dressed me in typical Ukrainian clothes, and Yosif Mikhailovich described to me in detail how to get to Fitkiv, a village nearby. This was in spring, some time before Easter.

In those days many children wandered around the place trying to get a job for a living. I was very small and weak. I wandered around houses for many days, begging that someone would hire me to watch over their cattle. Finally, at night, completely desperate, and terrified by the thought of crossing back through the forest at night, I went to one house, and started crying and begging the peo-ple there to let me stay. This family had a fifteen-year-old daughter, and later we made good friends with her. Here I was outdoors, and nutrition was much better and included milk and vegetables. I lived with this family for about eight months.

Later, a girl whose mother had died took me to live with her. Her name was Paraskovya Semenovna Dutchak, and she was seventeen. She told me, 'You are an orphan, and I am an orphan too. Let us live together.' She treated me like a sister. I was then only a child, bereaved of motherly care, and didn't know whether my parents were still alive.

After the Soviet army liberated the Stanislavshchina, my father found me. My mum had died earlier.

The memory of these people, and their honest hearts, has warmed me throughout my life. During those difficult times, not everybody would risk losing their lives and the lives of their family for the sake of saving somebody else. We still maintain friendly relationships with these families. We are helping each other with whatever we can, and often recollect everything we had to go through.

2. We survived thanks to the kind people – Ukrainians and Poles

Nyuma Anapolsky (b. 1926)

We passed all our school exams, and with the sunrise, on 22 June 1941, we all gathered in our schoolyard to go to the beach. There were twenty of us, thirteen- to fifteen-year-old boys. We had a tasty breakfast, with bread, butter, eggs, green leeks and radishes. Then, we went to play ball at the stadium. We had hardly played a few strokes when we heard the noise of revving engines. With 'hoorays', cheering, we ran towards the road, and to our delight we saw real tanks and lorries with Red Army soldiers in them. They were moving from Novograd-Volynsky towards Rovno.

A few days passed, and the first bombs started falling on to our town, followed by the burial of the first victims of the Fascist invasion. They were laid to rest in an old Jewish cemetery, with *Eimolerachamim* and *Kaddish*. And at the very same time, the tanks with red stars on them were now turning back to the east, towards Novograd-Volynsky.

A few more days passed and Koretz was occupied by the German troops. And even then Jews did not know what the Germans really were, and on the first day of their occupation everything was still calm and quiet. Yet the second day brought the news: we stopped being equally human. All Jews older than thirteen were forced to wear yellow *Magen Davids* [Stars of David] on the back and the front of their clothes. The Ukrainian *polizei*, together with the Germans, were breaking into Jewish homes. Accompanied by shouts, *'Jude'*, *'Schweine'*, without any consideration for gender or age, people were either thrown out into the market place, or thrown into the building where the police and government were currently based, or into the German commander's headquarters. There, being beaten, they were forced to pick rubbish, shattered glass, all with their hands, with no brooms or shovels. The *Judenrat* was established, which directed Jews towards slave labour, following the enforcement and demands from the Ukrainian police and new government.

The occupiers started to lay the surface cables for communicating with Berlin. Thousands of Jews were forced to dig trenches; dying daily, in dozens, from hunger, beatings and from enduring hard labour. The most difficult was the period when they had to lay cable in a narrow deep trench running for many miles. When farmers began to take beetroots over to a nearby processing plant, they tried to secretly throw a few to us. People were picking them up greedily and eating them raw, dirty, covered with soil. If the guards noticed this, they beat poor people brutally, and sometimes to death. Those who died were buried right there, in the middle of the field.

Erich Koch, who picked the city of Rovno as the capital of the Ukrainian Reichskomissariat, demanded that the local commandant's offices speed up the cable works. Ill and weakened people could not complete the deadly labour that was assigned to them in a short time. Then the Nazi started to force women and ten-year-old children to labour on digging trenches. I was one of those children. Together with my father, we were forced to slave under the beatings of *polizei*.

On the fourth day of the occupation of Koretz, 120 Jews were ordered to report to the new authorities or *polizei*. Their names were included in a special list. None of them ever returned and nobody knew what happened to them. For many years they were considered 'missing'.

My memory preserve a terrible day in the summer of 1941. This was a day of a Ukrainian religious holiday, *Prechista*. On that day the SS soldiers, together with the Ukrainian *polizei*, broke into our Jewish neighbourhood. They picked 350 Jews, men only. For many long years, we did not know what happened to those poor men. In the period of June 1941 through September 1942, some five thousand Jews of the town of Koretz died from horrendous tortures.

I am describing only a small portion of what I had to live through and what I saw with my own eyes. thirteen- to fifteen-year-old girls were raped before their mothers' eyes; wives and mothers were raped in front of their children and husbands. The infants, pulled from their mothers' arms, were thrown up in the air and shot at as targets; the same was done to the children tied up to pillars. When breaking into the ghetto, drunken Fascist killers were shooting at anyone they saw, commonly aiming at the *Magen David* we wore.

One day, all the rabbis were taken to our big and beautiful synagogue. They were split into groups of two to three men each, and then taken to other synagogues. There, they were forced to take out the Torah, and other holy books, to pour petroleum over them and burn them. There were rabbis who refused to follow these orders. They were beaten to death or shot. Some of them died right there, from heart attacks, not able to endure trial and torture. Those alive were photographed against the backdrop of the burning Torahs. The torturers forced those poor people to cut off each other's beards and cut out crosses in their hair. The big synagogue burned down completely, after they had rolled a big barrel with petroleum into it and started the fire. An ornate metal fence around the synagogue was taken down and put up around the place with birch crosses on the graves of Fascists. The rabbis, old martyrs of the ghetto, were harnessed into pulling a water barrel for the Ukrainian policemen, authorities, commander's staff and the hospital where wounded German soldiers were treated.

The winter of 1941/42 was the most horrible for us all. The walls of our flat were covered with ice; people did not wash for months, and were eaten up by lice. A few families now shared one flat, since we were permitted to live only in houses along the streets designated for the ghetto. We burned everything that could be burned in small furnaces: furniture, clothes, wooden floors. But police and SS men would break into those houses where they could see smoke rising from a chimney, and forced residents, numb from cold, to pick up snow in the street and put out the fire with it.

Every night dozens of the poor and miserable died from unbearable cold and starvation. Dead bodies lay for days in sheds, or on the porches. Once a while they were collected and taken to the cemetery where they were buried, again a few bodies sharing one grave. No matter how horrible death was, those alive envied the dead for whom the suffering was finally over.

Pretty girls aged eighteen to twenty years disfigured their faces with various ointments and cut their hair so as not to draw any attention and not be raped. Every day, the ghetto was flooded by various bandits who tried to take valuables from the Jews. Those bandits even used to take off door handles.

The time passed, yet we did not know what happened to the first 120 people taken away by the policemen, and those 350 taken away later. I remember well a group that included Velve Gilman (under the Polish rule, he had owned a clothes shop), Syoma, his son, Yosl Kleiner, Pirkes, Zise Segal, Pearle, his wife, my father, Birl Anapolsky, and myself. We all gathered in Velve Gilman's shed and discussed what we should do next. Segal told us that one shoemaker, a sect member and a Ukrainian, with whom he had business contacts under the Polish rule, knew one policeman well. If paid, he would be willing to provide the necessary information to the group. We started to get our valuables together. I was told to hang out in the centre of the city, near two marketplaces where the German soldiers stopped to rest. I had to be especially attentive in watching out for those who wore skull logos on their caps and SS letters on their collars that looked like '44'. As soon as I saw lorries with such soldiers I had to run down Shilgas Street and shout in Yiddish, '*Fir und firzick are in town,*' so that people had enough time to hide.

Our group got together for a second time when we had collected all the valuables. These were gold coins from the tsarist mint, rings, teaspoons and candlesticks. Nobody knew the name of the person this was all intended for. After he was presented with the 'gift', the policeman told us that all of the 120 Jews from the first list were shot the very same day, two kilometres away from Koretz, near the village of Shitnya. This list included the most intelligent and educated people of the city, both Communists and Zionists. The Germans and the Ukrainian police were afraid of these people getting up a five thousand *kahal* (congregation) of the Koretz ghetto to fight the occupiers and that they would organize and head the resistance.

We also found out the tragic details about the other 350 Jews taken on the *Prechista*. They repaired roads and then were shot there, right on the spot, in groups of twenty to thirty people, within a period of two months. Their remains were buried in five common graves, dug out with their own hands. These graves are located approximately ten kilometres away from Koretz, on the road towards Novograd-Volynsky.

The second year of the 'new order' began. In the summer of 1942 (I don't remember the date), early in the morning on the eve of *Shvue*, screams, laments and shots were heard everywhere. All Jews were marched to the Ukrainian town council located in Staromonastyrskaya Street, urged on by whippings, bludgeoning and beating. My parents, with their daughters-in-law and grandchildren (six-month-old Sheisele and three-year-old Goldele) were among those people taken. The children's fathers were at the front, in the army. I was together with my family, and then I was barely fifteen years old. Many men wore *tallisim* [prayer shawls], just like my father, and with their arms stretched to the skies prayed '*Shma, Yisrael.*'

We were put in close rank columns, 150, 200 and 300 people each, and were surrounded by the SS soldiers with dogs and by police that had come from Zhitomir. It was terrible to see children being pulled away from their parents and taken into different columns. Laments and screams were everywhere. Women fainted, and some died right there from heart attacks. Those who fell to the ground died under the feet of the crowds of people driven by their killers.

Away from the road there stood four carts on to which dead bodies were thrown, as if they were just logs. The way of the miserable people lay towards the forest about eight kilometres away from Koretz near the village of Kosak. Graves had been prepared there in advance. I witnessed this all with my own eyes, and I keep jumping, startled, at night when terrorized by this nightmare coming back to me.

When we came to the town council, and they began putting people into columns, I noticed some 200 young Jewish girls and boys whom I knew well. They were sitting aside from the place where our column was. I had a fleeting thought that maybe they had been put aside for some work. Stealthily I managed to leave the column that was about to start moving towards death, and crawled towards the group of youngsters. A few girls immediately got on top of me, covering me with their dresses. I spent four hours sitting like that. During this time, all columns (later we learned that there were some 2,500 Jews in them) were marched out. Only after that were the young people allowed to go back home. When walking back, we saw carts filled with the clothes of those killed: the belongings were brought back to the town council.

During that night some two thousand people who managed to survive this time gathered in the ghetto. Later we learned that the execution of our neighbours and relative had been over by four o'clock.

The following day, a group of thirty people, including myself, and accompanied by members of the *Judenrat* and Ukrainian police, took shovels and was marched to the place of death of our loved ones. There, at the end of the forest, about twenty kilometres away from the road, we could see the bodies of the murdered. There were twenty-two bodies there, including children who had been shot in their heads. They most likely had tried to escape from the column. Near the place of death, in a forest glade, there were prams, toys, little shoes, socks, shells from machine-gun bullets, cigarette butts and schnapps bottles. Everywhere there were traces of blood, and those killed floated in pools of their own blood, which were quickly evaporating under the blazing sun. We brought the first twenty-two bodies there as well. We measured the graves with steps; they were twenty metres long and twenty metres wide. We recited *Kaddish* and went home exhausted. By the time the sun went down we were back in the ghetto, not believing that we managed to avoid the fate of those who lay now in those dreadful pits.

After the first 2,500 ghetto prisoners were shot, there were another 2,000 people left. The suffering was not over for us yet, neither was hunger nor misery. But this was nothing compared to what happened to our family and friends. We were again forced into slave labour. After the killings there was not a single family who had not lost members. Almost all the old people, who had survived the massacre on *Shvues*, were killed. After the first *Aktion*, we managed to celebrate *Rosh haShanah* and *Yom Kippur*. We got to pray on these days in the apartment of Yuckle Zavodnik, who had been killed among the first 120 Jews. On the first day of *Yom Kippur*, during prayer, eight women died, from suffering and grief. We put them into another room and continued praying.

A few months passed by when, on the eve of *Sukkes*, we found out that new graves were being dug out in the very same forest, near the village of Kosak. I don't know how we got this news since the group, including my father, that was getting information from the unknown policeman, had been killed. We decided to run away from the ghetto. We were five close friends, and even more closely connected through our life in the ghetto – Avrum Golender, Avrum Lerner, Muma Esterman, Yankel Milrud, and myself, Nyuma Anapolsky. At night we secretly crossed the city and went towards Novograd-Volynsky. We went through the forest, which we had never really seen or known before, being town children.

A day after another went by, and we were still hiding and afraid to come out to the people. We quenched our thirst with moss; we ate different plants and sometimes picked black berries. Once we went out to a clearing in the forest, and came to a stand still: we saw farmers digging out potatoes. Hiding in a covered place, we waited for nightfall and went out to pick potatoes. We dug them out with sticks, branches, our hands, getting them out and eating them raw. Our wanderings continued for a long time. We walked across the forest without knowing where. We tried to stay unnoticed, hiding away from villages and farmsteads.

But then, autumn came with rain, mixed with snow and night frosts. Clothes grew wet during the day and then froze during the night. Once, finally exhausted from the cold and hunger, we lay down close to each other, under pine trees. We lay on the ground for a long while, not knowing whether our friend next to us was alive or dead. And suddenly there were three men with hatchets in their hands and sacks on their backs. Even today I cannot figure out where we got the energy to jump up and run towards the strangers, forgetting all our fears. We started kissing their feet, begging for help. We kept saying one thing to them, 'Please, for God's sake, don't kill us …' The farmers tried to calm us down and asked us not to make a noise. When we calmed down, they got pancakes, pota-toes out of their jackets, and milk out of their sacks, and offered all of this treasure to us. We started eating with some agitation. The men watched us in silence. It was obvious that this sight shocked them. They invited us to join them; yet again we were seized with fear. However, understanding the futility of our situation, we fol-lowed them. They took us into deep forest, showed us how to build a shelter where we could hide from rain and snow, and inside this shelter we started a fire. They told us to look for birch trees only, since wet birch tree would not smoke. They showed us how to find birch trees, how to use splinters to makke the fire. They left a piece of metal, a flint and some dry moss, telling us not to go into the village because of the village headman and police. They gave us a hatchet, two knives and their sacks, and departed.

For the first time in the two months of our wanderings we were warm and fed and, most importantly, we started to think about life, regaining our trust in people.

The winter of 1943 came, bringing severe frosts and heavy snowfalls. Our hunger became more and more accute. Once we saw tracks of a sleigh and horse hoofs on the snow. We decided to take a chance and follow the tracks. We walked for about ten kilometres until we heard dogs barking, and soon saw small village houses. What was to be done? Again we decided to try. We knocked on a door of the first house. Seeing us, the owners of the house began crossing themselves. Then they finally realized that we were not some forest-goblins but only desperate and starved boys, and let us into the house. They sent their daughters, eight and ten, outside to watch out for any unwelcome guests.

We did not know their names or surnames. I remember that, only once, the name 'Petro' was mentioned. This wonderful Ukrainian farming family warmed us up, and gave us a meal of potatoes and sour milk. When we were leaving, kissing their hands in gratitude, Avrum Golender saw near the door a trough of chopped straw mixed with boiled potatoes (food for pigs). We asked them to give us a little of this food to provide ourselves for a few days ahead.

I remember one episode. We were crossing a bridge across a river, when two men with rifles and white armbands on their rolled-up sleeves stopped us. These two were policemen. Suddenly a few women attacked them screaming 'Run!' to us. We ran away, and could catch our breath only when we had safely reached the forest.

But then hunger won over fear again, and though it was dangerous we used to go to villages in hope of help from kind people. We met those who gave us food and warmth and even sent their children out to watch over us. Years have gone by, and today I feel so sorry that I did not know the names of all the places or all our saviours, but I'm sure God is kind and favourable towards them all. They helped us in our wanderings, warning us of dangers from headmen or police. We were advised to get across the River Sluch; they showed us how to find our way through the forest, start a fire and which wood to pick for it, avoiding aspen wood which sent out sparks when burning.

In the spring of 1943, having walked hundreds of kilometres, we reached the forest in Bereznoye district about which we were told by kind people from the villages of Storozhev, Ustye, Bilchaki and Mishakovo (I found out the names of these places much later). But we could not rest even there. A few Polish villages were nearby, and there, the Germans ruthlessly burned alive and killed whole families. Poles were also hiding in the forest.

Many Jews who survived killings in the ghetto were captured in the forest. Some professionals (tailors, blacksmiths and shoe-makers) were used for work, yet killed later.

In this forest we met partisans from Shitov's detachment. They seemed to have accepted us into the unit, but they didn't give us any weapons, and told us to look after the cattle. Soon we were all ill with typhus. Only Muma Esterman stayed in the group. When armed, he fought against Fascism until the end of the war, and later hunted down the bandits who had killed our parents and other martyrs of the Koretz ghetto.

We were ill, and continued to live in the forest. We built a shelter. There were villages within an eight to ten kilometre range from our 'home', the names of which I remember well: Levachi, Sivki, Kozyarnik, Mochulyanka, and Zaitsy farmstead.

In these places we encountered people who had also fled from the Koretz ghetto: Azril, Malka, Hersch, Liniki, Zilik and Moishe Kharif, Glyuzman, a father with his daughter, and other Jews. Besides these, there were about twenty people from the Selishche (now Sosnovka) and the Bereznoye ghetto. They also lived in huts and tents.

The Poles lived in villages nearby. They shared potatoes and milk with us, and we helped them in their rural households (we ground grain on millstones, crushed millet in mortars, and brought wood from the forest). For us fifteen-year-olds, this was hard work but it earned us a living.

That was how we survived, thanks to the help of these kind people – Ukrainians and Poles. We survived death and went on with our lives. I bow and salute to all of our saviours, whose names we do or don't know.

They let us into their homes, gave us food and warmed us, and sometimes even allowed us to get cleaned up. All this was done under the eye of their prying neighbours and relatives, thus they were taking the risk of being denounced to the headman, the police or a representative of the *Landwirt*. In all villages posters were past-ed on the walls (we saw them on fences, near church gates), in which the local population weren warned against helping and hiding Jews. If caught, all the family would be killed and their house – burned down, while for a Jew turned over to the authorities a person would be rewarded – with a cow, salt or money. There were many honest and kind people living in those villages who were not scared by these orders; the proof of it is in us living today in different countries. Nevertheless, we cannot forget other disgusting individuals who brought suffering and misery on to Jewish people.

No, we shall never forget those who relieved our suffering and saved us from death by starvation and cold. I think that streets in Israel should be named after the 'Righteous among the Nations', and the whole villages hiding Jews deserve even greater appreciation than individuals, since, acting as a community, they were able to save hundreds of Jewish lives at the same time. I will never get tired of telling my grandchildren of how children of their age were out in the cold, watching over us resting in safety, and when we left, they were playing with dogs outside, rolling in the snow, and thus covering our footprints.

But fate was not favourable towards us. In the autumn of 1943, the Nazi killing squads attacked these villages. They burned houses down with their residents locked inside alive. If somebody managed to flee then and survived, I want to wish them health, kindness and well-being from the depth of my heart, from all of my family and on behalf of all other Jews saved by them.

We were completely exhausted. Trying to relieve our suffering caused by injuries and lice, we rubbed each other's backs with snow, learned to weave bast shoes from the tree bark and removed clothes from the dead.

In February 1944, the Red Army liberated these forests and the town of Koretz. We were barely eighteen then, but we enlisted in the army. It was the first time in many long years we had a chance to wash ourselves in a *banya* [bath house], put clean uniform and shoes on. We started to eat tasty soldier's *kasha* [thin gruel] with salt and bread, the taste of which we had forgotten, and had sweet tea; yet the biggest joy of all was that we got automatic rifles and went into battle. The minutes of the first battle were unforgettable for my friends and me. Until that moment we had been nothing but helpless persecuted boys, and now this was a happy moment when we could aim our first shots at our torturers, showing our invincibility and independence.

After many battles on the Second Baltic Front within the 379th Riga Division, when approaching Riga, Yankel Milrud, my friend, was gravely wounded, and died on the battlefield. In the following battle, Avrum Golender, another of my ghetto friends, was severely wounded (he now lives in Ashdod, in Israel). Then it was my turn: after a serious wound, I had my arm amputated. Muma Esterman, my third ghetto friend, continued to fight for many years in the internal security forces, and now he lives in Rishon leZion, Israel. Avrum Lerner, the fourth of us, moved over to Eretz Israel before its independence and then fought in many Israeli wars of independence.

All that I had to go through cannot be put on paper. Now, I have just finished my memoirs, and other episodes come up. Once, together with my friends, I violated the German orders and left the ghetto. We were immediately caught by guards and put into the police prison. A cell was filled up knee-high with water mixed with blood. The head of the Ukrainian police, Mitka Zaverukha, a sadist and bandit, beat us up badly, together with his aides. But then, two days later, a miracle happened, and we were let out.

After demobilization because of my wounds in 1945, I came back to Koretz. There was not a single home left on Shilgas Street where the ghetto had been located. A few Jewish families out of those who hid in the forests or served in the army returned to the town. About ten of us got together in the first days of our return and we went to Kosak, to visit the graves of our family and friends. It was a depressing sight to see. Everything was covered with tall weeds, and the place of burial could hardly be located. In Shitnya, the situation was somewhat better: a small memorial was put up there with an inscription, '*Here, 120 Soviet citizens were killed by Fascists.*' There was no mentioning that those citizens were Jewish. And we could never find a grave of the 350 people killed.

The Jews who returned got back to work. Among them, there were Communists and those who had held administrative and official positions, but they were all afraid of being accused of Zionism, and they never dealt with the issue of the Jewish graves. Moreover, there were no memorials then in Babi Yar or in Sosenki. However, the ten of us continued to take care of the graves, and annually, on *Shvues* and *Sukkes*, we went there to recite *Kaddish*.

The first two memorials to the Koretz Jews were put up in 1991, with the money left to the community in the will of Avrum Shikhman. In 1992, a generous and compassionate Fanya Vedro came from Canada to Koretz. Together with us, she had gone through all the suffering of the Koretz ghetto. We met and went to the village of Sukhovolya, which is located outside Koretz, towards Novograd-Volynsky, that is in Zhitomirshchina. There we saw five common graves, located two to three metres from one another. The total burial area was about three hundred square metres.

When the excitement was over, and having wept at length, we sat down to discuss what to do next. Fanya said, 'I am going back to Canada, and will talk with my husband. We shall think of how to build a memorial here.'

And in a short while, we got the news that the Vedro family would give money to build a memorial in Sukhovolya. The construction was put in the hands of a good person and a professional, Ilya Kuperschmidt.

In 1992, I met an 82-year-old resident of Koretz. He did not tell me his name or the name of the village he was originally from. This is what he told me:

> In 1941–44, I was a member of the Koretz Ukrainian police and I was present at the killing of Jews from the Koretz ghetto. I did not shoot, our unit was standing encircling the forest nearby the place of the *Aktion*. People were marched here in columns, beaten by truncheons, whips, rifle butts, with no consideration for age or gender. They were forced to undress completely. Their clothes were put on to carts, and the people were marched further into the forest. There, in a forest glade, two huge pits were dug out, about three metres deep each. The executioners put eight people into the pits; forced them to lay down, and shot them, while holding a cigarette or a sandwich in the other hand. Some were still alive when the next layer of the doomed was put on top of them. Some rushed to the pit themselves, to die faster and not see all this. If police noticed such 'violators', they returned them back, beating them severely. Children were pulled out of their mothers' hands, and thrown into the pits alive. The laments and screams of many people were heard far away from the place of this horrendous action.

There are three common graves in the village of Kosak, twenty by thirty metres each. These graves contain remains of 4,500 ghetto martyrs killed or buried alive by the German Nazis and their collaborators. For fifty years these places were neglected and used as rye fields. When we started to restore burials, it was the first time that the fields were not ploughed and rye sown.

After my long-term correspondence with the Koretz community in Israel (as well as after the funds that had been raised by the children of those killed, who now live in various countries), in 1994 all graves were restored. Now each of them has a memorial set up and, in the field where rye was grown for fifty years, there is a menorah, eight metres high.

A few participants in these events, who survived miraculously in the inferno of those days, attended the memorial opening. The children and grandchildren of those who perished had come from America, Canada and Israel. With the sounds of *haTikvah*, *Kaddish* and *Eimolerachamim*, the flags of Israel and the Ukraine were lowered and the ribbons on the memorial were cut. All those who gathered saw the monument with the Star of David on it, the tribute of mourning and respect to those 4,500 Jews who died in this place as martyrs.

3. On this day the Germans decided to completely destroy our camp

Grigory Bassovsky (b. 1927)

My name is Grigory Solomonovich Bassovsky, and I was born in 1927, in the village of Shenderovka, Korsun-Shevchenkovsky district, Cherkassy oblast. In 1938 my father died and before the war my mother got remarried to Fischel Kaminsky, who lived in the town of Olshany (then, it was the district centre). We moved to live with him.

In the second half of June 1941, the Germans occupied our town. Their first action was to kill all Jewish men, including my stepfather. All remaining Jews were forced to move into a ghetto, which took up one quarter of a street. Our belongings, clothes as well as the house, were taken away from us. The Germans and the police guarded the ghetto closely and we were not allowed to leave it.

They made us work from dawn to night; food was not provided at all, and they tortured us in any way they could. Those ill and weakened were shot to death. We lived, or rather existed, in this way until the spring of 1942. In May 1942 we were all brought together and they marched us in a column in an unknown direction. By the end of the day we reached the town of Zvenigorodka, and were 'accommodated' in a local prison. The following morning they started to sort us. Women, young girls and teenagers (including my mother and myself), were put into one group while old people and young children were put into another group. Children were pulled away from mothers and thrown to the old people. Laments, cries and moaning were heard everywhere.

We were taken to a concentration camp, first in the village of Smelchintsy, Lyssyansky district; then my mum and I were transferred to the village of Nemorozh, Zvenigorodka district. Both camps were located along a highway then under construction. Those who were left (elderly and children) were taken out of town and killed.

What was our concentration camp like? It was a yard of a former collective farm [kolkhoz], fenced off from the local population with barbed wire. We were put in a pigsty, where we slept on the

ground. During the day we worked in a stone quarry, on the highway construction. They gave us food once a day (some watery soup
and 100 grams of bread from millet). Every once in a while, they
would select weakened people and shoot them. When we returned
from work, they forced us to run around the pigsty while beating us
with truncheons. After shootings, they brought clothes taken off the
dead to the camp and distributed them among us.

Local people supported us as much as they could, sometimes
managing to smuggle food into the camp.

Thus we suffered until 23 August 1943. On this day, the Germans
decided to completely destroy our camp. When they were taking us
to be executed, my mum and I managed to escape. For a few months
we hid in forests and haystacks. Grigory and Anna Kulik of the village of Budishche helped us a lot; may they rest in peace now.

My mother died on 18 October 1943. Basyura, a local teacher,
betrayed us. The village leader together with two policemen, came
over, put a rope around my mum's neck and took her away to the
village police station at Shevchenkove, three kilometres away from
Budishche. I escaped.

4. This happened in Kiev[1]

Doba Belozovskaya (b. 1912)

My parents were ordinary people; my father worked at a *bagasse* – a processing factory.[2] We were seven children in the family: three boys and four girls. I was born the fourth child, in 1912.

I came to Kiev in 1933, studied at the RabFak, and then got married. We lived in a thirteen-square-metre room, at 25 Chkalov Street. On the first day of the war, I went, together with my children, to my mum, who lived on Tverskaya Street. My sister, with her deaf-mute child, was already there. In the meanwhile, the Fascists entered the city.

One day, without knocking on our door, our neighbour, Zhora Veryovko, with others, walked in. Even though I was present in the room, they took whatever they liked. Zhora went up to the couch on which mum was lying, pushed her off, and took the couch away. After the war, I saw this man.

Gita, my elder sister, had a Russian husband, Ageyev, an honest man. They had a son, named Igor. He is alive. When the war began, Gita's husband sent her away with their child, to his parents, in Podol, where they lived at 22 Konstantinovskaya Street. His sisters were married to Jewish men, and his brother's wife was Jewish as well. It was a very big family. They hid Gita.

Once I went to get water from the water pump at the corner of Zolotovorotskaya and Vladimirskaya Streets. And there I saw at a distance a column of people, guarded by Germans with dogs, coming along Vladimirskaya Street. All the people were carrying shovels on their shoulders. And suddenly I recognized my dad with *talles* under his arm. I wanted to run up to him, but then remembered my children left at home. They said that the column was marched beyond the Goloseevsky forest and everyone was shot there.

An order was posted everywhere commanding all Jews in the area of Syrets to report near Lukyanovskoye cemetery. Shura, my sister's husband, came to us. He walked us to a small square in Artem Street (at the place of a modern monument to Kossior). We sat down on a bench: my mum, my sister, our children and I. The children became quiet. Shura went to Babi Yar, and then quickly returned, 'Don't go there.' He took away our children, and we went back to Tverskaya. We didn't sleep that night and lay on the floor in the hallway. In the morning we had to leave. I gave my sea-bear fur coat to our neighbour in exchange for an old jacket; I did the same with my shoes, exchanging them for some felt boots. It was 1 October and the weather was good. The three of us went towards Stalinka, but then mum returned to Tverskaya.

Shura took the children to Podol. The deaf-mute son of my sister was taken outside and left in the street; they did not want to hide him. He was probably taken away and shot. They hid my children. Then people said that they eventually were brought back to Tverskaya. My mother was there too. Then the Gestapo came along in a car, and took them all away.

But I also know something else. Throughout all the years of the German occupation of Kiev our children were hidden in Podol. When the Germans were leaving Kiev, people were all forced from Podol to Karavaevy Dachi. My sister left the children for a short while to get something. At that moment, a neighbour came in and announced that these were the children of a Jewish soldier. They were taken away immediately, and that was all. Igor, the son of Gita and Shura, remembered how they were taken away. Now, I don't know where my children were or how they died. But this happened much later.

Yet now Rosa and I were leaving Kiev. People said we could cross the Dnieper. The bridges were all blown up. They thought we were Russians, and a fisherman took us in his boat across the river, to Darnitsa. Rosa gave him her watch. We stayed overnight with a lone woman. She kept telling us all about the Jews, saying that Jews were to be blamed for all that had ever been wrong or bad. At dawn, we moved on. We went from Poltava to Kursk along the railway tracks. It was very terrifying. We could see exploded and crashed trains all along our way. Once I saw two Germans in the distance. I told Rosa, 'Rosa, this is our end. Let us walk on but don't look back, as if we haven't seen them.' We walked past by them, and they never called us. But then we heard shots.

In Ukraine we were mostly treated well. People let us in to stay overnight. People knew what the war was like. There were places where people sheltered us knowing who we really were. There were villages where one part was already occupied by the Germans, and the other – not yet. We walked fifty kilometres a day. I envied beggars: they could beg, and we couldn't. Rosa tried to find something. Only when we almost reached Kursk did we get onto a train.

I don't know what happened to my husband. I received only one letter from him. For thirty years, I have searched but have not found where his grave is.

NOTES

1. This testimony appeared in the *Jewish News*; it is also in the appendix to *The Voice of the Ukraine*, a special edition of *The Supreme Council of the Ukraine*, No. 4 (the Society for Jewish Culture of the Ukraine, 1999).
2. The dry, pulpy residue left after the extraction of the juice from sugar cane, usable as fuel, or to make paper, etc.

5. Don't be afraid of me, little boy, I won't betray you

Victor Berezin (b. 1930)

When the war began I was eleven years old. My father was Ukrainian and mother Jewish. My parents divorced in 1936 because my father had a serious drinking problem. My grandma (my father's mother) visited us frequently and took me to stay with her. My mum had two older sisters: Aunt Gita and Aunt Tena, and two brothers, Meer and Misha, who enlisted in the army immediately.

When the evacuation began, my mum, together with her aunts, departed, and left me behind. I still do not understand why she did so. I stayed with my grandma, under the German occupation.

During that time, my grandma's oldest son lived with her, together with his wife, Lida, and two children, Valya and Lena (by his first wife, who had died).

One autumn day, when the Germans had already occupied Kiev, Lida came home and said she had joined a *Volksdeutsch* organization (she was an ethnic German born in Povolzhye). Then, pointing her finger at me, she said: 'If this little Jew doesn't leave, I will turn him in and will get an extra ration for it.'

I fled immediately, not knowing where to, and went wandering and begging. The first place I reached was the town of Belaya Tserkov. I walked there along the streets, in the markets, begging for a piece of bread. I spent nights wherever I could, and it was already getting very cold during the nights.

Once I came to a big grey building. Later I learned it was a *soldatenheim* [a soldiers' house]. At the back of the house, in the yard, there was a shed with open doors in it, and I saw an elderly man chopping wood there. I asked him for a small piece of bread. He told me he didn't have any, and started asking me who I was and where I was from. I told him I had been evacuated from Kiev together with my mum, but then the train was bombed, I got lost, and now I was walking around places, begging for bread.

Then, 'Uncle' Vasya (the man's name) explained that he worked there as a joiner and also supplied wood to the kitchen. He allowed me to live in the shed and help him saw the wood. I was afraid to tell him I was Jewish. I was afraid he would betray me and turn me in. I lived through the autumn and winter in this shed until another man, named Ivan, was hired as a yard-keeper. He got drunk all of the time, kept saying I looked Jewish and that 'measures need to be taken'. Not waiting until he finally took the 'measures', I left. So that people wouldn't think I imagined all this, here are the names of the people who worked there: Larissa Semenovna, a *Volksdeutsch* administrator; Wanda, their cashier; Vassily Ivanovich, chef; Natasha, a barmaid; Galya and another Natasha, waitresses.

There were many people working at the kitchen but I don't remember their names. Three German women were in charge: a thin, tall, dark-haired woman named Eleonora, *oberschwester* [head nurse] (they said she was a countess, and generals kept paying her visits); Louisa, a red-haired, plump, round-faced woman; and Mariana, short, thin and dark-haired with wicked grey eyes.

The latter two loved to slap waitresses and cooks, especially if the countess had slapped them before. I remembered them so well that I would recognize them among dozens others, even now.

Having fled from the *soldatenheim*, I again went on wandering around and begging.

Thus, in the spring of 1942, I reached Zhitomir. Hungry, weak and heavily covered with lice, I knocked on one door. A woman (Vera Fedorovna) came out, asked me who I was and where I had come from. She said, 'Don't be afraid of me, little boy, I won't betray you.' She had very kind eyes and I told her the truth straight away. Aunt Vera took me into the house, cleaned me and began taking care of me. Uncle Sasha (Alexander Nikolayevich, her husband) and their son Boris, a boy of my age, lived in the house. Together with Borya we went to the market and sold water, matches and cigarettes that we bought off the Hungarians. Even now, I remember their names – Livato and Guniya. In time, their neighbours started to say that I really didn't look like their relative but more likely as a Jew. By then I had fallen ill with pneumonia and couldn't get well for a long time. Then, Uncle Sasha took me to his relatives in Rakitno, Rovno oblast, as if to be treated. This was in December 1942.

Thus, I entered the family of Anishchuk. Boris Mikhailovich Anishchuk was a doctor; his wife, Evgeniya Fedorovna, a housewife; and their daughter Tamara was of my age. Uncle Borya treated me, and often partisans came in the middle of the night for his help too.

When the raids for partisans and Jews began in town, Tamara's parents wanted to take me to their friends who were hiding Jews in their cellar. But I became scared and ran away without saying a word to them.

And again, there was hunger, cold and lice. Then I developed scabies. My body started to rot with the itch, and I got very weak. Again I went through many villages begging for food. Sometimes people gave me some food, sometimes they simply chased me away. It was understandable: who would want to let a dirty, itchy beggar full of lice into their house?

Thus I wandered and almost reached Odessa, coming to the village of Krasnoarmeyskoye or Krasnozvezdnoye, I don't remember exactly. Here, a very poor woman with three children picked me up, and took care of me using her own folk remedies.

It was in this village that I saw the liberators. When I learned that Kiev was freed, I went back home. I found my grandma. By that time, Lida and Uncle Vitya had moved to Vinnitsa, and I never saw them again.

In 1944, a letter from my mother found me in Kiev. She was in the town of Chkalov. She lived there with her sisters Gita and Tena. My two cousins, Zoya and Vera, Aunt Gita's daughters, were there as well. Then, my mother sent me money for the trip, and in late 1944 I went to her.

In 1945, I was given a job as an assistant to the shoemaker at the Chkalov Fifth Grain Processing Factory. My Aunt Tena worked there as a commercial agent. In 1946, we returned to Kiev.

Everthing I have described is not the fruit of my imagination but, unfortunately, the bitter truth. I don't have any documents to prove my story, and I couldn't have obtained them from anywhere. The only people who could prove that I was living under the occupation were Zoya and Vera, my cousins, Boris Alexandrovich Mitrofanov and Tamara Borisovna Khomitskaya (Anishchuk), the 'Righteous among the Nations'. Their families saved me during the years of occupation. I met Boris and Tamara accidentally, in the 1980s, in Kiev. They moved here after the war.

6. We were in distress all of the time

Maria Bortniker (Averbuch) (b. 1930)

My name is Maria Yogannovna Bortniker-Averbuch, and I was born in 1930. Before the Great Patriotic War I had just finished the fourth form at my school in Shargorod. When the war began I was eleven years old. Everything we had to live through during the three years of the Fascist and Romanian occupation in the Shargorod ghetto left an indelible trace in my memory.

I lived with my mum and brother in the house of our aunt and her husband.

When a group of the SS arrived, the Jewish community was required to pay a 'contribution'. More and more various demands and conditions were established with each and every day. Failing to meet these demands entailed a death penalty. And even though before the war people had been mostly poor, all demands were none the less met.

Besides this, SS soldiers came into our houses, accompanied by police with their dogs, and robbed people. If doors were closed, they broke in, and smashed everything in the house. That was why, when leaving the house, we left our door open. The SS went through our clothes and things in the closets, in the wardrobe, in the attic.

I remember that we were in distress all of the time. We didn't take our clothes off for the night, grown-ups never slept and we were always ready to run any minute to our hiding place – the so-called 'secret chamber'.

The SS left suddenly one night, having packed all they had robbed into boxes specially prepared for this. Then, some time later, we learned about the mass slaughter of Jews in other districts of Vinnitsa oblast. Those Jews who had miraculously survived and came to us (the Padva family, and others) told us of horrors.

The ghetto prisoners were not allowed to walk along the central street or leave the ghetto. We had to wear armbands with yellow Stars of David on them at all times. We couldn't earn our living anywhere, and had to trade clothes for food from farmers.

Our neighbour, Raya Shtekkel, was shot for helping her seven-teen-year-old daughter and a friend run away from the soldiers who were bothering them. Long before the curfew, the local police-men were hunting Jews in the streets, throwing them in prison, beating and torturing them, and demanding ransom. Thus Alter Lopata, our old neighbour, was beaten almost to death.

Those who were fit to work were taken away to work in a *kolkhoz* for some time. These people lived with farmers who generously shared their food with the prisoners. My mother often recalled these people with gratitude.

While Mum and my brother were working in the *kolkhoz*, I was left at home with the old people, and starved. Once, in the middle of the night, a terrible racket on the door announced the arrival of the police. They began to beat the old people with truncheons, demanding more money.

When the Romanians took over the area, Shargorod was filled with Jews deported from Romania, Bukovina and Moldavia. Beside the five of us, eleven more people were now put into our house. Other houses were also packed with newcomers. Jews lived in all the synagogues, and they had come from as far away as Dorogoy, Suchava and other places. People slept on the floor. An epidemic of typhoid fever began, killing people in dozens. People were dying from cold, hunger, and the absence of medicines.

Every morning the cold bodies of naked dead people were taken away from the synagogue, which was across the street from our house. They were put on a sledge, covered with a black blanket, with their legs and arms sticking out. The clothes were taken off the dead to be traded for food. There were so many dead people that they were buried in common graves.

I remember another episode. During a raid on youngsters, who were to be sent to the labour camp of Trikhaty (and others), my brother jumped through the door in the kitchen to the cellar and knocked a boiling samovar over himself. He was burned badly, especially on his head and shoulders. He was put into bed and cov-ered with wet towels. A policeman who entered the room saw a moaning young man with a wet towel on his head, and, thinking he was ill with typhoid, left quickly.

Over the course of three years, six people died in our house alone. On the victory day, my uncle died. Our people could endure more than the Jews from Romania. A factory owner, together with his wife and parents, died from typhoid fever, while his elderly brother and sister died of cold.

When the Germans were retreating, the ghetto seemed to be empty and dead. People hid away in specially made hiding places, which they didn't leave until our troops entered the town.

7. Under occupation[1]

Alexey Brick (B. 1935)

My childhood memory retained well the events of the first year of the war. At the end of August 1941 the Germans entered our village of Kuzmintsy, Gaisin district, Vinnitsa oblast. I remember how my mum, my grandma and myself, as well as a few other families, hid in a bomb shelter constructed in our kitchen garden while the battle lasted. But the battle was short, and our troops retreated. When I came out into the street with the other children, the Germans were already in the village. It was a hot day, and many of them having taken their uniform shirts off, were pouring cold water down on themselves. A few days passed.

And then Stars of David appeared on our doors, and on the doors of my aunt's house, the only two Jewish families living in the village. My mum, aunt and grandma were made to wear armbands with *Magen Davids*. Two to three months later we were shocked by terrible news: in Balandiyka, in Gaisin (a place similar to Babi Yar), about 1,000 Jews from places nearby and from Gaisin itself, were slaughtered, and good, young professionals were moved into the ghetto. It was then that our close family, who lived in Gaisin, died. When we heard about it, we hid at one of our neighbours' homestead. In the shed where the cattle was kept and hay was stacked, special recesses were built and we hid there during pogroms.

Following the first pogrom, my mother turned to Vassily Shaydyuk, the village headman, with a request to leave us alone. We knew him well, because he had frequently visited us before the war, and grew up with my mum's brothers who helped him since his parents were sent away to Siberia and their wealth taken away. He said, 'I won't take you to the Gaisin ghetto if I am not ordered to do so; but if I am, I will take even my Kilinka [his wife] there.' We didn't doubt he would do what he said.

During the day Mum went to work, and at night we didn't sleep at home – we were afraid of being 'taken away'. Two military divisions were stationed in the village: the German Kommandant's office and a Tatar division who served with the Germans. People said that the Kommandant was a humane person. Maybe that was why we survived. He not only knew about two Jewish families living in his territory but also recognized us.

We spent three years under occupation. We survived a lot of different things. And although some things may be forgotten now, there were some events that I could never forget.

We survived a few pogroms. And how could I ever forget my mum's cousin, Uncle David? He escaped from a German concentration camp, and walked more than a thousand kilometres. A neighbour denounced him to the Germans. My uncle came to us in the middle of the night, spoke with Mum, and after he had left the Germans surrounded our house. We survived only because he had gone. In the morning they caught him, sent him to the ghetto, and then to Balandiyka.

I remember an episode with Boris, my mum's brother. He also escaped from German imprisonment, and returned home. His wife was Russian and he had two children. She said the Germans wouldn't take him. Before the war he had worked as a veterinarian in a *sovkhoz* [collective farm] near Gaisin. When he returned, they took him back to work. He wanted to join the partisans, and Grandma asked him to do so, yet his wife cried and said that if he left, she would be shot, together with their children. He listened to her. One day having sold a few pigs in the Gaisin market, he was walking back home. A certain Stasyuk, who had been his sanitary assistant before the war and then became a German policeman, betrayed him. The Germans were taking another group of victims to Balandiyka, when Stasyuk, who was escorting them, saw my uncle, pointed at him and said, 'Here's a partisan!' He was taken, with no explanations, and shot.

I will never forget another episode with a young man (I don't know his name now). Before the war, his family, which lived in our village had moved out to Gaisin. Now they were all in the ghetto. And then he came back to the village. The very same neighbour betrayed him. She was a paid informer for the Germans. The young man was put near the cages containing the German shepherd dogs. And one night he was gone. The rumour made the rounds that a local person, who cleaned the cages and fed the dogs, had let him out. The man was threatened that if the following day he couldn't catch the boy himself, his own son would be shot. The following day, with the dogs, he caught the boy in a rye field. The boy was sent back to Gaisin and on to Balandiyka.

In 1942, my grandma fell ill with typhus. We had to keep that a secret because the Germans killed all those with contagious diseases. She had a high fever and was delirious. We couldn't turn to a medical assistant either: he wasn't local and served the Germans far too well. My mum came into the house secretly during the night and gave Grandma different herbal concoctions. My grandma survived!

Once, when my Aunt Lisa was going home at dawn (she had spent a night somewhere, hiding from the Germans), she encountered the German patrol sitting on a bench near her house. She wanted to run away but it was too late. They stopped her. She asked them to let her go. One of the soldiers hit her with his rifle butt in her face, kicked out her teeth, and then pushed her away. He left saying something, probably that it was forbidden to show up in the street during the night. While lying there, my aunt moaned and cried loudly. At the very same time, my mum and I were also returning home from the 'sleep over'. When we heard her moaning, we ran away. I don't remember how we reached the other end of the village. We didn't return for a few days and had been hiding in a haystack until we were told what had happened to my aunt.

On the eve of 1943 my mum could have died: she was shot at. It was the winter of 1942, the end of the year. At that time we didn't live in our house – rumours were that the pogroms were about to start again. My mum decided to go and check how things really were. At that time, Frantz, a drunken German, was walking along our street, with his local girlfriend. He was getting 'practice' in executions. When he saw the Star of David on our doors, he kicked the door down, and when he saw my mum in the room, he fired his gun. He missed because he was very drunk. Hearing Mum screaming, his escort rushed into the room, took him by the arm, and pushed him out. She was drunk as well, because if sober, she would have been afraid of doing so. In the spring, I found three bullet shells in that room.

And how could I forget a mass raid when young people were taken away to Germany? Once I was caught during the *Aktion*, along with other children. They let us go only because we were too young. It is difficult to write now about all this.

In March 1944 our village was liberated from the Fascists. Two of our families miraculously survived. It was over a year before the Great Patriotic War would finally be over. My father didn't return home; three sons of my grandma perished at the front and she mourned them for the rest of her life.

My mum passed away a long time ago. I will be indebted to her for ever. She not only gave me life, but she also saved me with her incredible efforts, raising and teaching me. I am thankful to all those people who during those horrible years saved us, while endangering their own lives.

1. Originally published in *Tkhi*a, the monthly newsletter of the Chernigov Jewish community.

8. One hundred and six members of our family perished in the ghetto, and thirty-eight at the front

Yelisaveta Brusch (Moschel) (b. 1925)

I was born on 25 June 1925, in the town of Bar, Vinnitsa oblast. My father, Froiko Moschel, was a tinsmith, and my mum, Revekka Moschel, was a housewife. I also had a younger sister whom I loved very much, Manya, aged twelve. When the war began, we lived in Bar, near School No. 2, and next door to our teachers, Molchanovsky, Lerner, and Kuperman. Two families of our relatives, the blacksmiths Kauman (my mum's brothers) lived in our house as well. I was going on sixteen and I remember everything clearly and well: how the Germans entered the town, and how our troops left it.

The Germans entered the town at 11 a.m., without any battle, taking it over from all four sides. I saw them marching along the central streets, in columns four abreast, in shorts, with blue ties over naked torsos, with no shirts on, with automatic guns in their hands, and without hats. They were tall, blond and athletic. We immediately went into hiding in a cellar where we lay with our relatives for a day until a neighbour came and told us to get out because the Germans hadn't touched anyone. When we got out of the cellar we saw many Germans stationed in our yard, and thought that they would kill us. But they didn't touch us, and said they were in the military, and would leave soon; one young soldier cried at our home, saying, 'I am only twenty-four, I want to live, but we have been sent away to fight. I have parents at home, my things…'. I felt very sorry for him.

My aunts, the Kauman family, kept cows, and three times a day they milked them, and the Germans took all the milk away. All of the time someone was coming in to get a bucket or something else, but it was relatively quiet and we were happy. I was taken to work: I washed floors, carried bricks and water. One officer started picking on me to clean his boots. I became very scared because I couldn't understand what he wanted from me, and he got furious, got out his gun and wanted to shoot me. Fortunately for me, an older woman was nearby, she pushed me away and started shouting that she would clean and polish his boots. And I ran away to the street and thus was saved.

I worked all the time, very hard, outside in the yard, and was afraid to go into the building. This lasted until the end of July (they entered the city on 16 July). And then they began forcing us into the ghetto. There were three big ghettos in Bar, each surrounded by barbed wire. We were put into the ghetto behind a monastery, near to a Roman Catholic church. When they moved us to the ghetto we were not allowed to take anything with us. And we had to live somehow. It was forbidden to go outside the ghetto. But Manya, my younger sister, was not afraid of anything. She crawled under the wire and brought us something from the people that we knew. Sometimes Ukrainians came to the fence and brought us things to eat – potatoes, peas and beans, or whatever else they might have.

It was a horrible time. Together with other people, every day, under the escort of guards (police, dogs and German soldiers), I went to work, every time to a new place. When we left in the morning, we didn't expect to be back because every day someone was killed, beaten or shot without any reason.

My mum had a heart disease, and she was fainting all the time. This lasted until 19 August 1942 (it was the *Spas*, a church holiday), when at 4 a.m. they all forced us out of our houses, telling us to take our most valuable things with us. We didn't have anything at all. The Gebietskommisar ordered us to hand over all our valuables, pointing to a chair they had set up. He told us that those who would do this would stay alive. I started crying and, asking my dad to give them everything, began searching through his pockets and begging him to do as they told us. My mum fainted immediately, and neighbours covered her, understanding that if discovered she would be shot immediately.

Our fears were not groundless, because one local *schutzmann* [policeman] started asking Yanover, a supplier, where his three handsome sons were. Yanover said he didn't know, and this was reported to the Gebietskommisar who ordered the supplier to be killed immediately. He was taken to the wall, and shot in the head. His wife went mad in front of everybody, and she was shot as well. The most terrible was the killing of Sophie Faershtein, a sixteen-year-old, incredibly beautiful girl. The Gebietskommisar saw her and ordered her to be killed, saying that beauty didn't last. It was sheer terror.

I kept crying, and begged Dad to put at least something on the chair, hoping that this would save us. And my dad, crying as well, tried to calm me down, and said, 'Leikele, I don't have anything, please calm down!'

The sun burned down ruthlessly. They started picking out young boys and girls for slave labour. An inconceivable lament started. Three daughters of my father's elder brother, aged sixteen to twenty, were taken away, including my beloved cousin, Manya Moschel. They were sent away under the pretence of herding cattle, but in fact they were all killed *en route*. Two daughters were taken away from Bondarevskaya, a widow. One of the girls used to work in the pharmacy and had studied to be a pharmacist and the other was a very good student and a very beautiful girl, aged seventeen. Like hundreds of others, they died in the Yakushinetzky camp, in 1942.

We heard shots coming from the second ghetto: its residents were being killed. Many lost their relatives on that day, and their children were taken away, but mostly, in our ghetto, people survived that day. However, everyone realized that this was only a matter of a couple of days or weeks. Every day we waited for another pogrom and every day we were marched to work. At that time I worked in the fields, behind the local sugar plant. Once Dad came (he worked putting a roof on some village church) and said that a priest told him that the following day the Germans wanted to do something bad to the Jews. Then Avrum Kravets, my dad's elder sister's husband, a tinsmith, came to us with the same news. He had two daughters, Dora and Lisonka. And my parents decided to take me, Dora and Lisonka to Benzion Kauman, Mum's eldest brother, who remained as a black-smith in the city and lived in our old house. Dora didn't want to go; her mum had been killed in the first pogrom, and she said she wouldn't leave her dad alone. My sister, Manya, who was twelve, wanted to go with us, but Dad asked her to stay because Mum was bedridden and very poorly. And she cried that she wanted to live, wanted to hide somewhere, that they would kill her. And Dad replied, 'Mum and I will be with you.' And she stayed behind, because we had to try to get out and get a job, and she was too young.

Uncle Avrum, Lisonka and myself went to the Kaumans; this was in the evening. Avrum asked them to let the children spend the night with them because, as people said, everybody would be taken to the work. Uncle Benzion agreed, but his wife, Aunt Lyba, said that they would be going to the farmsteads themselves and didn't want to take 'strange' children with them. Uncle Benzion became angry and left the room, and Uncle Avrum took Lisonka and left the house.

After Uncle Benzion's wife refused to put us up for the night, Uncle Avrum took us to our neighbours, the Dombrovskys, and asked them to hide his daughter. They could not tell him 'No' because Aunt Momuya, Uncle Avrum's wife, was like a mother for Dombrovsky. He was a Czech who didn't speak any Russian. I don't know how he ended up with them, but I remember that he had lived with them since I was very young, when everybody lived in a temporary house near my Uncle Benzion's smithy. Avrum taught him the profession, and they went around together taking jobs, and they got him married off to a local Ukrainian girl. So they treated him as a relative. All my relatives, when moved to the ghetto, left all their possessions with his family. When I returned to Bar, a neighbour told me that Dombrovsky's wife had accepted Lisonka (she was nine or ten then) but, two days later, she took her out into the street, and said, 'Go away!' and Lisonka was captured by a *schutzmann*.

I was left alone, and decided to go to the Shtarkmans, our relatives who lived at the edge of Bar. They were also *kolkhoz* blacksmiths, and they stayed out of the ghetto for the same reason as my Uncle Benzion, and their smithy was next to the house. I went to their house in the middle of the night. When they saw me, they became frightened. I told them how I had reached them, and how I was scared to go back home – at 5 p.m., with the curfew just started. Aunt Shtarkman knew me very little, but she took me to spend the night in her granddaughter's bed, which was small for me (she took her granddaughter into her own bed). I couldn't fall asleep that night, and at 4 a.m. I decided to leave. My aunt started persuading me not to leave the house so early but I told her I wouldn't go back home, but would head towards the fields. To do so I had to cross the road behind the northern barracks (built just before the war), get into the sugar processing factory's backyard, thus reaching the fields. There I would wait for the girls who were supposed to come to work. It was October, and it was cold in the morning. I had left my home lightly dressed and with bare feet. I was very cold, it was foggy and I was walking through the fog.

Suddenly, Podlisotzkaya, a young woman who lived near that field and was tending to her cow, called me. She said, 'Lisa, where are you going?'

I told her I was going out to the field, to which she said I should not be going there but should hide in a *bagasse* pit (a few remained near the sugar factory). She also told me not to go back home, that nobody was there any more.

Before meeting her I saw the Germans and *schutzmann* in the distance, and realized I had to hide, but I was in a kind of stupor. Her advice and the place of hiding that she pointed out to me brought me somehow back to my senses. I jumped down into one pit, and found Idochka Pinelis there, a girl I knew. My family met her and her mum in the ghetto. I don't remember her father. She was my sister Manya's friend, and they were of the same age.

When my Uncle Avrum came to us to take me away into hiding at Uncle Benzion's place, Idochka and her mum came to us too. She wanted to tell my parents what she had heard during the day, and discuss what to do next. Seeing what was going on in our room, she started crying and begging Uncle Avrum to take Idochka with him, too. An impossible lament and cries followed; Mum fainted. He told her that he wasn't sure whether he could leave us at Benzion's since he knew well what kind of person Benzion's wife, Lyba, was. But Idochka's mum decided to save her child no matter what and told her how to reach the pits, since this was the only thing she could think of. Idochka was afraid of going out alone at night, and didn't want to leave her mum at all; she was the only child. But her mother shouted at her and threatened she would be killed tomorrow if she stayed. Crying, this child reached the pits, jumped down and hid there.

I don't know for how long we stayed in the pit. The only thing I remember is that I heard shots – machine-guns and automatic rifles shooting – and I didn't feel any cold or hunger or the dampness of the pit. When it got dark, I went towards the Ivanovetzky forest from where the sounds of shooting had come; towards the pits. I heard the screams of those buried alive, I saw their naked bodies, blood, drunken German soldiers – and I fainted. I don't know what happened next. And I don't remember how I came back to my senses. I only remember that I couldn't get out of the pit. But when I reached the board on which poor naked people stood before they were shot down, I managed to get out and went back, towards the field.

Again, Podlisotzkaya was tending to her cow, and called out to me, 'Lisochka,' she said, 'where are you going, you are naked!'

I hadn't realized that. She took me to some old barn, and then brought an old dress of her daughter and a neckerchief.

Then, her mother ran in screaming, 'What are you doing? You will get us all into trouble, destroy me, yourself and your own children!'

But she gave me a loaf of bread, telling her mother: 'Leave me alone, maybe she will survive.' She started to explain to me how and where to go in order to cross to the Romanian side, and pointed at two trees in the distance, that I should keep my eyes on, but I couldn't think clearly. There was only one thought pulsating in my head, I was lying there, with the dead, in one pit; I was covered in blood. I was naked just like them, and killed: yet I was alive!

Suddenly, a woman came running across the field. It was Manya Foldberg, a typist. Podlisotzkaya knew her well, called her and said, 'Take Lisonka with you, you see what a state she is in!'

I somehow came back to my senses, remembered about Idochka Pinelis in the pit, and told Manya we had to take her with us. We went to the pit and told Ida to get out and we would go to the Romanian side. But she didn't want to get out; she didn't pay attention to my begging, pushed me away, and fought me back.

Manya took me by the hand, and we went away. I was walking and crying; I was hysterical, I felt so sorry for Idochka, for my little sister, and for my poor parents.

We crossed a river and entered the village of Golotki. Then we walked up the hill, into the forest and, suddenly, came out on to a German sentry box. They were chattering merrily there, and, fortunately, we passed by unnoticed, because there were no dogs.

We entered the suburb of Matleikovskaya, and then a local shepherd told us that we were already on the Romanian side. Here people surrounded us, and we found out there was a community headed by Grinshtein, an uncle of my dear Aunt Lyba. He put me into the home of a very good couple whose son was at the front. They boiled some water, bathed me, gave me clean clothes, and – not having eaten for three days – I fell asleep. They wouldn't wake me up. When I finally got up, they gave me cheese and sour cream, some sweet tea, and started saying that after all I had gone through and told them, I should stay with them as their daughter. Their only son was at the front, and God knew whether he would be back or not.

However, I was in a hurry to go to Kopaigorod. We had some family there, I heard, a very wealthy uncle, Melech; he was my dad's cousin. When he had come to Bar, my parents tried to welcome him as best as they could. On such a day, my mum baked and cooked and laid the festive table. When I arrived at their house his wife only opened their door a bit, not inviting me into the house, and called out for Melech, saying some relative was asking for him. I felt that things were not turning the way I had hoped for. But, as my mum used to say, God was helping me. Out of nowhere, an aunt I had never met, Momuya Zaleznyak, Melech's own sister, came up to me, took me into her home, understanding that her brother and his wife wouldn't let me in.

She was very poor, raising six children herself: daughters Tuba and Brana, and David, her son. Itzik, Yasha and Avram were at the front. All three were killed. They lived very poorly, ate thin soup and had no bread. The most horrendous thing was that the Germans demanded that those who had escaped from the other side be denouced. The question arose of how to save me from this, and the family tried to do their best. Their little house was on the road running down towards a small bridge, near a cinema. I spent nights taking turns at homes of some 'aunts', Gafiya and Nastya, Ukrainians, who lived at the edge of Kopaigorod, at the side of the station. Very often the Germans would catch people and send them to work in Trykhatky, Pyatikhatki. Each and everyone tried to save their own children, and nobody cared for an orphan like me. It seemed that everybody was watching me and hunting for me near the house. Once I was going in the evening to 'Aunt' Gafiyka, when I noticed a *schutzmann* follow me. I ran into her yard and told her about it. She told me to go to a shed, and burrow deeply into the haystack. He came in and started threatening Gafiya, but she was a courageous woman, and told him, 'Go and look if you want to, but don't threaten me, since there is nobody there!'

He rushed into the shed and started poking his ramrod through the haystack, and it was a miracle that he didn't poke me. He got angry, spat, and left. After this scare I decided to stay at home overnight, and was immediately caught, and put into the basement of a prison, along with other poor people.

David did his best to save me. Somebody told him that the Kommandant had a mistress named Sabina, and she could ask him to do anything but she liked money. He went through the town, from home to home, to Jews, Ukrainians and Poles, and got 300 lei,[1] and then fell at Sabina's feet, and she asked the Kommandant to let me go and not to send me to the camp.

The morning of our departure we were put into marching columns, and I was told if the Kommandant pointed his glove at me, I should take two steps forward. And so I did. A total of three people came out of the columns, and we survived. All the rest died.

I stayed with my dear relatives until the liberation on 24 March. On 27 March I went back to Bar. Our flat was looted. Half of Uncle Benzion's house was still there. His children survived – Kolya Kauman, a Soviet officer who was imprisoned in early days of the war; his eldest daughter, Lisa; and his granddaughter, Galochka. Yankel, my mum's other brother, was killed, together with Benzion, Lyba and their younger son, Duzik. A total of 106 members of our family perished in the ghetto, and thirty-eight at the front.

Right after the liberation, their son, Yosif, returned. Before the war he had been a problem child, both for them and for the school. During the war he was promoted to a major, in 1944, and was decorated many times. I stayed with them, but was 'free' for a short while only: a local military commissariat enlisted nineteen girls into the army, including myself. I served in Lvov and Sambor.

In 1947, I was demobilized and got married. We were poor but we tried to build a new life. Somehow we repaired our flat. I gave birth to two sons, and have worked all of my life, just like my husband, who passed away a long time ago. I'm disabled and have four granddaughters.

After liberation, in 1944, I met Idochka in Bar; she told me her story. She had spent another day in the pit, and on the dawn of the following day, frozen, she got out and went towards the two trees pointed out by Podlisotzkaya to Foldberg and me. When we were leaving, Foldberg told Idochka: 'You can't stay here for long. If you decide to go, go this way.'

So she went the way she was told, crossed the river, and got to Bar station, and this was already on the Romanian side. But she didn't realize that. She hid from all people she saw, and behaved as if insane. People were noisy, the *schutzmann* were running around, she even saw a couple of German soldiers … It was a station! At that time one of the freight trains stopped. The engine driver had been observing the child's abnormal behaviour for a long while from his train. He watched her, then got off the train, came to her unnoticed and said, 'Don't be afraid of me, follow me.' He put her into an empty place and told her, 'Be a good girl, wait for me here. I will get into the station, register, and will come and take you to the train to Mogilev; there are a lot of your people there.'

Ida waited for some while. He came, and as promised, he took her to Mogilev. There, the Red Army liberated her, and she returned to Bar. Her mother had been killed and she stayed alone, with no means of support. If I hadn't been enlisted in the army, she would have stayed with me. For some time, Idochka worked for one local man, and then her aunt came from Kharkov and took her away. She graduated from evening classes there, then from a technical school and went to Grozny. There she met her Marat, they lived very happily and raised a daughter. She lives in Astrakhan now. Idochka wrote to me that they dreamt of getting together with her daughter, because of the Chechen war, but I don't know whether they have managed this or not. I want to hope for the best.

NOTE

1.　The Romanian currency; singular, leu.

9. A lot could be recalled, but the memory is very painful

Mikhail Burd (b. 1932)

I was born in 1932, in the village of Dzygovka, Yampol district, Vinnitsa oblast. When I was seven months old, I became an orphan. My mum died in 1933; my father remarried and never recognized me as his son, although he lived nearby, in the neighbouring Chernovtsy district. My grandma raised me until I reached fourteen years of age. My grandma was everything to me.

Our village was very big. Jews lived in the centre of it. They were all busy doing their own business. There were also professionals in different trades among us.

The war began, and planes with black crosses on their wings were humming threateningly above our heads. People said that we had to run away, hide, and some people from the village went to Bezvodnoye, a place nearby. They thought they would find shelter there. They stayed overnight with some local Jews (there were five families), and in the morning returned home: it is better to die home than in some strange place.

A couple of days later we learned that local Ukrainians assisted and took part in the execution of those five families. After the war, we buried them at the Jewish cemetery of the village of Dzygovka. It is very painful to recall all this. I shall remember it all until my dying day.

In July 1941, we were all put into one place, and the ghetto was established. Jewish refugees from Bessarabia and Romania were also put into this ghetto. After our place was liberated they left for their homeland immediately. I am not going to describe how we lived there. Jewish people everywhere in the world know this well, since many of them went through the inferno of Fascist imprisonment.

Together with my uncle, we worked in the *kolkhoz* as woodcutters and tried to at least bring some splints home to burn them in the stove and cook something. I remember the following episode. An old threshing machine was in the *kolkhoz*, and I started to take laths off it. I had made a first bundle and put it on my shoulders when, at that moment, a German saw me, and motioned with his finger for me to approach. My blood chilled in my veins. I thought this was the end. I acted very fast; I threw the bundle of wood to the ground immediately, jumped up on to the machine, and from there I jumped over the tall fence. At that moment I heard shots, but it was too late. I was already down, all in the thistles, and running home across the gardens. They were pulling the thistles out of me for two days.

Once the Ukrainian police broke into the ghetto and captured one man, named Donik Bondar (we called him this because he was a cooper), some fifty years old. Vovk, a drunken policeman, ordered him to make twelve barrels by the morning. Donik said, 'I will make one barrel only.'

Then Vovk put his rifle into Donik's mouth and fired. The bullet blew his head away. He was a very respected man in the Dzygovka community. All the community wept for him.

I recall the Giter family, our neighbours. Avrum Giter was a photographer; he had a wife, Gitl, and two boys, Yasha and Itzik. Avrum went into the army in the early days of the war, and soon afterwards he was killed. And his family suffered in the ghetto. My grandma and I went around the neighbours, collecting bits and pieces to support them. Thank God, they survived, and after our district had been liberated, they left for Almaty immediately, to go to their family. Soon afterwards Gitl died. The boys grew up, had their own families, and left for Israel.

In 1949, I graduated from the Borislav technical school and became an oil industry worker. I served in the army in 1951–54. And I have worked in the Drogobych Oil Refinery for forty-one years. I retired at fifty-five, and had a son and a daughter who have their own families now. My wife, Busya Shoilovna Trunyanskaya, and I are listed as former young ghetto and concentration camp prisoners. A lot could be recalled but the memory is very painful. The heart still bleeds.

10. Two mums[1]

Yuri Weinberg (b. 1938)

I was born in Kiev, in 1938. Together with my mother, Clara Alexeyevna Gorelik, I lived in Yagotin when it was occupied by the Fascists. My father, Grigory Isaacovich Weinberg, was enlisted in the army at the beginning of the war, and fought all the war years as a private soldier. We met with him again in 1952, when I was in the sixth form. Before getting married, my mother had graduated from the Kiev Medical Institute. She began working as a paediatrician in Nikopol, Dniepropetrovsk oblast. There she met with Anna Vassilievna Puzyreva, who worked there as a nursing assistant. In 1940, my mother was transferred to the post of chief of the paediatric clinic in Yagotin. Anna Vassilievna moved with us too.

In a new position, my mother demonstrated her qualities as a good administrator; she brought together a good team, and residents and patients alike respected and loved her. (That was what local residents of Yagotin told me after the war, including doctors who had worked with her until late 1942.)

In the first days of the war, the Germans killed almost all the Jews in Yagotin, including my relatives. The Skoversky family and Anna Vassilievna Puzyreva hid my mother and me in their flats. Life under such circumstances was full of various unexpected things. We feared being discovered because, along with us, those who hid us would be executed. We had lived this way until late December 1942. All of this time, my mother was helping as a medical doctor for residents of Yagotin.

On Sunday, 22 December 1942, two policemen came and took us to prison, where two Russian girls – parachutists – were already being kept, as well as Galina Alexandrovna Tzarik, who had some Jewish relatives. I spent five days in prison, and was saved by Anna Vassilievna. She went to the Kommandant of Yagotin, telling him I was her nephew and she asked him to give me to her to be brought up. Kommandant Schultz agreed because, in his opinion, I didn't look Jewish. On the way to the Kommandant's office, Anna Vassilievna tore up my birth certificate and ate it. Thus I became

Yura Babichev, and Anna Vassilievna was my second mum. We lived together until she died in 1988.

My own mother, Clara Gorelik's, fate was tragic. On the eve of the New Year of 1943, she was taken to be killed, along with Tzarik and two parachutists. Petr Kolodiy, a policeman, was in charge of the execution. A pit was prepared in advance, near the prison. The executioners first tortured them, then undressed them and shot them dead. In 1959, Peter Kolodiy was tried and sentenced to serve fifteen years in prison; he pleaded guilty. Many years later I managed to commemorate my own mother with a monument put up on the site of her death.

Anna Vassilievna, a simple Ukrainian woman, saved me. During all the years of the occupation she never parted from me, raising me in the spirit of international tolerance, acceptance, humanity, kindness and compassion. Every year, together with members of our family, we visit her burial place. We frequently recall Anna Vassilievna's righteous soul. The kindly and bright memory of Anna Vassilievna will always linger in my heart because it keeps beating only because of her saving my life. She was awarded the titles of the 'Righteous of the Ukraine' and 'Righteous among the Nations'.

In my hard life, I had two mothers. One gave me my life, and died untimely; the other risked her own life to protect mine. After the war I entered the construction technical school in Poltava (1956–59), then worked as a subcontractor. I served in the army, then entered the Poltava Construction Engineering Institute, and graduated from it in 1970. When I was a student I met a doctor, Lyudmila Sergeyevna, a wonderful person. We got married, and raised three children. My children live because I live, a boy who could have been killed in 1942, at the age of four. I put a monument to my own mother and her inmate friends on their grave. A second monument was raised for Anna Vassilievna Puzyreva, my named mother. And I go on living with the memory of my two mums, Jewish and Ukrainian.

NOTE

1. Professor Anatoly Vanukevich, a former Auschwitz prisoner, recorded the story of Yuri Grigoryevich Weinberg. This originally appeared in the *Jewish News* and in the appendix to *The Voice of the Ukraine*, a special edition of the *Supreme Council of the Ukraine*, Nos 3–4 (Society for Jewish Culture of the Ukraine, 1999).

11. The terror of the Jewish population began in the first days of occupation

Grigory Weinerman (b. 1927)

When the war began, I lived in the small town of Rogachov, Baranovka district, Zhitomir oblast.

The terror of the Jewish population began in the first days of occupation. At first all Jews were moved into one street; they were not allowed to leave their houses without wearing Stars of David on their clothes. If somebody coming out to get food or water was noticed in a 'Ukrainian' street without an armband, this person would be shot immediately and other Jews were made to bury victims in their vegetable gardens. All good clothes and valuables were taken away.

It all lasted for a month or two, and then they began selecting young men. The men were taken to the forest and shot. One day, in September or October, in time for *Yom Kippur*, it was raining heavily. It was so heavy that it made the day dark. Nature wept when all Jews were forced into a local club. First, a list of people with different professions – tailors, shoemakers, barbers and others (about two dozen names) – was read. We were taken aside and put into three houses. Other Jews were put (or, to be more exact, pushed with bayonets and thrown) on to lorries, taken to the forest, in the direction of Kamenny Brod (about four to five kilometres from Rogachov), and shot dead. The pits had been prepared in advance.

Small children remained in the club. For two days the club was closed and nobody was allowed to get close to the building. Their cries and screams sounded throughout the whole town. Then the Ukrainians asked that something be done about these children. The headman and the Kommandant ordered carts to be brought to the club. Then the children were thrown on to these carts, taken out of Rogachov and thrown alive into pits or shot. The earth there was moving for the whole day. One cannot describe in detail all the terror we had to witness.

After this mass killing, the families of professionals lived still for another month or two in Rogachov, then lorries were brought, and we all were taken to the ghetto, in Novograd-Volynsky. Jews from Baranovka, Yarun, Novograd-Volynsky and villages nearby, were already living there. The ghetto was comprised of wooden barracks of the former flax collection station. These barracks were surrounded with barbed wire and with guard towers. German soldiers and the national police guarded the ghetto.

We lived in inhuman conditions, if one could call this living at all. The barracks were not heated, and the winter of 1941/42 was very harsh (-30 to -32°C). A meal was provided once a day only, and included a bowl of some soup and a piece of ersatz bread. There were no bowls – we ate out of military helmets – and the food was given only to those who worked. We, the children, got our meal from whatever people would throw to us.

Every morning the Germans, together with police, took all healthy people to work at the station. They loaded wood and stacked hay to send it to Germany. They laboured until exhaustion, with no food. Everywhere, there was cold, dirt and insects. People were collapsing due to hard labour, and every week the most exhausted were selected and taken towards Gorodnitzy, to the Sukhovolya forest, where they were killed.

Once the rumour spread that the ghetto would be liquidated. The winter of 1942/43 was very severe. I don't remember the date but I remember the Sunday night, when there were fewer guards than usual and they were all drunk. A partisan contact came over and took all the healthy men, and a few women, away. For children, an opening was cut out in the barbed wire, and they scurried around the place, starved and frozen. Some of them were caught the following morning and killed.

But we managed to reach the village of Kikov, Novograd-Volynsky district. This village was not far away from Rogachov. A few people we knew lived there, and we hid there until the Soviet Army liberated the village. People in the villages were different: some saved our lives and risked theirs (and these were in the majority), yet there were police, too, who were getting soap, sugar and money for each Jew or POW caught. Our lives were in constant danger, since anybody could denounce us and nothing would happen to them. But there were more good people than bad; otherwise we wouldn't have survived.

I cannot describe in detail how we lived, and how we hid after our escape from the ghetto. In summer we lived in the forest, in winter in villages. It was hard for the Ukrainians too: they were sent as slave labour to Germany. Villages were surrounded by the

Germans and together with police they were catching people and sending them away. But for us, it was even more difficult. In every flat or a house there was a list of residents, family members, and if someone extra was found, this person would be killed instantly, especially if Jewish.

We had to go through new suffering after the liberation. In 1944, on New Year's Eve, the Soviet troops won the battle at the village of Kikov and entered it. We returned to Rogachov. Everything was ruined and looted in the houses where we had lived before the war. Starved, poor, with no documents, we returned to Novograd-Volynsky. Nobody wanted to hire a young kid, there was no place to live, and everywhere was in ruins. A person we knew who worked at the dairy factory helped me with a job there. I washed tubs, cleaned everything, swept up dirt, did all the 'dirty work', but still I thought I was in heaven. The factory had a diner and a small farmstead; I got food there and worked hard and honestly. The factory's director, a kind person, felt sorry for me, and provided me with a uniform to wear.

Thus I had worked until 1947, and at the director's advice I went to the military commissariat: they were selecting younger workers and professionals to study in an aviation school. I was admitted, and finished the school with the rank of senior sergeant. I was sent to an aviation regiment as a plane mechanic. In 1950, I was referred to the two-year officers' school because of my good service. There, I studied until April 1952. At the time, the persecution of certain Jews began (as in the case of the Kremlin physicians and the Leningrad case), which affected my life too. A month before I was supposed to be promoted and get an officer rank I was expelled from the school, together with six other Jewish students, and we were sent back to our regiments. I returned, and served in the regiment until 1953, when I left the army.

I went to Baranovka, to my wife-to-be. We were neighbours before the war, and met each other in the ghetto. She worked at the Baranovka Porcelain Factory, and I found a job there as well. We got married, without any big ceremony, rented a room and lived there until 1954. Then we moved to Polonnoe, and found jobs at a local porcelain factory. I worked there in hot production, as an operator of the tableware slide. There was little automation in those years; the work was hard, and each case that I had to move weighed 200–250 kilograms.

In 1959 I began studying at an evening school, completed the course and entered the Kiev Industrial Technical School. After graduation, I worked as a controller and, from 1964, as a master of production.

In 1961 I received a one-room flat as a reward for good work (before that we had lived in rented private rooms).

In 1985, I had an accident, had surgery on my right eye, and in 1988 I retired.

I lost my childhood, didn't have any youth, and all we had lived through will stay in our memories for ever. It affected not only my wife and myself, but also our children.

Everything I have told includes only a few brief episodes from all that we lived through; these were separate muments, episodes, cases, but even they were terrible enough.

12. People starved and turned into skeletons

Semyon Weisblei (b. 1930)

My name is Semyon Aronovich Weisblei, and I was born in 1930, in the small town of Chemerovtzy. My father was a tailor, and he made caps. There were three children in our family: my elder sister, younger brother and myself. My mum died when I was seven years old. We were extremely poor and didn't have any money to get food. After school, I went to a collective farm, collected manure together with the ostler, and this person gave me some food. Then my father remarried.

When the war began, my sister went into the army, and we stayed behind. After the Germans entered, they took all the Jews and marched us over to Kamenets-Podolsky. We reached the town of Smotrich, spent a night there in a basement, and in the morning they marched us further to Kamenets-Podolsky. There, about twenty-nine or thirty of us were taken to a German named Barisch (people said he was the town's Kommandant), who ordered us to be put into the ghetto since there he hadn't received an order to kill us yet. They gave us husks from barley and buckwheat grains to eat as well as meat from dead horses. People starved and turned into skeletons. I spent about three months there.

Then they began to kill us: at first, the elderly, the disabled and the children. When they started killing children of my age, I decided to flee. I found some gutter, and crawled through it under the ghetto's wire. I didn't manage to go far before a *schutzmann* saw me. Fortunately, he thought I was Ukrainian because I was blond, and drove me away from the ghetto. I went away to Chemerovtzy district to the farmstead of Relekovetzky [now Zalessye]. I hid at Ivan Brizhak's, who was also hiding three other Jews for a long time. I spent the winter there, and in spring I went to the village of Dubivka, in the same area, telling people I was an orphan, and became a shepherd there. Only Volodya Shkandyuk and his sister, Lida Bolosetskaya, knew I was Jewish.

Thus I lived with different people, until the Victory Day. After the war my sister returned back from the front, and we lived in the house of our grandma. All other members of our family were killed.

13. This was a horrendous tragedy

Mikhail Weinschelboim (b. 1928)

My father was a painter, and he loved his job and our family, comprised of eight people. Our big, friendly family enjoyed getting together in the evenings and loved to sit out in the street near our small vegetable garden.

But our peaceful life ended on 22 June 1941. Black birds with crosses on their wings darkened a beautiful sunny Sunday morning. They bombed a sleeping town. There were the first victims and the first blood shed. And, on 7 July, the coarse boots of the Fascists were already treading our land. We loved it as much as we did our life. From the very first days of the invasion, they began robbing and killing civilians, and Jews were among the first victims.

The first orders of the Fascist government told all Jews, Communists and Comsomol (Communist Youth) members to get registered at the town council; those who disobeyed would be killed.

Jews from all over the city were ordered to move into one area of the old town, into the ghetto, and to put yellow Stars of David on their backs, again under the threat of being shot for disobedience.

Our family included my father, Aron Moiseevich, born in 1896; mother, Faina Efimovna, born in 1889; my older brother Efim Aronovich, born in 1921 and died in 1941 at the front; my sisters Polya and Tsilya; and my younger brother Syoma (born in 1923, 1925 and 1936, respectively). The Fascist bandits shot them all in 1941.

I was the only one who miraculously survived and didn't share the destiny of my parents, brothers and sisters. I survived three times by escaping execution. I cannot believe I'm alive.

The first time happened when my mother was baking bread at night, and at dawn, at four o'clock in the morning, they began pounding on our doors and windows. They ordered us to go out in the street with our valuable things, to go 'to work'. She left me at home, to take the bread out of the oven. She thought she would return home from the so-called 'work'. At first people were marched to a local market and, from there, the majority of them were marched to the airfield where the pits had been already dug out. The dead and the living were thrown into them. A few days later, the earth there still moved as if in an earthquake.

When I got the bread out of the oven, policemen came over to our house again, and started beating me up with a whip. 'Why are you still here and alive?' one asked me. I told him that my mother left me at home to get the bread out of the oven, to which they said, 'You won't be eating it; earth is your bread.'

While they went searching for the valuables in our closets, I didn't deliberate for long and ran out into the street. I had to run very fast for a thirteen-year-old in order to run away from the police. But there is always someone kind around. When I got to the stables of the sanitary transport, an old man whom I had never met in my life came up to me. He understood everything, took pity on me, and hid me in a big box where horse forage was kept. At the end of the day he let me out and told me to keep away from the Germans and the police. I went to the village of Grishkovtzy, where we had friends.

A woman who was friends with my parents told me that my father was at home. It turned out that before the execution the Germans selected Jewish professionals and workers who could be useful for them in the restoration of the barracks and other necessary construction. I returned home. My father began kissing me and crying; he told me of all the horrors that he had to witness. It was a horrendous tragedy, and although fifty-eight years have elapsed since then, my hair still stands on end when I recall all this.

We lived with my father for some two months. He was painting and they gave him food in their kitchen; out of which he would bring me some *kasha* and bread.

On one of the rainy autumn days, the Fascists decided to execute all the remaining Jews. They had to get us all together. For this, they used the basements of an old fortress. They started getting people together on Monday, and only on Thursday, having kept people without food and water for three days, did they march us in columns to the place of execution. This time they took us to the former machine and tractor station of Sukulino, near the airport.

About 200 metres from the final destination, in a garden, they ordered us to undress. My father managed to tell me that we would finally be reunited with my mother, sisters and my five-year-old brother.

We do not appreciate and do not value our life enough, and we often think it is worth nothing, but it is impossible to explain how great is the desire to live in moments of danger. It is especially great when you're only thirteen years old and you haven't accomplished anything important in your life yet.

At the fatal moment the solution came in an instant: I had to survive. When this nightmare was over, I had to tell future generations about the evil force that was ruling our beautiful land. The desire to live is hard to explain, but perhaps it was some higher authority that saved me that day to allow me to relate the story of it, albeit now, fifty-eight years later. But this was more than a story; this was the truth.

In the space of a moment, while taking off my shirt, I threw myself under an old harvester standing nearby, in the bushes. I hid quietly. I was waiting for someone to take me back to the place of the execution. But fortunately, nobody saw me escape. Listening to the screams and shots of the automatic weapons and machine-guns, I understood what kind of 'work' was prepared for all Jews that bloody Monday. I had only one thought throbbing in my head – to survive and tell the whole world about the trouble that had come into our home.

Some time later, I crawled out of that place and went away. I found myself a few kilometres away from the place of murder. Until darkness fell I stayed in the ditches, and then ran away from the city lights. Finally, I reached the outskirts, and since I was naked, I decided to knock on the first door I saw.

An elderly woman opened the door. She was scared but then realized where I had come from – she must have heard the shots. She put me up to sleep on a Russian stove, having given me bread and milk to eat. I couldn't sleep; at dawn she gave me old clothes, and having thanked the woman, I went towards the village of Bystrik.

I was walking through the fields, away from the roads, and reached the crossing of an old road going towards Terekhovo. I didn't know where to turn, and stood there for a few minutes thinking. There I saw a man who was a brigadier in a local *kolkhoz*. He spoke to me, understood what my problem was, and suggested that I go with him: 'I will take you to reliable people, they will give you shelter.' We reached the end of the village where there was a hut covered with straw about 200 metres away from the rest of the village.

The brigadier, Andrey Scherbatyuk, turned to the owner of the house, an elderly woman who emanated kindness and warmth. This woman, Filona Ignatovna Korshevnyuk, became my second mother.

In this hard and dangerous time, there were people who risked their own lives and the lives of their children, but who weren't afraid of the invaders and saved a life of a Jewish boy.

Filona Ignatovna lived with her two daughters. The house had two rooms, and you could move from one half of it into the other. The older daughter, Dora Trokhimovna Kurilina, had three children (two daughters aged five and two years old, and a month-old son), and she lived in the second half of the house. When the Germans entered the village, I moved into the part that faced clumps of rushes and if danger was near I was to go into the thick bushes, through the vegetable gardens, in a matter of minutes.

After a family council, with Filona Ignatovna being the oldest, they decided to save me from the occupiers, despite the fact that danger was hanging over them all now.

That's how I'd lived all through the years of the occupation in the village of Terekhovka. There were dangerous muments when the Germans would suddenly enter the village, and as the house was near the road I had to hide fast: in a cellar, or an attic, or the bushes.

Then, the winter of 1942 came. Hunger and starvation threatened us all. The food was very scarce, and the family, including me, consisted of eight people. What was to be done? I spoke with the people dear to me, and we decided to go and ask for bread in villages nearby.

Having gone through villages that were close, I had to go to distant places. In August of 1942, I entered a house in the village of Vovchintsy, Vinnitsa oblast (then Komsomolsk district). There were two men at the table drinking vodka. I asked them for some bread. They turned out to be two local policemen. They immediately saw what kind of catch they had. One of them said, 'We will take you to the Kommandant's office in Komsomolsk, and we'll get 5,000 German marks each for your head!'

I denied being Jewish, I told them I was Ukrainian (I spoke Ukrainian well). Then the policemen took me to the village council and called the headman. To determine whether I was Jewish or not, they took my pants off me by force. Before the war, in Berdychev, all boys were circumcised, and thus they determined I was in fact Jewish. Thus this tradition almost cost me my life.

'Now,' the police said, 'everything is clear, and we'll take you to a place with no return!'

I thought that this was my final hour. Who would tell the descendants about the tragedy of my people? And I wanted to live so much, being only fourteen years old.

I wore a military jacket, and there was a small strap on the back. One of the policemen didn't trust his ability to hit me with a bullet [if I ran], and held me by this strap. We reached a bridge across the river, and at that moment I realized that this was my last chance. And within a second, leaving the coat in the hands of the policemen, I jumped off the bridge into the water.

I tried to stay under the water for as long as I could, and swam away, with all my strength. When I felt that I had no longer any energy to do so, I gulped in some air, but then, hearing gunshots, I swam farther and farther from that place.

Darkness started to fall fast. But not trusting anyone, I decided to keep on swimming until the night came. When it was completely dark, I stayed for a long time in the reeds and listened to noises and whether there was a chase. When I was certain that all was quiet I decided to get up on to the riverbank. Then, I thought, this is my third survival. Again I was completely dirty, with no clothes on.

While I was swimming, I had to take all my clothes off. But how could I get out to people looking like that? Going across the gardens and listening to every noise and sound, I overheard farmers talking as they were sitting in the street. They felt sorry for a poor man who had been killed by the police. They said he must have drowned. I understood then that not everybody was a traitor and I could trust these simple people. I came closer, and not to scare them away, I said, also in a whisper, 'Kind people, I didn't drown, I'm here, alive. But I'm sorry I'm naked, I had to take all my clothes off to swim away.' In a few minutes, they brought me old trousers, a shirt, and rubber shoes, as well as a piece of bread and a glass of milk.

When I was dressed, I thanked those kind people but left the place immediately because I was afraid of getting into the police's hands again. I knew the streets well – I had gone begging for bread there many times – and I decided, the darkness notwithstanding, to return to Terekhovka, to my second homeland, to the people who saved me and were twice as dear. Terekhovka was eight kilometres away, and I had to go through the dark night, across the fields. But what could be done? There was little time left before the dawn. I came to my grandma (that was what I called my saviour) with the sunrise. They were waiting for me; everybody cried because I had never before been that late. Everybody was very worried but when I told them the story of my third escape they were terrified. They felt very sorry about me and kept kissing me.

Grandma said that I was born lucky and that luck had saved me each of the three times. 'Now we won't let you out any more. We had better stay hungry, but you have to survive, as God tells us so,' she said.

Thus the village of Terekhovka and the family of Filona Ignatovna Korshevnyuk became my second home until Berdychev was liberated on 5 January 1944.

I returned to the town, got a job in a repair and construction department. We rebuilt the ruined city council's building. In June 1944, I went to work in a mill. In April 1950, I was drafted into the army, where I served until October 1954, and after I returned home, in December 1954, I got married. I worked until 1988. Now I'm retired.

14. From the ghetto to the partisans[1]

Golda Wasserman

In the autumn of 1942, there were more than 3,000 Jewish families from the Ukraine, Bukovina and Bessarabia resettled to the Tulchin ghetto. Every dawn, all those who were able to stand on their feet were marched to work. Nothing was paid for it, and no food was given. We had to provide our food ourselves. At the same time, it was strictly forbidden to leave the ghetto. If the Romanian police found a farmer in the ghetto, they would beat him up violently and take away all the food. Only on the way to work or back to the ghetto, were Jews able to buy some food from the farmers, or to trade the last clothes they had for it, and then secretly bring it in.

Every day, new groups of Jews arrived. These were people who had been hiding in the forests for a long time or had been trying to reach the partisans, as well as Jews from other countries of Europe which had been occupied by the Germans earlier.

Every day, between fifteen and twenty people died in the ghetto from hunger, typhoid, and other diseases. The Romanians killed anyone who looked weak or could hardly move. Dead bodies lay unattended, sometimes for weeks. Tortures and beatings of grown-ups and children happened daily.

About fifteen kilometres from the ghetto, there were Italian and Hungarian reserve divisions. As demanded by the commissariat-officers of these divisions, the Romanian gendarme who was Kommandant of Tulchin selected healthy young girls from the ghet-to, and sent them away, under the official pretence of working in the kitchen and bakery of those divisions. The girls returned from there having been raped, ill with venereal diseases. Many commit-ted suicide back in the barracks, while some of them were killed when resisting or attempting to flee.

Then the Kommandant selected new girls for 'work'.

Selection was carried out every fifteen to twenty days. It is impossible to describe what was happening in the ghetto – the des-perate screams of the girls, the pleas of their parents. Some girls tried to run away along the road. The Fascists shot them in the back. Only a few managed to hide in the villages, pretending to be locals, or were saved by partisans after long wanderings in the forests.

I belonged to the latter group.

Among twenty-five other girls, I was picked to be sent to 'work'. Two soldiers were escorting us – a Hungarian and an Italian. The road went through the swamp, over narrow bridges. Silently, without any agreement, Zhenya Fuks, Sore Vital, Clara Meidler and I decided to push both of them into the swamp, and run away. One of the soldiers drowned immediately in the marsh, the other managed to get out. He got hold of some stump and began shooting at us. Blume Krieger, one of the girls, was wounded. She fell into the marsh and drowned.

The soldier's gun became empty. While he was reloading it, we threw stones at him and lumps of mud. He lost his balance and fell, getting stuck in the swamp.

For two weeks we wandered in the forests around Tulchin, eating berries and wild plants. Then we reached a village but didn't enter it: we heard noises of machinery and tank engines. On the fields adjoining the forest we picked up potatoes and corn, and went deeper back into the forest. Barely alive, we were found by partisan scouts and saved from starvation and death. Only Berta Kimmelman survived out of all the wounded girls. Sonya Fuks and Regina Zalkind died of severe blood loss.

We became partisans. Sima Chabad of Sikuren, Rosa Grinberg of Chernovtsy and Leya Kuperman of Cisinau died heroically in battle. All three were twice decorated. Regina Kotesman, Hanna Beker, Lily Schekhter, Sonya Kurtz and Golda Wassermann were also decorated.

NOTE

1. This appeared in the *Jewish News* and as an appendix to *The Voice of the Ukraine*, a special edition of *The Supreme Council of the Ukraine*, Nos 5–6 (Society for Jewish Culture of the Ukraine, 1999).

15. This must not be forgotten[1]

Eva Gladkaya (Khamara) (b. 1924)

When the war began I lived in the small town of Baranovka, Zhitomir oblast, in Western Ukraine. I had just finished school. I had wonderful dreams, and hoped to enter a medical institute.

My family comprised my father, Avrum Nysselevich Khmara, born in 1896; my mother, Leya Ruvinovna Khmara, born in 1902; myself, Eva Abramovna Gladkaya (Khmara), born in 1924; and my brother, Naum Abramovich Khmara, born in 1926. In Baranovka we also had my uncles, aunts, cousins, other relatives and friends.

And suddenly the war began …

We didn't evacuate immediately, and when, on 2 July 1941, our Baranovka was bombed, we left on a cart for Zhitomir (there was no railway station nearby). But the Germans entered Zhitomir earlier, so we went back …

And back home everything was ruined and looted. The house was empty. All Jews were moved out to one street, Zhaboritskaya, where a ghetto was established. Each Jew, no matter what age, was persecuted, beaten, tortured, taunted and humiliated in every possible way. Everybody had to wear an armband with a *Magen David* on his or her left arm. We lived sharing one room with seven families, in terrible conditions. We starved, were freezing, and experienced inhuman fear continuously. Every morning, the Germans and police marched us, weakened and hungry, to the building of the former district authorities and from there we were sent to different works. Primarily, they took us into the forest to cut down trees and make roads for German transport. People were exhausted, but when people fell down, they were shot immediately.

The most horrible things began on 28 August 1941. At dawn, somebody knocked on the window and ordered all men to get together in order to elect the 'Jewish headman'. My father had to go. They were all thrown into the basement of a former prison, and beaten up.

A witness, who was let out from there for work, told me that my father was violently beaten with truncheons, and as thrown from one torturer to another. Then they were taken to their execution.

The place was in the marsh. They dug out a pit that was immediately filled with water. My father and a few more men were thrown in there alive while others were shot down above them. The pit was poorly covered with earth, and rumours started to make the rounds that dogs were digging out the bodies. Together with a few other youngsters, risking our lives, we went there secretly. The pits indeed were barely covered, and everywhere there were clothes and things left by people before they were killed. I suppose they left them so that the relatives could identify them and the place of their death. Uncle Kiva, my father's brother, left his jacket, my cousin Nyssel his shoes; many left passports and other things. My father didn't leave anything; most likely he was thrown into the pit among the first.

Another *Aktion* followed soon. Teenage boys were killed. We hid my brother in a cellar and blocked the entrance so that no one would guess. The boys were put on to lorries and taken away to be executed. The Germans who escorted them gave little mirrors to each of them to look at themselves before they died. One good-looking little boy, Munka Weinshtein, my brother's friend, was thrown out of the lorry by a German who took pity on him. And this boy survived.

The third *Aktion* was in the autumn of 1941. All mothers were killed and children were left to certain death. And again, my mum, brother and I hid in the attic, and when all this was over we came out of our shelter. We found out that the wife of Shlyoma Schwartzman, Dad's cousin (who couldn't stand this any more and had committed suicide earlier), was killed in this pogrom, and they had three children. The oldest was five years old, Bronya, his sister, was three, and Romochka, the youngest one, was only a few months old. We took the children to our place. The older children couldn't walk and speak. They sat silently for whole days without any movement. If we managed to get a couple of potatoes or a piece of bread, we gave it to them. They were putting food into their mouths in tiny crumbs. Only their eyes, full of sadness and grief, screamed. And the youngest, Romochka, was crying day and night. There was nothing we could give him. No milk, nothing. We all felt sorry for him, and especially my mum. She gave him her barren breast, to calm him down a little, and he tore it until she bled with his gums. Sometimes, risking her life, she left the ghetto and went to the Ukrainians she knew – and didn't know – to ask for a little milk for him. But this couldn't last for long, and Romochka died.

In November 1941, Germans and the police broke into our house and took my brother (he was younger than fourteen then). We were sure they took him away to be killed. But then we learned that, together with other able men, he was taken to the concentration camp in Novograd-Volynsky, to build the railway. He was taken away almost barefoot, in torn shoes, half-naked, and the winter was very severe that year.

My mum, two little children and I were all who were left from our family.

From time to time, Mum would get out of the ghetto. It is difficult to imagine how she managed, half-naked and starved (she never touched the food that she got for my brother), to get to that concentration camp. On 5 January 1942, Mum returned. The veins on her legs were obstructed by burst clots and were bleeding. Around noon, she came out to our neighbour, to tell her that her husband was alive so far and that she had seen him in the camp. At the same time, a friend of mine came running in with her mother. She said that the next pogrom was planned, and this would probably be the final one. The Germans were getting people out of their houses. The children were thrown on to the carts, one on top of the other, while the elderly and women were marched along as one crowd. There were ten of us in the house, and we hid together in the attic. I didn't want to go with them, I wanted to wait for Mum, but they told me she could have hidden in another place, and I agreed. But while in the attic I heard how my mum was captured at the door. I heard her screams. I wanted to go down, and struggled, but people kept me in. I never saw my mum again.

From the attic there was a doorway to a shed; we hid in this shelter, and there was a policeman standing at the door. We had to sit quietly and not move, but my Aunt Sheindl (Dad's sister) with her two-year-old granddaughter was with us. The child was cold, and wanted to eat. When she started to weep, they would give her a small onion that my aunt had kept in her pocket. She would suck on the onion and stop crying.

I spent only one night with them. I suffered terribly and felt awful about the death of my mother. My nerves were shattered. I couldn't stand it any longer, so I got out and left the place. That night there was a nipping frost. I knocked on the doors of the Ukrainians I knew asking them to let me in but they told me 'No'. They were afraid for themselves and for their families. The Germans and the police were searching through houses looking for Jews. Finally, on the outskirts of town, one family let me in and promised to hide me. They put me to sleep but at dawn they woke me up, apologized, saying that they were frightened for their family. They gave me a piece of bread and sent me away. All the time that we lived in the ghetto, there was a wonderful Ukrainian family that helped us with food and sometimes even hid us: Aunt Mariana Syabruk, Uncle Petro Syabruk and their son Nikolay, who was my

brother's school friend. Nikolay Petrovich Syabruk now also lives in
Baranovka. But at that time, even they were afraid of hiding me. I
didn't know where to go. And again, I was on the road. I was
dressed very lightly for the autumn. I went on without really knowing where. At the outskirts of Baranovka, where the final execution
took place, I saw a huge pit with poorly covered bodies of massa-
cred children, women and old people. The witnesses later were said
that the victims were ordered to undress in the hard frost. Then children were thrown into the pit alive, and grown-ups were shot and
thrown on to them. The moaning and screams of the poor people
were heard far away.

I stood there for a while, crying bitterly. I bowed to the martyrs.
Then I went to the village of Virlya, where I knew there were people who knew my father. They didn't let me in. I asked them to let
me stay in their shed just to get warm, but alas. I was very cold and
went on further, asking people to let me in to get warm. I walked
through the fields, as I was afraid of being on the road; everything
was covered with snow, it was blinding, and I didn't notice how I
stumbled when crossing the river and fell into an ice-hole. I still cannot understand how I managed to get out of there. All covered in
ice, again I turned towards the lights of the houses but nobody
would let me in. I spent the whole night hiding behind the last
house of the village, afraid of the Germans who came to collect
warm clothes from the farmers for their soldiers. My hands and feet
were frost-bitten, I couldn't take a single step, but it was very dangerous to stay and, overcoming pain, with frost-bitten and swollen
feet, I walked away towards Novograd-Volynsky, where my brother
Naum was with other Jewish men. Not really believing that they
were still alive, I nevertheless walked there because there was no
other place for me to go. After a few days on the road to Novograd-
Volynsky, I walked into the Olshanitzkoye forest where a husband
of my classmate, Galina Pilipenko, worked as a forester. I barely
made it there, ill and exhausted. There, they offered me shelter and
hid me in a bathhouse within the forest. But soon police got to know
about my hiding place, and that meant death to me and to their
family.

And again I had to leave. For a week I walked along old abandoned roads. I reached the camp. Some prisoners were still alive –
but they were hungry, covered with lice, and ill. They laboured very
hard, and were fed very poorly: half a kilogram of bread was the
ration for a week, along with a few frozen potatoes and some soup
(or rather grey-coloured water). I had to hide in the camp as well,
because it was a male camp. And still the Germans found me twice.
The first time they tried to rape me, and it was a miracle that it

didn't happen, and on the other occasion, a German beat me violently but didn't kill me. My inhuman suffering continued until November 1942 when partisans freed us. Together with my brother, I became a partisan in the unit of Major-General A. Saburov, fighting there until March 1944.

It has been over fifty years now, yet haunting recollections, illnesses, and nightmares don't let me rest.

NOTE

1. This originally appeared in *Shalom* [a publication of the Kharkov Association of Activists and Friends of Jewish Culture], No. 2 (1997).

16. Noble people were saving us

Leonid Grips (b. 1936)

For many years I've been trying to cast away all those recollections that were related to the first months of the war as a nightmare, as well as all those horrors that I had to witness and survive. But since I have written the first lines, I have to try and complete my story.

I was born in Zhitomir, on 5 November 1936. My mum, Tatiana Abramovna (Jewish name Gitlya) Grips (née Kamenir), was born in Zhitomir, on 15 November 1913, into the family of a cabinet-maker, Avrum Aronovich Kamenir, a native resident of Zhitomir. My dad, Grigory (Hersch) Avramovich Grips, was born in the town of Troyanov (twenty kilometres away from Zhitomir), on 15 June 1907, in a working-class Jewish family where he was the fourteenth and the youngest child. My parents got married in February 1936, and lived in one flat with my mum's parents at 58, K. Marx Street. This was a small house, a former wing of a mansion belonging to Minchenko, a tsar general. My parents' neighbours were people of different nationalities. Everybody was very friendly and respected my grandfather, who was very religious, could speak a few European languages fluently, and respected the traditions and customs of people of other beliefs and faiths. My mum was on wonderful terms with their neighbours' children, who were her age. In 1941, my dad worked as the head of a department on the machine-repair plant, and Mum was an accountant in one of the city's offices.

On 23 June 1941, my dad volunteered for the front, fully confident in our speedy and complete victory, and Mum, my ill grandma and I stayed behind. It was primarily because of my grandma's illness that we couldn't leave on time.

On 9 July 1941, the Germans were already in Zhitomir. It is a well-known fact what happened soon after they entered the city. My grandma, Mum and I were registered and told to relocate to the ghetto. The ghetto, organized in the centre of the city, was fenced by barbed wire. During the day we could go almost freely back to the city (provided we wore armbands), and get our clothes and food, since rumours were spreading that all Jews would be sent from the

station by train down to Odessa and then on to Palestine. It was all
staged to look as if it was for our salvation, since the same rumour
had it that the Ukrainians had intentions of killing all Jews. Our
neighbours insisted that Mum and I didn't go there, but should stay
at home and see what was going to happen next. But my mum went
beyond the wire with me: our bedridden grandma was there.

A few weeks later, Jews were allowed out of the ghetto less frequently. At that time, the place for our execution was picked, and
those Jews who were digging ditches for graves on the outskirts of
the city, Bogun, were among the first killed.

And then a day came when a decision on killing thousands and
thousands of Jews was made. We were already starved; the old
people were dying, the police had begun beating people just for no
reason at all. They were already robbing and taunting people
because they knew that our fate was decided and we were doomed.
Innocent people were hanged. Mum didn't let me look at the blue
feet and swollen tongues of the hanged.

But many people from beyond the wire were throwing food,
bread into the ghetto, and were searching for the people they knew.

On the day when all people were taken to their execution, my
mum and I were outside the ghetto. She managed to ask a policeman to let us into the city as if to bring in the gold that we had hidden, while in fact she went looking for the medicine that Grandma
needed. When we were coming back, we saw two girls in their early
teens, running towards us. They had managed to escape from a column of Jews being marched to the slaughter, and to get mixed up in
the crowd of people standing on the pavements. They were in torn
dresses and blood was on their faces. One of them had a bunch of
hair in her hands, and all her head was bloody. Mum ran with me;
we were looking for my grandma but couldn't find her anywhere.
People who were able to walk were marched off in columns by the
Germans and taken out of the city, while ill, weak and old were
simply thrown into the lorries and taken out. When we reached
Bogun, it was almost dark. The distance from the centre of the city
to the place of the killings was about six to seven kilometres. All the
way we were under the guard of policemen and the Germans. Long
before we reached the forest, we heard continuous bursts of fire.
When Mum and I entered the forest, it was obvious what awaited
us. For the smallest disobedience or resistance people were killed
immediately.

We were approaching the ditches and waited for our turn to
stand on the place of our slaughter. Mum put me up on her back.
She then explained to me many times that she did that because if I
was killed, then she didn't want to go on living, and if she were to

be killed, then I wouldn't be suffering alone. Headlights from cars
and lorries lit up the place of the execution. When the dead people
began falling down around us, Mum took me and, alive, jumped
into the grave, covering me with her body so that I wouldn't scream
(a bullet scratched my leg; I still have a scar). The bodies of the killed
were falling on to us. When everything or almost everything was
over we were covered with earth. It became quiet; nobody shot or
screamed, but the moaning lingered – the wounded were dying.

My mum was very strong physically, so she got out of the grave
together with me, and we crawled from the forest, to a field. We
spent the whole day in the bushes in the marsh, and heard how the
Germans and police 'worked' in the forest continuing to kill people.
At night we walked to the town of Troyanov, to my dad's hometown, and hoped we would be able to hide there. We walked for
two nights, and spent the day in the bushes. In Troyanov there were
no Jews left alive: all of them were lying in a grave beyond the town
limits. People gave some food to my mum for me, and told her how
to get to Zhitomir fast, where they believed it would be easier for us
to hide.

On the second day, closer to nightfall (there was already the curfew established), we came to our neighbours. Our houses were near
a small church, in a so-called monastery garden, next to deep
ravines covered with bushes, and a cemetery. Our neighbours, the
Mayers, could not believe we were alive. By the order of the Fascist
authorities, anyone who was found hiding a Red Army
commander, or Communists and Jews, would be shot or hanged.
Our neighbours knew the order well, yet they let us in, gave us
food, cleaned and took care of my wounded leg and hid us in the
attic. Anastasia Ivanovna and her husband were very afraid of
Minchenko, one of our neighbours, learning about our hiding place,
but told our other neighbours, the Pilezkys, about us.

The Mayers were also hiding partisans, and Kirschon, another
Jew, but I found out about that only after the war.

Those were horrible days. We lived either in the attic of the
Pilezkys' house, or in the basement of Anastasia Ivanovna's, or
spent whole days in hen houses or ravines. There were many hen
houses and sheds for rabbits. The days went by, the Red Army was
retreating further to the east, and it was more and more dangerous
for our neighbours to hide us, and there was less food. So, when the
Germans entered Kiev, our neighbours made the decision that we
had to leave and go and follow the front line. We found Alla
Schwartz, a friend of Mum. Her father was German; her mother
Ukrainian. She had been married to a medical doctor whom she had
divorced before the war. She was a very beautiful woman and my

mum's close friend. She knew some people who could forge my mum's passport. Now in passport 1-R3 50429, instead of Grips Gitlya Avrumovna, it was written 'Grepsunova Nina Andreyevna', and we have a document issued by the NKVD in January 1942 stating this, when the forged passport was taken away from Mum. The passport was forged professionally, since at numerous inspections by the Germans and police it didn't raise any doubts or questions.

There was another problem, yet clever people also solved this. When I was an infant, my grandparents, without my dad's consent but with his silent approval, did what was supposed to be done to a newborn Jewish boy. (My dad sympathized with the Communists but could not join the Communists for a year then.) To hide my Jewish identity, I was dressed up as a girl and had to learn to go to the toilet as a girl. I knew the Lord's Prayer better than many current observant Christians do. I wore my fair-coloured hair long. Nobody ever suspected that I was a boy and not a girl. The smallest mistake in my behaviour would have cost us our lives. (I couldn't get rid of the 'bad habit' of going to the toilet as a girl – sorry for intimate details – until the second or third grade.) Since those days I have had a rapid tic in stressful situations – the frequency of winking corresponds to the frequency of shots when they tried to kill us – and a scar on my right leg.

Further, under detailed medical examinations (I served almost thirty years in the air forces of the Soviet army) curious and attentive doctors inquired about the reason for, and origins of, my scar and winking, but the reason was left out [of their medical reports].

She [Mum] named me Alla (for Alla Schwartz, who helped forge her passport), and we set out on our way.

Mum walked and I was either in her arms, or getting a ride, or sometimes walked too. Sometimes farmers would give us a ride and sometimes – police (but Mum only got on wagons carrying one person). Sometimes even the Germans gave us a ride. We walked along small country roads, keeping away from central roads and highways, and bigger places and railway stations.

Mum spoke Russian and Ukrainian well, but the instinct for self-preservation made her order her speech in such a manner as to avoid words with an 'r' sound in them. She was afraid that the accent might betray her nationality. (Many years after the war she wouldn't use words with the letter 'r' in them.) She kept saying we came from Kiev and not from Zhitomir; that she was from a teachers' family, etc. My mum was an exceptionally clever, observant, careful and intelligent woman. She analysed any situation instantly, was not very demanding, but physically strong, enduring, persistent and patient. She was afraid of nobody and nothing. She smiled if a grown-up screamed at seeing a mouse. When spending nights in basements and haystacks, and in the fields covered with snow, she would throw a mouse or a rat off herself and didn't make a sound because this could have cost us our lives. She loved the sun: even when she was very old, she never hid in the shadows – that is because of how cold she got in basements, forests, shelters and dugouts during her young years. For her whole life she preserved the dislike of 'big water', she didn't like to go on boats or ships and explained it all by one accident. In the late autumn of 1941 when we were being taken across the Dnieper, I pointed out to her a gun sticking out of the rags on the bottom of the boat. It was clear that the boatman was a soldier, and it was not clear which side he was on, but it was as dangerous either way. Two or three other men were waiting for him on the left bank of the river. It was the end of the day and they were in a great hurry to return to the right bank. They let us go, but first checked Mum's passport and discussed something among themselves. When we alone and they moved away from the bank in the boat, each moment we expected to hear shots at our backs. But we were 'experienced' by then, so we didn't hang around there for long, but lay down on the ground and crawled away from the water. *Achtung, Minen* [Attention, mines] notices were everywhere. How could we leave any faster when the bank was all planted with mines and it was October or November? Mum pulled me closer to herself and tried to keep me warm with her body, taking the force of the wind herself, and thinking how to get out from there. We spent the night near the river, and in the morning we followed the footsteps of those who had gone to the other side of the river, and reached a country road, and this meant life again.

When we managed to spend nights in houses as a rule people gave my mum something for me – a few potatoes, a piece of lard, some bread or baked beetroots. My favourite place for sleeping was a haystack near a cow. There was the warmth coming from the cow, nobody would search for us, and it was possible to talk in whispers with Mum. And Mum was telling me for the thousandth time how I should act or what to say in this or that situation.

I was scared when compassionate people would put us up overnight on their Russian stoves: if the Germans or police broke into the house, the first places they checked were attics or basements, and then people were thrown off the stove, and they would go to sleep there themselves. People were different: some didn't let us in, others threatened that they would go to the village headman and report on strangers roaming around. It was good that at least they warned us; yet there were some who would let us in, and tell us to 'sit and rest' while they went to find the police. Mum, as a rule, would enter a village at twilight and ask that we be put for a night in the houses at the edge of the settlement, closer to the forest, so that when danger threatened it would be possible for us to leave immediately. If we saw that someone secretly left the house, Mum would instantly decide to take me out to the toilet, and we would run away to a field, or the forest, further from the house and that village.

However, there were significantly more kind, honest and compassionate people around and this helped us a lot. There were people who were willing to hide us at their place, and we stayed there recovering for a day or two and then went further on, to the east. Neither Mum nor I fell ill a single time. It was much later, when I was in the fourth and fifth grades, that my joints hurt so badly that I couldn't walk or even get up from the chair, and Dad took me to Odessa to a spa to be treated. Mum gave me food three times a day, even if it was only a piece of bread. It was a common thing for me to drink water from a pool or a swamp. The most important was not to stir so that mud was everywhere, and I learned to do it perfectly. The Germans poisoned wells and it was dangerous to drink from them.

There were many horrendous things but the most dreadful were the hanged, decomposing corpses of cows and horses, and announcements that *Judeh* were being hunted for. Cold, starvation and dirt were taken for granted. Another common thing was to spend a night in a small forest or a haystack, or in a burnt-out Soviet tank, while listening carefully to the smallest noises.

At dawn we usually were on the road. The Germans didn't pay attention to a lone poorly dressed woman with a girl in her arms. But the police were a threat. They saw a source of profit in any stranger. But Mum behaved wisely. She learned their habits, and didn't give reasons for unnecessary questions, telling them what they wanted to hear in advance.

A terrible thing happened on one of the crossings. It was raining heavily. There were many lorries and cars on the road, both German and national police. They were trying to catch runaway POWs and those who were found were killed immediately. The pile of corpses was very high. The police 'worked' and the Germans stayed in lorries under their tent covers. When a policeman was checking Mum's passport, a drop from the hood of his raincoat fell on to the page with the last name. He closed the passport and gave it to Mum; they felt sorry for us and put us into the lorry with the Germans and gave us a ride. They brought us to another village, and I asked to go to the toilet. They let us out, the lorry left – we stayed a long time because I was feeling sick. And when Mum opened up her passport again, she was shocked. The name was smeared. But her passport was never checked again.

For the first time in my life I saw my mum crying when we heard the noise of cannons and artillery clearly and realized we were close to the front line. There were almost no civilians, there was no food, and there were lots of military people. During the day we slept in abandoned houses, and during the night Mum walked closer to the front.

It was decades later, having been an officer myself and having seen much in my life, that I realized the degree of self-preservation, courage, and intellect needed to accomplish what we did. After having lost her mother and getting out of her own grave alive, my mum was able to find the way across two front lines, minefields and barbed wire, and to search for the way to safety and life.

Our way was towards Berdychev, Belaya Tserkov, Kremenchug, where they 'forced the Dnieper', and towards Kharkov. Near Kharkov, my mum caught up with the front, and crossed it near the railway station of Volubki, where they thought she was a German spy and wanted to kill her. Only after my mum showed I was a boy and not a girl did they feel sorry, but questioned me for a long time as whether she was my own mother or some strange woman. The Soviet counter-intelligence didn't believe her and took her back to the front line, so that she showed how she had crossed it. According to her story, the scouts went to the German rear, returned, and only then were we allowed to go to Voronezh to an evacuation station.

Later on everything was chaotic. We hardly made it to Voronezh, as the Germans took over Kharkov and almost reached Voronezh too. Mum didn't wait for long, and we tried to reach Astrakhan in freight containers or empty carriages. And there was typhus, dysentery, and piles of dead bodies at the transfer stations. Mum ran away with me from there to Nemchenovolzhye. There, barely alive and ragged, she went to send a letter to Buguruslan in search of Dad, and at the post office she was recognized by Graipel, my Uncle Grisha, Dad's cousin. He had seen my mum only once in his life, in 1938–39 when he visited his home town of Troyanov and stayed with my parents. He was an air force officer. Through Buguruslan we managed to find my father at the front.

Again, we were in the area near the front. We lived with my uncle's family. His wife Rosa, he and their two children lived in a dug-out hut. My uncle served in the aviation school that once had been in the deep rear of the country yet now was near the front. As I found in a reply to my query in 1985, the military division where Mum went to work was among the divisions that were in the area of military action. My mum got the certificate for 'A veteran of the Great Patriotic War' and many decorations. My father came to visit us during his leave for a week, and my uncle wanted to transfer him to his own division using his position and connections. But my dad said if he had managed to survive the nightmare of the first year of the war, he would continue sharing the fate of his comrades in arms.

He came back home in November 1945, alive and well, and died senselessly, in March 1973 – killed by a drunk driver. We buried my mum on 6 November 1994. She died nine days before her eighty-first birthday. Both my parents were buried in Zhitomir: my dad at the Jewish cemetery and Mum in the Druzhba cemetery. They had lived their life in peace and accord, never speaking much about the horrible years of war they had to live through, but they always highly respected courage and endurance, loyalty and faith in each other.

We returned to Zhitomir in 1944 and I completed ten years of schooling and attended a navy and air force school there. My course commander, the kindest person, advised me to list my nationality as Russian. I didn't do that and have never felt sorry, though my nationality cost me a lot in my career as an officer. Yet I didn't trade in my conscience.

Noble people were saving us, risking their own lives every minute. They did not do it for any material benefit but because their consciousness told them to do so. We stayed close with them after the war, helping each other. They are no longer among the living. But their descendants are alive.

17. The Fascists used to beat people and torture them

Hanna Gritzevskaya
(Dainicheva) (b. 1933)

My name is Hanna Abramovna Gritzevskaya and I was a young ghetto prisoner in Mogilev-Podolsky, Vinnitsa oblast, as well as in the concentration camp in the village of Pechera, Vinnitsa oblast, and the camp of Ananyevo, Odessa oblast, in the period of July 1941 till April 1944. I was there together with my parents, my sister and brother.

When the war began, I was less than eight years old. In the middle of the night the invaders arrested all our big family, including my mother, Manya Moiseevna Dainicheva, born in 1906; my father Abram Iosifovich Dainichev, born in 1906; my brother, Mikhail, born in 1940; and my sister Sara, born in 1938. We were not allowed to take anything with us except for the clothes we wore. This happened in July 1941. We were taken to the ghetto in Mogilev-Podolsky, and from there on to the Pechera concentration camp. There were many people there from all over the Ukraine. Nobody gave us any food, our feet were swollen with hunger, and many people were famished with hunger. My parents were taking off their clothes and trading them for food. The Fascists used to beat people and torture them.

In the winter of 1943 we were taken to Ananyevo. There my parents were forced to work; they were beaten badly and were not given any food. And children had to go to nearby farms begging for food. People gave us whatever they could. We were all kept in a school building; we slept on the floor covered with straw, all together, covered with straw as well.

I remembered well how my father and other men were forced to dig out a grave for themselves. When they were taken to be killed, I turned away so as not to see how they would be killed. But then partisans saved us. They killed the Germans and buried them in that grave.

Some time later, the Germans sent in other soldiers but we had been forewarned, and our men hid in the forests. Thanks to the farmers who brought them food, they survived.

Many people froze, died of starvation; many men and young girls were taken away by the Germans, and were most likely killed. My father and all our family survived by some miracle. A few very good farmers who were helping us saved us.

On 26 March 1944, the Red Army freed us. Everybody was surprised that we had survived. My father was enlisted to the front, and we went back home. My father returned home in 1946, wounded.

18. And at nine o'clock in the morning a miracle happened

Bronislava Grushko (b. 1921)

I was born on 15 October 1921, in Volodarsk-Voloshskoye, Zhitomir oblast. This was a quiet and peaceful little town with a beautiful park and a river, attracting people from other larger places in summer. We called them *achniki*. Jews formed the majority of the town's population. Until 1936, there had been a Jewish seven-year school in town. Of course there were the Ukrainians and people of other nationalities as well, with all of whom Jews had always been on friendly terms.On the whole, people were not very rich. Frankly speaking, all the talk about the good life before the war is exaggerated. There had always been deficiencies in this or that, 'temporary' difficulties and continuous promises of a 'bright future'. Political repression started in 1937 and couldn't help but involve our little town.

In 1938 I finished my schooling with honours and entered the Chemistry Department of the Shevchenko State University in Kiev. The life of the capital, with its wide cultural opportunities, seemed very attractive; besides, the studies were important and interesting.

And then peaceful life was over at four o'clock in the morning, on 22 June 1941. Kiev was bombed violently. But it was only at noon that we learned that a war had begun, from Molotov's radio address. However, the summer exam session continued and we managed to complete our third year, and our exams in German were passed even earlier. Zinaida Nikolayevna Boyarskaya, a wonderful teacher, taught us German. We had classes twice a week, with much interest and enjoyment. I had to use the knowledge I obtained there very soon and under very tragic circumstances.

The evacuation from Kiev wasn't going on yet; and I received a letter from Volodarsk, from my stepmother, asking me to return and join them in the evacuation. My brother, born in 1929, lived with her as well. Because of certain circumstances, when I studied in Kiev, I very seldom visited my hometown, and going back there on 23 July, I saw many new people. My friends had been enlisted in the army, or had left the place to study somewhere else, or just left in search of a better life.

We didn't have enough time to leave the place. When our troops retreated, there was no law enforcement in our small town. Robbery of shops and homes began. There were many people who behaved indecently. An announcement appeared inviting all residents of the town and villages nearby (except for Jews) to get together for a general assembly in the theatre. The objective of this meeting was clear, judging by the changed behaviour of its participants.

However, the most dreadful events began when, after a few gunshots, a German division entered the town on 2 August, in the middle of the day. Until 21 August, that is, until our liberation, the Germans had authority over our town. These were three weeks in which any hour could become our final one.

By then, there were many Jews in town, beside local ones, who had come from other towns and villages and who had to remain here when attempting to go further to the east.

The Germans were 'pleasantly' neighboured to our house: they set up their headquarters in a building of a local Communist Party Committee and its newspaper, publishing 'For the Bolshevik Progress'. We had a big house with a large basement, which had an entrance from the kitchen and an entrance from the yard. During shelling, very many people went down into this basement, and we saw the first German soldiers out of its window.

Our house had two entrances: one from Rosa Luxemburg Street and the other from the backyard. When a persistent and hard pounding was heard on the door, my uncle and I came out of the basement and opened the door. An armed officer came in, escorted by three soldiers. Most likely the feeling of being doomed and prepared for the worse added to my courage, and I asked the officer in fairly fluent German what he was looking for in our house. And an unexpected thing happened. The officer was surprised at my knowledge of German, apologized, introduced himself, and said that it was a part of his responsibilities to look around the house, see who lived there and whether we kept any weapons. I introduced my uncle to him, asked him into the room, assured him we didn't have any weapons, showed him other rooms, opening cupboards and sofas. There were no questions about Jews or Communists, but I had to tell him about the people in the basement. He ordered them to come out one after another, and commanded soldiers to examine the basement.

The Germans had a brave and victorious look. On the buckles of their belts the words *Gott ist Mit Uns* [God is with us] were inscribed. This, however, didn't prevent them from doing unseemly things. It is still horrible to recall that feeling of despair, detachment from the whole world, uncertainty, and impossibility to change anything. And all this when you were only nineteen!

In an audio classroom where we used to have our German lessons, there was a saying by Karl Marx: 'A foreign language is a weapon in the struggle for life.' I had many occasions to verify this with my own experience, and especially in the period of the German occupation.

Soon the town headman and the chief of police were chosen out from the local citizens. The persecution began. About seventy men were shot immediately, including all shop assistants with whom people were angry because of continual goods deficits. Jews were taken out to dig trenches, clean streets and do other work. There was no food for us, and we had to depend primarily on remains of potatoes that we picked in the night.

To be fair, I have to say that the Germans from the stationed military division did not hurt us and even tried to feed us. I would suppose it was the influence of their commander. Future developments proved to us that he was a noble person.

When we got to know each other better – and he was continually trying to befriend us – the German officer turned out to be a cultured and educated man. His attitude towards me was not only one full of respect and dignity, it was that of a true gentleman. There were other honest and decent people among them, too. My address *Herr Hauptmann* [Mr Captain] hurt him, and he asked me to call him by his first name, Woldemar, in order to remind him of peaceful times. I think his last name was Krepe. He was a fifth-year student in the law department at a university and knew literature well. I could not comprehend what made him take the steps to save us. He could not have expected any reward, or even simply expressed human gratitude. Hence humanity, kindness and non-acceptance of the cruel ideology of Fascism led him in to his actions.

He didn't exactly save us in a manner of Schindler or Wallenberg. The Soviet soldiers rescued us in the same way as all our people. But without his plan of rescue, and his advice for its practical realization, our salvation would not have happened and we would have faced certain death.

On the evening of 20 August he came to say goodbye to us. He said that at sunrise he would be leaving our town, and for the first time he spoke of Jews. He told us plainly that soon after their departure a killing squad comprised primarily of Ukrainians would enter the town, and the 'Final Solution to the Jewish Question' would begin. And he couldn't bear even to think about my death and the death of many innocent people, so he had developed a plan for our possible rescue. He mentioned a small place called Kropivnya (I didn't have any idea there was such a place, but local people knew of it), where, according to his sources, a Soviet army division was still stationed. A few men had to get there during the night and tell them that after the Germans departed only a small local police unit would remain and there would be basically no resistance. We had to ask the Soviet military command to save many Jews who would otherwise inevitably get killed.

But it was very hard to accomplish! When people learned about the source of the information, they didn't believe me. I had to convince them, to call on their courage, saying that there was no other option, and we would all be dead here, very soon, and we should use at least this tiny chance to survive. Finally I managed to convince three men, and in the night they went towards Kropivnya.

It is understandable how we spent that night. Nobody could sleep. At dawn we saw that the Germans were indeed leaving the town. And at nine o'clock in the morning, a miracle happened: we saw a huge lorry with our armed soldiers and three of our messengers. It was impossible to express the feeling of joy and excitement. I only remember how I hugged the first soldier I saw. We were given thirty minutes to get our things. We could take only things we could carry. Small children and the sick, and old people, would have to get into the lorry. Some people ran around informing all those who might wish to leave, and a few men went to search for the headman and the chief of police. They managed to hide, but three, the most violent and ruthless, were brought and shot.

And then, on 21 August, we were literally fleeing from death towards life. There were very many of us: people said, thousands. Escorted by our soldiers we marched in a few columns, taking different roads. This road didn't seem difficult for us. In the military division, they greeted us well, gave us food and some bread for the road. On behalf of the saved, I thank those who saved us.

The following morning we went towards Korosten, from where we were supposed to be evacuated. Going through the town of Ushomir we told the Jews we met to join us. But, alas, nobody did.

Why did many Jews, and even perhaps the majority of them, never get evacuated? I think this happened for a few reasons: first of all, the mass evacuation wasn't organized well at all. Those who had such an opportunity simply hired wagons or carts, and these people set off on the road, making stops along their way, as happened in Volodarsk. Second, many still remembered that during the First World War, the Germans treated Jews well, protecting them from pogroms. That was why people didn't really believe in German brutality.

All Jews who stayed behind in Volodarsk were killed. Those who believed in God and survived kept saying that God heard their prayers and sent His angels to save them. And those few, who really knew the details of how it all happened, believed that we owed all this to the German officer. Unfortunately, very few participants and witnesses of those events still survive. Not only those who were older, but many people of my age, died long ago, while some have become scattered all around the world. My brother lives in Orenburg, Leibson is in Germany, Bunis and Farber are in Israel. They remember everything, although they were children in those days.

In Korosten they put us into freight carriages, and we left. I got to the town of Rudnya, Stalingrad [now Volgograd] oblast, where I had lived until June 1944, when I returned to the Ukraine. I can't help but recall with kindness the people in Russia who accommo-dated us, sharing with us everything they had, demonstrating their kindness and generosity. Throughout all my life I have remembered Grandfather Faloley and Grandma Dunya with whom I stayed. I kept in touch with them until they passed on, helping with what-ever I could. And among the Ukrainians there were people who were saving Jews and risked their own lives, and the lives of their loved ones. Their heroism is now acknowledged. They are indeed the 'Righteous among the Nations'.

During the evacuation I worked as a schoolteacher. When, in 1942, after the defeat of the Sixth Army of Paulus near Stalingrad, a temporary POW camp was established, I worked as a part-time translator there. How drastically different they were – ragged and frost-bitten now – from those victorious winners of 1941!

I anxiously looked through each group of POWs, although I clearly understood that such a meeting would have been possible only in fairy tales. There were many Woldemars among them, but, alas, none of them was the one who had saved us.

19. Books could be written about any separate day survived during the war

Lev Gurfinkel (b. 1937)

When the war began, I was four years and three months old. In my pre-war recollections I see my father on a sofa, in a military uniform. He had me sitting on his chest, then raised me above him, and we laughed at something. That was how I remembered him for the rest of my life. He left our Ternovka on 22 June 1941, and after the war we received a notice from the military commissariat that he was missing in action in 1944.

My war recollections are episodic. But I have a good memory and I remember many things in smallest detail. I think if a child was fed with whipped cream and chocolates, he would remember very little from his childhood. But when a child witnessed the hanging of Andrey Voskoboinikov, a Jewish partisan from the Korniychuk unit (I can't be absolutely positive of his name; it happened in the autumn of 1943), this could never be forgotten. We lived in the Ternovka ghetto, in Bershad district (formerly the Dzhurin district). Mum, together with other women, was taken to work in the fields. Together with Leonid, my older brother, we stayed in the room, and ate beetroots baked over the bonfire. A door opened, and a few policemen and German soldiers entered the room. Some of them kicked over a chair with my coat on. Silver spoons were sewn behind its lining. The treacherous, quiet noise sounded. The lining was immediately cut open, and the spoons taken away. We went to Mother in the field, running through hidden pathways. I was choking on tears and asked Mum, 'What shall we now be eating with?' Mum gave me a wise reply, 'I wish we had something to eat in the first place!' Mum was the centre of our universe, with all life revolving around her. We didn't have any clothes, just some rags. But my mum was a seamstress, and from a quality German sackcloth she made a skirt for herself, colouring it with elderberries. But berries could not overpower the quality German paint, and an eagle with the circled swastika was soon showing again on the skirt! Mum made a shirt for me too, from an old home-made cloth, and coloured it with the berries too. When I ran a lot, my shirt changed its colour with the sweat, and all my body was coloured blue. In the evening I ran through all the rooms of our tightly packed house, and anybody who saw me laughed. It was laughter through tears.

In the summer of 1941, typhus spread in the ghetto. Out of all the residents of our house only my mum and Grandma Granovskaya were not ill. The Germans entered the ghetto wearing gas masks and this scared me. When these monsters approached our little house, my mum and Grandma Granovskaya tried to get up everybody who was ill. I remember how one old man refused to get up, and he was killed. Even now, after many long years, the smell of burnt gunpowder is associated with death.

In the spring of 1942 they marched us from the ghetto to the gallows where a stranger (without an *ausweis* [ID card]) from Uman was being hanged. He had come to Ternovka with his son, blind from birth. We stood around the gallows, and when the hanged man twitched and wheezed on the rope, his son rushed towards him from the crowd. Having perfect hearing, he picked the exact direction, ran up towards his father and caught his legs. He was a boy of about fifteen years old, thin, tall and red-haired. I saw how a few bullets from an automatic gun tore the blood out of his body which splashed on to his white shirt. I still can hear his scream, drowned with blood, '*Tote-e-e!*'

On 27 May 1942, the Germans organized mass killings, but Mum, my brother and I hid in the rubble. We were found only on 28 May in the evening, and were taken to a local pharmacy. There were many people already gathered there. Now I understand that they were tired of killing us, it was dark, and the grave was some three kilometres away. So the Kommandant said, 'Those of you who have gold, hand it over to us, and I will release you.' He realized that our fate was already decided. My mum tore open the lining of her clothes and gave to him a gold wristwatch and her wedding ring. We were released. This time, we were saved.

The children from the ghetto were ill with 'night blindness'. Once, a German military doctor brought into the ghetto three champagne bottles filled with cod liver oil. He told us to put three drops of this into our food, saying that those who survived would not be blind. He said that he had three children of his own, and he didn't need the war. I searched for a long time in the archives, and asked people, but have never been able to find the name of this honest man. But I know the name of the Kommandant – Kurt Emmel.

The winters were very severe. But if one could get into the half-dried manure, it was warm there. I know this from my childhood experience. It is true that I smelled bad, but at least I didn't freeze.

Speaking about the food: when the Germans retreated, a man on a horse stopped at a ruined house. He took a loaf of bread from his saddlebags, and fed it to his horse. Then he started eating himself. He wore an armband on which there was a letter. Now I understand he was a soldier from the Romanian Liberation Army. I stopped not far from him, and was looking at the bread as if I was mad. Maybe he had a younger brother or a son at home, but suddenly he cut this loaf open, put a package of ersatz butter inside, and threw it to me, saying, 'Hey, boy, catch this!' I caught the bread. I ran to my home, and a crowd of other boys and girls followed me. I realized that they would catch me and take it away. While running, I managed to take a few bites and swallowed some bread, but didn't taste anything. Older children kicked me off my feet, and took everything away. They shared it among all the children, giving a small piece to each and every one. I didn't get anything, because when running I ate a portion bigger than what was supposed to be mine.

When the Germans retreated, after two days with no law enforcement, the Red Army division entered the town. Machinery and soldiers were coming over the hill and across the pontoon bridge. Those of us who survived stood along both sides of the road in a packed crowd. Children were happy at seeing anything, feeling that the fatal danger had finally passed. Grown-ups smiled a little: each of them had someone in the army, everybody hoped to see a familiar face in the crowd, sometimes cries were heard filled with hope and despair, 'Has anybody seen or heard anything about Misha Wortman?'

It was perhaps on the third day, when a lorry was revving trying to get up the hill. There were about ten people in it, all dressed in dirty military jackets and tank helmets. Literally next to us there was a woman with a girl, aged twelve or so. Then, suddenly one of the men in the lorry screamed, 'Fira!' He jumped off the lorry; ran towards the girl, knelt down and began to hug her.

Such a commotion began! The soldiers stopped the lorry, I remember how much they rejoiced, saying: 'Semyon has found his family!'

I also wanted to see my father very much. I pulled one soldier's sleeve, and asked him whether he had seen my dad. The soldier took me into his arms and gave me a packet of dried biscuits and a lump of sugar. Ever since then, the smell of machine oil, which was coming off the soldier's coat, makes me feel better.

Once, some of the soldiers gave me a package of tinned meat. I'd never tasted anything so delicious. However, it seemed salty to me and with a strange taste. But perhaps that was the taste of blood from my lip, which I cut on a poorly open tin?

My mum frequently recalled our neighbour who was a veteran of the Finnish War in 1939. After six days of his war experience he was wounded and put into a military hospital. Then my mum was annoyed when, for years, he would talk of what his experience had been during those six days. After the war she used to say that books could be written about any separate day survived during the war.

The same thing applies to me – but I have to limit myself to a few episodes. But I would also want to recall what happened to Shurik Farber's family, a survivor of my age. All his aunts, brothers and sisters, the total of thirty-two people, were killed in a forest and thrown into a dried-up well. Another story could be told about the Bliender family. And it is very difficult to be writing about it – going through this all over again.

I still hope that David and Nathan, my grandchildren, will never experience the terror of war and genocide.

My mum, Adelya Yonovna Gurfinkel, passed on. For me she was an example of courage and of a true '*Yiddishe mamme*'.

20. Seven people risked their lives to save mine

Yosif Gussarov (b. 1932)

When the Germans occupied Kiev, I lived together with my mother, Nadezhda Iskorovna Gussarova, at 149 Saksaganskogo Street. On the second day of the occupation my mum sent me to her good friends, the Patyut family. This big Ukrainian family kept me with them. Moisey Kharitonovich, the father, and Anissya Korneevna, his wife, had five daughters – Maria, Nataliya, Oksana, Praskovya and Olga. A month before the occupation of Kiev, Praskovya gave birth to her baby son, Dmitry, and Maria lived in the village of Kobyzhcha, Chernigov oblast.

I never saw my mum again. The Patyuts tried to convince her to stay with them, and promised to send her further away to some other village. My mother refused. Two weeks later our neighbour turned her in at a Jewish market. Mum was killed in Babi Yar.

The Fascists ran a rule of real terror in Kiev. There was an order threatening all those who helped hide Jews with the death penalty. Notwithstanding all this, these brave and honest people kept me within their family, as a relative. Seven people, including a young mother with a baby, risked their lives in order to save mine. There were many examples of horrible executions of local residents but this never prevented Moisey Kharitonovich and his family from demonstrating the best of human qualities in difficult times.

Some time later, someone from their neighbours reported to the Germans that the Patyuts were hiding a Jewish boy. A big man, an SS soldier, together with his Czech translator, came to check this. I don't know how old Moisey convinced him and how much home-brewed vodka he gave him. All this time I was out in the yard. Only for a minute I was called into the house so that the Fascist could check my nationality, by taking my pants down. I survived.

I am not going to describe all the difficulty, danger and tragedy of life during the occupation. Much has been written, and movies have made about it. I would like to note one thing only: I never experienced any bad or unkind feelings towards me from the Patyut family. I was their son and grandson. I shared all the hardships of that life with them. I had everything that this family had. For the rest of my life I would remain their relative, as well as for their children and grandchildren. And my family (my wife, my daughter and granddaughter) would be their family too.

Old Moisey died in the difficult year of 1942. Grandma Anissya lived a long, bright and kind life, and died in 1965. Their oldest daughter, Maria, is gone now too.

According to the standards of our society my post-war life went fine. I have a wonderful wife and friend, Lyudmila Yisrailevna, with whom I have lived over thirty years now. We raised a good daughter, Galina. My granddaughter is named after her great-grandmother, Nadezhda (1908–41), who suffered an untimely death at the hands of the Fascist invaders).

I have recalled the tragedy of those distant unforgettable days with only one purpose: to commemorate the Patyut family, a wonderful Ukrainian family. I want to salute these people and keep a memory of them living through all upcoming generations. And I do this now with much gratitude.

21. We were the only survivors

Miron Demb (b. 1931)

Everything in this world has its end:
Excitement, joys and suffering.
And only memories have no end …[1]

By a wicked twist of fate, the German troops entered Uman on 31 July 1941, the exact day I turned ten (although officially Uman was occupied on 1 August 1941).

I remember well how I was standing near the gate at house no. 5, on Proletstud Street (now Zatonsky), and saw the first German scouts on motorcycles. I quickly ran into the house and told my mother and our neighbours about this (only Jews were living in the house). Some time later, on the very same day, following the scouts, military German divisions entered the city.

The headquarter vans and some other machinery was stationed in our yard. German soldiers didn't touch anyone, didn't beat anyone, and were only inquiring whether there were any Russian soldiers hidden anywhere.

My neighbours, together with my mum, did laundry and cooking for the Germans (people were afraid to refuse). They brought home tinned meat, sugar and bread as payment for these services. At that time, they had bread in plastic packaging and their sugar was white and crystalline, and looked like salt. The Germans thanked us for the services and said, *'Danke'* [thank you]. Some were even saying, *'Hitler, Stalin – kaput!'*: meaning that Hitler and Stalin were fighting, and what did we need that for? The soldiers showed us their photographs. They sincerely missed their *frau* [wife], *mutter* [mother] and *kinder* [children]. They were not interested who was Jewish, Ukrainian or German; they didn't care much.

It may sound as if I am idealizing the Nazis, but to be just it is necessary to say that there were normal people among them too.

But when the military division moved on, the SS, SD and Gestapo divisions entered the city. And then the horror began.

Within two weeks, six Jewish doctors were hanged in the most conspicuous place in the city. I remember the surnames of the two well: Dr Burschtein and Dr Gitis (people in Uman still remember his daughter, Assya Lazarevna Friedman, well; she is a dentist and musician and now lives in Israel).

All power in the city was centred in the German Kommandant's office. The Kommandant picked a few local traitors to form a new local 'government'. A person named Marzin, a former school principal (School No. 3) was appointed the head of the city council. Tonkoshkur was appointed the chief of police; and there were a few other people such as Ryabushenko (a former schoolteacher), Vladimir Palamarchuk (a former college worker, of whom I shall speak separately), Voropaev and others.

A local Fascist nationalistic newspaper was published in Ukrainian, called *The Voice of Uman.* 'Judeo-Bolsheviks' was a common word in this publication, as in 'six Judeo-Bolsheviks were hanged'.

About two weeks after the doctors' hanging, the first Jewish pogrom was held. There were three pogroms: as if in some horror tale, Jews were caught and beaten right in the streets and houses, and then they were taken to the basement of the former Palace of Pioneers, in the centre of the city, in Lenin Street (now, it's Diner No. 16). The basement was packed full, mostly with women, children and old people. Then, the gas was let in, and people suffocated. Rumour had it there were around 1,000 people killed, there is no exact number. According to the words of a witness, Maria Pavlovna Kovalenko, born in 1906 (who helped save me), the bodies were removed out of the basement, and local people had to take them on carts out of the city and put them all into one pit. The pogrom lasted for one day.

For some time the Jews who survived the first pogrom were left alone. The Kommandant issued an order obliging all Jews to wear a white armband with a black Star of David on the left arm. Those who wouldn't wear it were killed, in the best case. Jews were forced to move to the area of the market (Vostochnaya, Nekrasov and other streets): that is, to a ghetto. We lived in very bad conditions, a few families sharing one flat. My mum, a one-year-old brother, and I 'lived' in a two-room flat together with six or seven other families.

From that time, the black-and-white armbands were changed for bright yellow circles, about eight to nine centimetres in diameter, worn on our fronts, where the heart was.

Young and middle-aged residents of the ghetto were used for difficult labour. A policeman watched them, or sometimes there was a German guard. The old and ill people stayed 'home'.

What did we get to eat in the ghetto? I don't remember now. By all means, we were hungry. Sometimes we were given flour or millet. Also, Jews tried to secretly trade their clothes and valuables for some food. The Ukrainians from the city and villages nearby came and even entered the ghetto. Our pre-war friends from the village of Dmitrushka visited my mum, my younger brother Kim (born in 1940) and myself. These were two sisters and Yevdokia Kravchenko, who still lives in the same village. Their father, Roman Kravchenko, sent them. He later miraculously survived and returned from the Stalinist labour camps.

The ghetto was not surrounded by any barbed wire and it was practically unguarded. It was just that the finding of a Jew outside the ghetto, as well as 'visitations' to the ghetto by the Ukrainians, could be severely punished (they could even shoot the person).

The head and assistant head of the Jewish Council were appointed out of Jewish residents of the ghetto (Sambursky and Tabachnik, respectively). I remember them well because we lived in one house (it is now 5 Vostochnaya Street).

The ghetto headman had a beautiful daughter aged seventeen. One Ukrainian boy risked his life to keep coming to visit her in the ghetto. I saw them seeing each other in a small hallway of our house. She must have been in love with him too. That was true love. I don't remember the names of these two, and don't know exactly what happened to them, but people were saying that the young man saved the girl, and after the city was liberated, they got married.

Also two or three Jewish policemen and one policewoman were appointed. I don't remember the men's surnames, but her name was Ite Gleckele (that was either her surname or nickname). She was very cruel, and tortured her own people. People said that she survived but after the liberation Jews caught her, beat her up, and turned her over to the militia. Sambursky and Tabachnik died during the final pogrom.

From time to time, the Germans and the police would come into the ghetto and demand gold and valuables from the headman of the ghetto. If we failed to give them what they wanted by a set date, a pogrom would follow.

Then the headman with his assistants would gather the wealthier Jews together and demand the requested amount from them. If they refused to give gold, then the Jewish policemen beat them up. They put them on a couch, face down, and beat them with rubber truncheons or sticks on their naked backs until the victims agreed to give whatever they had. My granddad, Chaim, was beaten up like that too. But everything has its end; and finally all the gold had run out, no matter how severely they beat people. And then the terror began.

On an early autumn morning a pounding on doors woke the residents of the ghetto up. It was mainly local police armed with rifles captured from the Soviets who carried out this *Aktion*. Women, children and old people were taken out into the streets for *appel* [roll call]. Our family was about three to four minutes late while I was looking for my hat. It was cold in the street that early morning and although I understood where they were going to take us, I didn't want to get cold.

A policeman, who had made sure all the Jews had gone out, was eagerly looking through chests with clothes in the common room (at that time many people kept their best clothes and valuables in those chests). My mum asked him whether we could go and get the boy's hat in a distant room. I remember what my hat looked like – it was an aviation hat, with flaps like the Soviet aviation hats had. The policeman waved his left hand (I remembered that well), either in agreement or for us to leave the house faster. But we interpreted that gesture in our favour.

When we found my hat and came out into the common room, the policeman was gone. I don't know whether he had forgotten about us or left us on purpose. My mum took my hand to go out into the street, to join everybody else (where else had we to go?). She took me by the hand, and took my brother Kim in her arms, and from our yard, we went first down and then uphill, to a local spa (now, a psycho-neurological hospital). From there we went to the yard of School No. 1, and there we managed to hide in the school vegetable garden.

All the Jews who were lined up in Vostochnaya Street have, ever since that day, rested in a mass grave in Sukhoy Yar of Uman, where there is now a monument standing, commemorating over 20,000 Jews tortured and killed there. We were the only survivors.

We waited in the school's backyard, and I remember the dried weeds of potatoes that had not been harvested yet. We were cold and hungry. Mum decided to go to our empty flat at 5 Proletstud Street, which we had owned before the war. This house is still there.

Aunt Zina, Mum's good friend and a wonderful person, lived in the same house from the very first days of the occupation. Her husband, Vladimir Palamarchuk, had become a policeman. Somehow, secretly, Mum let Auntie Zina know where we were hiding. I remember how she brought us some very tasty stewed meat in a pot and bread but left very quickly so that her husband didn't suspect anything.

We stayed in this empty flat about an hour or two. Most of the furniture and things had been stolen. And suddenly somebody was persistently knocking on the door. We thought it was Auntie

Zina. But when we opened the door we saw Volodya, her husband. On the left sleeve he wore a police armband (in the first months of the war, the police hadn't received their uniform yet), and he held a Soviet rifle.

I remember well how he entered with a smile on his face and didn't look really angry or menacing. He took out a gun magazine with five bullets from a hidden bag, held it in his open palm so that we would see it, and then loaded the rifle. 'Get ready!' he said. Mum was shocked, 'What? Volodya! Don't you remember we worked in the same college?' (He was a janitor and Mum was an accountant, and she also studied there.) 'I beg you, let us go. I have children.' To which Volodya Palamarchuk said, 'No, I can't, it's my duty. And even if I let you go, other policemen will catch you anyway.'

So he escorted us along the highway, as if he were escorting arrested criminals, towards an ambulance station. Near the spa he noticed another Jewish woman, and he ordered her to come up to him. Somehow he took us all to a local prison. We were lucky that he didn't kill us there, in our house. They took us into a cell fully packed with Jewish women, children and the elderly. One woman was lying on a stretcher, paralysed. People were suffocating from the lack of air in the cell. In the corner of the room, there was a toilet, or more precisely a cut-out metal barrel. My year-old brother Kim sat on the floor and was putting all the awful things into his mouth. And to all comments from other people, Mum kept saying that it no longer mattered. Everybody was certain they would shoot us in the evening or morning.

In the evening, a German soldier opened the door to the cell and gave us a few loaves of bread. I was near the door and managed to catch a few mouthfuls of fresh air, not thinking of bread then. We stayed in the cell the whole night. In the morning the Germans and the police opened the door. We thought they would take us to be killed but the Germans shouted, 'You are free. You all go home, to the ghetto. Nobody will ever touch you again. Let this be known to all those in hiding.'

And again we were lucky since the Germans liked to play tricks. Of course, nobody believed in their promise, but that day we were still alive. In fact, the Germans expected all Jews to come out of their hiding places and return to the ghetto. They thought that our group, when released from the prison, would spread the news among all other survivors.

The Jews were in fact going back to the ghetto – they had no other choice. The usual 'life' in the ghetto resumed again, continuously under the fear of being beaten, shot, hanged; yet everybody was hoping to survive. There were almost no men left, and young women were forced daily to hard labour. My mum (she was in her early thirties) worked at the construction of a motorway. To repair the roads they often used gravestones from the Jewish cemetery. There, where my mum worked, a German soldier was a guard. Since Mum spoke relatively fluent German, the soldier often talked with her. He openly spoke of his home, his life, and how he hated the war. Mum told me this when she came home from the work.

I don't know exactly how long Jews 'lived' in the ghetto following the second pogrom – probably, another five to seven months. In any case, one day when Mum was at work, the German guard told her secretly, 'Raya, tomorrow early in the morning, you will all be killed. Go anywhere you can, tonight, together with your children.'

I would like to note that the soldier risked being executed for the disclosure of the information on the planned *Aktion* against *Judeh*.

Mum came back to the ghetto and shared this news with family and friends, but nobody believed that the German was telling the truth. Then Mum said, 'I have warned you. Now it's up to you whether to believe me or not but I am leaving together with my children.'

Once darkness fell, with Mum holding Kim in her arms, we went downhill, to the right of house No. 5 in Vostochnaya Street, and came to the city centre through Ostrovsky Street, reaching an old bathhouse (after the war, this building was used for vinegar production). Mum had taken off our bright yellow circles, tell-tale signs that we were Jewish, before leaving the ghetto. As I said, the ghetto was not fenced and there were no patrolling guards around.

And the following morning (I think it was the autumn of 1942), the third, final, pogrom began.

Where did we have to go now? The city was packed with the Germans, police, and even any passer-by seemed to us to be a policeman; besides, very little time was left before the curfew. And now there were 'impertinent and criminal' Jews wandering around the city, with no identification 'marks'! The situation seemed to be with no way out, but again our mum planned it all. I can surely say, without any exaggeration, that for all the ingenuity and risk that my mum demonstrated while saving us, she really deserved the title of Heroine. So, Mum took us through back streets, to an old friend of hers, an elderly woman, Stanislava Pavlovna Novak, at 17 Lenin Street. This house is still there; and before and after the revolution this house belonged to Yuri Lvovich Kramarenko, a well-known doctor. My mum and brother stayed with Stanislava Pavlovna until the morning, and her niece, Stasya, took me, an eleven-year-old, to Vera Mikhailovna Batzmanievskaya, who lived in a private house at 55 (now 39) Gorky Street. Before the war, she had worked together with my mum as a teacher in school No. 11. This was a beautiful young woman, who lived with her daughter Galya, who was my age. Her husband was politically repressed in 1937 as a fighter for an independent Ukraine. Vera Mikhailovna was an activist of the Ukrainian liberation movement, and she equally hated the Soviet regime and the Nazi invaders. For about a year I lived with Vera Mikhailovna, as her nephew. She called me Vasya Melnik, and I still have this name, although in my passport Miron, my true name, is written. She had a small farm near her house, including a cow which I tended all the time. She taught me to work although I was a city boy, and she treated me as if I were her own son.

I frequently took the cow out to the pasture near a POW camp and saw all the suffering that they had to go through. Mostly they were dying from cold and diseases; and they were dying daily.

During the time that I was a herdsman, many daily accidents happened to me. I fell out of trees, and I once jumped off a cart and its wheel ran over my two legs, but half an hour later I was able to walk and no bones were crushed. But what if I had a fractured bone or another trauma? Even now it is hard to imagine what would have happened. Where would I be treated? If taken to the hospital, they would have known instantly who I was and that would have been a silly and unfortunate death.

The further ordeal of my mother and brother occurred as follows. It was very dangerous to spend any extra hour at Stanislava Pavlovna's house because if they were found, they and herself would be killed immediately. So, in the morning, my mum walked towards the village of Podvysokoye, where her brother-in-law's parents were. Her sister was married to a Ukrainian man. They couldn't give a shelter to a woman with a child but gave her food and advised her to go to Golovanevsk, where a former *sovkhoz* was and anyone could be hired there. (*Kolkhoz* and *sovkhoz* structures continued to run during the occupation.)

It was easy to say, 'anyone', but Jews were not included. Where could you go without documents proving that you were not Jewish? Mum went to Golovanevsk, but she didn't know the road well and was asking people for the directions. Some good people gave her food to eat and take with her. It worked out fortunately that no one turned in a suspicious-looking woman with a child in her arms to the police. (Mum spoke good Ukrainian with no Jewish accent, as she used to teach Ukrainian in the fifth to seventh forms of the school at the village of Polyanetzkoye.)

Once, as my mum told me later, on the way from one place to another, she sat down to rest in a forest glade, near the village of Semiduby. She was suddenly overcome with complete apathy, and everything suddenly became indifferent to her, both her baby and her life itself. A woman in a coat, very unfriendly-looking, was passing by. Mum asked her to trade some documents for a new and good coat she wore. The woman agreed, went home and brought a document issued to Maria Snitzaruk. My mother gave her the coat, and got the old coat from the woman. Dressed like that she suddenly looked less suspicious and conspicuous. And she went on further to Golovanevsk. In one of the villages she saw a pleasant-looking woman near the gate of a house. The woman asked her in, gave her some food, feeling sorry that Mum had to go around suffering with a baby in her arms. Mum told her she was a refugee from Donbass. The woman offered to wait for her husband who would soon be back from work as maybe he could give some advice to her.

You could imagine Mum's emotions when the husband who came from work turned out to be a policeman! However, he didn't suspect anything – or at least pretended he didn't – and advised Mum to give her child to the orphanage in the village of Lebedinka. He took them there. My brother spent almost a year in that orphanage, and the conditions there were terrible.

An ethnic German [*Volksdeutsch*] was in charge of the *sovkhoz*. After the liberation it turned out that he was a partisan.

Mum had to go through a lot in the *sovkhoz*. One man, a former POW, started suspecting Mum was Jewish so he went to the farm manager with his report. The manager reminded him that he, the informant, was a 'Red Commander' himself, so he'd better stay quiet about others.

Having worked for seven or eight months, my mum got a room in a hall of residence and decided to get me over from Uman. She received a document from her work place to say that she went to visit her family in Khristinovka. The manager issued her a pass [*ausweis*]. When Mum reached Polyanetzkoye, a woman she knew sent her fifteen-year-old daughter to get me from Uman. And she brought me to Mum. From that village we went back to the farm, where she worked and lived. When we went through the forest near the village of Sobkivka, we suddenly saw a cart coming towards us, with ten or twelve policemen sitting in it. One of them, who was their chief, was sitting next to the driver. I started to pull mum to the forest and kept saying, 'That's it! We're dead!'

But the policemen saw us, and ordered us to approach them. 'Who are you and where are you going to? Your documents?' they asked rudely and abruptly. Mum showed them her pass and the document she had traded.

The chief policeman looked at Mum and said viciously, 'Don't tell us your tales! You worked and studied in Uman Education College.

Get on the cart, now!' They took us to Sobkivka, to the village council. I still cannot understand why they didn't kill us there, right on
the spot, in the forest. Perhaps we were fated to survive. There was
a meeting of village residents in the council. Looking at us, many
women had tears in their eyes (one of them said, 'Poor things,
already dead!') The women brought us some food, and they were
crying. I want to interrupt myself, and say, that the Ukrainian
people were wonderful, good, kind-hearted, hospitable, and often
risked their lives to save and help others. I know this from my own
bitter life experience when I encountered them in trouble. Yes, bad
times showed who your friends really were. And of course, there are
scoundrels in any of the nations.

So, we sat on the sofa, waiting for the worst to happen … and
again, there was a fortunate circumstance for which we couldn't have
hoped. The chief policeman (I think it was Ryabushenko, deputy chief
of police) was called to Uman and he left us to be executed at night by
a local village policeman. We waited until late night. I fell asleep. Then,
Mum woke me up and I saw a policeman in front of us, with a rifle in
his hands. He took us out into the yard, put us into a cart, sat next to
us, and we rode away. I remember that horrible and happy night very
well. The night was quiet, and the moon was bright. Neither Mum nor
I was crying, or screaming. We sat quietly, since we knew well where
we were heading. And suddenly my mum started talking along this
road to death, in Ukrainian, 'Is this the last time that I shall see this
wonderful night, this moon, that lights up my last way, this wonderful forest or hear the birds singing? I shall never see the sun rise again.'

And suddenly the policeman (I saw this) took my mum by the
hand, and said, 'You will see night, day, moon, and everything
around. But be very careful in future.'

The policeman was about twenty-five years old. He told us about
his hard childhood and youth. His parents' property had been
repossessed and they had been sent off to Siberia, and he had to go
'among the people'. I can't understand how he wasn't afraid that
the cart driver wouldn't report him. He gave Mum all of our documents: he probably had known from the very beginning that he
would release us. We didn't know his name or surname. After the
liberation, we went to Sobkivka to tell people about his action, but
he had already been put in jail for twenty-five years and we were
late. Why didn't my mum appeal for him? I don't know …

We reached the *sovkhoz* fairly safely.

But still we had to be very careful out there. That was what happened to me when we lived in the *sovkhoz*. At that time Ukrainian
youths were being taken away to Germany to work, and there was
a period when they were taking children too. And so, as a Ukrainian

boy, I received a draft notice. I had to hide myself twice: Mum took me to some people she knew, at a remote farmstead. This was a teacher from Leningrad who had come to visit her sister and couldn't get back home because the war had begun. The *sovkhoz* manager told the Germans that such a person was missing from the farm's estate. I spent almost two months at the other farmstead, and then Mum took me back.

After my mum started working in the Svirnevo *sovkhoz* and took me away from Vera Mikhailovna, from Uman, she went to the orphanage and took Kim away with her. He was in critical condition, all covered in abscesses and seriously ill. Nobody believed he would make it, but Mum treated him, although no medications were available, with only folk medicine and herbs.

Our continuing life in the Svirnevo *sovkhoz*, in the Golovanevsk district, went on without any specific accidents or adventures, not counting the fact that any minute we were in danger of being denounced and killed.

Thus we lived till 1944. The Red Army was approaching, and we knew that the liberation was near. But there was a question: how to survive? Many retreating police units accumulated in our *sovkhoz*, and out of viciousness they could kill all the population of the farm. We faced another specific danger: one of the retreating policemen started telling my mum that he had guessed who we really were. We were very stressed before the liberation: it would have been sad to die at the very end, having survived so much.

After the police and the Germans left, we had no law enforcement for about two days. And then I was sitting near the window, on 16 March 1944, and saw four or five horse-riders seemingly dressed in Soviet uniforms but with shoulder straps. I thought these were the policemen. We didn't know that they had started to wear these straps in the Red Army, although we had heard something like that. I told Mum about this and we became really scared. Where to hide? And I saw people coming out of the houses, hugging and kissing the 'policemen'! We were shocked! Nobody was shooting or killing anybody. So we came out too … and only then did we realize who those riders were! It is impossible to describe the emotions of this encounter with our dear liberators. Such things have to be experienced.

The horse-riders turned out to be Soviet military scouts. A military division followed on. All the residents of the farm wanted to have soldiers stationed in their house. People tugged at their hands, pulled on their trench coats. We had eight or ten people around our table. We sat with them. We were supposed to rejoice and laugh, yet we cried … these were the happy tears of joy: was this only a dream?

22. Our life was growing more intolerable

Maria Zaslavskaya-Siginur (b. 1921)

My name is Maria Borisovna Siginur, and I was born in 1921, in the town of Bershad, Vinnitsa oblast. I was a teacher. When the academic year was over, I went to visit my relatives in Kodyma, Odessa oblast. I had spent a few days there, when it was announced that the war had begun. I tried calling Bershad but it was impossible to talk over the phone; German speech and shouting were interrupting it all of the time. I packed my things and went to Bershad, where my parents were.

The town was small; Jews had lived there from time immemorial, and everybody knew each other's name. There were a lot of old people who had never seen a railroad – for example, my grandparents, who were ninety years old. There were also young people who, like me, had completed ten years of school and dreamed of entering an institute or university.

The houses were located very close one to another, separated by narrow streets only. There was not a small plot of land for the outhouse or even the rubbish dump. The cobble-paved streets saved the situation, with no pavements but very good gutters for water and sewage, and small bridges that connected streets and entrances to the houses. The water didn't stay on the pavements and during heavy rains we children enjoyed running through quick streams, with knee-high water.

Before the war there had been approximately 10,000 people in Bershad, mostly Jews. These were mainly workers, tailors, shoe-makers, hairdressers, carpenters, woodworkers, roof-workers, and mechanics. Old paramedic Yurko was our medical source for many years. Young intelligentsia – teachers, doctors and nurses – started to appear in the early 1940s.

The pre-war industries included a spirits factory, a sugar plant, a mill, a bakery and a smithy. They were located in the centre of the town. The river split the town into a number of areas. When you crossed the Pelopenyovka Bridge, you could get into a quarter where

Russian Old Believers lived. The Ukrainians lived across the Berlovsky Bridge. Yet everybody used the services of hard-working Jewish professionals.

We lived together in a friendly manner and needed each other. For their work the Jews was paid with money and food. And people always thanked each other, and were happy to meet and greet each other. There were no quarrelling among the neighbouring children: we played, studied and grew up all together.

My mum, Ennya Berkovna, and Dad, Benya Herschkovich, had five children, all girls: Zhenya, Manya, Lida, Rita, Raya and myself. We all survived. The Nazis killed my dad. He was killed three weeks prior to the liberation.

On 2 July 1941, everything went quiet due to anxiety and fear. Our army retreated and the population started to break into shops. We were given sacks of flour from the mill storage. The army departed, leaving the local population to fend for themselves. At the same time the bridges were planted with mines, and then blown up: for town residents that meant complete isolation from the rest of the world. But the Germans who came in restored bridges in a couple of hours and entered Bershad with terrible noise, on their motorcycles. There were very many of them, they were shooting recklessly, but there was not a single person out in the streets: everybody vanished. They kept shooting through shop and house windows.

Big lorries, coloured green and with camouflage spots, followed the motorcycles. We had never seen such lorries before, and they were making a terrible noise coming down our paved streets. They all went into our ancient park and were stationed by the river, near a school, a former city council and the militia.

Some strange people came together with the Germans; they shouted, kept shooting and dragged people out of their flats and beat them up. With the help of interpreters they were forcing people to move to the square near a synagogue. Next morning they announced, 'All Jews should not leave their flats. They should not communicate with local residents. They should establish a community council and obey all orders of the German administration.'

Every day, we received new instructions by means of our community council: they demanded money, gold, a workforce, women, girls and so on. They started killings and the first dead bodies appeared in the streets. Three factory workers were hanged on telegraph posts with notices on them reading, 'This will happen to anyone who is hiding war prisoners.'

Then, an order was issued for all Jews to wear white six-pointed stars on their chest and back, so that it could be seen from a distance that this person was a Jew. It was a very convenient target to shoot at.

An eighteen-year-old boy who had escaped the German impris-onment became the first local victim. He went into a two-storey house, went out on to the balcony, looked out, and was immediately killed with an automatic gun. He fell off the balcony, but a gunman continued to shoot at him. I saw this myself, through a slit in the win-dow blinds in my flat. For a few days his body lay there, torn, and the community was not allowed to take him away to bury him. The looting and murder continued. The announcement demanded that the Jews select their community council (the headman, his deputy and a person in charge of burials) who would be responsible for the enforcement of all orders by the German Kommandant's office.

People were killed for anything: for being Jewish; for being alive. The mortality rate grew with each day: a typhus outbreak began and no medical assistance was given. The number of Hungarian and Romanian Jews who died was especially high: they lived in much worse conditions than the local Jews.

Then the Gestapo transferred our camp to under the Romanian Kommandant's supervision. New tortures were created; children were taken and killed in front of their mothers. The screams of those who were about to be killed lasted throughout the nights, and nobody could help them.

Life in the ghetto was getting more severe with every passing day. Our life was growing more intolerable. The guards watched over the ghetto. The typhus cases were everywhere. There were a few local medical doctors and nurses in the ghetto, as well as for-eigners from Italy and Romania. Raya Miemer, a local nurse, saved many lives, as did an Italian doctor named Gutman. We were young and helped with whatever we could for those who were arriving in our ghetto; we were housing them in the flats. In our flat we put two people from Italy and four from Romania. Raya, my little sister, was only eight years old then, but she saved two orphaned children, Borya and Manya Kon. They now live in Israel. I will relate a story of their rescue further on.

Raya Miemer, born in 1918, was saving people, not really having any medications, not caring for herself, and not thinking about her baby son at home, waiting for her while she could have caught a disease.

Doctor Gutman saved me. I had a typhoid fever of up to 40°C. His method of treatment was as follows. They put a dry towel on my back, then soaked a sheet in cold water and rolled me into it until the bed got hot and dry again. Then they kept changing it frequently until the fever went down.

In 1942, together with my husband, I went to Beta, my cousin. She had two small children. When we came out of the alley, we saw a big cart full of the dead people, and their arms and legs were sticking out. My husband took me to my cousin's home, but she was already dead. She had become ill with typhus and died quickly, leaving behind two orphans: Syoma a few months old, and, the one-year-old Maya. We helped them survive; and they lived to see the liberation and the victory. There were many orphaned children there, and many were dying. All those who could help orphans were helping them.

Raya Borisovna Zaslavskaya, my sister, born in 1932, saw two ill children in a basement. They were a boy aged four, and a seven-year-old girl. The girl sat next to her dead mother, pulling her and asking her to wake up, and the boy just moaned. The girl had swollen eyes and a big swollen belly. My sister Raya took these children to our neighbour who lived alone. She agreed to take the girl, who was unable to speak, and a man named Feldman, who was a cart-driver and worked picking up dead bodies, took the boy. He lived in a neighbouring street, together with his wife and two children of his own.

Haika Batelman treated the adopted girl very well and loved her. The girl was recovering, but never recalled she had a brother, as if she had never had him. As a grown-up and as a teacher, I felt very sorry they would grow and lose each other, not knowing where they lived. I decided to talk to Zelvey Feldman, the man who adopted the boy. The meeting took place. I met a very thin miserable boy, then again spoke with Feldman and his wife, and asked them to give the boy to us so that the children could live together. The first step was taken. My father brought the boy in his arms into our home. Then Haika adopted the boy too, and they lived together. After the victory, they went back to their homeland, to Moldavia. The girl graduated from the Institute and became an agriculture engineer, and the boy became a veterinarian. They moved to Israel in 1992. After the war, for over twenty years my sister lived in Yevpatoria and worked there as a maths teacher. Now she also lives in Israel, and is friends with both of them, Maya and Boris Kon.

This was one single episode of the ghetto life and of how we helped each other survive.

In 1942 I gave birth to my son, Alexander Siginur. Raya Miemer was an obstetrician and assisted in my labour. She held a kerosene oil lamp.

The Kommandant's office requested us to provide daily information about how many people died. Germans were mad with anger; they were running around the ghetto, catching people and shooting them.

In 1943, a partisan underground was established in the ghetto. The Soviet soldiers and officers, who had escaped from the prison, started it. Some of them survived: Yasha Talis, Farschtendiker, a lawyer, Mitzel and others. They were in charge of the partisan underground. We established connection with local partisans who were in the forests. When the Germans discovered the underground, they left for the forest too. But before they left, they had written a list of 250 names of people who were helping partisans. Yasha Talis and others put this list into a bottle and decided to hide it. They gave the bottle to two small boys, the Alevich brothers, to do this. In late January 1943, Germans surrounded the house of Busya, their sister, who was also a member of the resistance. Together with her two brothers, she was at home. The Germans tortured Busya in front of her brothers demanding they tell where the partisans were and who were in the groups. She didn't give a single name. Then the Gestapo turned to her young brothers – could they remember who came into their house? In return for an answer, the Germans promised to stop torturing their sister. The older brother agreed to help, provided they let their sister go. They went, together with the torturers, into the basement where they dug out the bottle holding the 250-name list. During the night all the people from this list were found, gathered together, tied up, and thrown into a prison cellar. They were beaten up severely and kept there until 10 February, and then at sunrise, they took these martyrs to their final destination, across the Berlovsky Bridge, and forced them to dig out a grave. On 11 February, these people were taken in groups of two or three, stood up facing the grave and shot down. The Berlovka residents heard how they prayed, cried raising their hands towards the skies, and said goodbyes to each other.

Here my father died too. He took his jacket off, remaining in a grey shirt, home-made felt boots. He didn't scream but he kept his teeth and fists closed tight. The tearing bullets hit him and half of his face and head was smashed and the other half had a bulging eye.

It is very painful to recall all that, especially because in three weeks' afterwards our ghetto was liberated by the Soviet army. This happened on 14 February 1943. Our partisans and Yasha Talis returned, and the town council allowed the grave of those killed to be opened. The German prisoners of war were digging the grave open with their hands; shovels were not given to them. The grave was in a hollow, and water ran down into it, so the dead bodies had decomposed fast. To go down into it, one had to close off one's nose and mouth. We couldn't understand why there were so many dead people there but it turned out that they had killed two groups here: 250 and 270 people, respectively.

In the summer of 1942, the community council called together all parents and announced that all those who wanted their children alive and out of the ghetto, should come to the square near the synagogue. There the carts would wait for the children. Under the guard of Romanian soldiers they would be taken to Balta, and then on to America. The children of Bulgarian, Hungarian, Romanian and Italian Jews were put voluntarily by their parents on to the carts. Free vacancies in these carts were filled up with local children. My sisters Rita and Raya asked our parents to let them go. They cried and wanted to go with their friends. I was absolutely against it, and being the oldest, explained to them that we had to always stay together, no matter what happened.

The children were taken to Balta. There a German killing squad waited for them and started killing them. They tried to flee but there was no escape. Only two sisters and a boy in his mid-teens managed to escape. When fleeing they got into a pit overgrown with plants. The pit was very deep with water at the bottom. The boy's surname was Rosenruch. Three days after the killings, somebody heard their cries and wailing. The children returned to the ghetto, to their parents, and told them everything about the Balta massacre. After the liberation, the parents went to Balta. They were shown a common grave where the murdered children were buried.

Assya and Zhenya Sikor, two sisters, were hanged in Balta. Also, Mortche Bramzuger and Lisa Luscher, the Romanians, were hanged for their connections with partisans. The witnesses later said that they were tortured ruthlessly and questioned about where partisan groups were, but they didn't say a word. Crippled and hardly able to move, they were taken out into the square, in front of all people, and shot one after the other. Their dead bodies were dragged up and hanged on the telegraph posts. They hung there for long time. The witnesses who buried them managed to survive, that is how it was possible to find their graves.

In the Bershad camp and the ghetto, the Nazis tortured and killed twenty thousand people. I have reasons to believe this figure to be true. Unfortunately, my memory has retained the names of a few people only. Among them there were Ben Herschkovich Zaslavsky, Grisha Batelman, Boris Batelman, Lyova Meyer, Yasha Naitshut, Isrul Naitshut, Moisha Wielderman and Mylter.

I also remember others who were in the ghetto with me: Lida, Raya and Rita Zaslavskaya, Leika Gvienter, Abrasha Toyvovich, the big Tzybelman family, Yankel Simedubersky, Isrul Simedubersky, Manya and Borya Kon. Among others there were Raya and Zolya Miemer, Shloylya and Frima Gutenmacher, Semyon Borisovich Davidson, Sara Fierer, Assya Feldman, with her daughter, a wife and a son of the murdered Mylter, Haika Landman, Alexander and Aron Chaimovich Siginur.

Russian and Ukrainian neighbours helped us to survive by bringing food and clothes, and often risking their own lives: Irina Bendyak, born in 1920, and Yurko, the paramedic. Our gratitude goes out to them!

23. I was wandering for so long

Polina Zaslavskaya (Soikis) (b. 1930)

Before the war, my parents, Boruch and Soikis, had worked in a *kolkhoz*. I had two sisters, thirteen and nine years old, and two brothers, aged four and one. My grandma had one leg only. Our family was poor. We survived the famine of 1933. We lived in a semi-basement flat, in a street with mostly Jewish residents. A synagogue was near our house.

When the war began, people started talking about Hitler's plans to destroy the Jewish people. My parents didn't believe these rumours. Besides, it was scary to go anywhere, having five children. Dad was not drafted into the army because he had small children. Yet when my parents finally decided to leave, it was too late. The Romanians captured us on our way and returned us back to our home place, to Kamenka.

Thus we had lived until early 1942, when the Romanians and the Germans forced all Jews into a marketplace. All those ill and crippled, like our grandma, were put on to carts and taken to the Dniester, thrown under the ice, and drowned. That was how our grandma died.

Those Jews who were gathered at the marketplace were marched along the road. Those who lagged behind were shot down immediately, or beaten with rifle butts, or hunted down by dogs. In January 1942, the frosts were very hard. When my father began getting behind, he was killed. This happened not far from the town of Kotovsk, but I don't know where his grave is exactly.

Not far away from that place, in a village, we were put up for a night in a horse stable. Mum told me, 'Go into the village, maybe you will get warm somewhere.' I went into the village, and somebody gave me shelter.

In the morning, all Jews were brought to the Kommandant's office. My brother was brought from somewhere (Mum had given him away to someone in hope that he would be saved). He was four, and the Germans shot him down right there, in front of the Kommandant's office.

We were all put into a column, two abreast, and guarded by soldiers with dogs. We were marched on to a ravine, where we were put on the edge of it. The Germans began shooting. I was pushed down. I was alive, among the dead bodies, but fainted. When local people came over, they heard moans and found me. My body and hands were frostbitten. The fingers on my right hand had gone dark. Another woman and a boy were found alive too.

Old Grandfather Dubrova came up to me and said, 'Come with me.' He took me into his home. Together with his wife, he cleaned me and changed my clothes, and in the early morning he took me across the forest into a village. 'Go wherever you want, but never return here again. The Germans counted the dead and are searching for three people who are missing.'

And thus I began wandering from village to village. During the day I went around but nobody would let me in, and in the evening when it was dark, people gave me shelter. So, I spent the night, and in the morning I had to leave again; people were afraid of hiding me – it was such a time.

In one house, a woman told me, 'You, child, will come here only at specified times. I will give you special treatment to save your fingers.'

She explained to me, that her neighbour served in the police and if he knew, she would be executed. Every day I would go over to her place, and she would make special baths and thus saved my fingers. She offered me some food but I never took it. I was very thin. Fear haunted me. I lived with this fear through the winter.

Once one family let me in to sleep. There were four children in it, and the woman kept me for a few days: where there were four, a fifth was not noticeable. Then, I went to another family. Everybody went to work, and I stayed home alone. She said, 'You will stay with us for some time', and left. Suddenly she ran back, took me by my hand and took me to another part of the village. She said only, 'I will tell you everything later.' So she left me there and went to work. In the evening she came to pick me up, and told that somebody betrayed her but she had been warned and was told me to get me out of the house. At the same time, the police came to her home to get me.

Thus I was going from family to family throughout the winter, trying to survive and not to be killed. I was wandering for so long.

I knew that I was left alone. I didn't know where my family was buried, and I don't know this even now.

In spring they had been the order to kill. All those who were caught were now sent to the ghetto. I was taken into the Tzurkan family. The father of the family, Yakov Tzurkan, and Grandma Anya, asked me whether I wanted to go to live with Zhenya, their daughter, who had a twenty-month-old son: 'You will babysit him, and later, you will tend to a cow.' Of course I was ready to do anything.

I got accustomed to them quickly, and they treated me as their own child. In the morning they took me to their daughter. Boris, her husband, was in the army. That was where I stayed. She went to the fields and I stayed with her baby.

Everybody span wool in that village, and as if sensing I would need it, I learned to make wool. Zhenya didn't approve of that. She would came home from work and say, 'What do you do that for?'

When Runya, Zhenya's sister, came (she was eight), she called me names, calling me a 'Jew-girl', and I cried. When Zhenya came home from work, I told her about it. And she said, 'Don't let her in.' But how could I not let her in? She was not doing that to hurt me, she was only eight, and everybody in the village was calling us those names, because they understood that only Jews could be roaming around the place. That was why she taunted me that way.

Then it was my turn to tend to the cows. I was sitting there and thinking, 'Well, now I will get my bullet in the back.' Although I said I was Russian, and my name was Olya (not Polya) Derevyanko, and I didn't look Jewish, still, every moment, I was expecting to be shot. That was how I suffered all of the time.

In the summer, Boris, Zhenya's husband, came home from imprisonment; he knelt in front of his wife, crying, and said, 'What a good deed you have done by saving this child. I was in similar conditions, and I understand it so well.'

They treated me very well, as if I were their child. I hoped this would be my family.

In September–October 1942, we received a notice from the Kommandant's office to bring me there. Somebody had reported Zhenya. It looked as if they had found those who survived together with me: the young boy and the woman. I was the only one missing. Boris and Zhenya dressed me, and tried to calm me down. They kept saying that perhaps I would see someone from my family there. When we arrived at the Kommandant's office, we were told that I might go free for now, they would send us another notice. It turned out they were still looking for the woman and the boy. A month later, we got the second notice. And then they took me and sent me to the Rybnitsa concentration camp.

When I was in Rybnitsa, my skill in wool spinning was very helpful. There, behind the barbed wire, I had to earn food for myself. I started spinning wool. People from the village used to come to me, and for the wool I had spun over the week, they brought me some food, and that was how I earned my living then.

About half a year later, there was an order to collect all orphans and send them to Balta. There was an orphanage in the Balta ghetto. I was also sent there. Life in the orphanage was better: I wasn't sent to work, I was given clothes and some food. This concentration camp was under German jurisdiction. But none the less, the attacks on the orphans were continuous, and many, including myself, were raped.

That was how we lived for a year and a half. Not long before our army approached Balta, I found relatives whom I hadn't known before, and it was an accident. I had met them before the war when Bessarabia was united with the Ukraine. They lived in Moldavia, - in Ustyuzhany, Beltsy and Cisinau, and came to the funeral of their relatives (our grandparents lived together with us). Then I got to know my uncle, my aunt and their daughter.

We were freed in March 1944. The liberation lasted for two days. Over these days, the Nazis managed to kill everybody. First, they took all the boys out of the orphanage and killed them, then all the remaining children. I was fortunate. One old woman hid her daughter and me in the basement. That was how only three of us survived out of all the orphanages. The Germans killed everybody.

When our troops came, they managed to catch one policeman who was hanged right on the grounds of the camp.

After liberation I decided to go back to my home town, to Kamenka. I was fourteen years old. I don't remember how I managed to get to Kamenka. Our house in Kamenka was destroyed. My parents' friends asked me to stay with them in Kamenka. But I went to my relatives in Maltyushany. There I went to school. My aunt left for work in the morning, she taught in school. When she came home, I put on her coat and shoes and went to school, to attend afternoon lessons. That's how I completed the seventh form. Then I found more relatives through correspondence: I had two aunts who lived with their husbands in Kharkov. They decided to take me to live with them.

In March 1947, I left for Kharkov. First, I stayed with one aunt who lived near the Kharkov Tractor Plant, and later I moved in with the other, who lived near the Luch factory. They were my distant relatives, but I didn't have anybody else. I lived with them from 1947 till 1956. They wanted me to continue my education. But I saw how hard their lives were and told them I would go on working and would study part-time.

In 1950 I began a part-time course in a local trade college. When I got married we lived in a tiny room, eight square metres and conditions were very difficult.

In 1963 I wrote a letter to the *Izvestiya* newspaper (it was a problem for me to write since I didn't have any fingers on my right hand). In the letter I briefly described the story of my rescue and asked the editors to help me find those who rescued me. After some time, I received the response from the newspaper and from my rescuers' daughter, Vera Kornya, who invited me to come and visit them. Soon afterwards, Kornya himself with his daughter came to visit us. Later I went to the village together with my husband and son. These were memorable encounters.

24. Thus all Jewish residents of Lyubar were killed

Efim Zakharov-Zaidenberg (b. 1927)

This happened in Lyubar, in a small town located on both banks of the River Sluch, about eighty kilometres west of Zhitomir, in the Ukraine.

About 500 years ago, the Lyubar Jews prayed in a wooden synagogue built in 1491 on the right bank of the River Sluch. In the early twentieth century, there were nine synagogues in Lyubar, as well as the Talmud-Torah, a Jewish theatre, and a Jewish hospital. There was a Jewish school. There were 116 shops and many professional workers and intelligentsia – doctors, teachers, actors and musicians. Over 7,000 Jews lived in Lyubar.

The revolution gave freedom to Jews – freedom to study, live anywhere and work. Many Jews left Lyubar. Then many books and newspapers in Yiddish were published.

In 1938, I finished the fourth form of the Jewish school with honours and my parents transferred me to Novolyubarsk Ukrainian comprehensive school so that I could afterwards enter a university. The very same year, the Jewish school was closed. In 1941 I completed the seventh form and turned fourteen years old.

Already, on 22 June, German planes bombed fuel stores and shot at the houses in our city. The panic began and only a few managed to get evacuated: for this you needed transport, money and permission to leave work. Many walked away but then returned because German paratroopers barred their way and many still couldn't believe the Germans would be murderers and torturers.

The battle near Lyubar lasted for a few hours; we heard shots and explosions. My parents, together with my little sister and me, were hiding in the cellar of a brick house that belonged to our neighbours, Aron and Meer Balk. Almost all our neighbours were hiding there, together with us.

When the shooting was over, the Germans entered the town on motorcycles and they immediately started going through Jewish homes and stealing whatever they saw. This happened on Sunday, 6 July 1941.

A few days after the Germans occupied Lyubar, a local policeforce was organized out of bandits and scoundrels who were capable of any crime. F. Yu. Kiyan, our former school military teacher, became the chief of police.

The family of Hirsch Galperin, four people, became the first Jewish victims. Their son, Ariel, was accused of setting wheat stacks in the fields near Lyubar on fire. Later, the police killed Nus Litovchik, Leib Kraidman, Yosif Druz and Shmul Barenberg, whose fault was that they were once members of the village council.

Kudimov, a teacher of German from our school, became the town mayor. Traitors served the Nazi in Lyubar. I remember names of a few of them: Lipinsky, Bilenky, Sukhach, Myssechko and others. They knew almost all the Jews in town, being their neighbours. Now, being in power, they got a chance to torture them.

In the centre of the town, a number of streets were assigned to be within the section of Jewish residents. Jews were not allowed to go beyond the ghetto limits under the threat of being beaten or killed. All this was done by the police, under the supervision of Kiyan, and later of Kulchitzky. The starvation began. Jewish children tried to get into the streets where the Ukrainians, Russians and Poles lived, and traded clothes or food, but police hunted down the children and took away the last crumbs of food. Many Ukrainians tried to pass some food to the people they knew, but the police didn't let them go into the ghetto either.

On Saturday, 9 August 1941, in the morning, the Nazis took all men whom they used to use to work, and marched them outside the village of Yurovka, near Lyubar. Near the Ladiva Vilshana forest they kept digging pits during the whole day, and by the end of the day all of them, about 300 people, were shot dead. There, my father, Meyer Yitzkovich Zaidenberg, died.

Suffering, violence and beatings of Jews continued day after day. At night, drunk policemen would break into Jewish homes, robbing and beating residents. The terror was all over the town. This all lasted until September 1941.

We lived in the centre of the town. We had a cow that I took out to graze on the bank of the River Sluch, near the ghetto border, closer to the village of Struzhevka. On Saturday, 13 September 1941, I took the cow out very early. When I reached the river, I heard shooting back in the town, so I left the cow and ran away through the bushes along the river, reaching the village of Karan, three kilometres away from Lyubar. Schika Geraschny, a boy of my age, was with me. We hid in a forest glade, among the haystacks, but even there we heard screams of people forced out of their homes and taken away to be killed. In the afternoon everything went quiet and we saw how clothes and different objects looted from Jewish homes were taken into villages surrounding Lyubar. Than we realized that all the Jews of Lyubar had been killed.

The following morning, after all this horror, having lost Mum, our little sister and all our relatives, Schika and I went to the town of Ostropol. Schika told me he had some family there. When we arrived there, the Jewish residents were still alive. But we thought that they would follow the path of the Jews in Lyubar, and left Ostropol. We went off without really knowing where.

In the village of Provalovka a farmer who was milling grain in his yard stopped us. He asked us where we were going. We didn't know what to say, but said we had come from Lyubar. He didn't have a leg, but had a wooden prosthesis instead. He told us to wait for him and promised to get us some food. Then he entered a house but soon came out with a rifle, put us into a shed, and locked it. We stayed there until evening, and when he finished his work and entered the house, we pried open the door and through a slit in it crawled out and ran away. He noticed us but we managed to reach a cornfield and hide there. However, the residents of this village, led by a policeman, surrounded the field, caught us, put us back into the shed and set a guard to watch us.

On the following day we were taken to Lyubar together with Pesya from Lyubar (I don't remember her surname, but I know that her mother's name was Haika die Gile). They took us to the police. There were about fifty people who had managed to escape or run away into the nearby villages during the mass slaughter of Jews. We were all locked up in the Starolyubarsk secondary school, kept under supervision and taken out to different works. Every day, a few more Jews were found in hiding, and they joined us. We slept on the floor on rotten straw. There was no food given; policemen treated us as though we were some kind of insects – they beat us and killed us just for fun.

Then they moved us to the building of a former orphanage and kept us there.

All Jewish homes were robbed and emptied. I managed to get into our house, to get some clothes, but I couldn't find anything there. Everything was taken away; only pieces of broken dishes, furniture and torn pictures were scattered everywhere. I couldn't even find anything to have as a keepsake. All my relatives and family, a total of twenty-three people, were killed in Pischane. On that day, 13 September, about two thousand Jews were killed and buried in the ditches from which we used to get sand.

I was left alone.

Fridl Koltun, my dad's friend (his family was also killed and he was in the orphanage), took me with him to work, and I worked as an assistant of a hat-maker. Tailors, shoe- and hat-makers worked in the building of a former military commissariat, near a big red-coloured mill. They made clothes and shoes for the police.

As children, we were sometimes let out so that we could go and beg people we knew for some food. At the same time, everybody was warned that if we didn't return, grown-up prisoners would be shot. That was how we lived and suffered until late October 1941. In the final days of October, before the work was over, the policemen came (they were from Chudnov) and we all were taken to the orphanage where we were kept locked up. When we were marched there, the police fired to the right and left so that local people wouldn't walk up to us. But they didn't kill us that night since they hadn't managed to gather everybody.

We were accommodated in the building of an orphanage, in a few rooms, where we slept on the floor on the rotten straw. On that final night of our stay there we were moved all into one room, and put on the floor. Drunken policemen were mocking us: they beat us, they took away and raped girls and young women. There was a baker named Lyova in our town. A policeman cut his nose off with a razor. The policemen were brutal. All those sitting there were numb with shock. Like all those sitting next to me, I realized that this was the end, but nobody dared to say that aloud.

When night came I decided to flee. We had been put on the first floor and the window was opened a bit. I thought it would be better that they kill me when I ran away rather than shoot me in my face. I got out of the window, climbed down the drain pipe, and ran away. The policemen didn't notice me. And in the morning they killed everybody who was in orphanages, about 250 people. Thus all Jewish residents (some 3,000) of Lyubar were killed, only because thei parents were Jewish. The majority of those killed in Lyubar were women, children, elderly, the ill and disabled, in other words, all the helpless.

The Nazi murdered teachers – Chant and his family, Kipnis and her family (her husband was Ukrainian, S. S. Bondarchuk, a maths teacher), Penda Borisovna Kofman with her children, Groisman and Goicher with their families. All the teachers from the Jewish day school, were killed. Among those who perished there were nurse Sarra Khasin, surgeon Gurfinkel, mother and sister of Aron Vergelis, a Jewish poet, as well as many other clerks, teachers, doctors , and actors. They are all in the grave that is located in Pischane, on the outskirts of Lyubar.

I don't know what guided me or which roads I took, but I reached the village of Glesno, about ten kilometres away from Lyubar. There, our family had friends, Yuchym and Vassilina, I don't remember their surname. They let me in, cleaned me and changed my clothes – my sweater was moving with lice. I spent a few days in their house

but they were afraid of keeping me there, fearing for their neighbours, and hid me in their shed. But it was already cold and frosts fell
at night. They gave me winter clothes, some food, and advised me to
go to the east to get across the front line. I did as advised, although
before the war I had never left Lyubar or even seen a train.

I came to the Pechanovka railway station and walked along the
tracks, keeping at a certain distance, enough to see smoke from
steam engines, and crossing villages, I finally reached Kiev. It was
already winter, but the Dnieper was not frozen yet. I couldn't cross
it because the bridge was ruined and the Germans were guarding
the pontoon bridge. I didn't have any documents with me. I lived in
Kiev a few days, in the area of the Pecherska Lavra (the Holy Caves),
with a solitary monk who gave me shelter and never asked me anything. I think he knew I was Jewish.

There was hunger in Kiev and my desire to live was so strong
that I decided to go to the Western Ukraine. I knew that there, in the
town of Varkovichi, Aunt Sarra Ossovskaya, my mother's sister,
lived. Listening to conversations in houses where I managed to get
a night's sleep, I knew that not all Jews had been murdered in the
Western Ukraine.

And again, going along the railroad tracks, on foot, begging for
food in villages but mostly eating frozen beetroots, hiding from the
Germans and police, in fear, hunger, cold, and with no hope to survive, I finally reached Varkovichi.

The Varkovichi ghetto was fenced with barbed wire, yet it was
not guarded very well. But my aunt wasn't there. I left Varkovichi
and came to the village of Zhornovo, located a few kilometres away
from the highway, between the towns of Rovno and Dubno.

I walked into one house and I asked for permission to spend the
night – I was very cold. I was allowed to, and in the morning, Vassyl
Gorobetz and Katya, his wife, offered to allow me to stay with them,
if I help around the house, for food. This was a thread to salvation to
which I clung immediately because I knew well that even if I managed to survive the police, the Nazis, and all other enemies, I would
nevertheless die from the hunger and cold. I didn't have any option,
so I chose to stay.

I called myself Fedor Mikitovich Zakharov, saving the first letters
of my real name and surname. I told my hosts that I fled when being
taken to work in Germany and I couldn't return home because they
would take me away again.

They treated me well, and I tried to work hard, but at nights I
almost never got to sleep: I was afraid of demonstrating that I was
Jewish (at home we spoke Yiddish, and in Lyubar, Ukrainian).

Here everything was different: the Bandera bandits were active,
coming into the village in the middle of the night and demanding

that farmers not give bread to the Germans. In the daytime, the Germans came and demanded that grain be handed over to them. Most people were hiding in various shelters and the Germans took away cows, pigs and horses, and warned that if they didn't receive grain, they would return and burn down the village. And they kept their promise by burning down a few streets. The bandits kept saying that the German rule would be over soon, that was why they were on the rampage. Many times, together with my hosts, I had to hide in the shelter dug out in and masked by our vegetable garden, during the time of German 'visitations'.

In such intense conditions I had to live from January 1942 till September 1943. In September 1943, a Soviet partisan detachment went through Zhornovo. Many POWs, who worked now for farmers, went to join the partisans. Later, those who remained tried to go away too, fearing engeance from the Bandera bandits.

I also left, having decided to go to the east. Again I walked along the railway, but now across Polessye, and various people joined me along the way. Going through forests, I reached the area of Chernoby, from where I walked to Kiev, in November 1943. The city was already free from the Nazis. That was how I got out of their ruthless hands and miraculously survived.

When the war was over, I came back to Lyubar. There I knew that only Polya Kantor, Esther Goltzman, Fischl Shmaiger and his sister Anya Shmaiger-Kiyanovskaya and Borya Schraer were among those who fled together with me from the ghetto and survived.

The Jewish town of Lyubar was gone and the houses were demolished. After the war, the surviving Lyubar Jews fought for fourteen years to obtain permission from the local authorities to put up a monument on the grave of our families, friends and compatriots; but that is another story.

Only in 1972 was the monument set up with the inscription, 'To the Soviet people – victims of Nazism in 1941–45'. In 1990, a *Magen David* was carved on the stone above the inscription. That was all that was left of the Jewish town of Lyubar, along with an old Jewish cemetery, with turned-over and broken *matseivoss*, and the forest that has grown over it, where later a gas distribution station was built.

I have told you all I have gone through personally – and I have not imagined anything. There are no Jews in Lyubar now. I want my story to be a tribute of eternal memory for the innocent victims who rest in trenches in the outskirts of Lyubar, in Pischane and Ladiva Vilshana. This, of course, will not heal the deep sadness that will live in our memory and in our hearts for ever.

Thank God, those who survived all the terror can and should preserve our roots in the hope that our descendants will inherit the same responsibility but the Almighty protects them from things we had to live through.

25. Our eternal gratitude to kind people

Lazer Zienger (b. 1936)

On 22 June 1941, at six o'clock in the morning, our little town of Lipkany was on fire. The fire would rage for three days. The hometown of Eliezer Schteinberg, Moshe Altman, Jacob Schteinberg and other well-known representatives of Jewish culture was set on fire. The residents were leaving the burning town; some walked, some rode carts, some were carrying crying children in their arms. Some were pushing pushchairs with their meagre belongings in front of them. Everybody was going towards Brichany. And a few days later, as a child of five years, I watched the entry of the Romanian occupational divisions from the attic of our relatives' house. The following morning, the Romanian Kommandant issued an order for all Jews to come to the central square with their belongings. The unit of Romanian gendarmes with automatic guns and a band of Romanian and Moldavian Fascists marched away a column of over ten thousand Jews. Where to? This was unknown to us.

They marched us from sunrise till sunset. Wherever we were when night fell we had a rest. People were tired and fell down on the ground. My brother, Moischele, who was only a year and a half old, was in a privileged position since Mother and Father were taking turns carrying him in their arms. I had to walk all the way from Lipkany to Mogilev-Podolsky and back to the Yedintzy camp, and then again along the Kosoutzky forest, Sokiryany; then, again, through Mogilev-Podolsky, Kopaigorod and Luchinetz, in the Vinnitsa oblast. This was late autumn, in November or December 1941. All the way, my father was holding my hand, and I kept asking, 'When we will finally be there?' My mum used to answer, 'Once we see the lights, we shall rest there ...' In reality, we were put into pigsties, which became our place of residence until the spring of 1942: a residence with no doors, and when frosts began, with no windows – the gendarmes shattered the glass so that we would not be hot (their words).

After one lots of shootings in the Kosoutzky forest, I saw with my own eyes how the ground moved because of the people buried alive.

I remember the bridge crossing from Ataki to Mogilev-Podolsky. The Germans surrounded the bridge. Soldiers were lining the rails on two sides of the bridge. They were the ones who pulled old people out of the marching column, and took children away from their parents. Before the bridge, an elderly German soldier approached my parents. 'Give me your children,' he said, 'I will take them to the other side.'

Mum didn't want to but my father insisted. On the other side of the river this German waited for my parents. Mum was crying.

The German said, 'Don't cry, sister. The German people will pay a high price for your people's suffering.' He gave my mother a loaf of bread, a bar of chocolate, and a few biscuits. I have kept this episode clear in my memory.

My father was a tailor. He began to work; in the spring of 1942 we were allowed to get out of the pigsty. An old Jew named Mendel, a blacksmith, gave us shelter. He had a big family, eight children, and a small house. Neveretheless, Mendel gave us a small room that for us seemed an incredible luxury. My father got bread, potatoes and beans as payment for his work. He got to know many new people and many kind and good people at that. Maria Vassilievna Starodub, from the village of Vinozh, allowed him to use her sewing machine. Darya Fomovna Shalomai, their neighbour, a wonderful and compassionate Ukrainian woman, allowed us to use her house when my father worked with customers and took orders. During two years, she virtually saved our family, sharing everything down to the very last thing that she had, although she basically had nothing at all. Her house, thatched with straw, had two rooms, a kitchen and a hall, and the floors were made of mud. During winter, the internal walls of the house were covered with ice. In severe frosts, when we didn't have anything to heat the house with, she took me into her room and warmed me. There was a vegetable garden near the house, a few trees, and her father, Granddad Foma, and three children, Kolya, Maria and Volodya, looked after it. They had a cow that gave us very little milk, especially in winter; yet my brother and I were getting as much milk as any of her own children. One day, Maria poured herself more milk than everybody else, for which she was immediately reprimanded by her mother, and she never did that again.

Granddad Foma was an amazing person. He rode a cart harnessed with oxen. Maria and Kolya were in the fields, working by his side all daylong. Together with my brother and younger children, we went out to greet them every night. Granddad Foma used to put us up on the cart and drive home. He always gave us something: either a plum, or a piece of a sunflower that he had saved for us. He was a quiet and very kind man.

In the winter of 1943, my father became ill with typhus. He lay in bed, in a high fever, and was delirious. One day, when Mum went to get a doctor and Darya Fomovna had stayed at home taking care of my father, a neighbour walked in and said, 'Why do you look after this Jew? He will make you and your children ill. Leave him …'

Darya Fomovna answered to this, 'Get out of my house. You may throw a man with his children out into frosty weather, but I can never do this.'

When the Nazis were defeated in the Vinnitsa oblast, in March 1944, we went home. In 1946, Darya Fomovna came to visit us in Lipkany. We welcomed her cordially. Almost every year we went to visit her. All the years my father was helping Darya's children and grandchildren with whatever he could. But how can we compare our attention and support with all that she did for us in those years? Our gratitude to her will be eternal.

26. This is inside me … and will only go away along with me

Ida Kalnitzkaya (b. 1932)

When the war began in 1941, our family (my parents and four children) and our relatives didn't manage to get out of our little Jewish town of Dzhurin, in Vinnitsa oblast.

It was already July when the Germans entered the town, and they soon moved all of us into the ghetto. Beside local Jews, there were thousands of people from all over Vinnitchina, the neighbouring oblast, as well as those relocated from Bukovina, Bessarabia and Moldavia. Being children, in the beginning, we didn't realizse all the terror that was happening. But, very soon, we too had to experience this bitterness.

I remember well the horrible bombing in the first days of the war. The skies were dark with the Nazi aeroplanes. We counted the total of twenty-seven of them. And then bombs started raining down on us. The adults were hysterical and shouted for us to get down, and all the children were lying on the ground. When the air raid was over, the town was unrecognizable: houses were burning, women were screaming in panic, searching for their children, and shattered glass was everywhere, as well as torn power lines. I think that everything was over at that moment, including our childhood: in the space of a few minutes we changed into little old people.

In the ghetto, fear and humiliation were our constant companions. The overcrowded conditions brought on epidemics of scabies. People were dying in hundreds and thousands – from diseases, cold and hunger. We wanted to eat all of the time. We were so happy when we managed to find a piece of goosefoot or a nettle! Once, a man was transporting beetroots in a cart, and I picked one up that had fallen down on to the ground. A policeman saw this and hit me with his whip – so hard that I will have a scar on my leg for the rest of my days so that I would remember the 'new order'!

Once, my sister was ordered to disinfect the clothes of the diseased, and I had to help her. I still remember the number of lice that were crawling over the meagre clothes. I developed a nervous itch, which even now, after so many years, keeps coming back.

For any minor offence we were punished. If somebody forgot to wear an armband with a six-pointed star on it, it was a crime. Or if someone went outside the ghetto, or didn't go to work because they were ill …

We didn't know that Hitler had headquarters in Vinnitsa called *Wehrwolffe* [Wolf's Den] and that all the local population had either been killed or removed to concentration camps. We were fortunate because the Germans went away and the Romanians took their place in our little town. There were no mass killings under their rule; howeve, pogroms were common.

The Romanians were looking for valuables and the 'dirty work' was performed by policemen: they turned everything upside down, cutting pillows wide open, beating people up. But the small town Jews were poor. That was why they threatened the ghetto residents with death. This probably would have happened, if the Bessarabia Jews had not paid ransom, and for a while we were left alone – until the next pogrom.

I remember how, during one of the raids (it was in 1943) they caught some teenage boys – David Barshtein, Kostya Rudyak, Naum Tzipman, Volodya Kapustyan, Yasha Furman and others – who were sent to a labour camp near Tulchin. Local residents told them that the previous group had been killed once they completed their work. One night, the boys managed to run away and return to the ghetto. They had to hide, paticularly from the policemen who knew them, and we had to help them and keep quiet.

But there were kind people on the other side of the ghetto fence who were helping us too, no matter what dangers threatened them. I will always remember Grandma Anya Polishchuk and her daughter Maria. If not for them, I don't think we would have survived. They were our saviours.

Once in the middle of the night we had a visitor: Auntie Malka, my dad's cousin, with her daughter Golda and a three-year-old son, Fimochka. They had escaped from the place of mass killings in the Pechera concentration camp, one of the most horrendous in the Ukraine. The child looked as if he were dystrophic, like a skeleton. We gave them shelter, hid them, sharing whatever little we had.

In March 1944, the Soviet Army liberated us. I will always remember 19 March, the happiest day in my life. We had spent two and a half years waiting for our inevitable deaths. However, in the ghetto, we still heard of what was going on in the Ukraine and what the Nazis did to people: killing, burning, hanging, wiping complete towns and villages from the face of the earth.

Many of the young boys I have recollected went to the army – one of them, David Barshtein, after the war got married to my elder sister. His father died at the front. His sister Leika was relocated to work in Germany. Along the way the Germans got to know she was *Judeh* and she was killed. We learned about all this much later.

In Dashev, a similar little town in the Vinnitsa oblast, my mum's parents and sister were killed: Yosif and Hannah Shutin, and Clara. They were killed right in their own yard. Their son Boris never came back from the war. Their second daughter, Zhenya, was murdered in Gaisin, with her two children. Her husband was also killed at the front. Almost all of the family was murdered. This mournful list could be continued for ever. When I grew up, I discovered that out of 185,000 Jews who remained in the occupied Vinnitchina, only 15,000 survived through to the liberation.

It is difficult to relate our suffering in the ghetto. If not for the victory, we would have turned into the smoke hanging over the crematoria.

How did our life go after the war? After the ghetto, the feeling of hunger haunted me, and having finished schooling, I entered the Odessa Institute for Food Industries. But I never managed to get a job that would adequately compensate for this deficiency. As a young specialist I was sent to Leningrad, to the biggest tobacco factory in the country. I worked there for twenty years, and in Leningrad I met my future husband, who at that time was a cadet in a military academy. In 1965, our family moved to his place of service, in Siberia. We lived there until 1985. In Leningrad, we had our first son, who grew up and became an officer too. Our second child was born in Siberia and is now a surgeon. When my husband retired from the military service, we came to live in Dniepropetrovsk.

27. It was heroism to survive[1]

Clara Kanovskaya

Like many of our neighbours, my family didn't have time to leave the town, and on the twentieth day of the war, we found ourselves in an occupied area. For three days, our city of Mogilev-Podolsky was robbed and ransacked by the Nazis, and innocent people murdered. Then people were relocated into the ghetto. Death was the punishment for crossing the ghetto borderline. In fact, death was the punishment for anything: for failing to obey the commands of the occupation authorities, for not wearing a *Magen David* ... A special labour team was put together comprised of children, and I was put into it. Under the whipping and beatings carried out by the policemen, we had to clear the wreckage, clean toilets and barracks, and perform other physical tasks.

On 15 August 1941, the ghetto residents were gathered in the station and it was announced that they would be resettled. They were all put in closed freight carriages. For the whole week they travelled, with no food or water, with no toilet. Finally the doors were opened and we saw the name of a small station, Shpigovo. They formed us into a convoy and marched us on to the village of Pechera. Here, as we found later, was a Nazi death camp for prisoners from Tulchin and other places. They asked for bread and salt, to cook soup from the tree leaves. They were completely indifferent towards anything.

We were put into a former horse stable with no roof. It rained continuously and there was no way to get warm. It was impossible to get food. People were killed for attempting to trade things. Swollen from hunger, we waited for the end.

Winter was approaching and there was no hope. But one day my mum told me in secret that a guard from the Ukrainian police, in exchange for some gold jewellery, promised to release a few girls.

I would never forget my farewell to my parents, their instructions, tears and kisses. I never again saw my beloved mum, Rachel Moiseevna, or my father, Leib Moshkovich. They were killed soon afterwards. And in the dark night, five of us, Jewish girls crossed the Southern Bug and found ourselves in the area occupied by the enemy. Local residents helped us change into old farm clothes. In the day we hid, and during the nights we walked into the unknown. Any moment we could be stopped by any local person, or the headman, and turned over to the police. But everywhere we were helped by Ivan, our guide, who was raised in the orphanage and who had Fruma, a girlfriend, in the camp. We were supposed to check whether he was trustworthy. When he went back to Pechera, his girl was already dead.

Having walked over 200 kilometres across the Ukraine, again we found ourselves in the Mogilev-Podolsky ghetto. There, Jews resettled from Bessarabia and northern Bukovina lived. We thought it was easier for us to get lost among our kind and wait for the liberation.

I was in the ghetto until November 1943. It was very difficult: I was an orphan, a lonely person in a city where power was in the hands of the police – German, Romanian and Ukrainian – and everybody was in charge of you, abusing you, while you – albeit hungry, ragged, barefoot – wanted to live and survive no matter what.

During the next pogrom I was caught and again put into a freight carriage. Together with other 280 other prisoners I was taken to the station of Balta, Odessa oblast. In the station square, people were selected to be sent to labour camps. I was fortunate to get into the Chapaevka farm, Ananiev district. And again, policemen beat us, and again there was this unbearably hard labour when I had to walk barefoot on snow, and had only one dress, made from an old sack. Yet again, this orphan hoped for a miracle in order to survive till liberation. You may imagine how hard I had to work when a Nazi farm owner said to a policeman once, 'Don't beat her, she has made the pigsty as clean as a church.'

In the winter of 1943/44, the rumours started spreading among the prisoners that the Nazis were losing in the war. A hope for rescue grew. In the evenings, after work, in a half-whisper, we were singing the song made up in the camp:

> On a faraway farm, in the Pridniestrovye steppe,
> We are destined to spend our days …
> In these difficult times, in a prison we stay,
> Yet the memory of our past never goes away …
> May the storms rage above our heads,
> May the cell be so tight and so dark,
> Yet we know well, that on those steppe ways,
> Our spring is approaching us!

And indeed, on 1 April 1944, our liberation reached us, and it was a joy hard to describe – before that, we had learned that a death squad was coming our way. Villages were burning everywhere through the region, and gunshots could be heard everywhere. Military fighter planes with red stars on their wings were flying quite low. By the time the evening came, our police guard had somehow disappeared. We also left our cells. We hid in the bushes and in the attics. I ran to the cemetery and lagged behind my friends. It was cold; shots sounded everywhere, so I sat down in fear on somebody's grave. I wondered whether the death squad would be searching for people under such circumstances. And, suddenly, I saw a big dog running towards me. At first I thought this was one of those trained to catch escaped prisoners. But it moaned painfully and came close to me. When I touched it, I saw blood. So I had to tear a sleeve off my only dress and bandage its wound. That how we stayed, keeping close to each other, keeping each other warm and waiting for our enemy. Time went by very slowly.

In the morning I found out the killing squad had passed by our farm, because the Soviet military scouts were already nearby (soldiers with stars on their helmets). We ran towards our rescuers without paying attention to the gunshots. When the first soldier on a horse rode into our village, everybody had tears of joy in their eyes. Everybody wanted to touch his trench coat or to shake his hand. It seems strange when now some people call them 'the invaders'. I will continuously refer to these soldiers with all due respect and sacredness: they rescued us from Nazism! We were prisoners and children, and we didn't demonstrate any heroism, but it was heroism enough to survive in the circumstances of the Nazi hell, in death camps and ghettos.

NOTE

1. This first appeared in 'People Remain Human: Testimonies of Witnesses', *Bulletin*, 1 (1991), pp. 48–50.

28. I got into Barrack No. 3

Movzesch Katz (b. 1926)

I was born on 25 December 1926, in the village of Koshelevo, Khust district; this place was then known as Transcarpathian Russ (Czech and Slovak Republic). I grew up in a worker's family; my father had two horses and was a cart-driver. He took parts made of beech from a saw mill in Nizhny Bystri to the Khust railway station where there were loaded on to the carriages and sent over to Poland. My mother was a housewife, and she looked after seven children.

Our family was observant, and there were two synagogues in the village and a *shoichet*. The Jews in the village observed all the holidays very strictly, and in particular Shabbat. I was the oldest child and it was my responsibility to help my parents. We kept our house kosher, and I had an obligation to go to farmers every morning so that they would milk the cows into our buckets. My mother made sour cream, soft and regular cheeses from the milk, and twice a week she took all this dairy produce on her shoulders to Khust and sold it to Jews there, carrying this all herself, sixteen kilometres one way. We had a couple of dozen geese to attend to. My mother fed them corn and when they grew fat, killed them, and salted her meat in a barrel as if it were a coleslaw. We lived very modestly. My sister and I (she was younger than I by one and a half years) helped my parents to work in our vegetable garden and babysat the younger children.

When I turned six, I went to the school and the *cheder* [Hebrew school]. I got up at 5 a.m. and went first to the *cheder*, then returned home to have breakfast, and then went on to school. After school I returned home, had lunch and went back to the *cheder*. During winter months, we went to the *cheder* in the morning and evening. Thus I completed seven years of school. When I was thirteen, I had a *bar mitzvah* (when I got a suit for the first time in my life).

In 1939, the Germans occupied Czechoslovakia and we were transferred to the rule of Nazi Hungary. Life became more complicated; food was rationed. In 1941, Jews became open targets of mockery and humiliation. In our village, people were good. But in the city they pulled Jews by their beards, *payot*, and for any offence their hair could be cut. Jewish families were randomly picked out and sent in freight carriages to Yassinya, Stanislav (Ivano-Frankovsk) oblast, because Hungary wouldn't agree to the exterminations of Jews on its territory.

In 1941, my father was taken into a labour battalion to dig anti-tank trenches. We remained without the head of the family, yet we had to survive somehow, so I started working instead of him. They didn't provide any men to load wood and, although only a child, I had to carry wooden parts through the forest on my shoulders, walking for fifty to a hundred metres. I came back home at dawn, slept for two or three hours, while the horses took rest too, and my mother gave them food and water. Then she harnessed them again, and sent me to Khust, to ship out the parts. The place was about thirty kilometres away from our village, and I had to unload the cart myself. In a week I could make three trips like this. The earning from the first trip went to buy oats for the horses, second to buy the hay and the third for the family – provided things went well, and the cart or wheels were not broken or anything.

Once, in the autumn of 1941, gendarmes came to Koshelevo and together with the village headman started putting Jewish families into lorries. We were taken to Khust, to the railway station, and put on to freight trains. The whole group was transported to the borders of Ivano-Frankovsk, which was the final destination on the railway. We arrived there in the middle of the night. In the morning we saw that far away in the forest, in tents, there were other Jews.

Two hours later, our carriages were opened up, and we were ordered to line up along side them. We were kept like this for about three hours, then we were counted, and put back into carriages where we had to stay until night fell. At night, our transport was attached to the train engine, and taken back to Khust, where we were allowed to go home. This caused great joy because we were the first transport to return home alive. Those taken out before had never survived – they were gunned down or drowned in the Dniester.

Thus we were back home again, and again work and life continued until 1944. Father was demobilized in 1943 because of illness. In spring, after the Passover, all Jews were taken to the ghetto. The ghetto was located in the village of Isa, which was nearby, about five kilometres away. In Isa, Christians were driven out of their homes in two streets in the neighbourhood of a burnt-out church, and Jewish families were resettled there.

We ate whatever we were able to bring with us. The ghetto was guarded and nobody was allowed out. Even when my granddad died, we were not allowed to bury him in Koshelevo but instead only in Isa, and only immediate family could attend the funeral. But I took a risk, and left the ghetto at night and, crossing the river and hiding in the fields and vegetable gardens, reached our home. I took there, from the attic, whatever I could carry (beans, flour, other food) and took it back to the ghetto, so that the children would have something to eat. The grown-ups struggled and endured but the young children were crying, asking for food.

We lived in this way almost a month and then, one night, we were all taken into burnt building of the church where there were no windows or roof. It was raining heavily and we all were wet through. Then, escorted by the guards, we were all put onto the carts and sent to Khust to the brick plant. There, for two days they tortured us, humiliating us, taking away money, gold jewellery; we were then put on to a freight train, with windows closed with barbed wire and doors shut tight. In the middle of the carriage, a hole had been made in the floor to serve as a toilet. All were put there: children, old people, youngsters and complete families. And they took us all to the concentration camp.

We arrived on the night of 29 May 1944, by transport from Hungary. In the morning, through the holes in the walls, we could see people in striped clothes. The guards surrounded the train, ordering us to get out and leave all our possessions behind. Then they started sorting us out. Men and young boys who were able to work went to the right, women and girls straight ahead, while old people and women with small children were taken to the left. I decided to go with my father. We were taken to a barn and ordered to undress. Then they shaved our hair, gave us striped clothes and shoes, sent us out to join the column and marched us to the Berkana concentration camp. There, numbers were tattooed on our arms. My father was A-8200, and I was A-8201. And this happened to each and every one of us. We lost our names and surnames and the morning calls went by numbers.

Then we were taken to Auschwitz. I spent two days there. There, again, they sorted us, and I had to tiptoe so as to look bigger and more able to work. Those who were too thin or ill were sent to the crematorium, and we already knew that. And on one hot day, escorted by guards, we were taken to another concentration camp, Monovets, across the fields. For me, this was not a very difficult journey, since older people from the intelligentsia (teachers and doctors) were giving me food.

During the air raid alarm, everybody was supposed to run to the shelter. But there were some miserable people who went through the rubbish bins during the alarm, searching for food, and if they were caught, they were hanged on the *platz*, in the concentration camp in front of all the camp inmates.

In the evening we received some food in the barracks. The oldest person in the barrack allocated the food, and if there was something left, he tried to give it to us, the youngest, and I tried to get it to my father. We lived in this way until 26 January 1945, when the final night came.

The front was approaching, and the plant where we worked was bombed the whole night through. One bomb fell in the middle of the camp, where we lived, but nobody was hurt. Next day they forced us again to work. At lunchtime, all barracks were ordered to assemble on the square. An officer came, and said that the front was approaching and we had to leave the camp, and those who could walk, should walk. Otherwise they would pour petrol around, and those who remained behind would burn alive. Each of us was supposed to take a blanket; then they gave us a loaf of bread and a roll of liver sausage for the road. We had to go out of the gates in groups of five, holding hands, and the guards escorted us. It was then that I lost my father and did not see him any more.

We went out to the highway along which we usually walked to work and saw that the plant was in ruins. We wandered in different directions as we walked; the Germans were leaving in lorries, cars and carts, retreating as the front approached. Those who became weak and fell on to the road were shot and dumped into ditches. Thus we marched in convoy for two days. Sometimes they allowed us to have a short break, but no food was given. I divided the loaf that had been given to us on departure into a few portions, and had one piece a day. At night they took us into the Gliewetz concentration camp, where there used to be people just as miserable as we were. But the camp was empty. Everybody tried to get into a barrack. It was cold; the blankets worn around our shoulders didn't give us any warmth and the three of us didn't get a room. We stayed outside and had to find something to sit on, to survive till the morning. We saw a corpse nearby, moved it to the wall and sat on it; we were exhausted.

We spent eight days in the camp and nobody gave us any food. We looked for the waste from the kitchen and ate that, including frozen potatoes and bones. My brother found a piece of a biscuit but didn't have enough strength in him to chew it, so he had to soak it in his mouth with snow. People were dying in droves.

Then 'open Pullman' carriages that were traditionally used to transport coal were pulled in. We each received 200 grams of bread and a piece of liver sausage. A ladder was set up for us to climb into the carriages. Then you had to jump down and move away fast so that the next person wouldn't jump down on you. The Germans ensured it was fast. Many were crushed: between 120 and 130 people were pushed into each of the carriages. We were packed tight and didn't have a chance to move. We spent seven days on the road, with no food or water. We wet our lips with the snow falling on to our blankets. When the train went under the bridges, some people threw bread to us. Each of us tried to catch it. There were many dead people in the carriage. On each stop they were taken out and put into a separate carriage.

Monowetz is an old labour camp. Jews from Poland had been imprisoned there since 1939, as well as political inmates, non-Jews. There were fifty-nine wooden barracks with wooden three-tiered bunks. I got into Barrack No. 3, together with my uncle (my father's younger bother), who was born in 1924, and my cousin (my father's sister's son) who was born in 1927. We were of the same build, small, and as we were a group of young people we were given less strenuous tasks.

We went to a plant that was located near the motorway, about two kilometres away. We went out in teams of two dozen or twentye, with the *kapo*,[1] accompanied by music, and we came back with music. The musicians stood at the gate. There, we were counted, again. The number of people entering had to be the same as the number of people leaving in the morning. We went to and from work, guarded. The plant was secured with barbed wire and guard towers. The guards didn't enter the grounds. The local population worked at the plant as well as British POWs (they were kept in another camp). The tasks we had to handle varied. I worked at the warehouse with one old German who was put into the camp for political reasons. I carried boxes with spare parts and nails. My father was sent to hard labour – he had to carry pipes for the sewerage system, also beams, or dig trenches for the sewerage system. We had breakfast in the camp, and the lunch was brought to the plant, separately for each team – *buno zyp* [nettle soup]. However, I managed to get to where the girls from the Ukraine worked. Then, we were moved to the Buchenwald camp. The camp was on a mountain, and we had to climb there on foot. There we were immediately sent to the showers, had to change our clothes and find accommodation in the barracks; but again, the three of us managed to remain together. They brought black coffee without sugar in barrels, and drank it greedily. When the lights went out, we were given tokens, which would allow us to eat once in a camp diner the following day. There were so many of us put into the bunks, that we stayed tightly packed. If one wanted to turn over, everybody else had to turn as well. Sometimes, when the lights went out, somebody would steal a food token from a neighbour, and then cries and laments would last throughout the night: someone would eat twice, and someone would go hungry.

For a few days we were repairing the road behind the camp and carring blocks. This was a transition camp, and again the three of us were lucky, we were put into one barrack where there were a few older people, about sixty years old, and young boys. We were also given food tokens but we were not sent to work, nobody would stole the tokens, and on that day we ate and rested.

But in early April the American army was approaching, and special groups composed of inmates surrounded one of the barracks each day, and under the supervision of a German officer these people would be forced out of the camp, into another one. Daily, the American planes would bomb the camp. The air raid alarm sounded, the Germans closed the gate and rushed into the shelter and those who didn't go to work that day ran into their barrack. The planes bombed the military barracks but not the camp itself.

This all lasted for a week. On the seventh day our barrack was surrounded and we were marched towards the gates. The three of us stayed together, and tried to get into the middle of the convoy because the first and the last were beaten up with rubber batons. And when we had almost reached the gate, one German officer who was responsible for keeping order told us, 'Young people, come and stay here, with me, you will be the final ones.' We stayed next to him, and nobody touched us, and at lunchtime the fighter planes flew overhead, and the gates were locked. The officer ran towards the shelter, and we ran into a barrack. Nobody did anything after lunch. At night we could hear that the front was nearby. In the morning they didn't touch anyone either. People were getting on to the roofs of the barracks and from there you could see that Germans were leaving along the highway, with the Americans following them. When American soldiers appeared, the guards abandoned their posts on the towers and fled. Immediately, some brave people found rubber gloves and cut the electric wiring, and also began catching the Germans. When the Americans were already in the camp, the phone rang. It was the German military commanders with orders to kill everyone who remained in the camp and to leave the camp.

That was how I got liberated, on 11 April 1945. American soldiers started giving us chocolate and biscuits, they cooked a heavy meal, and let exhausted people eat as much as they wanted. People started eating greedily, and as a result of this many had to go to the medical quarters, and died.

They started making lists of people, with names and addresses, so that they could be forwarded home. We said we were from the Czech Republicand the Americans started telling us to go to America. We refused, wishing to go home, and anxious to know who survived there. We hoped that our father reached home; as for my mother and brothers, I already knew they had been burned in a crematorium.

The Czech Tatra lorries came to pick up people, and we went with them. When we reached the border we were let into the Russian zone, and there we saw Russian soldiers. We were taken to Prague, from where the Czechs went home, and only twenty-five young men from the Transcarpathian Region stayed. They took us into a Czech military sanatorium, gave us food and clothes, and we were allowed to go around Prague for free. There we spent two weeks there.

They offered to let us stay in the Czech Republic but we refused that as well; we wanted to get home. The officer said that they wouldn't be able to send us all home because the Transcarpathian Region had been ceded to the Ukraine and they were no longer the hosts there. But they could transfer us to the Russian Kommandant's office, and they would send us home. We agreed. The officer took us to the Russians in a yard near the border and turned us in. There were many people there. The soldiers started mocking at us, taking away our clothes and suitcases. We asked, 'What's going on? Where are we?'

And they told us that people were being got together to be transferred to a labour camp in Russia, for three years, during which it would be established what we had been doing during the war. Knowing that, we had one of us go down a rope from the second floor and he went back to the Czechsto ask them to take us out.

The Czech officer came and said that he had earlier taken us there by mistake, that we were from Slovakia, and he got us out. He suggested again for us to stay there, but if we still wanted to go home we had to go by ourselves. So we took our clothes and went to the railway station and travelled on the top of carriage roofs to Bratislava. We had to change trains, but we saw how the Russians robbed people getting on the train and so stayed where we were.

Next day we got to Budapest with a freight train. There, there was a JDC soup kitchen, we got food and money, and went home. When we arrived home we found all the buildings reduced to rubble, nothing was left, everything was stolen. I found the walls only, and no one from my family. Later I found that my sister, Gitlya, who was one and a half years younger than I, was in a labour camp in Russia. She came back home after three months. Nobody else survived.

NOTE

1.   Literally, 'heads', chosen from among the camp inmates to enforce Nazi orders.

29. And our march of death began

Shaya Kleiman

The place where I was born, Vad Rashkov, was a small Bessarabian town on the right bank of the River Dniester. Before the war, over a thousand Jewish families had lived here.

Our family had four members: David, my father, Golda; our mother; my sister Beila, born in 1933, and myself.

When the war began, my sister was visiting my Aunt Miriam, a teacher in the village of Chinishauci. From there, they were evacuated, but were caught by the Nazis in Rostov-on-Don, where they were killed.

In the first days of the war our little town was murderously bombed, although there were no military targets or troops there. Many people were killed and wounded. We didn't have any information on the current situation at the front, but soon after the bombardment we began to hear shells bursting on the approaching front lines. Then the Jewish population began to leave. It was some time around early July of 1941.

The evacuation was organized in the following way: since people were afraid of possible air attacks, late at night, in darkness, a ferryboat was brought to the bank of the Dniester, pulled by a motorboat. People, with their possessions, were put on the ferryboat and taken to the village of Rashkov on the left bank of the river. On one such night, we crossed the river too. Together with our family, there was my father's sister, Maika Nusimovich, together with her family (husband Yosif, fourteen-year-old son Moisey, twelve-year-old daughter Bela, eight-year-old son Chayim-Shaya, and two-year-old daughter Noech). There was also the family of my father's sister-in-law, Taibl Kleiman, with four children (Ida, twenty-two; Rachel, twenty; Lev, seventeen; and David, fifteen). We all went to the Kodyma station, Odessa oblast, to get on the train and move out. My father went back to Vad-Rashkov to pick up more of our things, and we agreed that we would wait for him in Kodyma.

This saved his life. When we arrived in Kodyma, the railway station was on fire, and no more trains were dispatching. The following day the Germans entered the town.

In the first days of the occupation their attitude towards us was fairly 'satisfactory'. Things were limited to robbery; moreover the robberies were of an 'intelligent' nature. German soldiers could enter a house any time since there had been an order to keep doors unlocked. They went through our possessions quite contemptuously and picked out the most valuable things. I remember how they took a gold watch and a racoon fur coat. All Jews were required to wear white stars (later, yellow stars) on the front and the back of our clothes. But our relatively 'calm' life did not last for long.

Once our neighbourhood, settled primarily with Jews, was raided by a group of Germans dressed in black uniforms (probably, the Gestapo). They started taking men and teenage boys out of the houses, shouting at them and beating them. They were taken to the outskirts of Kodyma.

Over a hundred people were killed and buried there. Among those killed were members of our family: my uncle, Yosif Nusimovich, with his son Moisey, and my cousins Lev and David Kleiman.

A few of the arrested were allowed to go free, while others were kept, as they put it, as 'hostages'. They were horrendously tortured, their faces were painted like those of savages, and they were forced to stay that way. After a few days, they were killed too.

I would like to make a small digression for two recollections.

1. Among the so-called hostages, there was an acquaintance of my parents who managed to escape, thanks to one German soldier. He told us how one German approached him, gave him a bucket and told him to go to the well and get some water. When he came back, the German started shouting at him that he hadn't done his job well, and turned the bucket over. When he came back again, the German again turned his bucket over and again sent him to fetch some more water. Only then did this person came out of his stupor and realize that this was an attempt to save him, and hid.
2. Among those killed in Kodyma there were many of my parents' compatriots. After the war, in Chernovtsy, the former residents of Kodyma wanted to raise money and establish a monument there. They have never received a permit to do so.

And now, I return to my memories.

Soon after the pogrom, my aunt, Taibl Kleiman, with Rachel and Ida, her daughters, decided to leave Kodyma and secretly go to friends or relatives in a village on the bank of the Dniester (I don't remember its name now). Soon we got the news that all Jews there, including themselves, had been drowned in the Dniester.

Following the pogrom, my father came to Kodyma. He had suffered a lot too while searching for us but the fact that he was not with us at that time had saved his life.

Soon afterwards, the German Kommandant issued an order that all those evacuated had to return to their homes, and we were marched back towards Rashkov. We were not allowed to cross the Dniester to Vad-Rashkov, and most of the town had been burnt down. We were taken towards the little town of Kamenka, where we were accommodated in the houses of local Jews.

Here, Romanian gendarmes were already in authority. For two months, until November 1941, gendarmes and local policemen continuously humiliated us. It was a continuum of robberies, violence and murder. Frequently, adults were sent to work, and after their work they were drowned in the Dniester. I remember that following one such *Aktion* my father hid away and didn't want to go to work. A gendarme came to us, and started beating my mother violently, threatening to kill her if my father didn't show up. I knew where he was hiding, so I ran there and told him, my father came out, and the beating stopped. Thus we lived until November 1941. On 7 November 1941, all the Jewish population was marched out of Kamenka. Under the supervision of gendarmes we were marched towards Rashkov. Those who were slow were gunned down or beaten to death.

The horrible march of death went on through the end of 1941. We were marched during the day, and at nights we stopped at some farmyard, a warehouse, a stable, and so on. For part of the way we were walked along the railway tracks. I remember such stations as Kodyma, Sloboda and Borshchi. German soldiers frequently shot at us from passing trains, killing people. Along the way, and especially at night, we were robbed, often our clothes were taken away, as well as hats, and it was a very cold time of the year, and frost and snow were everywhere. Mostly gendarmes and their collaborators from the local people carried out these robberies. I remember how, in order to keep their clothes and stay warm, people cut them into pieces, made patches, soiled them, and so on. I shall always remember young women and girls who covered their faces with mud, shaved their heads and scratched their faces, in order to look as ugly as possible. I remember the laments and cries of the old people and children who begged for food. Along the way we were joined by Jews from various places we passed by, for instance from Kodyma. But nevertheless, our convoy became smaller with every day: some people were killed during the march, some died along the way or couldn't walk any more, and were killed where they stood. Some people fled; it was easy to escape but there was nowhere really to run. Every time, after the day's march was over, we couldn't locate some of our relatives or people we knew. Thus my aunt, Maika Nusimovich, died, together with her children Beila, Chaim-Shaya and Noech.

At Borshchi station, the gendarmes transferred us over to the Ukrainian police, who never made it a secret that we would be taken to be killed.

I remember a horrible village – I think it was named Gvosdovka – where we stopped. We were put into a *kolkhoz* barn, which had been already filled with bodies of the dead and those of barely alive and breathing people. Most likely, a day earlier, another convoy of Jews had gone by and the dead had not been taken care of.

By the end of December we reached a location called Krive and local residents told us that the place of the mass execution was near. Then my parents and another family of four and two men decided to escape.

On 31 December 1941, early in the morning before the policemen came after us (they had been spending the night out in the village), we fled and hid away. We decided to walk towards Krivoe Osero, the district centre (I don't remember why the adults in our group picked that direction). Along the way we entered a house where a single young woman lived. She agreed to give us shelter in exchange for some of our clothes. When we were accommodated, she left, and in the evening she came back with a group of young men. They were swearing and cursing, and threw us out of her house, taking away our remaining clothes and things that we had. Then they chased us and beat us up.

We soon lost sight of one of the men who had fled with us, and we never saw him again. We were eight of us, and on the night of the New Year of 1942 we found ourselves in an open field, in the frost. It was our luck that we had the time to get dressed otherwise we would have frozen to death. Soon we found a haystack in which we spent the night, and in the morning we set off to wander through the villages. In many houses people would let us in, to get warm and have some food; but there were nights we spent in half-ruined sheds, abandoned houses, and simply in the haystacks.

Once, in early January of 1942, we stopped to spend the night in an abandoned house, with no doors and windows, at the entrance to the village of Kruchinov. The residents of the neighbouring house brought us some food, closed the windows, fixed the door, and suggested that we lived there for some time. For a month this family provided us with food and fuel to heat the house. In early February 1942, policemen came to us, they beat us up; and threw us out of the house, killing one of the men. And again, our trials continued, in the cold and frost, and again kind people helped our family, and the other family that was with us, to survive. We were advised to go to the village of Baba Dzivka (or Baba Divka) where members of some Christian sect lived. I think they were the Seventh Day Adventists, so we went to them. These people hid us for two weeks in their village council. It happened that soldiers or police came to the village but nobody turned us in. They went through all the local places where Jewish ghettos had been established to search for a place where it would be the best for us to live. They chose the ghetto in the village of Peschana, Odessa oblast.

In late February, when frosts had somewhat diminished, and we had become a bit stronger, they put us on to a sleigh, gave us warm sheepskin coats and took us away, to the Peschana Jewish ghetto.

During our travelling we saw many horrible things. Here are two more examples that I remembered well:

1. When the Jews of Kodyma learned that they would be expelled, some parents who had grown-up daughters got them married to Ukrainian young men, and the girls stayed to live with their husbands. Later, these young women were arrested and killed.
2. And here is an example of cynicism. During one of the stops of our convoy, a German officer, who looked very intelligent, came up to us. He saw two women, a mother and a daughter, who were covered with very beautiful and well-crafted blankets. He told them that they would be killed soon, and it would be a shame that those valuable things would be wasted. That is why he would take away their blankets and instead he would send them a nice meal to have before their death. He kept his promise.

We managed to survive only thanks to kindness, humanity and compassion of many local people who did their best to save us, the threats of the occupiers notwithstanding.

I will never forget a forester who, after finding us in the forest where we had got lost during our wanderings, took us into his home. He gave us food, some clothes, his shoes to my father, and a warm coat to a girl from another family, and took us out to the highway.

By the summer of 1942, we had settled down a bit; we had made shoes from wood, found bags somewhere, put hay in them, and made 'pillows'. My parents started going to work, and received bread and some other food for it. Besides, they began working for local residents and Father worked a little in a *kolkhoz* that was still running in the village. This all gave us a chance to survive, although we did not always have enough food. We frequently heard the rumours that somewhere a ghetto had been liquidated or Jews had been killed. Unfortunately, these rumours were often true.

In the ghetto, gendarmes carried out frequent 'check-ups'. During those *Aktions* all ghetto residents had to go to the central square and hear, often on their knees, the 'complaints' and orders of the gendarmes. These were often accompanied by beatings.

During the check-ups we were very afraid that we would be sent out again, but everything was eventually over.

In 1941, when we left Vad-Rashkov, there were fourteen of us; by March 1944, only three remained.

30. Each day of our life seemed a year long[1]

Igor Kogan (b. 1938)

When I was three and a half years old I didn't know the meaning of the word 'war'. I could only see the changes in the faces of people – they now had fear written on them, and I couldn't understand why all the smiles had gone, and everybody seemed sad and concerned all of the time. I remember how Mum would take me in her arms and at night we would go out to the marketplace, looking at the red sky in the distance and listening to the artillery booming. This was the railway station of Zhmerinka, which had been set on fire, and we could see the fire from twenty-five kilometres away. It was then that I heard the word 'war' and felt it was a bad word.

The real meaning of the word 'war' became clear to me when planes with crosses on their wings flew over our heads and I heard the skies moan. It happened when I was standing in the street and waving a handkerchief on seeing our soldiers off. They were leaving us and it was then that small dots appeared in the skies – these were German parachutists. They were shooting from above, without distinguishing between targets – shooting at children, women and old people.

We all ran away and hid in cellars, There were many people with us in the cellar, it was stuffy and children cried. Suddenly the door opened and I saw strangers in helmets with automatic guns. Everybody had to go out with raised arms, and we were all taken to the marketplace – it was the centre of our village. They beat those who couldn't walk with gun butts. The Germans surrounded us; machine-guns were set up on the ground, with their black muzzles pointing at us. Everybody understood that this meant death, and the cries and laments began.

At that very moment, one of our planes appeared in the sky and started circling above us. Till now I cannot comprehend why the pilot did so; he probably saw the crowd of people on the ground. But the Germans got confused and started shooting at the plane. And when we heard the shots, we ran away.

A few days later, the Romanians entered our village and announced that a ghetto would be established and everybody had to wear a six-pointed star, both children and grown-ups, and those who didn't would be executed. We were driven out of our homes and resettled in the centre of the village. Nobody was allowed to leave the ghetto without a special permit. Zina, my mum, my sister Sima, Aunt Basya, and my brother, Mora, were taken away to the camp in Tyvrov. And my grandparents, my sister Raya, and myself stayed in Krasnoye. We suffered a lot, living through hunger and cold, until all of our family returned to the ghetto.

We were in a continuous state of waiting, day and night, afraid that the Germans would come any minute and kill us all. I don't remember when and how it happened that the Germans suddenly surrounded our ghetto. Mum hugged my sister and me and took us up into the attic, crying. We understood that we would all be killed. The Germans kept us surrounded from morning till night, waiting for an order. My sister, Sima, said, 'We had better jump down, so that we won't be tortured.' And she was only six years old. The Germans stayed for a long time, but somehow we were delivered that time. People said that a Romanian Kommandant in Krasnoye overturned the decision to kill us.

We were walking around, hungry, with bare feet, and naked. Each day of our life seemed a year long. My uncle, S. Kh. Bogomolny, Mum's brother, was a very handsome, tall man. Mum always asked him to hide away, and not to go out into the street. But the trouble followed him close. He didn't know that all of his family had been killed in Babi Yar. I always liked to sleep in the same bed as him. One day I woke up and saw a German soldier standing by the side of our bed. Another soldier was standing by the window. My uncle realized that they had come to get him; he said his goodbyes to us. They took him out of the village and told him to run. He ran, but a bullet caught up with him. My grandpa was not allowed to bury him, but he ignored them and buried his son.

Some people came to us and told us to run away because we would also be killed. But we didn't go anywhere. One evening, a Ukrainian woman came to us and said to my mum, 'Give me your son, he doesn't look Jewish. They will kill you and I will save him.'

Mum cried for a long time, keeping me close to her body. I cried too. Why would I have to go with a strange woman whom I had never met before? The woman took me, covered with a warm shawl, and walked away with me. She had warned her relatives that if somebody asked, I was her sister's son. I remember that tears were always in my eyes; I cried constantly. I don't remember how long it took, but I began to get used to my new family.

Once, in the middle of the night, I heard someone weeping above me. I opened my eyes, and saw my dear mum. She took me in her arms, and we cried for a long time. Mum thanked the woman and said, 'Thank you for everything, but I cannot live without him. Whatever happens to me, will happen to my son.'

No matter how that woman begged her, my mum wouldn't leave me this time. Unfortunately I don't remember the woman's last name, but may God grant good health to her, her children and her grandchildren.

We were hiding for a long time, yet expected to be killed any day. And this lasted until the Red Army liberated us in March 1944.

My father, S. Kh. Kogan, died at the front. I don't even know where he was buried. All his numerous relatives were killed in the village of Brailov, Zhmerinka district, Vinnitsa oblast, where almost everybody died, and only a few survived.

I'm writing my recollections and tears keep rolling down my cheeks. I ask myself one question only: why my people had to suffer so much?

NOTE

1. This originally appeared in 'People Remain Human. Testimonies of Witnesses', *Bulletin,* 3 (1994), pp. 86–90.

31. Days and nights of the German occupation

Leonid Korenfeld (b. 1927)

When the war began, I lived in the town of Alexandria together with Mum and my grandparents, who were than over seventy years old. We were very poor. My grandma had been disabled since childhood. Mum worked as a cleaner in a shop. My father had left us back in 1936 and at that time he already had another family and they lived in Poltava.

In early June 1941, the Germans entered Alexandria without a single shot. I remember there was this terrible silence, and tanks and motorcycles were the first things to enter the town. Thus the days and nights of the Nazi occupation began. Beside us, many in the town didn't manage to get evacuated.

First, the Nazi Kommandant's office was established in the town, followed by Ukrainian police and [officials in] the city hall. Orders, directives and commands were posted everywhere, each one more scary than another. The Nazi propaganda system began its work.

There was an order for all Jews living in the town to register at the Kommandant's office. It was mandatory. Those who failed to register would be punished in various ways or even executed. In these matters, the Nazis and their collaborators were very skilful and 'generous', in particular when it was a Jew in question. After registration, all Jews were commanded to wear six-pointed stars on their armbands. The Germans and their local collaborators humiliated and abused Jews in every possible manner, forcing them to do the hardest labour and to work from dawn till night. Poor people were severely punished for any minor fault. Almost every day police would storm into our flat and take away something from our miserable possessions. They never missed anything. One morning, on the walls of houses, on lampposts and fences, the orders were pasted for all Jews living in Alexandria to report immediately, with their belongings, to the Kommandant's office for relocation. Those who ignored this order would be killed, as well as all those who would help hide Jews from relocation.

Thus all Jews were forced to report to the Kommandant's office. Those who didn't go voluntarily were forced there. My mum and I understood what that meant and tried to hide wherever we could. For almost two weeks my mum hid with our former neighbours, the Ukrainian family of Ivan Alexeyevich and Polina Lukyanovna Kozhinets. At the same time I was hiding with my uncle's wife (my uncle had been killed at the front in the first days of the war). Thus, in less than twent-four hours, there was not a single Jew left there. All my close relatives were 'relocated', a total of nine people, soon followed by two more, though the mother of one of them was Ukrainian. One day, together with my mum, we left the town and went towards the east, hoping to cross the front line somewhere, to reach our side.

Thus, having crossed almost a thousand kilometres of Nazi-occupied territory, we reached the city of Orel. This was some time around October 1941. Along the way, a new surname was 'invented' – Mum called herself Galina Ivanovna Sigorenko and referred to me as Vladimir Alexandrovich Sigorenko. By then, the front had stabilized but, although we tried many times, we failed to cross it. In June 1942, I was captured in a raid and was forced to go to Germany for hard and slave labour.

They took us there in freight trains, with closed doors and tight security. There were between fifty and sixty people in each of the carriages. It was a long ride, and finally we got to Austria. Following long 'quarantines' and allocation I was sent to the camp for relocated individuals in Grosszolenshtein, the station of Sankt-Georgen am Reit, near the town of Amshtetten. I worked there as a labourer on the narrow-gauge railways for almost three years.

The camp was located in the sheds and barns of one Joganne Falman, a private innkeeper; it was surrounded with barbed wire and guarded by elderly *schutzbahnpolizei* [railway police]. We had to get up at four in the morning, and we had to work under tight security till very late at night, and then we were marched back into camp and locked in for the night. They gave us turnips to eat, punishing us very severely for any 'offence'.

Some time closer to the end of the war, the Hungarian Jews were brought in and accommodated in a specially designed camp, some thirty kilometres away from us. There were about 400 people there, and they lived together with their families. They worked in the depot. And then, almost at the very end of the war, early one morning, the camp was surrounded (according to the story told by Austrian railway workers). A German *Sonderkommando* [Special commando unit][1] surrounded it and burned it down with flame-throwers, while all the poor people there were still alive. This was perhaps one of the final mass annihilations of the Jews of Eastern Europe during the Second World WarI.

In April of 1945, divisions of the Red Army liberated our camp, and all of us, the camp prisoners, returned to our homeland.

My father was at the front from the very first till the very last days of war, and was a commander in many divisions. My mum was a volunteer at the front after Orel was liberated and fought there till the end of the war.

After the war was over, Father started looking for us, and in August of 1945 he found us in Orel, and brought us to Poltava, where my true name and surname were restored.

NOTE

1. *Sonderkommando* were SS units which carried out mass exterminations, disposed of dead bodies and erased the traces of mass murder. (Mr Korenfeld specifies 'German' *Sonderkommando* as there were also Jewish units comprising camp inmates who were forced to assist in the gas chambers and crematoria.)

32. We were left all alone in this wide world

Evgeniya Krestyaninova (Birman)

My name is Evgeniya Lvovna Krestyaninova (Birman), and I was born in the Ukraine, in the village of Novaya Sinyava, Starosinyavsky District, in Kamenets-Podolsky oblast.

My father, Lev Birman, worked as a blacksmith in a *kolkhoz*. Sophia Birman, my mother, was a housewife. I had three siblings: Yasha, Pinya and Izya. Our grandma Sosya was my father's mother. My parents got married very early. My mum was sixteen years old when she got married since she was an orphan: her parents, both teachers, had died in the Civil War during Petlyura's pogroms. I don't know where that happened. Their five children survived. Her youngest brother and her older sister lived in Moscow. One brother lived in the town of Proskurov and another in Balta. I only met her older sister, my aunt, who had come to visit us a year before the war began, with her youngest son. We don't know my mum's maiden name.

My aunt from Moscow wanted to take me there for education, but my mum wouldn't agree. My mum was a well-educated woman. I was four or five years old, and I knew all Pushkin's fairy-tales by heart as well as many folk stories. When Izya was born, in winter, my mum was laundering his swaddling cloth in the pond, and she slipped and fell into the icy water. She was only saved at the last moment (it happened near the mill and the whirlpool started pulling her in). She was sick for a long time after that. All the household was managed by Grandma.

My father didn't have any siblings. He started to work very young. I don't know anything about his father.

I don't know exactly when I was born, but I have a few starting points from others' stories. My mother's story had it that I was born on New Year's Eve, it was the time of a heavy blizzard, and it happened about eight years after Pinya. I didn't go to school before the war. I don't know whether I had to go or not. My friends say that Izya is three to four years younger than I am, and when the war began he was no older than two or two and a half years. I came back to the house where I was born only in 1987. I met with some of my brothers' friends and learned some facts from them. Yet, they didn't know where my mother came from originally. And all of our neighbours had died. Thus I had emptiness around me. Nobody can tell me anything now. And I can only trust my memories.

For me, the war began on an early summer morning. I looked out of the window and saw a cannon with a huge muzzle near our house, covered with branches of a walnut tree. It appeared quietly, during the night, and disappeared likewise, into nowhere.

The same happened with a tank, and soon afterwards I heard a clatter. People started to say that Shepetovka was being bombed. In Staraya Sinyava, a sugar factory was bombed. People were carrying yellow sugar that was still soft, as far as ten kilometres away.

One day, two planes appeared above our house, a German and one of ours. They started an air fight. It was a terrible noise, and everybody ran away and hid. Later, I found out that our plane had been downed and had crashed at the end of our village. I went with other children to have a look at it. It lay on one side, small, with one wing torn off. There was no pilot in sight. A few days later, our soldiers walked through Novaya Sinyava. They were young, very tired and hungry. They asked for milk.

Mum cried, 'Where are you going? The Germans will come, they will kill us all.'

The soldiers drank milk and calmed us down by promising to be back soon. I don't know where they went, but soon afterwards, trains of German wagons pulled in from the village of Lyadki. Huge horses with sturdy legs were pulling carts filled with something. Soldiers sat on them, and some of them were playing harmonicas. There was a monkey on one of the carts. They stopped in a carrot field. We went to see the monkey. I saw almost nothing because I was afraid of going up close. The soldiers took batons and went through the yards to beat chickens.

Once I became ill; I had a sore throat, and was in bed with fever. Suddenly, a German entered our house. He asked for eggs and potatoes. Mum said that the potatoes had not grown yet. She started talking with him and began crying. He calmed her down. He told her that nobody would hurt us. He took me in his arms and started carrying me around the room, singing some lullaby. I shrank with fear. He said, 'Don't be afraid, I also have children.' He put me back and left the room, without taking anything from us. He spoke German but I somehow understood him.

I felt the war when I saw that Polish refugees were going along our highway towards the village of Lyadki. They walked through the village silently and many did not have any things with them. We stood along both sides of the road and watched this huge flow of silent people. Anxiety grasped my senses.

A new flag was raised over the village council. New money was introduced. A rouble note had a picture of a girl in a white kerchief. Soon we had to leave our home and spend nights at other people's places. Finally, we were accommodated in a house, the owners of which had been evacuated. I didn't see any fear, nor did it in the attitude of my family. But one day, Father came and said we had been relocated to Khmelnik.

We put all our possessions on to a cart and, escorted by the police went to Khmelnik. This was some time around July 1941. All the remaining Jews who were residents of this village were killed on the premises of the sugar factory on 1 August 1941.

We stayed with some of my father's relatives. It was very crowded since there were seven of us: four children, our parents and Grandma. That is why Grandma Sosya stayed in the village of Sokolovka, in a local potter's house. There was a kitchen and a room with a pottery wheel, not suitable for living quarters. My elder brothers, Yasha and Pinya, went to Sokolovka a few times. Once they brought me a gift from Grandma: a small pot. I also wanted to visit Grandma badly. And then, one day, two women came to us from the village of Sokolovka, on their own business. When they were going to leave I quietly followed them. They were walking along and talking to each other, and they noticed me when they had gone quite a distance.

'Where are you going?' they asked me.

'To my grandma,' I said.

They took me into the village and showed me Grandma's house. It was at the very entrance to that village. Thus I began to live with my grandma. And my parents stayed in Khmelnik with my brothers.

One night, in winter, somebody knocked loudly on the door. My grandma went to see who was there. A completely naked man entered the house. He gesticulated, waving his arms to and fro around his head, and mumbled something indistinctly. Grandma wanted to leave him, but he was very agitated, and then jumped up and ran away. My grandma realized what was wrong, and I could understand it only decades later: the man had escaped the killing.

A few days later, my father came over. He spoke to Grandma and she left. I stayed with Father, and we spent a few days like that. Then, Yasha and Pinya came. Finally, Grandma brought over my mum and Izya. I don't know how my family managed to survive the slaughter. I remember how glad Mum was that she listened to a bird knocking its beak on the window, as if telling them to leave. I will never know now how they were saved.

We lived for some time in that place. Then, although my father was a wonderful blacksmith, a much-needed profession in any village, the headman demanded that we leave the village immediately. There was a heavy snowfall and blizzard and we were again travelling on a cart towards Khmelnik. There we found out that our relatives and their neighbours were not alive any more. Their houses were empty, burgled and with shattered windows. Many years later I learned that in early January of 1942, in the morning, the police and a special raid squad came, together with dogs, and stormed the Jewish homes. They threw unsuspecting people from their beds out into the streets, with whatever they had on them. Those who couldn't walk – the ill and disabled – were killed right on the spot. Hunted down by dogs, the people were surrounded and thus marched out into the field. Horrible laments and screams were heard everywhere. One section of the people was shut in the basement of the police station and kept there for a week with no food or water. Then, they were also taken out into the field and killed. A man who was thirteen years old when he ran away from the convoy related this story to me. That time, almost 3,000 people died.

The survivors were forced into one small territory close to the police station between the streets of Shevchenko and Sholom-Aleichem (their current names), into the houses of people who had already been killed. Yellow stars were placed on the houses, and it was prohibited to leave the boundaries of the area. Police guarded the ghetto. Once I was playing in an empty ruined house with a toy I had found. Suddenly, in the doorway I saw a policeman.

'What are you doing here?' he asked.

'Playing …'

'Where are you from?' he continued, pointing at the Ukrainian and Jewish parts of the town, 'There or here?'

I pointed to the ghetto, and then realizing the gravity of the situation, became so scared that I peed.

He said, 'Get out of here!'

I ran away, happy that he hadn't done anything to me.

My father was taken under guard to work at the sawmill, where he worked as a blacksmith. They didn't get any food there. Mum was also taken to different works within a POW camp. One morning when I went out into the street I saw many policemen coming along. They started to beat people with gun butts and marched them into the police station. There we were put into a basement already crowded with people. There I saw my mum, grandma and Izya. My father was put in a separate jail, with another man. There were so many of us that we could only stand. Izya was held in people's arms – taking turns – but I had to stand almost all of the time. Thus we stayed all night. Early in the morning the doors in the basement were opened, and an order to get out given. Women started to scream, followed by the children. The first were beaten down, and they moved towards the exit. Soldiers with fixed bayonets were standing along both sides [of the passage]. We ran through the passage, and stopped in the police yard. The German Kommandant and the chief of police went out on to the balcony. They started to read a list. First, the surname of my father: 'Birman, four children, wife and mother, go towards the exit!'

What followed was awful! All the women started pushing their children towards my mother. I was pushed away. I screamed with terror: Mum forced her way towards me, took two other children, since Yasha and Pinya were not with us, and we left the police station. Then, everybody else was let go.

This was in summer, since I was barefoot. Little less than a month later and I stood by the road and saw a few SS men in blue and black uniforms with bones on their sleeves heading towards the police station. Two women stood nearby. They spoke quietly between themselves, saying that it would begin tomorrow. I could barely understand what they were talking about but felt something was wrong. I decided to tell my mum about it. Still, I had my doubts and fears whether I understood things properly, and feared that I would scare my mum in vain. But then I told my mum what I heard. In the evening she dressed Izya and me and told Father that she was leaving. Father tried to persuade her to stay but she was firm in her decision. We went out into the street through the fence of a Ukrainian home that bordered the ghetto, and went into town. She took Izya and me to a house near a cemetery. A Ukrainian or Polish family: a couple with two girls lived there. They met us at the entrance. I thought that we had come to visit but we didn't enter the house. We went upstairs into the attic. It was dirty because of the bird excrement but we sat down on the floor and stayed like that until morning.

Early in the morning the host came and said he couldn't hide us any longer since a raid on the camp had begun. He was scared for his family. We became scared too, and went to the cemetery. There we found a hidden corner and spent the next night there. I was very hungry and thirsty and started to beg my mum to go back home. Mum couldn't decide. Eventually she let me go. I ran home through the yards, trying to stay away from the road. In the doorway of one house I saw a woman with a child. She asked me, surprised, 'Where are you from?'

I ran away from her. When I arrived home, it was dead silent, and everything was turned upside down. Though Father seemed to be all righ, as well as my brothers, Yasha and Pinya, none the less I felt some emptiness. I realized that Grandma was gone.

My father was scared when he saw me alone. 'Where is Mum?'

I said that Mum and Izya had stayed in the cemetery. He started to convince me to go and bring them back but I refused, with no explanations, since I was very frightened. In the evening Mum and Izya returned to the ghetto. Father told my mum how Grandma had died.

Once again, the police had acted in theirs preferred manner – secretly and unexpectedly. Early in the morning the police had broken into our house. Grandma, Yasha and Pinya were in the house. Grandma was awake and she shouted to the boys to run to the attic. While they were going to do so, police managed to catch both of them. Grandma charged the policemen, screaming, 'Don't touch the children!'

Then police caught her but Yasha and Pinya managed to hide in the shelter and pulled the ladder up. Grandma struggled but it was an unequal fight: the police pulled her off her feet and beat her head on the concrete floor. When she was unconscious, they dragged her to the police station. We never saw her again.

It was impossible to live in this ruined place, so we moved into another. After the final raid, my father grew very cautious. No matter what happened they ran away to hide in their birthplace, Novaya Sinyava. But there, they also had to hide, since there was a whole gang of police there along with their chief. It was warm then; we went around with no clothes and shoes, hiding them in holes, since everything was looted during raids.

One day, together with other children, I was at the corner of our house, and we listened to one boyof roughly our age. He told us how he had been left alone after the raid, since his parents and sister had been killed. I got frightened: how could one live alone with no parents? He lived with his aunt who, thank God, was alive.

Suddenly a twelve-year-old girl in a white kerchief came up to us and said, 'Go with me to Zhmerinka, they don't kill people there.'

I went to Mum and began telling her about the girl. But Mum wouldn't listen to me. But the boy decided to join the girl. And if they reached Zhmerinka, they survived. I don't know why my parents did not take the chance. Most likely they didn't have money to pay the guides, or maybe they simply didn't believe the story. In any case, those few from Khmelnik who survived had gone to Zhmerinka.

One day, Mum strictly forbade me to go out into the street because the day before the Kommandant had gone by and – having seen children – he wondered why so many were still left. He couldn't let it stay that way. Suddenly, in the middle of the day, Father came home. He called Izya and me and showed us a pit dug in the corner of the barn. We went down into it. It was not deep enough yet but he dug down more. And again, we went down. We sat down on the ground, and the floor was placed above us and something was put on top of that. Father told us to sit quietly and not even to whisper until he came back and freed us. We stayed thus for a very long time. Nobody came back to set us free. Finally, our father came and opened the shelter. He let us out of the pit but was very sad. It turned out there indeed had beens a raid on the children. They caught them, threw them into pits and buried them alive. After he had hidden us and cleared away the dirt he was unable to leave quickly enough and a policeman saw him. Father tried to run away but the policemen shot and wounded him in the leg. He hid in the basement, yet there he stepped on a big hidden nail, which went through his shoe and wounded his foot even more. He became ill soon afterwards and died after a few days. This happened some time in August or September of 1942.

We obtained permission to bury Father in the cemetery. My elder brothers, together with Aron Royach who worked with my father, buried him. Any connection with an outer world, as well as money, ended with the death of my father. We didn't have anything to sell for a long while. It was a time of real tragedy for our family. Starvation was in store for us. Sometimes, one of Mum's friends would bring potatoes, buttermilk left from making cottage cheese, or pieces of bread crust into the ghetto. Thus, we barely survived until February 1943. But although warnings were frequent, we hadn't been touched as yet. My brothers would run away, but it would be over soon.

However, the final time, in early March 1943, it didn't pass us by. Izya and I were in the street when we heard a command sounding from the speakers, 'All adults should come to be newly registered in the police station.'

We were alarmed. Suddenly, I saw the police surrounding the neighbourhood of the ghetto. We went into our house and started looking for Mum, but she wasn't anywhere. Sometimes she would hide in the attic, so Izya and I went upstairs and started calling her. But there was nobody in the attic. It was very scary. Some time later, Mum came up through the opening and took us with her. We stayed in a secret place which was like a well: it was cold and dark. We were hungry but fear was stronger than hunger.

At night we got out. Mum took us into another house. There she knocked on the floor. A manhole opened and we went downstairs into the basement. There were three men: two elderly and a young one. Mum talked with them and we stayed. I was coughing, and everybody was angry. Soon after that, the men left the place, one after another. We remained alone, and then Mum decided we should leave too. We went upstairs from the basement and returned to our house. Mum told us to wait for her in the street. When she came out, she put a package with pictures and documents into my clothes. Once we were outside on the road, we could hear the sound of hooves on the road pavement.

We quickly went up to a sentry box on the other side of the road. The patrol stopped near the box and asked loudly, 'Who is there?'

We went silent and the patrol went on without looking behind the box. Mum took us towards a wooden bridge across the Southern Bug. But the bridge was lit up and there was a checkpoint. Then she took us to the Zamok, where there was a stone bridge. The bridge had been bombed. Then Mum made me go down from the high slope to the river and see whether there was water or ice. I went down but couldn't see and told Mum that there was water. And again we went back to the wooden bridge. She was hesitant. I was afraid that the patrol would be back and started convincing Mum to cross the bridge.

She took the package from me and said, 'Take Izya by his hand, and go. Once you cross the bridge, go down into the park, stand behind a tree and wait for me.'

With fear in my heart, together with Izya, I walked across the well-lit bridge. We reached the sentry box. Nobody called us back. We successfully passed by the box and reached the park. There, we hid behind a tree and waited for mum. She stepped on to the bridge. We could hear her steps loud in the silence of the night. When she almost reached the sentry box, we heard, 'Who is there?'

Mum could only say, 'Oh …'

And a policeman took her back to the police station. We never saw her again.

We stood there and couldn't come to our senses. Then we began to cry loudly but nobody could hear us. The snow was deep and soft everywhere. It was very difficult to walk. I only knew how to go to Sokolovka, but we kept walking in circles and coming back to the river over and over again. Finally, we got out of the park to the road and soon found ourselves on a village street. This was the village of Mazurivka. We entered the first open gates and found ourselves in a country house yard. There was no dog. We sat down on the kerb and, being exhausted, we fell asleep. Soon afterwards, an old man came out of the house and, seeing us, he became scared and began crossing himself. I raised my head and he saw we were alive. He calmed down and took us into his house. His wife got up too. I told them everything about us. The old man gave us each a slice of bread with butter and honey. After we had eaten, he started asking where we were heading. I told him the first thing I was thinking about, 'We are going to Sokolovka.' Then he told us that his son, a policeman, was on duty, and it was by fortunate accident that we hadn't encountered him. We couldn't go along the road. He showed us another road to Sokolovka, through vegetable gardens. But snow was deep there, too. We continued with much difficulty and cried, since we were exhausted. Izya grew tired and kept asking to be carried. I couldn't take him in my arms, let alone carry him. With great difficulty we finally got out to the well-trodden road. We kept going forward. We could see people riding carts to the market. It was probably Sunday. One cart stopped and two young men jumped off. They were dressed in tall hats and long traditional coats. They started chasing us to catch us and turn us in to the police. We screamed and tried to get away from them. A few women came over and rescued us. We went forward again, asking nobody about anything. I don't know how long we continued in that way but one woman asked us where we were going. When she heard we were headed for Sokolovka, she turned us back and showed us another way, across the field. When we reached the village, I didn't recognize it because we entered from the other end. We approached some houses. A woman came out of one of them, and came towards us. She asked us what had happened and from where we had come so early. She took us into her house and kept us there until the evening. In the evening she took us to the house where we had lived earlier with our grandma. Yasha and Pinya were already there. I cried and told them everything. They listened to us in silence as if they had already known about this. Then they took us to the attic of the house. They put us behind the chimney and covered us with straw. It was very cold during the night. Early in the morning they left to go somewhere and came back in the evening. They called to see if we were still there and gave us a few pancakes. After we had eaten, they got us up and took us into the field. There they put us into a haystack and got into it themselves. Early in the morning they woke us up and took us out on to the road.

They brought us to some village and said, 'Go into it, and don't leave it. When the war is over, we will come and get you. And now we shall go back to our home and from there, we shall try to cross the front line.'

I became very scared. A lump was in my throat. They turned and walked away. I tried to scream but there was no sound coming out. Suddenly, my voice sounded, 'Pinya!'

They stopped and looked back. Pinya also began to cry.

Yasha hurried; he said, 'It is late now.'

And they walked away.

We entered the village. We approached the houses, but there was something alarming, strange, emanating from this unknown place. I took Izya by the hand and we ran out of the village. We wanted to catch up with our brothers but there was nobody in the field. I cried and called them.

We couldn't see anyone around, and there was no road. Suddenly we heard singing, and started to call. But the man, who was riding a cart, didn't hear us. Then we ran downhill, following the cart. Thus we came back to Sokolovka again.

Perhaps it was the following morning, or a few days after, that we stood out in the street, and a woman from this village came up to us. She whispered to us that the day before she had been to Novaya Sinyava and saw how police had caught Yasha, and Pinya turned himself in after that. The police beat them with gun butts on their heads, and they were pleading for them not to. Then, the police put them on a cart and took them away. I didn't believe this. It seemed to me that nothing could have happened to them so soon, and they would definitely survive. For many years we lived in hope that our brothers had survived and simply couldn't find us.

We were left all alone in this wide world. There was a whole year to go before the liberation.

Nobody wanted to take us and give us shelter since it was dangerous and difficult to feed two more children. For greater safety we walked from Sokolovka to Mazurivka and back. Once we were in a house of a teacher from the Mazurivka School. His wife warmed some water; I washed my hair and started to comb my long curls.

Suddenly the teacher ran into the house, all scared and shaking. He cried, 'Leave immediately! A drunken policeman is walking on the streets looking for you! He asks, "Where are the little Jews?"'

And so he took us out through the vegetable gardens, towards the river. But even here the police were searching. There was a raid on girls who were hiding from going as labour to Germany. We were completely frightened and walked up to some boys who were baking potatoes. I think they were cow herders. Although it was very cold and everybody was dressed warmly, there was no snow anywhere. Suddenly I raised my eyes, and saw a policeman heading towards us. My heart sank. He came to our group and asked whether we had seen any girls.

We shouted 'No.'

He stood with us for a while and then walked away towards the clay pit where people were getting red clay. After he was gone, the boys remembered we were there and started to send us away. I hesitated. Then they started beating us up with whips. The whips hit us on our faces, too. It was very painful.

Izya and I left them, although we didn't know where to head. I was frightened. I started hallucinating. There was nobody in front of us, and yet suddenly I saw a policeman, walking towards us dressed in full uniform. I would shut my eyes, then open them, and there was nobody.

But this time we didn't go to the village. We found a hiding place in some ditch and sat there the whole night through. It was very difficult for us. We didn't know where to spend our nights. Most frequently we slept in the cellars, sheds and barns, if the gates were left open. And once we got into a big kennel. It was very tight but warm. But then we were really scared by the very drunken owner of this place. He leaned down and saw children instead of the dog. We were woken up by the shouting and saw his face and smelled heavy spirits. During the day we hung around the village, walking through the mud and only thinking of where to get some food. Mostly people would not refuse, and gave us a bowl of borsch and a slice of bread. But there were also people who would say, 'Why are you wandering around here? Go to your Palestine!'

I didn't know what Palestine was but I understood it was a place for Jews. I felt bitter. 'Why Palestine?' I was born here, and nobody told me how to get there.

Once a young woman approached me and said with a smile, 'Zhenya, I would take you to watch over my geese, but your brother mucks things up. Let's drown him.'

I became very frightened. Perhaps she was joking, but it was scary. In the day we tried to stay behind the vegetable gardens so that people would not see us much. It was cold already and I fell ill. I lay by the road. I was very weak and felt sleepy. Izya sat by my side and cried. He wanted to eat and I couldn't get up. I don't know how it would have ended if a friend of our family had not found us. She gave Izya and me some milk and said that soon one of her relatives would go to Zhmerinka to sell something and would take us there, since here somebody could turn us over to police. She told us where and when to come. When the time came, we got on to a cart, were covered with straw and went away. Early in the morning, the cart stopped in a forest. We got out, and together with one woman we went towards Zhmerinka. She took us into the ghetto. Dr Gerschman was the Kommandant there. When we went to see him, we saw two men there. One of them was with his family. The Kommandant could not accept them since he was frightened. Jews were coming from all over the Vinnitsa oblast. Anybody who was alive was trying to get to Zhmerinka. The Kommandant was afraid the Germans would start fighting with local Romanian authorities. That is why he refused to accept adults, but he let Izya and me stay. But somebody from the ghetto would have accepted us. One woman, who was originally from Vapnyarka, gave us shelter. Others helped her feed us. We had lice. She decided into put us in order – she took me out to the street, behind her barn, and started combing my sticky hair. The lice were tumbling out as if somebody was spilling grain. A whole yellow trail appeared. Then she cut some of my hair with scissors. Thus we stayed on in Zhmerinka. I was very surprised that everything here was like it would normally be. Beds had linen on; it was warm and clean everywhere. People were trying to earn their living any way they could. Some made shoes, some made clothes or hats. We lived there the whole winter. There were many people here who were also worried, but virtually everybody survived. There was a school too, but somehow we didn't attend it.

When our army liberated Zhmerinka, people started to get ready to go on the road again. We also decided to go to Khmelnik, since we thought we would find someone alive there from our family. We came to Khmelnik and went over to the ghetto. We kept thinking we would see the house where we had lived, we would enter it and see our mum there. But ruins were everywhere. Our house was ruined too and the foundation was the only thing left. Not knowing what to do next, we went to a house where our relatives used to live. This house was outside the ghetto and was still standing there. I wanted to enter it and see what was inside but a woman with clean laundry came out of it.

I asked her, 'Our relatives used to live here, do you know where they are?'

She said she was a refugee from Taganrog. The house had already been empty when she settled here. And again, the emptiness was all over and around us. And again we began to wander, this time through the rubble.

We went to the militia a few times, to ask about our relatives, but the militiaman on duty didn't know anything. Another boy, who was deaf and mute, and a man were walking through the town too. They looked wild and we were afraid of them. Once the woman from Taganrog saw us in the street and said, 'Come to me into the kindergarten.'

Thus we began to live in the kindergarten. We slept in small beds where we couldn't extend our legs. Parents would come and take their children back home. Everything went on as if there had not been a war, and nothing had happened. And we stayed on in the kindergarten because all of our family had perished.

Soon, escorted by a kindergarten instructor, we went to an orphanage. They put us on to an open carriage loaded with lumber, and told us to hold on to the logs tightly. We came to the village of Kalinovka, and then walked on to Yanovka where the orphanage was. But they wouldn't accept us there because they had a pertussis outbreak, and we didn't have any documents. The woman escorting us was trying to prove that we were not her children. Eventually she left us behind and went back to the railway station. She told us not to leave. They put us into medical isolation quarters. Every morning they would take us out to the river, put us on a stone by its side in our shirts only. Thus we would sit until somebody came to pick us up. We were very cold and we cried loudly. But the pertussis outbreak was over. However, I developed pleuritis and I was put into a hospital far away from the orphanage and Izya was transferred into the younger group at the orphanage.

When I was back from the hospital, Izya was in medical isolation again. This time he was ill with measles. I felt sad also because many children had their fathers return from the war. These children received some special attention! By the time their parents came, the children were dressed in American clothes, and the staff treated them gently. When we went to eat in the diner we would meet the German prisoners of war. They ate with us. They would watch us attentively while we would watch them.

Once I was running around in the yard with other children and the orphanage's director called me to him and said, 'You will now go to another orphanage.'

My heart sank. 'How can I go when my brother is ill?'

'He'll get better and we shall send him too.'

Thus Izya and I were separated in different orphanages and didn't see each other for seven years.

In the summer of 1951, the group of children from our orphanage, headed by Fedor Savelievvich Ruzhizky, went to Vinnitsa to a school *olympiad*. We were accommodated in one of the Vinnitsa schools. Next to us, some other children were accommodated.

Once, our girls came back running to me and said, 'Go there; there is a boy who says he is your brother.'

I got very nervous but went out. A thin boy of about twelve years old was standing there in front of me. All his face was in scarred. I got scared and ran away. The girls started telling me that this was my brother. I returned. He approached me and I invited him to our place. We were embarrassed to hug since so many eyes were watching us. He told me that after the measles he had developed encephalic inflammation. He was saved by a miracle: a random commission of visiting doctors from Kiev performed surgery on his brain. It took a lot of effort for my group leader and Izya's group leader to persuade the directors to leave Izya in the Bratslav orphanage where I was.

Now we were together, in one orphanage, but it was still very different from being in a family. We felt ourselves rootless. When our elder brothers perished we lost the last opportunity of restoring connections with our relatives.

Many years have passed since. I am now a grandmother myself. Once I decided to go to my hometown of Khmelnik, although it was very frightening. I came there in 1987. My God, what happened to me there! It felt as if all the years were gone instantly. It was as if all my family was there only yesterday, and walked along those pavements, streets and the bridge. I was choking on tears. I entered the church and gave freedom to my emotions.

I called Izya. He came and together with him I went to visit tombs of our people innocently killed. There is one place in a field with three thousand people. There are five or six other sites in a forest and yet another three in another place. Where are our relatives, our grandma and mum? Where are our brothers? Are they in the forest between Staraya Sinyava and Novaya Sinyava or in a mass burial at the sugar refinery? Where were they killed? We installed a small memorial to our family at the Jewish cemetery in Khmelnik where our father was buried. Unfortunately, his grave has been lost. They are all now in our memory only.

33. Not a single Jew survived out of three thousand people

Ida Kritman (b. 1925)

On 20 June 1941, I graduated with honours from the tenth form of a Ukrainian school, and Lyusik Greis, my classmate, took his and my documents to apply to the Kiev Medical Institute.

My parents both worked at a railway station, and never had the time to be evacuated. The Germans entered the town on 3 July 1941. In September all the Jews from three little towns – Yampol, Belogory and Korchinets – were put into a ghetto in the town of Belogory. Two streets were assigned for this purpose (about fifty houses in total, mostly old with mud floors). These were surrounded by barbed wire. We slept on the ground, putting our clothes underneath us or wearing them when sleeping. Police with dogs guarded us and the Germans rarely came. The police started taking us out into the *kolkhoz* fields immediately to dig potatoes and sugar beet.

Winter was a time of great cold and hunger. My father was hired to work with horses in the Belogory hospital, due to friends' help, and when he came back to the ghetto at night, he would almost always bring leftovers from the hospital. This helped us greatly in our survival.

I studied in a Ukrainian school, and my parents had many friends and acquaintances among the Ukrainians. When the Germans came, my parents gave away some of their possessions to these people. And when we were relocated to the ghetto they would come, with much difficulty, and bring us bread and boiled potatoes and throw them across the wire fencing.

The regime in the ghetto was very strict, especially for young people, who tried to get out by various means. My friends were killed: Hannah Kornblit, a beautiful blue-eyed blonde; Izya Takhman, a wonderful young man, another honours student; and young men from other places too. The police also killed our neighbour, an eighty-year-old woman, respected greatly by everyone, and her son-in-law.

On 20 July 1942, Fedya Rudyuk, my former classmate, having spoken to a policeman he knew, got me out of the ghetto. He gave his new bicycle, presented to him in the early days of occupation, to the policeman to achieve this. During the night we reached Yampol. And on 27 July a week after my escape, all prisoners – including my mother and father, my mother's sister and their four younger children, my father's sister and her husband – were all killed in a forest near the village of Karasin. Not a single Jew survived out of three thousand people.

Kolya Voshchilo, a Red Army commander, knew about my rescue, and helped me at a later stage. (He became surrounded and went back to Yampol: he headed the partisans' unit.) Families of Kolesnik, Kapitonets, and Migal also hid me.

In the period of 20 July 1942 to 3 March 1944, I was kept in sheds, in attics, in haystacks, and in pits.

On 24 February 1944, Germans drove out all the local population of Yampol towards the west, the battle lasted for a week and I had to sit in a damp pit with no water or food. Only on 3 March when partisans entered Yampol, together with the regular army, did I call on hearing the voice of a partisan I knew, who was sent out by Kolya Voshchilo to find me.

'Come, get out, the Germans are gone!'

It was evening and there was a fire far away and everywhere there was black melting snow. I was taken to the house of Kolya Voshchilo's parents (I couldn't walk); I was given water and some food.

I don't know how I survived alone out of 3,000 prisoners.

To my deepest regret, Fedya Rudyuk is long gone (he died young, from TB); Kolya Voshchilo, Parfen Fedorovich Migal and his wife, Terentiy Kolesnik and his wife Praskovya, Dmitry Kapitonets and Maria, his wife, all passed away; to them I am deeply indebted for my salvation.

Out of the men and women of my age who studied in the Jewish school, only one girl and two men survived, because they had all managed to flee Yampol the day before the Germans entered it.

34. One day in the life of the ghetto was a whole tragedy

Alexander Kuperman (b. 1928)

Gaivoron, my hometown, is a small but very beautiful town located on the left bank of the Southern Bug. Twenty-five to twenty-eight thousand people had lived there before the war.

Our childhood in those pre-war years was wonderful. People of all nationalities lived as one family not differentiating between Russians, Ukrainians, Jews, Byelorussians and others. We went to school together, shared pioneer activities, played football, swam in the Southern Bug, and organized sports events. I remember how back in 1939, the best students of the fourth to tenth forms were taken for two weeks to tour Kiev: we received so many impressions then!

But this happiness did not last for long.

The treacherous aggression of Nazi Germany cut our happy life short. Five of my own brothers went to the front and three did not come back. My father was not drafted, being older (he was fifty-eight years old then), and he was put in charge of transporting young men aged sixteen to seveteen to the rear, in the east. That's why he was not able to evacuate our family on time.

However, we left on a horse-driven carriage when the Germans were already as close as twenty-five kilometres away from Gaivoron. In three day we managed to reach a village about thirty-five kilo-metres from Dniepropetrovsk. But we entered an area surrounded by the Germans and had to return home in early August 1941.

The Germans and Hungarians made my father labour at harvesting the fields. And then the most horrible time began. On 30 August 1941, at three in the morning, we heard a terrible knocking on the window and then something fell down. My father got out of the house and saw I. Feldman, a butcher, under the window on the ground, covered in blood. My father took him in his arms and carried him into the house. He put him on the bed and my mother ran across the vegetable garden to another street asking an old Ukrainian paramedic to come and help. He came, did his very best, and the butcher lived yet another day, till the major day of slaughter of all the Jews of Gaivoron.

My father believed in kindness and all that is good in people and in the great friendship of the Soviet people. On 30 August, he went to the local headman, named Chernushko, with whom he had worked before the war and with whom he was friends.

He calmed my father saying, 'Go home, Yosif, everything will be fine.'

My father believed him.

On the night of 31 August 1941 a few people got together in our house: my father, Faina Samoilovna, my mother, my brother, David (who had escaped from imprisonment in the infamous 'Uman pot'), my brother's wife, Faina, Yasha, a four-year-old boy, and me.

The same day, at two in the morning, police came and started knocking on the door demanding it be opened – claiming they need to check passports. But my father wouldn't open. He was a brave and courageous man, and quite strong. The police, headed by F. Chebatul, deputy chief of police, surrounded the house and started shooting at the roof. This lasted over an hour.

Then my mother said, 'Open it. They will never leave but will burn down the house with us inside it.'

My father listened to her and opened the door. The police barged in and, to keep up the pretence, asked us to take our passports with us. My father and brother made a seat out of their hands and put old Feldman on it, and the police took us all to their station which was housed in the building of the former railway militia. There we were locked in the cells and in the morning we all were all separated. My father and I stayed in one cell, David and Izya, our cousin, in another; the women and younger children were transferred into a building belonging to the former district militia.

In the morning these bandits brought us cocoa and white bread, telling us, 'See how kind we are; we shall sort things out and send you to work.'

On 31 August 1941, at 10 a.m., three policemen entered the room, headed by N. Khomenko, another deputy chief of police, and told my father to go with them. My father took me in his arms, kissed me, and said nothing but looked very carefully at me, then he looked at the policemen and left. When they were escorting him along the hallway, one of the bandits shot and wounded him in his leg. My father turned around and with one punch put three of his guards down. It was then that V. Lisitsa, the chief of police, and a few more policemen came running in. They killed my father with two shots to his head. Hearing this, I started to cry hard and scream, and this lasted the whole day. Frol Yanizky, a policeman on duty that day, took me out of the cell for a few minutes to get fresh air, gave me water and told me how things had happened. This police-

man didn't take part in the killings. He was forced into the police.
He knew me from the school – I played football for the Locomotive
children's team with his younger brother, Vassily.

Over thirty Jews beside our family were arrested on this horrible
night, including Menachem, my father's brother, his wife, son Izya,
and daughter Nelya. My uncle was killed on the bank of the
Southern Bug; my brother, David, and my cousin were killed in the
police station's basement. Nelya was taken into the police yard in
the night, shot and left. However, she survived, and, though bleeding heavily, she reached the German regional Kommandant's office.

The Kommandant ordered her to be put in a room and called
German doctors who carried out surgery. She was very beautiful and
she was seventeen then. (People said that this Kommandant was
killed later by the Germans for helping partisans with weapons.)

And so this Kommandant sent his major, who brought us all
together in the yard of the police station on the evening of 31 August.

The major spoke: 'We are not coming to kill civilians.'

But this turned out to be a lie. They kept us in the police station
till the midnight, and then took us into the chief's office, and he
started lecturing us, telling us that he was a son of a Russian noble-
man and now we could appreciate his situation. He told us that his
father was killed by the Soviets and he had spent fifteen years in
prison, lost all of his property and now had to restore everything. He
told us that we would go to work on the restoration of the railway.

At one in the morning were taken to the railway station, where a
trolley was standing along side the platform. We all were put in this
and policemen stood above us carrying machine-guns and pistols in
their hands. They took us to a place about eight kilometres away
from Gaivoron, called Khashchevatoye. Near Mukhovo, not having
reached our destination, the convoy stopped near a fifty-metre cliff
surrounded by woods. The first shot wounded my mother's chin
and we rolled down. She covered me with her body about three to
four metres away from the pit into which all the dead people were
falling. When these bandits were throwing bodies into the pit they
found out that a boy was missing.

M. Kazimirchuk, an old bandit, said, 'We counted these Jews
poorly.'

For an hour we stayed down with Mum, trying not to breathe,
and when they had left the place we went along the slope to the
opposite side of the ravine, and stayed there, in the bushes, until
five in the morning. Then we returned home. The house was
locked, so we broke the window and got in. Everything that
was good in the house we gave to our neighbours. This was all
accomplished within two hours, and then we went towards

Khashchevatoye, where my mum's younger sister lived together with her son, Milya. There my mum left me and a day later returned to Gaivoron, and went to Chernushko, the headman. And again he reassured her that there would be no more killings. But this gang of over a hundred policemen killed over eighty Soviet POWs, beside Jews. The very same policemen were killing Jews in Uman, Pervomaisk, Odessa and Kiev.

To justify themselves, the Nazis organized demonstrative funerals. They arrested N. Khomenko, the deputy chief of police, and three other policemen. On the day of the funeral of my father, my brother David, cousin Izya, old P Gorodezky, father of a local watch repairman, M. Velsher, baker, and E. Gurfinkel, engineer, their bodies were laid on two carts. People from all over the city were brought together, and these four policemen had to follow the carts, being beaten with rubber whips. Then at the corner of a Ukrainian cemetery, a grave was dug and a meeting led by the same German major who had spoken earlier at the police station.

A few days later, the Germans arranged another demonstrative performance. They shot these four policemen at the Polish cemetery, near a church. They were brought out and each of them had to dig his own grave. Then German SS men allowed them to eat chocolate candies and cross themselves and then shot them with machine-guns set up on motorcycles.

After that, Mum and I lived in my brother's house. But at the end of October 1941, all Jews who returned to Gaivoron from other place, and u, were again brought together at the police station. We thought that, again, killings would follow, but SS with shepherd dogs surrounded us and escorted us to the ferry that used to connect Gaivoron with Solgutovo on the right bank of the Southern Bug.

The chief SS officer told us, 'Go, Jews, wherever you want.'

And we went to the town of Bershad, where we got into the notorious Bershad ghetto.

What was the Bershad ghetto like? It included three or four streets no longer than one and a half kilometres, with mostly Jewish homes built back in the eighteenth or nineteenth century. The ghetto was surrounded with three layers of the barbed wire, with electric wiring in one of them. There was only one exit from the ghetto. In the winter of 1941/42, there were over 150,000 Jews in the ghetto, including 25,000 from Ukraine, 75,000 from Bessarabia and about 50,000 from Bukovina.

At that time, typhoid and famine began in the ghetto. I was sick with typhoid for over fifty days, and when I got up after the crisis there was nothing to eat. My mum would make me soup from potato peelings. People were dying each day, 150–200 daily. They were not buried but, instead, were put on to a cart and in winter dumped in the fields. My mum and I suffered through this hell for two and a half years, until 12 March 1944.

I think I was lucky for the second time in my life. The first time was when I survived the shootings. The second time was when I found a job in those unthinkably horrible and impossible conditions, when people lived with the continuous thought of death, and each and everyone of us was a walking corpse, while all ways to human life were closed. I was not yet thirteen then. The team that demolished Jewish homes beyond the ghetto borders hired me. Then my cousin found me a job as assistant to a private baker. (After some time I became a first-class baker myself.) When I worked for this man, I had to work seventeen or eighteen hours a day, and got paid with a kilogram loaf of barley bread, which saved my mum and myself from starvation and death. However, fears, tortures and horrors stayed with us every day and every hour.

Once, in the middle of the night, early in the winter of 194, when I was working at the bakery, I heard shots and screams in the rooms where the baker and his family lived. Five drunken Germans and a Romanian had broken into the flat, and started a real riot. It was fortunate that everyone managed to hide in the basement and the Nazis didn't go there. They were shooting their handguns into the basement and we hid in the side niches where they used to store potatoes and vegetables. They smashed and ruined everything in the house, and left, not taking anything with them.

When the Soviet army was preparing for the Korsun-Shevchenkovsky battle, the German Kommandant of Uman fled to Bershad. There were ruthless animals, but he was the worst. He used to go through the town with his dog. He was as small as a dwarf, and had a dog that was just as small. Once, when he was going along the street that led to the marketplace, a couple with a child crossed his path. He shot them for it. A few days later, in late December of 1943, he walked into a two-storeyed house in the ghetto, took twelve people out on to the balcony, killed them all and threw them down from the balcony. For a month, he didn't allow people to bury them. If anybody had moved their bodies, the whole ghetto would have been destroyed.

The Romanians were not much better than Germans. The ghetto was located in the territory occupied by Romanians, who tortured the ghetto prisoners day and night. On one summer day of 1942, a group of Romanians led by their 'platooner' [lieutenant] entered the ghetto, where the Jewish marketplace was established and where there were many people. They selected three or four young, very beautiful, Jewish girls, took them to their barracks, and made them go 'through their ranks'. The girls died.

Mikhail Kreiman, my uncle, went to his home in the winter of 1941, to get some food. Romanians caught him in the village of Ovsievka, beat him up severely, threw him into a shed, and locked him in there. It was very cold, the temperature was lower than thirty degrees. He had frostbite in both feet.

But people didn't stop hoping, kept their spirits high, and daily and hourly struggled for life, organizing partisan struggles. Yakov Lazarevich Dyshnevich, a Soviet major, and my cousin, Grigory Borisovich Kuperman, an artillery captain, headed this fight. Their partisan units were located in Bershad and Gaisin woods and were active throughout the Vinnitsa oblast. People from the ghetto were helping them with whatever they could – clothes, food, etc. … but fate was cruel to them. Only three and a half months before our liberation by the Soviet Army, during one of the military missions in Bershad, eight people were caught by the Nazis and hanged on the lampposts along the main street of the town. Another six people were shot. Partisans were killed in a barbarous manner: first, a person would be dragged behind a motorcycle at high speed along the highway, and then he would be hanged.

My cousin was shot three days before Bershad was liberated. One day in the life of the ghetto was a whole tragedy. Our biggest desire was to stay alive and to be liberated by the Red Army. And such a day finally came on 12 March 1944. Young Siberian soldiers, in white coats, told us at 7 a.m. that as of now we were free and beyond danger.

When the Great Patriotic War was over, Mum and I counted those of our family and closest relatives who perished at the front, in the Nazi prisons, death camps and ghettos. We counted ninety-three people. This happened in Gaivoron, Uman, Pervomaisk, Kiev and Bershad.

35. I was thirteen then

Sima Kuritzkaya (Zukher) (b. 1928)

When the war began, the town of Pryluki was occupied and, together with my family, we stayed in the occupied territories. From 18 September 1941, the very first day of the occupation, the Nazis began their ruthless persecution of the Jewish population. Everybody was ordered to wear armbands and soon all Jews were relocated into the ghetto. People were suffocating from the dirt and decomposing corpses everywhere, which Jews had to take away themselves on carts.

I was in the ghetto with my parents and brother in the period of September 1941 through to 20 May 1942, when the Germans posted an announcement commanding all Jews to proceed to Pliskunivsky Bridge for resettlement. On a wonderful sunny day in May when everything in nature was blossoming, a group of barely alive Jews was taken at gunpoint towards Pliskunovka, into a ravine. There, they were put in rows and shot. I hid behind my mum's back and when we fell into the pit I was not wounded. The Germans thought I had been killed. When it got dark, I climbed out of the pit and went away without knowing where. I was thirteen then, and my parents were killed.

By 20 May 1942, the Jewish population of the town of Pryluki no longer existed. All Jews had been killed.

My ensuing life was filled with wanderings. I used a strange Ukrainian name, and begged for food. I got hired in different places doing jobs that were beyond possible for my age. I was hungry, naked, barefoot, and in continuous fear that somebody would guess who I was and turn me in. I even cried when nobody could see me. I cried for my parents. But I kept telling everyone that I did not know my parents, that I had been raised at an orphanage.

My wanderings during the two years of the occupation took their toll on me. When thirty, I was disabled of the second degree, and at thirty-two I had complicated heart surgery.

36. I did not know where my mum and Dad were, I never saw them again

Klavdia Lepa (Bagmeiter) (b. 1929)

I was born in Berdychev. I lived with my parents and two brothers at 5 Shkolnaya Street. My dad's name was Petya, Mum's name was Riva, and my brothers' names were Isaac and Borya. My dad worked in a shop, and Mum stayed at home. Before the war I went to a Ukrainian school, studied with honours, and had an ordinary life of a common girl.

When the war began our family did not manage to leave.

First, they started to take away Jewish men. Germans went into the houses and wherever there were men, they took them away. My uncle, Mum's brother, was taken then. They were locked up in a museum and nobody was allowed in. But I looked Russian and could get in and take him some food.

He kept saying, 'Tell my family that I will survive.'

But two days later I went and he was not there – the Germans had killed him. There were also prisoners of war kept there.

Beside that, all Jews who dared to walk the streets in the town were seized too, since this was forbidden. We were allowed to walk only outside the town.

I helped Jews who lived at my grandma's – I went to buy everything they needed because they were not allowed to go out in the street.

September 15 was the day of the murder of the Jews in our town. My older brother could have saved himself – he was a friend of those who went into the police.

A day before he had gone to see some of his friends and they had told him, 'Tomorrow there will be a horrible atrocity. Stay here, you won't be able to save anybody there.'

But he didn't want to stay.

Then they told him, 'Tell your family to hide, everybody will be killed tomorrow.'

But where could we hide?

My mum told my brother, 'Go back to them, save yourself.'

But he wouldn't go … Perhaps, if he had known I would survive, he would have gone back there.

On 15 September about six o'clock in the morning, Ukrainian police came and began to force people out of their houses. We were taken to the marketplace where people sold fish. Those who couldn't walk were put on lorries and taken to the airport. From the marketplace we were also marched to the airport. They beat us very severely and everybody, hiding from the blows, tried to get deeper into the crowd.

I did not know where my parents were. I never saw them again.

When we arrived, we saw pits, already dug out. They started shooting near there. Everything was covered with blood and mixed up.

But one policemen looked at me and said, 'You are Ukrainian, how did you get in here?'

And he pulled me out and pushed me away. And I stood there, not knowing where to go or what to do.

Then he said, 'You go over there'.

I ran towards a beetroot field. The beets were still there, and I hid in the field.

It got very cold, and then one woman came over and said, 'Go, child, into the town. I would take you, but I can't because you're Jewish. Still, go to the town, maybe somebody will save you there.'

I went to the town but again didn't know where to go. I came to our flat and saw it all shattered. Then I found out that not all Jews had been killed. Tailors had been saved, as well as others with good professions. My Uncle Kleiman, Mum's cousin, was among them. I went to them. They asked me how I survived.

I said, 'I was pulled out. But I stayed out in the cold, and all my back is covered in abscesses.'

His wife decided to let me stay with them for a while.

One day I was sitting outside in the street when my aunt, who was a very neat person, brought a saucepan out to me, gave it to me and told me to clean it. So, I was sitting there and cleaning, when a woman passed by who used to live with us. Her surname was Golubchik. She told my aunt, 'Polya, I will take Klava for some time with me. Let her live with me for a couple of days. I will feed her.' And she took me with her.

I spent two days with her, and then I told her, 'Tanya, now I will run back to Polya. I don't want to be a bother to you.'

'Where shall you go, my child? They were all killed. If you had stayed there, you would have been dead too.'

Thus I stayed with her.

After some time she told me, 'I cannot keep you here any longer. Go wherever you can, I'll give you food to go.'

And I went out into the street. I met one of my friends. She told me, 'I would take you to us, but I'm scared. Go to someone else.'

I went to another friend, and her father was in the police. I stayed there a little while, and then she said, 'Go away because my father says you are a Jewess, and he will turn you in.'

I told her I had nowhere to go, and she replied, 'Go wherever you want.'

And I left them.

Then I met yet another of my former classmates. She said, 'I have an aunt, Yulia Adamovna Dombrovskaya. She will shelter you for a while, she has no one, but she drinks.' And she took me there. But it was very difficult to live there. When she got drunk, she battered her boy and me.

And then, to add to my 'adventures', I met another classmate, a certain boy named Durov. He looked at me and said, 'What is this, you are a Jewess! You are Bagmeiter, I know you well, you were a good student.'

And he ran to the police station, and they took me there. So I sat in the station, with a policeman. A German came up to me and said, '*Nicht, nicht Judeh!*' [Not a Jew]. But that boy stood there and kept saying, 'Yes, *Judeh, Judeh!*'

And the German, '*Nicht, nicht!*'

Then my hostess ran in, already drunk, with her passport. She had put me in it to receive a ration of bread for me. 'Look,' she said, 'this is my sister!'

But Durov continued to scream, 'I know her, I went to school with her, she is a Jewess.'

And they beat him up: she began it, and the policeman joined her. They let me go. The woman didn't know I was Jewish: 'If I had known you were Jewish, I would never have taken you. But I have got to like you and I will never turn you over to anybody.'

But it was not over yet.

Yulia had a husband, named Karl. Nobody knew he was a Polish Jew. He was appointed the chief of the ghetto. The ghetto was located at Bogdan Khmelnitzky Street. She sent me there, to take him some food and I didn't realize that Jews there could recognise me. And that was exactly what happened. I told Karl I was Jewish. And when I was out, he came and told his wife, 'Now, this Klava will come home, she is Jewish, I will take her away with me, she needs to be killed.'

To which she said, 'What are you up to?'

I was getting water at the pump. There were two neighbours, who told me to run away because Karl wanted to turn me in. But where could I run? I went to Khazhin, towards the Lysa Gora. I went into one flat and asked for some food, but then noticed they were whispering and going out into the yard. I thought they were going to turn me in, and fled, while they followed me. Then I hid in the high grass and they went by, while I stayed unnoticed.

I went into another flat and asked for food. They gave me food and kept me overnight, but in the morning they sent me out on my way, giving me a little bread and a small piece of salted pork lard. But again, where I was to go? I tried another home. Nobody wanted to keep me, and I returned to Yulia. She let me stay with her.

It was a very bad life there. She drank and brought home whoever she wanted. I cleaned, did the laundry, looked after her boy. Many things happened to me! Once she sent me to do the laundry on the river, and the ice moved, together with me on it. Everybody started to scream. Policemen in black coats guarded the bridges. One of them saw me drowning. He jumped into the river, right in his coat, got me out and resuscitated me.

Now I seem small but in those years I was bigger than most children of my age. I was not eligible to go to Germany to work because of my age, but nevertheless they tried to take me there.

The woman who fostering me did not want to let me go, and hid me in her cellar. I spent a few nights there while the raids lasted. But there were rats in the cellar and they bit my left arm. I screamed so loudly that her neighbours heard and came over. When they opened the door, they almost killed the woman. And she kept saying, 'But I have saved her.'

My arm would not heal for a long time. She brought some doctors, but they said the arm needed to be amputated – I had a blood infection, and nothing could be done about it. There were no medicines. But a Hungarian named Peter, a good man, was visiting Yulia. He said he would help me, and he took me to where the Hungarians were stationed. Their doctor told me that no amputation was necessary, and started putting on some ointment. And my arm slowly started to heal.

I remember Gestapo officers going through the village. They wore big boots, with wide boot legs and nailed heels, and 'God is with us' was inscribed on their belts. They would walk into houses and ask, 'Are there any *Judeh*?'

And although I sometimes would be there, they could not tell the difference, and recognize a Jew in me. One time, one of them caught me, took me in his arms, and said, '*Du bist Jude* [You are a Jew].'

But Yulia jumped up with her passport, and started saying, '*Nicht, nicht Jude, schwester* [sister].'

And he kept saying, 'All your neighbours say that is she a *Jude*.'

To which she replied that she didn't know who would say that, and she wanted them to leave.

And he said, 'I will now shoot you, and shoot her.'

And she replied, 'Go ahead, shoot.'

But he only shot into the ceiling.

I lived with Yulia for a long time. Later, I lived with her aunt, Mikhailovskaya. But there I had to hide in the cellar, and I couldn't stay there for long. I went to Filya Domanskaya, stayed with her for some time, helped her around the house and looked after her child. But neighbours started inquiring, who was the girl living at her place? She said I was her niece, to which they said, she had never seemed to have a niece before, while now she had one. And again I left. This time, I went to the Kozlovsky family. They knew I was Jewish, but Kozlovsky was with the police and they never came to his place, because they knew a policeman would never hide a Jew. I didn't live there for long; they didn't want to take risks. And I went to the Sidlezkys. They were Yulia's neighbours. She came to visit me frequently and brought over some food. The Sidlezkys also had quite bad neighbours who started asking where this girl had come from. They brought a policeman in, who took me to the Gestapo (who were based where we had the militia before the war). Sidlezkaya ran to Yulia, saying that Klava had again been taken to the Gestapo.

Yulia came with her passport again, screaming, 'She is not Jewish, look at this!'

The chief of the Gestapo walked in, and shot his gun near her. She was so concerned about me, she made neighbours cross themselves and crossed herself, saying that I was not Jewish, and they let me go. I lived briefly with the Sidlezkys.

When the war was over, I lived with Yulia. She took me back again, being afraid I would get killed.

All our neighbours – and there had been many of them before the war, – were killed. The Rabinovich family (seven people), the Shokolads, the Dolgonos, the Rudinskys … I don't remember now all of them, it has been over fifty years.

I didn't have any relatives left. But then I heard there were people with complete notebooks of surnames: they were searching for relatives who could have survived. I saw the Bagmeiter surname in one of these books. It turned out I still had a living uncle. They gave me his address, and I wrote to him. His family replied to me immediately with a telegram and came and took me away.

We lived in very difficult conditions, there was no place to sleep, and nothing to eat, but they kept me although there were six in the family. I went to school. I wanted to continue my education but it was impossible then. I started working as an accountant in a small local company.

Later, I got married. At first I worked, but then I had children. We have never lived in luxury, but we have good children, they studied well.

37. These were the first living Jews they met during the war

Regina Leshchinskaya (Sudobitzkaya) (b. 1930)

In 1933, my family moved to the town of Tulchin, Vinnitsa oblast, where we had lived before the war. My family consisted of my father, Mikhail Ilyich Sudobitzky; my mother, Sophia Lvovnay; my sister, Faina; and myself. I had completed three grades before the war, and my sister, nine. My father was a printer and he worked at the Tulchin printworks; my mother was a homemaker.

Two weeks after the war started, everybody began to evacuate. Families of party members and those in the military were leaving. On 20 July, my father printed the final issue of a newspaper and we left, and two or three days later our town was occupied by the Germans.

We suffered bombings along our way. The Germans caught us up near Alexandria, Kirovograd oblast. They humiliated us in every possible manner. My father was forced to look at the sun, and thus they kept him for two hours. We looked at our father and couldn't recognize him; his hair turned grey right in front of us. And then we got bombed again, this time by the Soviet planes.

In the village of Reshetilovka, Poltava oblast, they took away our horses and there we saw the first murdered Jewish man. From there we began our long way back home, to Tulchin. On 1 September, German lorries stopped us near the village of Tishlyk, and again they started picking on my dad, because he was Jewish and still alive. And then they took him away, put him into the lorry, took him out into the field and killed. We went on. And, a few days later, the mass killings began.

Early the next year (I don't remember the exact date), we reached Ladyzhin, Vinnitsa oblast, where 650 people had been murdered the day before. Local farmers warned us that the killing squad was searching through the town for more Jews. And traitors were everywhere. One old man with a grey beard sent his grandson to the police and we were arrested. There were thirteen people just like us.

They kept us for a few days and then announced that the following day they would take us to be killed. In the morning, the adults observed the Judgement Day.

They took us to be killed, but at that very moment a courier came and brought an order cancelling the murder of Jews on this side of the Bug. All the territory from the border to the Bug, including Odessa, Kherson and a part of Vinnitsa oblast, was under the supervision of the Romanians, and the Romanian king was against killing Jews in his territories.

When they released us, we all got settled in one house. It was very scary; all houses stood empty, with broken windows, burgled. In the night, people came to congratulate us because we had survived and to celebrate *Rosh haShanah*.

A few days later my mum was allowed to leave with her children for Tulchin. But on *Yom Kippur*, in the morning, all Jews were taken out to the central square – all women, children, and old people – and they were kept for the whole day outside, in the hot weather, with no water or food. Ten of the younger girls were selected and taken away somewhere. They returned home only late at night, on foot.

Then, we all were taken to the ghetto; they put us in one street, with two to three families sharing one room. But this did not seem enough for them either and, on 7 November 1941, they took us to the death camp, in the village of Pechera (then in the Shpikovsky district and now in the Tulchin district of the Vinnitsa oblast). We spent two and a half years there.

When we were taken there, weak, those who lagged behind were killed with batons. Policemen guarded us. One old woman committed suicide by hanging herself during the night.

During the first winter, many people died from typhoid, hunger and cold. Our family survived only because my sister managed to go to the village of Pechera, villages and further afield, where she asked for food. Local farmers would help her, sharing whatever they could, though they risked their lives immensely.

I remember how once a Romanian from the Kommandant's office came to our camp with the dog. We had one person who was deaf and mute. The Romanian set his dog on him because this man didn't say 'Hello' to him. Screaming broke out all over the camp. But this Romanian demanded that the deaf and mute man say 'Hello', claiming he was an imposter.

We got water from the Bug. The Germans were on the other side of the river. It frequently happened that they would shoot at a living target and once they wounded a woman. People were on the bank, so they picked her up, brought her into the camp, bandaged her with some rags and hid her away. The Germans came over some time later and searched for her, but nobody turned her in, so they left.

In 1942, many Jews from Romania, Poland and Bessarabia were brought into our camp. But they soon died. They didn't know the language and couldn't find any common ground, even with our local Jews. I remember there was one young man among the Romanian Jews: tall and handsome; it was said he came from a cultured and very wealthy family. Because of all the horrors he had witnessed, he had gone mad – so he ran around the camp, with a small box, and begged everyone for some money. He died soon afterwards.

In the summer of 1943, they suddenly began to feed us – which hadn't happened before. They said that it was the Red Cross of America that sent this food over; yet, again, they humiliated us. We were given pea soup and pea pies that were so salty that – even being continuously starved – we couldn't eat them. And they wouldn't give us any water, and they set guards and wouldn't allow us to go down to the river to get any water. Only during the night could one boy (unfortunately I don't remember his surname) and I go down to the river and bring some water. We gave it to the children first of all.

In the autumn of 1943, during the holidays, lorries came. We were told that younger and healthier people would be selected first to go to the ghetto, yet eventually everyone would be taken. Of course, each and everyone tried to get into the first group. But my sister didn't like something about Mum's clothes; I think she wore a skirt made from a torn sack. While Mum was tidying herself up, we didn't manage to get into the first group. Each of them received a loaf of bread for the road and they were taken away. Two days later we learned that they had been taken over to the German side to repair roads. Two or three weeks later we learned that they had all been killed.

The village of Burty was not far away from the camp; a policeman named Prigoda lived there. Even the local people were afraid of him. Another policeman, Mukha, lived in another village, and he was worse than the SS. These policemen killed so many Jews!

One night, in winter, a fire started, the third floor was burning. The Kommandant said that if we didn't extinguish the fire we would live in the yard. All the people from the village came to help us. We all stood in a chain, two abreast, and passed buckets with water. Thus we extinguished the fire.

In the town of Braclav, not far away from Tulchin, in the German territory, there was another Jewish camp. They killed people all the time there. But then they changed the chief of the camp, and the murders stopped. When, in March 1944, our army started approaching Vinnitsa oblast, the chief of the Braclav camp received an order to kill all the Jews. But he didn't obey the order, and during the night he brought all of them into our camp, thus saving their lives, and he was arrested.

When our army was really close to Pechera, Germans surrounded the camp in an attempt to kill all of us. They put soldiers with machine-guns at all corners of the building. One hundred and thirty steps led down to the Bug. When the soldiers with guns went towards their posts and the wall remained open, my mum shouted to us, 'Girls, run to the Bug,' and ran herself.

My sister and I ran after her. A few more people ran too, after us. We successfully reached the stairs, about 200–300 metres away, then went down a bit and took a turn. In the fence, there was a secret entry, and we went to the village through it. When we were going down we heard gunhots, and bullets flew above our heads. One girl saw us running and also ran but it was already too late. The Germans noticed her, and she was killed when she reached the stairs. Two or three steps, and she would have been saved too.

This happened either on 9 or 10 March. We went home, to Tulchin. All those who fled with us went their own ways.

The peasants to whom we turned, asking for help, gave us some food but were afraid to let us stay overnight. We slept in a hut.

We entered Tulchin with the first Soviet tank, out of which Colonel Konev got. My mum went towards him and started kissing him. When we came to the ghetto, everybody was hiding in cellars and could not believe that Soviet soldiers were already in the town.

The village of Pechera, together with the camp, was liberated on 12 March 1944. And two days later people returned to Tulchin. They told how soldiers and officers, having liberated the camp, knelt down in front of them and cried, being shocked, since these were the first living Jews they had met during the war, especially in the death camp. When retreating, the Germans didn't have time to destroy the camp.

Nobody is able to define precisely how many people had gone through the camp, and how many were killed. Hitler never tallied the number of killed Jews. In our family, two complete family lines were destroyed: my father's relatives (all his brothers and a sister, with their families in Dubny), and all Mum's relatives. My grandma lost two of her daughters and two of her sons, five grandchildren, a daughter-in-law and a son-in-law. She herself went mad. One of Mum's brothers fell into the ditch during the killings and stayed there unconscious until the night fell, among all those killed.

He got out of the pit in the night, and reached the nearest house. There, people cleaned him and got him dressed; he crossed the front line and joined the army. He was severely wounded but again he asked to be sent to the front. He died in 1946, of complications from his wounds.

In 1949, I entered the Lvov Printer's College, and graduated from it in 1953. From August 1953 through to May 1988, I worked as a shift manager of the printing department in the Kremenchug town printers. Now I'm disabled.

There is a Jewish community in Tulchin, until recently led by Mikhail Bartik. His wife helped him a lot. I cannot help but mention them, since they did a lot to preserve the memory of those perished in the camp. They initiated raising funds and established a monuments in those places where, in 1941, the first person was killed when we were marched to the camp, as well as above those trenches where there are mass graves for the dead, and in those places where Mukha, the policeman, murdered Jews. On the gates of the former death camp there is a memorial plaque. We got together when it was erected, and came back in 1991 to observe the fiftieth anniversary of the day when we were taken to the camp; and on 12 March 1994, the fiftieth anniversary of our liberation from the camp. We went to Pechera, to the graves … There were many memories.

38. I was the only survivor
out of all our family

Galina Lissitsyna (Faerman) (b. 1928)

Each person has his or her book of memories and recollections, but one's view and assessment of the past changes along with a person's age. I would like to speak of what I went through from the point of view of the girl at the age I was in those days – because the child's memory keeps facts best preserved.

I was born on 28 November 1928. When the war started, I was a fifth-form student, and my family didn't have enough time to get evacuated. The Germans were approaching very fast and in July they were already in my hometown of Vinnitsa.

Within a month, the pogroms had begun, following which people vanished without trace. In the first raid, on 19 September 1941, my mother's brother's family was taken. He was away to the front, and his wife and two children were killed.

In January 1942, an order was issued by the town's Kommandant for all Jews to report to a stadium in order to be registered. My parents went there, having sent me away to the country. We thought that we were seeing each other for the last time then, but they let everybody go.

The second *Aktion* started on 16 April 1942. According to a new order, all Jews had to report to the stadium bringing valuable possessions, clothes and jewellery with them. Families were coming in loaded with their possessions. Many policemen were there who used truncheons to make people walk faster. We couldn't believe that they might kill all these innocent people. This day became the darkest day in my life – the terrible date when I lost everyone. This day has left its despondent trace throughout all of my life.

The issue of sorting people at the stadium was resolved promptly, since the system had been well worked out. First, all the men were selected. But still there lingered some hope that we would only be deported. Then everybody was taken out of the town in closed lorries and mobile gas chambers, to the place where graves had already been dug out. I was thirteen years old but I remember well how my mum was gripped by fear and how this fear was transferred to me. But, in all the confusion, when everybody was ordered to strip naked, by some miracle, I managed to escape. The survival instinct was so strong: I fled that horrible place where my parents were left together with my three-year-old brother. I couldn't help him in any way. I was terrified; the forest was filled with screams, laments and shots. Thus, the 'Jewish question' in Vinnitsa was 'finally solved'.

Much later, the Germans and the policemen – not completely satisfied with the murder in the forest beside the Litinskoye highway – searched for new victims. They were killing civilians based on any information.

It was dangerous to return to the forest. For a whole day and night I stayed in the forest, numb with cold: it was a cold April in 1942. I didn't have any money, or documents, or a place to live, and hadn't eaten anything for over a day. I closed my eyes, remembering my parents and brother, and cried bitterly. During that morning I poured out my whole reserve of tears and became numb, having lost the ability to cry. The death that had scared me so terribly passed me by. But this was only the beginning of my trials. I felt the persistent will towards life in me: I could not relax; I had to do something, at least not stay in one place.

Then there was a long road through the villages. Then autumn came, followed by winter. I had to think how and where to spend the winter. It was easier to get lost in a bigger place, and so I returned to Vinnitsa.

God brought me to Stanislava Nikolaevna Savitskaya, my mum's friend. She cleaned me and treated me. My feet were covered with abscesses and hair was full of lice. Savitskaya introduced me to Valentina Frantsevna Martynovskaya and they decided to send me to the village of Obidnoe, Nemirovsky District, to the mother of Martynovskaya – Maria Porfirievna, a very religious elderly woman, who asked God daily to save my life.

The village was secluded, away from the roads and railway. She taught me how to pray, to read the Bible, and to believe that only God could save me. During this dangerous time, I was offered shelter, they gave me clothes and shoes, whatever they had, and fed me for a year and a half. They lived poorly, but even in this poverty shared every last thing they had with me. The Germans were retreating and it became dangerous to remain in the village. Valentina Frantsevna gave me her sister's birth certificate so that I had at least one document on me, and sent me to our distant relative in Zhmerinka, in the ghetto, which was under Romanian supervision. And, indeed, this birth certificate saved my life for the second time when I was stopped on the road by a patrol.

There was a terrible hunger in the ghetto. Eighteen people had to share one small room and lice were everywhere, as well as fleas and rats. I became ill, and had abscesses and scars on my head.

But our army was approaching and, on 20 March 1944, they liberated Zhmerinka and Vinnitsa.

Perhaps my story may seem a simple listing of facts of my biography, but for me these were the landmarks of my hungry and destroyed childhood. Is it possible to compensate in any way for the loss of people dear and close to my heart? When I come to visit the graves of my innocent family, I kneel down and cry bitterly.

The Nazis had many collaborators among the policemen. But under the conditions of the Nazi occupation there were still many honest and decent people, such as the Martynovsky family. I am deeply grateful to all of them, and salute them. I submitted all of their names to be considered as the 'Righteous among the Nations' in Jerusalem.

The place of mass murder has been fenced in and kept in order. Fifteen of my dear and loved ones rest in these graves. May their memory stay for ever … I was the only survivor out of all our family.

39. The most horrendous days began

Evgeniya Mazhbitz (Spektor) (b. 1934)

My name is Evgeniya Zyuzevna Mazhbitz (Spektor) and I was born on 17 September 1934, in Bratslav, Nemirovsky district, Vinnitsa oblast, into a family of workers.

My parents had eight children: my oldest brother was born in 1932, and the youngest brother was born in 1950, my sisters were born in 1943 (in the camp) and in 1945. We had lived very happily and well before the war. My father worked, Mother was a housewife and raised us children.

I remember well the most terrible day: 22 June 1941. Together with my elder brother we came running home, and saw people standing listening to the public announcements and crying listening to the voice of Levitan. Literally only a few days later, my father left to go into the army. I remember the difficult minutes of farewell at the door near our gate.

My mother remained at home with the small children, and she was expecting at that time, too. She gave birth to a baby in July 1941. My father's parents managed to get evacuated. Mum's parents stayed near us and didn't leave. A week later, the Germans entered the town and the bombings began. We all, together with neighbours and family, were hiding in our cellar near the house. The cellar was big since it had been recently built; there were many children hidden in the cellar. One day I went out into the street, and when I was there I became terrified: bullets were flying by, and shells bursting. I knew where the key to our house was. I got into the house and took off my dress, since it smelled badly of the cellar. It was very hot outside, and I remained in my underwear. Then I got the key from our wardrobe and took out new shoes which my dad had brought from the Finnish war for my elder brother (they were small for him, yet big for me). I quickly put the shoelaces in them and got biscuits and pancakes that Mum had managed to prepare. These were the last things Mum had cooked before the war; she would never cook again. I went downtown; I heard shots everywhere and the German divisions were already marching into the town. There was a library not far from the cinema; windows were shattered and portraits of Stalin and different books were lying scattered in the street. On the pavements, I saw dead people, cats and dogs. I began to pick up portraits of Stalin, filled my top with them, and cried bitterly. Across the street, there was the house where my mum's parents lived. The house was locked; everyone was in our cellar. I was very scared. I went to their small garden, and hid there under each and every garden bench. My grandma used to have a beautiful little yard. It was always sprinkled with sand before Saturdays, and in summer evenings we used to have tea there. But now there was nobody to be seen anywhere. I felt even more terrified because of that and I went on searching for my relatives. Everybody was hiding and flats were locked. When I was going back, I met two sisters, 'old maids' as everybody would call them. They took me into their home and hid me. (Later they were brutally tortured by the Germans.) I started crying and wanted to go home. They couldn't stand my tears and decided to help me and take me home. When we went by my grandpa's house, we heard voices; there were people hiding in a cellar. Everybody who was hiding in our cellar had to move in here when the Germans found them there.

Then, the most terrible days began: the Kaparnik couple, our elderly neighbours, were killed by the Germans a week later, and dogs tore their bodies to pieces. In July 1941, my mum gave birth to a boy, named Sasha, and notwithstanding all circumstances, he had to be circumcised according to the Jewish tradition. Rabbi Rabinovich performed this ritual, assisted by Genya, a midwife. (Rabbi Moishe Rabinovich survived the horrible death camp in Bratslav-Pechera; he died many years after the war. His wife died in the camp, his younger son Gedal was ruthlessly tortured in the camp, and two sons died in the military.) During the circumcision, SS soldiers with dogs entered our house but stopped at the door and told us to continue the procedure. Genya lived with us for another week. During that time the Germans didn't persecute us. Later, they tortured Genya to death.

It is very painful to recall our Soviet POWs. They were humiliated, hungry and almost naked. They were housed in Bratslav prison and in the school. And when the Germans approached, there were many dead bodies everywhere, on the roads and streets, and I don't know even now where they were buried.

In October 1941, we were already living in the ghetto. We lived in the house of the Kelmensons, who gave shelter to us as well as to their family. There were many Jews from Poland, Romania and Chernovtzy oblast in the ghetto. The road to Uman was blocked, and they were all relocated to the Bratslav ghetto. We didn't have food, and were tortured by hunger and cold. Once, my mum reached our house but she met a woman, German by origin, who was the wife of the director of a local brewery. Before the war they had been good neighbours but now she took out a dog chain and beat my mum with it till she fainted. When she came back to her senses, she still managed to pick some frozen potatoes near the house and returned to the ghetto.

Once a week we were allowed to get out of the ghetto to get food and water. To get water we had to go in a group, since we were frequently attacked by non-Jewish children of our age, who humiliated us as much as they could. And after the war we went to the same schools with them. And although now they have grown up and became prominent people, one cannot forget those days. I was very weak then and could not carry two pails of water by myself. Mozya Kelmenson helped me: he carried his own two pails on a yoke and my pail in his hands.

The ghetto was located near the prison, and had fifteen houses in it. The Germans and local people destroyed all other houses. However, we all lived very closely and friendly there. The Manelis family had been very helpful to us throughout the war. They didn't leave us when the war was over, until our father was back from the military.

Once, the Germans brought a lorry to the camp, and interned POWs there, and my two brothers and myself were taken from the ghetto. We were taken towards the village of Semenki where all the POWs were buried alive in pits. But my brothers and I were brought back. Many years later I found out that the Manelis family paid the Germans to have them release us.

The Manelis family while in the ghetto, gathered food from among the Bratslav residents – whatever people were able to bring – and took it to the Bratslav and Pechera death camps. The family had a grandmother, a very religious and kind woman. She sent me to take biscuits and throw them to the prisoners working on the road construction towards Semenki and Tulchin.

The German Kommandant's office and their kitchen were located not far from the ghetto. Young men brought from the Bratslav camp worked there. They chopped wood, brought water, peeled potatoes, and cleaned everything. There were many of them, including even a girl once. They were either Polish or Romanian Jews, and spoke European languages well. They were aged fourteen to eighteen. I think they were connected to the partisans – they gave assignments to my younger brothers to take small packages and notes to designated places, and put them under stones. Later, these young men were all brutally killed in the Grenensky forest. After the liberation their bodies were reburied at the Bratslav Jewish cemetery. Many years later, Alexander Miroshnik, a Polish Jew, donated money to erect a memorial to them.

In 1942 my dad returned from the prison. He hid with our neighbours, the Suprinovichi family, for the first two months. When they could no longer keep him, he came into the ghetto. The ghetto residents were afraid that everybody would be killed because of him. So, he went to the Kommandant's office and told them he was a prisoner. They beat him half-dead and threw him to other prisoners in the camp. Two days later, my father was taken to labour, and then he was taken to the Kommandant's office where they wanted to kill him. He asked for only one thing: to be killed by a German and not a policeman. The Germans could not understand why he wanted that, and began again to beat him, giving him fifty lashes of the whip instead of twenty-five, then poured water on him. But he survived. When he was asked later, he said that the Germans didn't beat people as severely as policemen would. Eventually, they let him live because he was a good worker.

In February, when the ice on the river was at its thickest, my grandparents were removed from the ghetto and put in the Bratslav prison. Many people were also put there under the pretence of their relocation to the Pechera concentration camp. They spent a week in the prison. Once a day, it was allowed to take them hot water. On one such day my mum took hot water, but there was nobody in the prison. Mum was told that everybody had been marched to the concentration camp, but then in the evening, a policeman we knew came and told us how he had been killing all these people. All the prisoners, including my grandparents, were brought to the Southern Bug, near the Bratslav brewery. The prisoners had to cut the holes in the ice themselves; then the Germans and the police ordered everybody to strip naked. My grandparents were killed first because they asked to be killed with one bullet. Then they were thrown into the ice holes. One neighbour's fiancée was the next victim, followed by the wife of Lyova Granatovsky, with her baby. She held the baby close to herself and they pushed the child away with a bayonet and threw it on to the ice. He lay there for a long time. And his mother was killed and thrown under the ice. I do not list the names of victims: they were numerous and I was a child and do not remember all of them.

Once we were all formed into a column – prisoners from the camp and the ghetto prisoners – and they marched us to the Pechera concentration camp. Those who couldn't walk were killed instantly. We, the children, tried to walk in front of the convoy so that if they started killing people from behind we would be able to get out later from under the piles of dead people. But our family was returned to the ghetto, where we remained alone. A week later, now on a cart, we were taken to Pechera, where we spent a month in the basement of the Pechera concentration camp. A month later, people from villages of Bortniki, Vyshkovtsy or Papanka (I don't remember who exactly, but do remember the surname Ryaboshapka) moved us to the Bratslav concentration camp from where we were eventually liberated. A German, a very kind man, saved the camp; children used to call him 'Uncle Fritz'. He warned prisoners that the camp guards had left and that the SS killing squad would arrive within an hour. During this hour, old people, women and children tried to save themselves in any way possible. This happened during the winter solstice of 1944.

In the camp we were put on the ground floor – it was the second or third room to the left of the stairs. In the yard of the technical school where the camp was set up, there was a marble sculpture of a lion. This was a place of execution for the children.

We ate some skilly[1] and bread made from straw, and pea powder. In the mornings and evenings we could have hot water. The camp was fenced by barbed wire, over two metres high, and nobody could get out of it. But once, I don't know how, our neighbour, Aunt Nyusya Pyasezkaya, got me out of there, and took me to Suprinovichi, since she had no girls and was afraid to keep me. Later she got my two brothers out of the camp too and they stayed for two weeks with her. Somehow, the Germans found this out and she (in fact, her late mother) had to take me back into the camp. I don't know how she did it because it was forbidden to enter or leave the camp.

It was very terrifying in the camp, because people, both dead and alive, lay together on the bunks and on the floor. David, our neighbour, let us stay on his bunk. He warmed us as much as he could and prayed continuously for our survival.

Our Ukrainian neighbours were helping us in the camp with whatever they could. Some brought food, and some brought clothes. These were the very kind and compassionate families of Suprinovichi, Ostrovsky, Pyasezky and Baranovsky, Aunt Marina Kushnir, with all of whom we still maintain family-like relations.

On 18 March 1943, my mother gave birth to a girl who was named Esther because of the Jewish holiday of *Purim* and in memory of my grandma, tortured, killed and thrown into the river. Somehow (I don't remember now), Mum approached a Romanian priest with the request to have her delivery in a hospital. Everybody was surprised by Mum's decision to turn to a clergyman of a different faith with this request. But she was very well received and helped. She delivered my sister in the hospital and received some rags in which to wrap the baby. When Mum was in the hospital she was visited by Gitlya Muchnik, who brought her some soup. (When she was going back, the Germans beat her up severely.) This kind woman was helping everybody with whatever she could, although she herself was very poor; she shared her final piece of bread.

Prisoners from the Pechera camp were taken to Bratslav to work. When somebody tried to escape, they were killed instantly. Thus my friend's mother, Dvoira Kabazkaya, died. She left her two children, Sima and Polina, in the camp. After the war they lived in the orphanage until their father came back from the military. Now they live in Tulchin.

A German who was good to our family visited us back in the ghetto and later in the camp. He used to come in the evenings and tell us of the events on the front lines. We, the young children, tried to eavesdrop although we couldn't speak Yiddish. We then related the news to our older brothers. Then he stopped coming, since he was under suspicion for treating us well. Yet, still, it was with his help that we managed to survive: he warned camp prisoners about the planned *Aktion*. Within two hours, everybody managed to escape from the camp. Those who could not walk were pulled through the snow and ice but nobody was left behind helpless. There were two villages next to the camp, Chernyshevka, a Ukrainian village on the one side, and Sloboda, a Russian village, on the other. The residents of both places treated us all very well, and there was not a single home where people from the camp could not hide.

When we escaped, my father was not in the camp: he was hiding with other men of various nationalities in the underground built long ago by the Turks, near the Jewish cemetery. Boris Polikarpovich Romanenko and others were in hiding with him. They were hiding because they were supposed to be taken away to Germany.

Before the liberation of Bratslav by our army they managed to leave this shelter, because the Germans had discovered them, and hide again in the Shuryansky and Gninensky forests. There they stayed until the town was liberated and then they joined the army and went to the front. By the end of the war, my dad had been wounded four times and was decorated with medals.

When we walked out of the camp's gates, we went towards the nearest village of Sloboda. There were five of us. Mum carried my newborn sister in her arms, and I had to carry my youngest brother, born in 1941. He was very heavy for me, it was cold and slippery and we had no proper clothes. I told Mum I couldn't carry him any more, and she said, 'Leave him on the ice.' We walked another hundred or two hundred metres and Mum turned to us and started crying and begging us to try and pull him along. When I went back, I couldn't take him in my arms, since his arms were glued to the ice, and when I tried to pull him, his skin stuck to the ice.

Nobody could shelter such a big family as ours. People took one or two people. Thus Petya Rosenberg was saved. He was orphaned, and a woman from Sloboda took him, and for many years after the war she treated him as her own son.

Old man Tymko from Chernyshevka was the first one who took three of my brothers. (His own sons had been killed at the front.) He washed them, warmed them, and gave them food. And when they were revived they began to cry and ask for Mum. Tymko was searching for us throughout the village but nobody would say where we were since people were afraid of each other. When he found us, we were living in Sloboda, hiding at one woman's house – unfortunately I don't remember her name. Later, we went to the Ulyanovy family, but again we couldn't stay all together, and Kseniya Ivanovna Borisova took me to her place. She hid me above her Russian stove, she gave me 'poorer' clothes, cut my hair and made me look as if I were a slow child. She made it look so real that when the Germans entered the house in search of Jews they would immediately leave, thinking I was gravely ill. Thus Kseniya Ivanovna saved me, but in the final hours before their retreat, the Germans discovered her secret and wanted to kill me. But she bought me off, by killing all her chickens and giving them whatever she had in the house. However, they didn't have time to take it all since our troops entered the village. Then I went home but didn't know which home exactly was mine. First, I returned to the camp. The building was there, destroyed, with broken windows. Then I went to the ghetto, and there all the houses were in ruins too, and across the street, near the open prison gates, there were huge gallows.

Then I went to my home and saw our soldiers there. Mum had not come back yet. A woman who lived there gave me shelter. A few days later, Mum returned home with all the other children. They had spent the final days before liberation with the Baranovsky family. We had to replace everything from scratch. Our friends and neighbours helped us with whatever they could.

It is very difficult to recall all this, let alone to describe it.

NOTE

1. A thin broth or soup, or thin gruel, usually made of oatmeal flavoured with meat.

40. A train to the unknown[1]

Zigmund Meizler (b. 1930)

In early June 1941, the German army occupied Chernovtsy. The Romanian and German Fascists, as well as some local 'volunteers' with swastikas on their sleeves, stormed Jewish flats, and raped, robbed, beat and murdered people. These were innocent people – teachers and tailors, doctors and shop assistants, carpenters and barbers, professors and shoemakers, engineers and students, women and elderly, schoolchildren, clergy and newborn infants. Many were thrown out of their houses and marched in columns down the street guarded by armed soldiers and local policemen, being taken to the suburb of the town towards the Prut River. Others were taken out to the Jewish cemetery, made to dig ditches and pits, and then brutally killed.

I remember the day of 8 July 1941 well, because I turned eleven years old then. In the centre of the city, Nazis burned down an amazing creation by architects of the past century built in Byzantine style. This was one of the major architectural monuments of Bukovina and a sacred Jewish place – the Temple Choral Synagogue. The chief rabbi of the synagogue, Dr Mark, and many other synagogue workers were murdered.

Continuous robberies, pogroms and murders lasted for a few days. Soon a curfew was established, effective for the Jewish population only (8 p.m. through to the morning).

To tell Jews from non-Jews in public places, the Kommandant ordered all Jews to wear an 'identification sign' – a six-pointed star, yellow in colour, sewn on to the front of the coat or on to the back. The *Magen David*, the traditional symbol of Judaism, was turned into the star of shame. If a Jew went out in the street without this mark, he or she would be punished: in the best-case scenario by a big monetary fine, but most frequently by being taken to the police, beaten and humiliated. Often, people simply vanished.

I remember one tragic day: 11 October 1941. It was a Saturday, perhaps intentionally picked as the day for the *Aktion*. Our family lived in Kobylyanskaya Street (formerly Yanku Flondor Street). In the morning we heard that:

The Jews have to leave their houses no later than 6 p.m. and, with a minimum of possessions, be resettled in the ghetto (the lower part of the city). In case of disobedience, they will be subject to physical punishment, or executed.

And groups of miserable people, scared to death, were moving off and carrying their possessions in quickly packed sacks, bags and knots. People started looking for shelter in strange homes. Many had to stay right there in the yards, outside, or in the streets. Our family reached our relatives' flat – they lived in Pereyaslavskaya Street (formerly Shteingasse Street), which was a part of the ghetto. Under the threat of the death penalty, groups of people were flooding into the ghetto right into the night. People were robbed during the time they packed, right there in their flats, and on the way to the ghetto, in the streets. The very same day, rumours started circulating that people from the ghetto would be deported to the concentration camps and people had to prepare backpacks since you were allowed to take with you as much as you could carry. People were terrified. They were scared of everything: what would happen tomorrow, where and when they would be relocated, and whether they would survive.

Three days later, on 14 October 1941, at about 5 a.m., gendarmes, police and soldiers stormed the house where we lived, and drove everybody out into the street. Alongside the street, in the direction of Kalichanka, there were armed columns of soldiers and policemen, as well as a few local residents. The chosen people had to walk through these columns. They were beaten and robbed right there, as they walked. A fur coat was taken off my grandma's shoulders while her handbag was pulled out of her hands. When people tried to resist, even a little, they were beaten to death. Cattle carriages had already been prepared in the area of the railway station. between a hundred and a hundred and fifty people were put in each carriage, and armed guards were everywhere. It was stifling and crowded in the cars, and people didn't have enough room to sit let alone to lie down.

Screams of terror, cries of babies and prayers of the religious elderly … The train went into the unknown.

Our family of thirteen people was separated into a number of groups when boarding the train.

The train went very slowly, and had frequent stops; people lost their feeling of time. Only once a day were people allowed out under guard to attend to their physical needs. On the sixth day of travel, the train stopped, cars were opened and everybody was ordered to get out – or to jump out, to be more precise. The railway embankment was surrounded by knee-deep mud. This was the village of Ataki, flooded by water and mud, on the bank of the Dniester. And again, the violence and robbery resumed. Everybody spent the night outside. Only a few days later, people were transported in small groups by boat to the other side of the Dniester, to the Transnistria concentration camp.

People were marched on to Mogilev-Podolsky, where the camp was located. Many could not endure this exhausting march and died along the road. Our family managed to run away when we reached the outskirts of the city and it was dark. We hid in a half-flooded basement of an abandoned house. We stayed there for quite a while.

This was the beginning of our trials. Our family eventually went into the ghetto. In the winter of 1943 my father was severely ill with typhoid. My mother lost her sight completely. My brother's feet were frostbitten. There were neither doctors nor medications available. I climbed over the walls of the ghetto-camp and went to a Ukrainian market to get milk for my ill father. There were many 'violators' like me in the market. Then there was a pogrom. The Nazi officer named Barbulesku and his assistant, Dan, with a huge German shepherd dog, forced everybody who dared to leave the ghetto into the basement in the gendarmes' office. There we stayed for three days with no food or water. Then, being beaten with gun butts, we were put into German lorries to be sent into the German territory as a punishment. While getting into the lorry, amid the confusion, I ran away together with Binder, a Chernovtsy violinist, who begged at the market. The gendarmes started shooting at us but we managed to escape. I was twelve years old then.

NOTE

1. This first appeared in *People Will Remain Human: Testimonies of Witnesses*, Vol. 2 (1992), pp. 59–61.

41. Babi Yar kept haunting me after the war

Raissa Maistrenko (b. 1938)

On 12 September 1941 I turned three, and on 19 September the Germans entered Kiev. September 29 became that tragic day which Second World War.

We lived with Mum and my half-brother, together with my father's parents. My father, Vadim Petrovich Lymarev, a Ukrainian, was studying in Poltava, in the artillery college. He left for the front straight from there when the war started. My mum, Tsilya Meerovna Lymareva, was Jewish. She worked in a small company producing medical equipment; she was a metal worker and cut medical weights. My mum was my father's second wife. My half-brother, Valentin, was born from his first marriage. Valentin's mother died when he was nine months old.

Petr Alexandrovich Lymarev, my grandpa, was a well-known stove-setter in town. He was very widely recognized as an artisan and he was asked to go and build ovens in the houses of scholars, professors and important people. His stoves were indeed extra-ordinary samples of tile-setting craft and heated well. He was respected and often elected a people's juryman before and after the war. Tatiana Ivanovna Lymareva, my grandma, was his second wife. After his first wife died, he was left with two children, a boy and a girl. The girl died, but Grandma managed to save the boy, my father, and raise him. She had never had her own children, and she directed all her motherly love towards us, my father, myself, my brother Valentin, my younger brothers and nephews, and grand-children.

She used to tell me, 'The mother is not the one who gives birth, but the one who raises and brings up.' And indeed, with her whole life she confirmed the title of 'true mother'.

In the first days of the occupation, the Germans started humiliating and torturing the city residents, and Jews in particular. And a week later, announcements appeared on the walls of the houses and on the fences:

> All Jews of Kiev and surrounding areas! You have to report on Monday, 29 September, by seven o'clock, with possessions, warm clothes, documents, and valuable things to Dorogozhitskaya Street, near the Jewish cemetery. If you fail to appear, report, you will be executed. If you hide Jews, you will be executed. If you take over Jewish flats, you will be executed.

Many people, having read the announcements, wanted to believe and indeed did believe that they would be deported. But events that were unfolding in the city put fear and terror in their hearts. My grandparents wouldn't let my mum go, promising to hide her, my brother and me. She almost agreed to stay, but at the last minute her parents came, and some relatives, with a cart. They persuaded her to go, saying they had the cart, and for her it would be easier to go with the children and with them. There were eighteen people in total: her parents, two of Mum's sisters, their children, Mum's aunts, and so on. Their surname was Kovkiny, but unfortunately I don't know their first names. Although, judging by mum's patronymic, my grandpa's name was Meer. One of the sisters' surnames was Kotlyar; her husband Boris came to us after the war. Grandma couldn't remember other relatives' names.

Mum gathered our belongings quickly, put all our clothes and things on the cart and we walked away, saying brief goodbyes to our grandpa. My brother stayed with Grandpa, who said he would bring him along later, after Mum had settled down in a new place. And Grandma came to see us off. We walked along Saksagansky Street towards the Jewish market, and then along Brest-Litovsk highway to Kerosinnaya Street, and further on along Kerosinnaya towards Babi Yar. I was very small and my memory preserved only individual episodes of this terrible walk. There was an enormous number of people; cries and laments rang out everywhere. I clearly remember sitting under a brick wall, among jars containing jam covered with paper and tied up with white rags. I thought they were so big. I was sitting among these jars, and saw legs, legs, around me, and then heard screams. A group of old men with white beards, dressed only in underwear, was taken away in front of us. A woman hugged one of them. He was pulled away from her, and she screamed terribly. These were the rabbis, as my grandma later told me.

When we reached the place where clothes and documents were taken away, and where machine-gun shots were clearly heard, Mum began to ask Grandma to save me. Grandma took me in her arms and went up to a policeman. She showed her passport and, crossing herself, told him she was Ukrainian. He wanted to hit me on my head with his gun butt but Grandma shielded me with her shoulder, and fell on the ground when she was hit, covering me with her body. A German came, picked my grandma up, and pushed her into the crowd. I clutched Grandma's neck with my hands. Going mad from pain and horror, she ran away. People in front of her let her go, and having run for a while, she turned towards the Jewish cemetery.

The shot at us a few times, but missed, and we hid among the trees of the old cemetery. We ran for a long while, but nobody chased us and we hid in the bushes among the graves. Thus we stayed until nighttime listening to the continuous gunshots. When it was dark, we came out of our shelter and started to look for the road back home. Grandma didn't know this area of the city well, and she became completely lost in the darkness. We walked around the ravine and, silently approaching, saw people who had survived the murder and were sitting on the ground and on dead bodies.

Grandma's sister, together with her mentally ill husband, lived in the same flat as we did. The flat was on Malo-Zhitomirskaya Street, but the Germans declared it a forbidden area, and moved all residents their flats. Beside this, due to different reasons, Grandma's nephews, Grandpa's sister with her daughter and grandchildren came to live in the same flat. Only a few families out of the old residents in our yard remained (two seven-storeyed houses), who knew that the Lymarev family had saved a Jewish child, but nobody would turn us in.

When raids happened we were warned and together with Grandpa we would go to the basement of our huge house. I remember this terrible dark basement well, with a pile of broken bricks and different trash. The walls of the basement were very thic, and light could barely get in through the narrow windows. The basement had many niches where we would hide with Grandpa and try to merge with the walls and dirty floor.

The Germans would never enter the basement. They would step in the doorway, shouting, '*Rus*, get out!' then fire from their automatic guns, and leave.

Once from the niche in which I was hiding, I even saw soldier's boots; then a gun, and heard shots.

That was what my childhood was like.

During the day we would often go with my grandma and brother to search for Dad in the camps for the war prisoners, somewhere in Darnitsa and Syrets. We took with us whatever we had, sharing our last bits and pieces – a couple of potatoes, an onion, a piece of bread. Sometimes we managed to pass this on to the starved prisoners. And we were always starving as well. Once, Grandma's sister brought some sour dough that was all over the street after the bakery was blown up. She didn't have anything to put it in, so she took off her knickers and got them filled with the dough. We baked cakes from it. They were sour and half mixed with soil, but we thought they were delicious.

Soon after the Germans occupied the city, our street was also turned into a forbidden zone, and I remember how we walked through the night to our relatives in Solomenka. Somehow we walked through the night. That night, according to German law, we were supposed to be killed four times: first, we were out in the night (violating the curfew); second, we had a Jewish child with us; third, we had a mentally ill person, the husband of my grandma's sister (and they were killed in the very first days); and to top it all, my brother was carrying a red-feathered dove (those who kept pigeons were shot, too). For the rest of my days I would remember this griev-ing procession walking through the night city. Grandpa was pulling a wheelbarrow, Grandma Frosya (that's what we called my grandma's sister) was pushing it from behind. Grandma held me by the arm, and my brother pulled the stubborn, ill, old man. Now, remembering it all, I'm surprised how amid all this horror we tried to keep our bird. But we all loved the beautiful smart dove. When somebody knocked on our door, it would fly into the half-open cup-board, and sit there quietly until the stranger left the flat.

We stayed with our relatives until the liberation. Before their retreat, the Germans drove all residents out of Kiev. They wanted to leave the city dead behind them. I remember how we were sitting on suitcases in the hallway of our relatives' home, dressed and ready to go. There were many people. A group of Germans entered without knocking. One of them was, as we called them, 'a black German', an SS officer. He shouted something pointing at the door. The 'translator' pounded the kitchen table that was in the hallway, and 'translated': 'This way – leave out of one door, enter another, don't leave the city, our soldiers will be tomorrow here.'

And the German would pat the 'translator' on the shoulder and say, '*Gut, gut* [Good, good].'

And the very same night our 'brave team' wandered back to Saksagansky Street. We entered our house, going through the back-yards. All the remaining residents got together on the ground floor of one wing. We comprised eight or ten children, and they put us all on an iron bed. Nobody could sleep. We felt joy: we messed around on the bed, laughed and were happy. But the grown-ups were wor-ried. Somebody continuously pounded on our closed iron gates with gun butts, trying to get in.

At dawn we heard tank chains rattling, and somebody cried out, 'These are our tanks!'

The gate was opened and we went to welcome the tanks.

The semi-basement – or to be more exact, a pit beyond the gates

– where now there is 'The Chocolate Bar' – was filled with corpses of half-naked Germans. People were hugging the tank drivers who stopped near our house to ask for directions. Grandma was holding me in her arms, covering me with her kerchief. One of the soldiers in a tank picked me up in his arms, kissed my face and kept crying.

Yes, 700 days and nights are far more than one day. How can I describe them? Which words do I use to put them on paper? There was cold and hunger, every day. Somehow I never remembered the summer – all my memory kept was the feeling of horrible cold.

The war orphaned many children; destitution and grief were in store for the whole nation. That is why I never stop admiring the nobility and courage of people who were saving Jews, putting their own lives and lives of their loved ones at risk. They were unarmed, poor and hungry, but they shared whatever they had.

Babi Yar kept haunting me after the war. Grandpa was ill all the time. With much difficulty I managed to finish school, but my brother managed to finish only seven years of school. We had to go to work. First I tried to work as an assistant on a construction site although I only weighed forty kilograms [eighty pounds] and was one and a half metres tall [about five foot six]. Then I went to the factory and worked as a metal worker, a milling-machine operator. But I was happy and optimistic. After work, in the evenings, I used to attend the factory's dance group, where I met my future husband. We got married, had a son, and when he was four, we were invited to become professional dancers. We worked there for twenty-one years. This was also more than one day. We had to take care of our ill, elderly grandparents and our son; later we had a daughter, overcoming all these difficulties, struggling for the survival of our family and us. We took care of the elderly and raised our two children. Now, together with my husband, I have retired as an actor, but we continue working – we created 'Dnepryanochka', a children's group of folk and modern dance, which has been performing for over ten years now. Our daughter is a ballet dancer and our son is the director of stunts at the Dovzhenko Film Company. Life goes on.

My family and I are for ever indebted to my grandparents, who gave me a second life. My first would have ended with my mum, her parents, and other relatives, a total of eighteen people, whom my saviours have now joined. May they rest in peace. And we shall remember them always. And if God is willing to let me survive, I will continue telling my children, grandchildren, great-grandchildren, and all people about the horrors that took place. So that it may never happen again! So that there may never be another Babi Yar where innocent people and children were killed just because they were Jewish.

42. I cannot forget those difficult years

Semyon Meller (b. 1930)

I was eleven years old when the war began. Our family had six people (Father, Mother, and four children), and we all fled from Volochisk, Khmelnitzky oblast. But, on the way, Nazis near Zhmerinka bombed our convoy and we had to continue on foot. In Zhmerinka, my father's sister lived, together with her family.

The Germans occupied the town, and soon a ghetto was set up for the Jewish population. Three streets were fenced off with barbed wire and all Jews from Zhmerinka were resettled there, two to three families sharing one room, with no right to leave the camp.

Life in the ghetto was very difficult because of the overcrowding, and lack of food and clothes. Cold, hunger and diseases resulted in high mortality among the Jews who lived in the ghetto. In 1943 our father died from starvation, and our life became even worse than before. Only once a week were Jews allowed to leave the camp for the market and to use special permits to trade their clothes for food. However, when going out of the ghetto we always had to wear armbands with six-pointed stars. Those who violated this requirement would be punished with twenty-five blows from a rubber baton.

Adults and children alike were forced to repair the railways and clean the railway station, and in summer we were put on agricultural assignments. I remember an instance when we were made to collect caterpillars off the cabbages and if a supervisor saw a caterpillar missed, he would make us eat it. By the end of the work, children were starting to vomit and they weren't able to stand on their feet.

The boys were forced to roll cigarettes filled with gunpowder; then they would be lit and their faces burnt. There was no limit to the humiliation and abuse of Jews. Twice a year, in summer and winter, documents were checked for all of the camp's population, and everybody – ranging from the elderly and ill to the youngest infants – had to line up in front of the communal building. In summer people would suffer from the heat, and in winter from the cold, since they had to stand outside for hours, frequently fainting. That was what life in the ghetto was like. The Jews of Zhmerinka were able to survive only because the town was under the jurisdiction of Romanian gendarmes who – although they abused Jews brutally – didn't murder Jews in large numbers the way Germans did in other locations around Zhmerinka.

In 1944, when the Soviet army began to advance, the Germans who guarded the station received the order to liquidate the ghetto. But because of circumstances, fortunately for us, they never managed to do it. In March 1944 the Soviet army liberated Zhmerinka, and thus we survived.

I cannot forget those difficult years.

43. My father was killed in Babi Yar

Vassily Mikhailovsky (Cesar Katz) (b. 1937)

I was born on 19 November 1937 into the family of Petr Solomonovich and Tzima Pavlovna Katz. My father was the manager of a café on Kreshchatik, and my mother was a homemaker. My mum died soon after my birth, in December 1937. Anastasia Konstantinovna Fomina, our nanny, looked after my older brother Pavlik (born in 1931) and me.

Before Kiev was occupied, my father had got Grandma, Pavlik, and me evacuated, together with our nanny but, together with her, I was late for the convoy, and had to stay in Kiev.

My father went into the army, and when defending Kiev he got surrounded. Having escaped from the Darnitsa camp he came home to 9 Kostelnaya Street. Seeing my father, a woman who was our yard-keeper brought two policemen. My father was killed in Babi Yar.

In the morning she told my nanny, 'Take the Jew kid to Babi Yar.'

My nanny was illiterate, and didn't really understand the dangers, so she took me to Babi Yar. When we got behind the first ranks of guards, and had heard the machine-guns firing, she realized that we would die. I was crying and screaming.

A German who was walking nearby pushed us away and pointed at a small alley, saying, 'Just sit the child down there.'

She went to the alley. The doomed people continued their march, and the German lost sight of us. Nanny stayed there with me till it got dark. When the guards left, she got back into the city. We didn't go back home to Kostelnaya Street though.

For two weeks my nanny wandered with me across the city. She would go to her friends, but couldn't stay anywhere longer than one night. Sometimes she would spend the night in the ruins of the department store on Kreshchatik Street or in other places.

She heard from people about the orphanage in Predslavinskaya Street. She was afraid they would not take me so she left me on their steps with a note saying, 'Vasya Fomin'.

I spent all the years of the war in this orphanage, organized by Nina Nikitichna Gudkova, a paediatrician, who founded it at the local children's hospital. Almost all the medical staff from the hospital were evacuated. Two nurses, three nannies, a janitor and an administrator saved those children who remained in the hospital, together with Gudkova. The personnel and older children were searching for food through the rubbish near hotels occupied by Germans. Workers from the meat factory would also help us by sometimes bringing us meat by-products and blood.

Children younger than a year died, while older children survived. Over seventy children were saved, including twelve Jewish children. In case of danger, they were hidden in the laundry room under the staircase, and everybody risked their lives.

After the liberation of Kiev, in November 1944, a doctor, Vassily Ivanovich Mikhailovsky, and his wife, Berta Savelievna, adopted me. I didn't have any documents, my age was determined from my looks, and they received a new birth certificate dated 15 September 1940.

Before the war, Vassily Ivanovich had lived with his family in Kirovograd. Because of severe illness, he couldn't get evacuated and stayed there with his Jewish wife and her mother. They were turned in to the occupiers, but some kind people saved them. They were going to Kiev where Vassily Ivanovich had relatives. In the village of Peschany Brod, he hid his wife in a morgue, and her mum in the typhoid ward of the hospital where the Germans were afraid to go. He saved many local people from being taken away to Germany, and treated partisans.

In Kiev, they hid with his older brother's wives. His three brothers were repressed in 1937 and died in the gulags, and they had no children. They took me when I was weak and ill, with a stomach oedema, and they treated me, raised me and brought me up.

In 1957, I finished school with honours and, in 1962, I graduated from the Kiev Construction and Engineering Institute with honours. I built power stations on the Dnieper, as well as transregional gas and petroleum pipelines in Tumen and the Ukraine. I also worked as a senior research associate in the Research Institute for Constructive Production. I took part in reconstruction of the stadiums in Kiev (Central and Dynamo), in the construction of the Ukrainian Home. In the recent years I have been the director of the Project, Construction and Technology Bureau of the Institute.

Pavlik, my brother, and my paternal uncle knew that I lived in the Mikhailovsky family but, because of an agreement between my parents and them, I learned about this only when graduating from the Institute.

My nanny, Fomina, died in 1980; she has always been a welcome person in our family. Vassily Ivanovich died in 1968; Nina Nikitichna Gudkova died in 1995. Berta Savelievna, my mum, lives with me. I will always remember these modest people who are dear to my heart; they gave me the gift of life.

A. K. Fomina, N. N. Gudkova and V. I. Mikhailovsky, my saviours, each received the title of the 'Righteous Gentile of the World'. They were awarded with diplomas and medals of the Yad Vashem Institute (Israel) (posthumously), as well as with diplomas of the 'Righteous of Babi Yar' (the Ukraine).

In 1993, I survived a myocardial infarction. As a young ghetto prisoner I qualify as the second category disabled of the war.

44. In those horrible days[1]

Leya Osadchaya (b. 1925)

Before the war our family had lived in Kiev. My maternal grand-parents' surname was Polyak. Before the October Revolution, my grandfather was the director of the Jewish Day School (later, School No. 19 was located in this building). According to my mother, he never charged tuition fees for poor school students. My grandma had her own cardboard factory. All my mother's brothers and sisters finished school.

Our family (the Osadchys) lived on Podol, at 9 Bratskaya Street and, after the famine of 1933, we moved to 89 Sagaydachny Street. My parents were tailors. My father was a very good suit tailor, everybody respected him, and he frequently received awards. He had the 'Stakhanov Red Book'. The whole river fleet knew him because he made suits for many of them.

We didn't manage to leave Kiev. I remember when the Germans occupied the city, many people were afraid of going out into the streets. Everybody lived with a premonition that something horrible was to come.

On 28 September, an order was posted on every corner for all Jews to report to Melnikov Street. Nobody knew then that this was the beginning of the road to the terrible Babi Yar. At that time I was in a village in Dymersky district, together with a friend, Maria Filippenko, trading clothes for food. Even then, my life was in danger. When, together with Maria, we were walking through the forest, a policeman stopped us and requested our documents. But my friend acted quickly; she gave me her own birth certificate and told him she had left hers at home. I showed him Maria's document and he let us go.

We came back to Kiev. It was unbearable to see the Kreshchatik on fire, and to watch military prisoners being marched to Darnitsa, and Jews walking along their last road.

It is not a secret that many people gloated over our destiny, say-ing that the Jews should have been removed long ago. They turned in everybody they knew to the Germans. Our family was shocked;

yard-keepers and neighbours could turn us in any minute. A traitor who called himself 'Mr Berezovsky' moved into our house. On 18 February 1942, a black car came and arrested all of my family. Maria Filippenko, my friend, and Tamara, her sister, witnessed this. At that time I was working at Zhulyany station, loading sand into carts to earn a loaf of bread per week. (When the Germans introduced bread rations, my parents could not receive it because you had to present identification documents.)

After my family was arrested, Maria came to me and told me about this, and warned me against returning back home since the police had set up an ambush there. I lived for some time in the dorm, in Zhulyany. The yard-keeper's children were searching for me everywhere in Kiev, and my picture was on billboards in Podol. My friend secretly removed it. However, these people tracked me down. But there were honest people among the Germans too. A German supervisor noticed the 'efforts' of the janitor's children, and told me to 'leave before they arrest you'.

Later I learned about my family's tragic fate. My parents and three sisters – aged fourteen, three years, and seven months – were all murdered in Babi Yar. My grandma, my two uncles with their families and an aunt all died there too. Thus I became an orphan, but I didn't know that another tragedy waited for me. From February through to 14 May, I led the life of a hunted animal: I hid in the forest during the daytime, and at night I asked people to let me stay in villages or remote farmsteads. When I came out of the forest into the road, Germans arrested me, put me in a car, and took me to the station to be sent to Germany with other teenagers. They took us to Warsaw, and from there to the Auschwitz death camp. I escaped along the way, but I didn't have a place to hide in Poland, since the Poles were not very friendly. I was arrested at the border and sent away to Magdeburg and, from there, to Burg. Farmers picked out the stronger-looking country boys and girls, and fifteen of us, weak and miserable, were left in the camp. We worked at the defence factory. I was exhausted, and every day I would faint, and they would pour water over me.

You cannot tell everything … I would like to say that the French patriots saved me from being killed. French friends made sure I was transferred into an Italian camp where there were fewer Russians and conditions were better.

On 6 May 1945, the Red Army liberated us.

When I returned to my home, in Kiev, I found out that our flat had been seized and burgled. 'Mr Berezovsky' made a fortune robbing many of the Jewish flats. Maria Filippenko and her sister told me about this, since they witnessed it. I turned to the prosecutor a few times, but to no avail. Until now, I have lived without my flat, and 'Mr Berezovsky', with his family, has lived in a flat occupied by him during the war, in Khorevaya Street, near Zhitny Rynok [the Rye Market]. I stayed in a dormitory, worked at the printers. Then they asked us to leave the dormitory. I wandered through railway stations, and in the autumn of 1947 I left for Zakarpatye (Transcarpathian oblast). I live in a room, only thirteen square metres shared by five people. My grandchild is disabled. We sleep on the floor. I have written letters to different organizations, including the Supreme Council of the Ukraine. For me, the war is not yet over.

NOTE

1. This first appeared in the *Jewish News* and as an Appendix to *The Voice of the Ukraine*, a special edition of the *Supreme Council of the Ukraine*, Nos 15–16 (Society for Jewish Culture of the Ukraine, 1996).

45. This can never be forgotten

Sophia Palatnikova (b. 1927)

On 26 July 1941, the Germans occupied the village of Teplik, Vinnitsa oblast, where I lived together with my parents and my sister.

In the first days of the occupation, all Jews were forced to wear white armbands with the Star of David on them. We were not allowed to walk across the town freely, and all Jews were resettled to the two streets closest to the river. Every day, at any time, they would come and take us to work: to wash floors at the rooms where the German soldiers stayed overnight, to do laundry for the soldiers, to clean toilets and so on. They humiliated us, not accepting us as people.

During the winter all the Jews were taken out to the roads to clear them of snow, so that the German transport could proceed without any delays. The winter of 1941/42 was cold and snowy. German soldiers and Ukrainian police guarded us. The latter abused us, beating us with their whips. And we had to labour hard until darkness, cold and starved. After the work we were marched like cattle, hastened on by whips. Workers included old people and young children aged thirteen and fourteen.

Before being sent to work they would form us into a circle, and then make us run fast. The old people, who were last, would be beaten with whips and batons. Some of them would never be able to get up again. Young people also left the *Appelplatz* [assembly square] violently battered, all covered in bruises and wounds.

In April 1942 all those aged thirteen to forty-five who could work were put on to lorries and, together with Jews from Sobolevka, were taken to a concentration camp in Raigorod, Vinnitsa oblast. Here we had to work in the quarry cutting stones for road construction. My older sister, Tanya, was there with me, in the camp.

After all those who could work were taken to Raigorod, on 27 May 1942, the Nazis and their collaborators killed all the remaining Jews of Teplik. My parents survived the murder by hiding among the trees.

In the winter of 1941/42, my dad, together with a few other Jews, was taken to work at a hotel for Germans officers. Mykola, a Ukrainian man, worked with them; he told my father that forty specialists (tailors, shoemakers, etc.) were left alive in Teplik, and that Yogahn Koch, the manager of the hotel, was looking for him to assist him in his work (my dad was a butcher). He went to Yogahn Koch, and Koch's boss, named Schweitzer, issued him a document certifying that he worked at the hotel in different capacities. Koch and Schweitzer, both Germans, treated the five Jews who worked with them well.

My mum was hiding among the trees, as well as with the families of saved craftsmen and artisans, or with good Ukrainian friends. Later, my dad sent her to the Bershad ghetto where his relatives gave her shelter.

My dad stayed in Teplik, while my sister and I were at that time moved to the Bratslav camp – marched there from Raigorod in the autumn of 1942. We lived in inhuman conditions, hungry, with no clothes or shoes, working at road construction, and other slave labour.

In 1943, my sister and I escaped from the camp to the Bershad ghetto. Our father, who was warned by Yogahn Koch that he had to leave, later joined us there. He was told that, when retreating, the Germans would kill all Jews, including the craftsmen.

We didn't work in the Bershad ghetto; we were famished with hunger, and lived in very crowded conditions. There were 14 of us in two rooms.

The Romanian Jews established an orphanage in the ghetto. My sister and I receiving from there a piece of thick polenta that we split into four portions. My father was already swollen from hunger and when there was already no hope for us to survive, fortunately, the Germans began retreating fast.

On the dawn of 14 March 1944, the Soviet army liberated us. We lived near the bridge that on the night before had been blown up by the retreating Germans. However, only the top surface of it was destroyed. With the help of the local population it was restored in a couple of hours, and our troops marched over it.

It is impossible to describe the commotion at the bridge that day. People were hugging soldiers, kissing them, crying with joy. I cry even now when recalling that liberation day. I didn't cry when began to write my memories; I'm crying now when recalling liberation. I remember my mum and dad who came to the bridge to welcome our liberators; they were swollen from hunger, cold, half-dressed, but together with other people they rejoiced in freedom. This can never be forgotten.

A few days after our liberation we walked back home to Teplik. The

Germans had destroyed our house. We stayed in an empty, abandoned house, which survived after its owners were killed. Ukrainian neighbours gave us wood to heat the house. My parents' Ukrainian friends brought us a bed, a pillow and a mattress filled with hay, a blanket and so on. They also brought us a few dishes, helping us with whatever they could, and we began to slowly come back to senses.

My father and sister went to work immediately; I was accepted as a trainee in a state bank. It was difficult to begin from scratch, and the war went on for over a year. But we were free.

46. There was a lot of humiliation

Polina Pekerman (b. 1927)

I was born on 8 March 1927, in the town of Chudnov, Zhitomir oblast. Efim Grigoryevich, my father, worked at a local spirit distillery. Polina Moiseevna, my mother, was a homemaker and also a seamstress. I had a twin sister, Asya.

Once, in the summer of 1941, I was playing with other children, and somebody came and told us to go home, because the war had begun. And, although we didn't really realize the seriousness of the tragedy that had just befallen us, every child ran to his or her home. At home, my mother was crying; hugging and kissing us. Confusion ensued, yet immediately, within two hours, everybody was mobilized into the military. My father went into the army too, and we never saw him again.

Three days later they started to bomb Chudnov. Together with Mum, we hid in a steep ravine behind our house. We went home after the bombing was over (it lasted for two to three days). And then the evacuation began. But only those who had the money could be evacuated, and we were very poor.

Mum kept saying, 'Where, my little babies, shall we go? We don't have any money or transport, and we are nobody, just plain workers, we didn't do any harm to anyone. You are very young, I don't have any money. And where shall we go, my babies? We will die anyway … See what kind of people is staying here, all engineers and doctors, and even wealthy people stay. And where shall we go?'

And we stayed …

And then the Germans came. My mother was not very well educated, and we were very young and could not understand why everybody was screaming and crying. Five or six days later, we were all gathered together, and a headman was appointed who said that we had to wear a six-pointed star because we were Jews. We were not allowed to go into the town, we had only one street to live on and separate shops. At that time we saw what big trouble was ahead.

Mum kept crying and saying, 'Kill me! It is because of me that you stayed here, and now you will be killed!'

Soon, the killings began. And how did we survive? Only because my mother could make clothes, and for some time the Germans kept different specialists they needed – about two weeks, a month, not for longer. So, in fact, we didn't live together for much longer, maybe for another month or so.

One morning we got up and saw policemen running from house to house and taking all our neighbours out, taking them all away to be killed. We saw a neighbour go out, who had many children. Her daughter had come to her from some other place, her name was Raya, and she was a teacher. When the war began, she was here, with her mother. She had two children – three-year-old Petya and Polinka, eight months old. When we were all brought together, she carried Polinka in her arms, and held Petya by his hand. The baby kept crying. Bryukhanov, a policeman, ran up and pierced this tiny baby with his bayonet, then threw her up into the air and shot her. She fell to the ground like a stone. And we couldn't cry, we held back; our hearts were like stones and nobody could cry.

We were all taken to a cinema building. The lorries kept pulling up there to take us to a park to be killed. And the graves had already been dug out in the park. The Germans put a board on the top of each pit; then they put five to ten people on the board and shot them down with machine-guns. Some were killed instantly, but some were only wounded. Yet everybody was covered with dirt. The ground there was moving for another three or four days.

We stood together with Mum. She hugged and kissed and us and cried that it was her fault that we hadn't left the town, and now it all would be over. There was no return. Then she would hug me and say, 'My little daughter, are you listening to me?'

'Yes, my dear mum, I am.'

'My sweet daughter, I have a request for you. Now go to that policeman and tell him, my baby, that you're not Jewish.' (I had braided blonde hair, and didn't look Jewish at all.) 'Tell him that they were taking everyone, and they got you. And maybe he will let you go and you will run away.'

'My dear Mum, how can I leave you, and go now?'

'Please understand,' my mum told me then, 'it will be easier for the two of us to take turns and get out of here.'

'No, Mum, I won't go.'

But she kept begging me, saying that the three of us would never be able to leave. I stood by her, she kissed me all over, holding me tight to her heart as a mother would in her last moments, and said, 'Run, baby, run. We'll join you later.'

And my sister came up to me, and also told me to go, and they would come to me afterwards. I asked Mum where I should wait for them, and she told me to go to 'Aunt Tanya's' (I had gone to school with Lilya, her daughter). And she told me to hurry up …

I was a child then, and didn't really understand what to do but I ran towards the policemen and told one of them I was not Jewish. 'And how did you get in here?' he asked.

And I said, 'I was walking along the street, and these people were being taken some place, and I was taken too, and I didn't know where these people were taken.'

The policeman told me to go with him to their chief, who had a table and was marking something down on paper there. The policeman approached this man – his surname was Lozovoy – and told him about me. Lozovoy told him to take me to town so that I could show them where I lived. It was a beautiful warm day, the sun was shining brightly. We went together for some time, and then I started asking him to let me go and not to kill me because I wanted to live so much. He became a policeman after he was surrounded by the military, and he looked at me with pity, gave me a hug, and told me to run away to the field and forests, in the hope that God would save me.

He went back and I ran to Aunt Tanya. She asked me where I had come from. I didn't tell her anything except that I was walking by and decided to come to them. I glanced at a wall, and saw a rifle on it. I asked, 'Aunt Tanya, why do you have a rifle?'

And she said, 'Uncle Fedya went to serve in the police.'

This was her husband. I felt so bitter, and I said, 'Aunt Tanya, my mum said you would give me shelter until she comes to get me.'

'And where is your mum?'

'My mum is in the cinema building; she was taken there, together with Asya, my sister. She told me to come and wait for her here, with you.'

And she said, 'Oh no, little girl, your mother and sister will never come; you will never see them again.'

I started to cry bitterly. She then asked me if I wanted to eat something.

'No, Aunt Tanya, I don't want to eat, I want to go to Mum and Sister, to them.'

'That is impossible; if you go there, the same will happen to you.'

It started to get dark, the sun set, it was evening, and she said, 'So, Polinka, I'm afraid of keeping you here, because now Uncle Fedya will come home, and I will get into trouble together with you.'

'Where should I go?' I asked her. I hadn't been anywhere before and didn't know anything beyond the home and my mum.

But she took me out to the road, and it was dark already. I was thinking to myself, 'No, I won't go anywhere, because maybe tonight my mum and my sister will come.' And I went to her barn, where she kept a cow and pigs. I sat there and cried for a very long time, calling for my mum. But I never saw my mum again.

Thus I stayed there until dawn and at first light I left, walking without knowing where. But Anya, one of her neighbours saw me, and said, 'Polinka, where are you going?'

I told her I didn't know and asked her to take me out to the road so that I could go to the forest or somewhere else. She took me out to the road and told me to go to Volosivka, a village. And I went along that road. I walked through forests and fields, and spent nights in the haystacks. But I couldn't sleep – any noise would scare me. With the morning, I continued on my way, and kept going in circles.

Finally, I reached Vilshanka, a place two kilometres away from Chudnov, and I didn't know the road. The Czechs lived there. I entered one flat, it was dark, and I hoped that they would give me some food. There was one Czech, and some other people who looked Jewish. The host asked me where I was going. I told him (somehow God put this thought into my head) that I had come from Kazatin orphanage, which had been bombed, and that now I was wandering from place to place. He told me to spend the night there and in the morning to go to Yakushpol. There was not a single Jew left in Chudnov, yet they were still living in Yakushpol. I sat down on a bench; he gave me a piece of bread and a glass of milk. I had it but I was so worn and exhausted that I fell asleep right on that bench.

In the morning he told me to go, and I didn't know how to get to Yakushpol. He told me to go through certain villages to Sharkovtsy and ask people the way, but I should stay away from the roads because they could catch me there. I went for two days to get to Yakushpol, and I was tired. I remember I didn't have any more strength to walk and stopped near one village. I thought of going into one of the houses as maybe they would give me some food. There was some old woman, a Pole. She asked me where I had come from and I told her that I was walking from Kazatin orphanage, that I didn't have any place in which to spend the night, and that I was cold and hungry. And then we saw a policeman coming. She told me to run and hide in her shed. He walked by and probably didn't see me. She started doing something in the yard, then went into her house, and brought me something to eat. I only stayed with her for two days, because she was scared – there were good people, but there were also people who would tell she was hiding someone. And if they told, the house would be burned, and she would be killed. And nobody wanted to die for someone else's sake.

Finally, with great difficulty I reached Yakushpol. All the men there had already been taken to the Lysa Mountain (in Berdychev), but the women and children were still alive. I stayed with them. About a week passed by. Then, one morning, I saw Germans about and policemen running around (and I didn't have a notice of residence registration). But a milkman lived across the street: people were carrying milk there. And, as I was small, I ran towards them, and stood with those people. I stayed there until all the Jewish families had been taken away and all murdered near a local plant.

And, again, I wandered on. And then, on the roads, you could meet either Jews or runaway prisoners. Because only these were without a place to live.

In one village a policeman caught me and took me to the Yakushpol prison. He brought me there and said that, finally, this would be over, and they would tear me in pieces. And I told him I didn't mean any harm, and asked why they would tear me in pieces. I also told him I was Ukrainian, not Jewish. Then he asked me for my passport. And I told him we didn't have passports in the orphanage, and it was bombed and everybody ran away, and there were many wandering like me. Than he told me to sit there and wait until they decided what to do with me. He put me in a cell, and left a policeman to watch over me. And he had a little reddish-haired dog with him. I thought they had gone to dig a grave for me, so I sat there and waited for my death. So I was crying and calling for my mum, asking her why she had left me to be tortured. I wished they would kill me but not torture me. People said they raped victims, took out their eyes if you got into their hands.

The policeman near me was drunk; he was sitting on the chair, and there was a little window in the cell. I looked at the window and the policeman was asleep and snoring. I wondered what to do. I could not leave because I was afraid of the dog barking. Yet, there is God above us all! When the policeman took me into the cell, I didn't hear the door locked, so I decided to give it a try. The door was open, and I saw the corridor. So I opened it quietly to make sure it didn't creak and went out. Now, I thought the dog would start barking and the policeman would wake up. But he kept snoring. I went out and the dog followed me. I saw a bucket in the corner; I took it in my hands and kept walking. The dog was following me, and the corridor was very long. I came out of the building and saw a policeman at the gate. I thought if he asked me, I would tell him I worked here. We looked at each other, I came by and the dog followed me. He didn't say anything to me, so I didn't either. Once I had passed between the houses, I heard shots and knew that they were after me. There was some sort of ravine behind the houses, so

I jumped down, and there was a river, so I crossed it and started to think where to go now, and was this the end of my life?

I wandered for some time again, until I got back to Chudnov. They caught me there and put me into prison. I told them I was from Zodovka; I could not talk about Kazatin any more. And they asked me how I got there, to which I said that I was originally from Zodovka, but then lived in an orphanage and was wandering around the town now begging for bread. I was wondering what they would do with me, and he [the policeman] pushed me to the fence and asked a big German to look after me. So he stood there, looking after me, and started to talk to me. I told him I didn't understand a word what he was saying to me. The fence was very high, covered at the top with barbed wire. Policemen were standing nearby but perhaps it was destined for me to survive. The German left for a minute (somebody called him), and I climbed the tree that was there, and got over the fence, and there was a ditch under the fence. I jumped into it, and there was some shattered glass so I cut myself, but I ran towards Dubishche, which was about two kilometres away from Chudnov. They were digging out potatoes and beetroots then, and people were going back from their vegetable lots. There I saw Nadya, my classmate. She was walking from the garden, carrying a jug, a shovel and something else.

She asked, 'Polinka, where have you come from?'

And I told her, 'Just walking … ' and I didn't see that I was covered in cuts.

I asked her if she could give me the shovel and the jug to carry. She lived near the road and we ran to her place. She asked me why I was so bruised. And I couldn't feel that I had bruised all of my head, arms and legs when I fell off that high fence.

So I told her, 'You know, Nadya, I was walking and a dog chased me, so I ran and fell down.'

Then I asked her where her parents were. She told me they had gone to a wedding. Thank God, I thought. She gave me some water to clean up, and then she asked if I wanted something to eat. 'No, Nadya,' I said, 'I don't want anything.'

It was getting dark when I saw her parents walking in. Her mother entered the house while her father stayed out somewhere. Her mother was somewhat drunk, like people after a wedding can be, and asked, 'Nadya, who is this girl?' And Nadya said, 'Mum, do you remember Polinka? We went to the same class together, and I also went to her home, and … '

'Oh my God, this is her! We were just walking along and the police stopped us and asked if we saw a girl like this. She must have run away from the prison!'

'Aunt Marusya, no. I didn't run away from anywhere. I was in one village, but night was falling, and I saw Nadya, and that is why I came to you.'

'No, child, go away, go wherever you want.'

It was night, and I didn't know where to go. And I knew they would catch me once I went out of the house. If she said they were looking for me that meant that at every crossroads the policemen would be standing and waiting for me. But on the very same day they said that some paratrooper girl had come down and they had missed her. Maybe they thought I was she. Who knows … ? But the fact was that patrols were everywhere, and she was throwing me out. I was begging her, 'Aunt Marusya, please, I will stay somewhere on the floor.'

But she would't agree, and turned me out.

So I left. She had a huge garden, and she took me beyond it. It was pitch black in the garden, nothing to be seen. So I sat down and started to cry. I was thinking where to go. Now if they caught me, they would torture me, rape me, stab me, execute me, gouge out my eyes – that was what people said they did. Where to go? Then I heard the doors closing, and she went in. I frequently went to see Nadya because we were friends. They had a dog called Belka [Squirrel], and she knew me. The dog was tied near the shed.

So I quietly came to the shed and opened it, and kept saying to the dog, 'Belchik, it's me, Belchik.'

And the dog didn't make a sound. I went inside; it was a hen house. I lay down quietly and began to cry.

About twenty minutes passed, or half an hour, when I heard the doors open. I thought they were coming to get me when I heard, 'Polinka, Polya, it's me, Nadya. Don't be scared, tell me where you are! I won't turn you in.'

'Nadya, please, don't send me out, I am here,' I said.

And she told me, 'I won't send you away. Mum has gone into the house, and they are in bed. I brought you a piece of cloth.'

It was already cold outside and I didn't have anything really. She brought me a piece of bread and a glass of milk. I told her I didn't want to eat but I asked her to give me the cloth to cover myself because I was bruised all over. And I promised her to leave at dawn. And I did so. Her name was Nadya Kosenko.

I was wandering this way for the whole year, sleeping in haystacks. In the second year I had almost no energy or strength. I was covered in wounds, and had lice; it was unimaginable. I already wanted to turn myself in to the Nazis so that they could kill me fast. But I was afraid they would torture me as people said. I wanted to poison myself.

I woke up one morning and saw people going to the market. I got in among them, and kept walking too. I thought that I would get into their hands sooner or later because the winter was approaching, with cold weather. Thus I reached the village of Bolotovka. It was getting towards the evening, so I decided to go to the village council, tell them I was from the Kazatin orphanage, and maybe they would give me some work. Many people were milling around the council, and I stood with them. It turned out they were taking people to work in Germany. I walked in. There was the headman of the village, an obese man of average height. People were sitting on benches. I greeted them. They greeted me back and asked who I was. I told them I had come from the Kazatin orphanage, which had been bombed, and that I had been alone, and no longer had the health or energy to keep going on. So I asked him [the headman] to let me work at least somewhere until they could check this. To which the head of the council responded that he didn't know where to take me because I was so young.

I said, 'Please take me, I can do anything.'

And he asked me to wait. So I sat down and began to wait when a woman came running in and crying because her only son was being taken to Germany.

She begged the head of the council to leave him alone, and he quietly told her, 'Take this girl. Clean her, give her food and clothes in a sack and we shall send her to Germany instead of your son.' She took me to her home and washed my hair and combed it. I asked her to cut my hair but she wouldn't. She gave me a shirt and a dress, and I washed all I had. In the morning, they shipped us out to Germany.

This was in 1942; it was cold, late autumn. They sent us to Auschwitz. First they put us on carts and took us to Berdychev, to the transit station, and from there we were taken to Germany in the cattle cars. I wanted to run away *en route*. It was extremely crowded in the cars. I was sitting in the corner and crying. Eventually they brought us into the Auschwitz camp.

Each morning we were taken to work guarded by soldiers with dogs. Everybody went – those who could walk, and those who couldn't. You couldn't stay in the camp – you wouldn't be left alive; they would take you to the crematorium immediately and incinerate you. I was not dressed. We received army-type blankets there. So, if the guard were good, he would allow me to go out covered in the blanket.

I worked at the cement factory. I was uploading sixty to eighty kilograms of cement on to wheelbarrows. A wheelbarrow was tall and I was very small. Sometimes I would throw and miss, and then a German would approach and whip me. I was frightened and worked the best I could. Once I fell ill and had wounds all over my body. I thought I would die. But they put me into a hospital, and I survived.

I spent three years in Auschwitz, from 1942 through to 1945. There were very many Jews there, and many camps within the system. We had *ost* in blue letters on our clothes, signifying that we were workers from the East. Those who were in the concentration camp had a star and striped clothes as well as a tattooed number on their arms. We didn't have that because we were considered to be a Ukrainian camp. Nobody knew I was Jewish. That's why I survived. I called myself Olga Ivanovna Sevruk. Why this name? I studied in school with a boy, whose name was Oleg Ivanovich Sevruk, so I decided to use his name so as not to forget or to say it wrong.

We were all swollen, exhausted, tortured and starved, and had to work in the factories. We used to come back in the evening and get only 350 grams of bread with straw in it. They tortured us. They would come into the barracks and if something seemed to be wrong they would beat us, take us out into the frost, and pour cold water over us.

I cannot tell you about everything that I had to go through. These were the three most difficult years. I only survived because I was very young: I was only fourteen years old. Only because of my young age could I endure all the torture and all the grief.

Yes, there were very many Jews there, but they were all kept in another concentration camp. We worked together with them but we were not allowed to speak. Sometimes they would say a word in German, but at first we didn't understand a single word in German. They were tortured even worse. Anybody who became ill would be taken immediately to the crematorium. They were beaten on the way to work and on the way from work. Germans let the dogs out to tear them in pieces. And when taken to the crematorium, they were not told why, but instead they were told they were being taken to have a shower. They would get a piece of soap and be put into a room, then locked in, and the gas would be siphoned in. Here, die … And then they used special carts to pick up the bodies and put them into the ovens. In the morning we used to go out to work and smell the burning, as if hair was burning or something was being tarred. That was how the human flesh smelled.

There was a lot of suffering. For instance, I was in the eleventh barrack, and it had a hundred or more people; nobody knew for sure since nobody ever counted. There were three-tiered bunks. So I used to come back from work barely alive and asked people to lift me to my bunk, because if you stayed on the floor for a while, they would burn you. It was a very difficult life.

We were liberated. When they tried to find out who we were and where from, whether voluntarily or forced, I told them my story and that I was Jewish. They wondered how I managed to survive. Our army questioned us.

When we were leaving Auschwitz, we received passports including surname, name and date of birth. My passport had the name I gave: Olga Ivanovna Sevruk.

When we came back to Chudnov, I went to the militia, or whatever it was called then … I told them my story and I received a new document issued in my real name. I didn't think then that I had to keep the original passport issued in Auschwitz. Children were playing with it and took it somewhere. This was a common occurence with many, not only with me.

We went back home in cattle cars; it took two or three weeks. Somebody would leave at each of the stops. Some people got off the train in Zhitomir, some in Berdychev, some in Novgorod, because people had came from all over the place. Thus I came home too. But I didn't have anybody left. I was lonely and miserable. What did I have to do? A couple named Fey took me to live with them. They are gone already. I stayed with them for about a month, and then I went to work as a waitress in a café. I didn't have any education, nor had I parents. I had to earn my daily bread, pay for a place to live … that's how I lived – it was a lot of grief. Then, when I was eighteen years old, I got married.

What did I know? I never had a childhood or adolescent years, I had nothing. It has been over fifty years now, but the horror I had to live through is still in front of my eyes – the way they took us to be killed, the way police were killing people and burying them alive … In Chudnov, there is a well in the park. There, in that well, little babies lay who were thrown there alive and then chlorine was poured down on to them while they were still alive.

There were fourteen pits in the park. When I lived in Chudnov, there was not a single day that I wouldn't be there. My feet would take me there. I know where the third grave was; and there my mum is. I was shown. There are fourteen pits there. No matter that they have a stadium now at that place, and a few buildings, I still know the place of every single grave. There are fourteen graves. I couldn't leave because my eyes saw it, how earth moved above the people who were still alive … I told my children all about this, and I took them there, to the park and showed the graves to them. They saw it, and know it all, but what's the use? This horror is beyond their imagination. They say, 'Mum, could such brute violence ever be possible?'

I remember when they took us to the pit, there was a woman named Genya Blyudaya. She was a teacher, and a neighbour of ours. She was blonde, very beautiful and tall. Her brother, who had a limp, and her parents, were already dead and already lay in the pit, and then Bryukhanov, the policeman, went up to her, and wanted to shoot her.

But a German went up to her, pushed him away, and shouted to her, '*Shön Mädchen, hey, zu Hause* [Hey, pretty girl, go home].' But she stood there with her hair let down, and screaming as if she had gone insane: 'Kill me, bandit, kill me faster.'

And this German couldn't do anything, and Bryukhanov shot her twice. And she fell down there where her parents where.

Then the Germans went to get another group of people – those who were still alive or were only wounded tried to crawl out of the graves. There was a little girl, aged two or three, I don't remember well now, I still see her before my eyes: she climbed out of the grave and she was walking in circles as if lost around the grave. One of the policemen jumped up to her, and this bandit kicked her with his foot so badly that he tore her belly apart … and then he pushed her down with his foot as if she were a dead animal. I also remember how I saw a boy aged eight or nine, sitting on a tree. A policeman noticed him too; he was standing on top of a lorry, behind us, and he shot him like a bird, so the boy fell like a stone down to the ground. And the policeman threw him into the pit that was already full of bodies. This was a Jewish boy, who also perhaps climbed out of the grave, and wanted to sit on the tree until everybody left.

We had a neighbour named Leya. She was very young, twenty years old. She had recently got married, and her husband had to leave to the front soon afterwards. She was pregnant, and was expecting a baby very soon. A policeman started kicking her with his foot in her stomach, and she began going into labour. And one policeman said to another, 'Go see how this Jew-girl will give birth now to a Jew-baby!' They waited till the baby was born, and threw her like a dog on to a cart with her baby. She cried and called her mum, and he took her alive, and threw her into the pit with her newborn child.

We couldn't believe that those same people with whom we had been friends, having shared food and everything, could be that violent and ruthless. The policemen were the worst. When those young bandits, policemen, who sat at the same desk in school with us, were killing people, a German who was there couldn't even look. Bryukhanov, the policeman I mentioned, was killed later by Germans themselves, who tied him with his legs to two birch trees and tore him apart for all his violence and atrocities. And there were thousands of people like him. And then they moved to America and Canada. And they live now, and come over here, important people, with a lot of money.

47. I escaped from Babi Yar[1]

Ida Pinkert

It is known that, on Monday 29 September 1941, on *Yom Kippur*, the German killers murdered 70,000 Jews from the city of Kiev and 30,000 Jews from all over Kiev oblast. In Babi Yar, there were 10,000 elderly people and women and 2,000 babies who were thrown into the deep ravine alive.

I am one of those few who were able to survive, having escaped death by a miracle. In Israel, I am the only one who managed to escape from Babi Yar. I am one of those who can remember that horror. I'm a living voice of the tortured victims of the Nazi executioners. I cannot forget or forgive all the suffering and pain inflicted on people, by the Nazi murderers and their collaborators, just because they were Jewish.

Until now, I've been haunted by the horrible blood-curdling screams of the victims of Babi Yar, the words of *Shma, Yisrael*, day and night. I cannot laugh, carefree, when in front of my children and grandchildren. Right before my eyes, my six-year-old child and my sixty-nine-year-old mother were thrown into the ravine alive. I cannot feel myself as fully as any other human. I am a shadow. I still cannot believe that I am alive or was saved.

Babi Yar was the first experiment in this kind of mass murder of Jews. Those who had not managed to get evacuated fell into the hands of the Nazis.

In the first days of the occupation, the Nazis began to abuse and torture any Jew that they met in the street.

I was shocked when they bombed the city. When I heard that the Germans were killing Jews, I decided to return to Kiev, to save my child and mother. I hardly reached Kiev. Near the Dnieper, I met a young Russian nurse who had escaped from the surrounded area. At a distant farmstead, I got some peasant clothes, having left my uniform behind.

I noticed the SS were everywhere around the pontoon bridge, and I saw arrested people who were carrying boards. Together with the nurse, we picked up the boards and joined the crowd of the arrested.

I was walking along the Podol, trying to get home. I saw the notices on walls, in Russian and Ukrainian, that said:

All Jews of Kiev and the areas around Kiev have to report on Monday 29 September at 7 o'clock in the morning, to Dorogozhitskaya Street, near the Jewish cemetery. They have to bring warm clothes, valuable things, and money with them. Those who won't come will be executed. Those who hide Jews will be executed as well.

On one of the trams I saw a poster on which a Jew with a long hooked nose was eating fish, and a man was sitting nearby begging for money. And the poster read, 'Jews eat at your expense'.

Instead of going home, I returned to Babi Yar, hoping to see my mother and my child among the Jews there. That how naïve I was. Not far from Babi Yar I saw a few Jews with shovels, escorted by Germans. Their faces were covered in blood. Behind my back somebody said that the Jews were being taken to dig their own graves (pits). I was going in the direction where all Jews were being taken. SS were everywhere. On one side of the ravine, an orchestra was playing, and on the other there was the sound of shooting. Old people, women and small children were thrown into the ravine alive. The *Aktion* lasted for three days. I arrived on the third day, 2 October. The earth trembled as if breathing. And the Germans kept bringing in more victims. Some people cried '*Shma, Yisrael*', some cried … And the Germans kept shooting.

It was a true hell. It began to get dark. I pretended to be dead and lay at the edge of the pit. The patrols were everywhere. At night I decided to run away. I crawled like a dog, trying to get around the patrol. I found myself on a little street and went through backyards to the Vladimirskaya Hill [*gorka*]. I wandered around the whole night. It was impossible to go across Kreshchatik since the street was all in rubble and ruins. I found a tap with running water and started to wash the blood and clay off my face and clothes.

On 17 November I suddenly reached the village of Megeya, near Pervomaisk, Odessa oblast. There, a month later, gallows were set up to hang all suspicious – looking people, and I was among them. I called myself Lydia Vladimirovna Tishchenko, an imagined name. Using this name I collaborated with partisans. The local partisans, headed by Masenko, helped me get out of this hell, and saved me.

At night the local population buried the bodies of the killed. By then my heart must have been made of iron since I managed to get out of this hell and go through so much pain, seeing death every-where. In the town of Uman the Jews were killed with the help of a special mobile gas chamber. I heard this along the way from a young man who was saved by a miracle just like I was.

When the Germans sensed their defeat, they forced all prisoners in Kiev to dig out the graves, pulling out the bodies of the killed and tortured Jews in Babi Yar, burn them, and spread their ashes over the river. But they didn't manage to dig them all out. The prisoners refused to do this; many broke off their chains and jumped over the fence with its high-voltage electric wire.

In 1961 (I don't remember the exact date), the dam was broken. Water flooded through Babi Yar. It washed off the earth, and skulls and bones floated to the top. The bones were knocking on the win-dows of the houses. The local population said this was the revenge of Babi Yar.

NOTE

1. Translated from Yiddish by H. A. Berman. This originally appeared in the Jewish newspaper *Renewal-91*, 1997, issue 9.

48. I witnessed it all

Ichel Pogranichny (b. 1931)

I have lived all my life in Shargorod. I happened to go through very difficult times in the ghetto (1941–44). Although at that time I was only a child, I cannot erase from my memory all that I witnessed and lived through.

We lived in the ghetto, in a house shared by twenty people. We also had refugees from Romania living with us. Almost everybody died from the typhus that was taking the lives of many then. It was cold and people were hungry. I saw how the dead were taken out of the houses. thirty or forty bodies were put on the carts and taken away. Arms and legs were hanging out. It was scary and painful to see all this. People were buried in one big grave. I can still hear the screams of people and the shots.

We were allowed to be outside only during designated hours, but even then we were afraid to be seen. I remember the kitchen of the SS killing squad located in a small park near our house. I was a child, and wanted to go outside badly. A German, who saw me, called me and told me to wash his boots. But he obviously didn't like my job and he began to beat me. I still remember his fists.

I saw their tortures of our neighbours and their children. I saw how severely the Germans beat a girl, who died two weeks later. Many people died from cold and starvation.

Everybody was exhausted and hunger forced people to steal. One boy ran to the mill to beg for some flour, he got in through the window. A German noticed him, shot and killed him – and I witnessed this too.

Frequently we would hide at the home of the Samborskiye family, our Ukrainian friends (they are gone now). They gave us whatever food they had and saved us.

The headquarters of the Romanian Kommandant were nearby. He issued orders to force us to work, and if we didn't obey, twenty-five lashes were given to everyone. I once got them too.

These are my brief recollections.

49. We endured everything[1]

Shelya Polishchuk (b. 1931)

The time has come in my life when I have suddenly found out that events considered by my children as distant history are in fact pages of my own life.

I was born in Zvenigorodka, and lived there during the first three years of my life. Later, I lived in Kiev. Before the war, there were four of us (my parents, a housekeeper, and me), and we lived at 32 Ostrovsky Street, in flat no. 2, in Kiev, Solomenka. My childhood was carefree, happy and joyous.

In the very first days of the war, my father left to join the people's guard; there he became ill, and returned home. After getting well, he went to the military commission and joined the active army.

My mother, who was a doctor, had worked in the Kalinin hospital until Kiev was surrendered to the Nazis. Her department was turned into the military hospital for civilians. Kiev was surrendered and, on 19 September, the Germans entered the city.

A day later Mum went to the hospital, and the Germans were already everywhere there. One of her former colleagues, a nurse, threw my mum out of the hospital. A couple of days later we heard terrible noise and screams outside, in the street. Our housekeeper ran in and said that a lorry was on the street and they had taken all the Jews. And the screams were of a blind Jewish man who lived with many children in house no. 10. Mum grabbed me by the hand, and we ran out of our flat and went upstairs, to flat no. 5. But then a woman came, and pushed us out, because she was afraid. Another neighbour, in flat no. 6, then opened her door and told us to come in. She had an open sewing machine in her room, and she sat my mum down to sew something, and I stood nearby. Then Varvara Gavrilovna Stepanovich (the woman's name) faced the window and began to pray. The entrance door was slightly open. Then it flew wide open, and two Germans came in.

The officer asked, 'Are there any *Judeh*?'

And she said, 'No.'

He looked under the bed, and seeing no *'Judeh'*, left the flat together with the soldier. The lorry left our house, turned into an alley and stopped at the house across the street. I looked out of the window. Germans entered the yard, and brought out an old Jewish couple. The old man helped his wife climb into the lorry. Somehow I remember that well.

At that moment, all our neighbours went outside into the yard and they were wondering why we had not been taken away yet. The husband of Stepanovich was outside in the yard too, and he came back into the house and said that we had to leave now; go somewhere.

In the yard, he told our neighbours that we would leave now (Mum and I), and nobody would say a word. Alexander Pavlovich walked us to the end of the block on our street.

Starting from this day, my mum fully realized what it meant that we were Jewish. We were afraid of being home during the day. We wanted to go somewhere and be with some people. We lived with the family of Doctor Grigory Trofimovich Buvailik, and with the family of Mum's patient, Evdokiya Grigoryevna Mikhailova.

It was then when we saw an order according to which we had to report on 29 September, by eight o'clock in the morning, to the corner of Melnikov and Degtyarevskaya Streets. Mum was asking herself and others the question, 'Where and why are they gathering us together? Is there a railway?'

That day arrived. The weather was good. We didn't hurry to arrive on time by 8 a.m. We put our best clothes on, took two suitcases and went there. Two of our neighbours and our housekeeper went with us. We went along Vozdukhoflotskoye highway, and then Kosior Street. There were a few people in these streets but when we got into Artem Street, there were many people there.

Mum sent home those who came to see us off; we met the doctors she knew. Nobody was in a hurry to go forward, people walked forward, then back, and everybody was asking, 'What is happening?'

It was scary when empty carts started to come out of the cemetery. People were rushing towards the drivers and kept asking what was happening behind the gates of the cemetery. The drivers whipped their horses with all their might, as well as the people who were asking the questions. Mum felt that something terrible was going on. And we didn't go forward.

Mum met a couple of young doctors she knew; he was Ukrainian and she was Jewish. They got married before the war. They didn't know what to do; he went somewhere, and came back with the news that the doctors were to stay, but one had to report to the Kommandant's office. We believed that and went back. At

1 Melnikov Street, there lived nurses whom Mum knew – Polina, Maria and Leonida Levchuk. We left our things at their place and went to the Kommandant's office.

I remember how we were walking downhill, and the street was empty. Germans on bicycles were riding towards us; they carried automated guns, were drunk and whistled some tunes. Mum told me they were going to kill people. This was around 2 p.m. The square in front of the Kommandant's office was filled with the Ukrainians and Russians who had been called there on the very same day, too. It was impossible to get through. Mum walked up to a German patrol soldier and asked him whether Jewish doctors were to stay in Kiev. The answer was absolutely negative, and we went back.

Artem and Melnikov Streets were empty by now. Silence fell everywhere and we could hear machine-guns shooting. We came back to the Levchuk sisters, and they started to convince us not to stay there. We took our suitcases and umbrellas and went further along Melnikov Street towards the cemetery.

Some young men started shouting at us from an alley, 'Give us your cases and umbrellas; they will kill you anyway.'

We kept silent and walked on. Far ahead we noticed a family stopped by a patrol and then the soldiers escorted them somewhere, but without the things they had carried. We came up to the patrol, two Germans – one was old, and the other young – and immediately we were surrounded by a group of young men.

The German asked, '*Judeh?*'

To which Mum replied, 'No.'

Then the Germans broke up the crowd that had expected to peruse our things and clothes. The soldiers asked why we had come here and Mum, who spoke fluent German, told them that she was Ukrainian, and her husband was Jewish, and she didn't know what to do with her child. They didn't demand any papers then, and said that there would be a separate order regarding children from inter-faith marriages. 'And now,' they said, 'go home, the curfew begins soon.'

We walked back home fast and again we stopped with the Levchuk sisters. They were happy to see us and let us spend the night with them. We couldn't stay with them for long because they were sharing their flat with other people. A day later we decided to go home. When home, Mum started telling people that she was returned because she was Ukrainian, and only my dad was Jewish. Of course the neighbours who lived in our house knew well this was not true but kept silent at that time.

Our neighbour, A. S. Dovbysh, reached an agreement with the house manager who changed – for money– the record of my mum's nationality in his register. I. G. Mikhailova was looking for a draughtsman who could change this record of nationality in her passport. We were afraid of being at home, so we hung around for whole days in other places. We sat for hours at the Solomenskoye cemetery, and went to stay with G. T. Buvailik. He kept warning us that we had to leave Kiev as soon as possible until police or local authorities became effective in the city. We were hiding in the yard of the private house owned by Mikhailova. When we were there she used to send her twelve-year-old daughter to stand at the gates to watch if somebody was coming our way. Sometimes, she would send her to our home to see what was going on there.

This lasted for about ten or eleven days. A neighbour from flat no. 1 was expressing his indignation, asking why we were still there to our housekeeper, who still lived with us.

On one of the days when we went back home, a plain-clothes policeman was waiting for us. He said he had come to arrest us and take us to 15 Korolenko Street to investigate our identities. He said they had received information that Mum was not Ukrainian, as she claimed to be. And he took us to an investigator named Ishamovsky. He was a young, tall and handsome man who spoke very good Ukrainian. Mum said he was from the Western Ukraine. My mum persevered in convincing him that she was Ukrainian and he started to doubt the report. He let us go but ordered us to come back the following day, saying that if we failed to do so, our friends would be arrested.

While we were absent, everything except furniture – even our photographs – was taken out from our flat. The following day we returned to the investigator. But this time he had our family album on his desk. Mum showed him 'Russian' faces and told him these were her relatives, and that the 'Jewish' faces were those of Dad's family. He asked Mum many questions about religion and asked me whether my parents had spoken Yiddish.

Of course I answered no.

The investigator then asked whether they had taken me to church, and I said, 'Yes.'

Mum asked him to question witnesses who had known her for many years. The following day he called in Mum's witnesses. Doctor G. T. Buvailik signed a testimony that he had known Doctor Maria Isaakovna Konstantinovskaya since the early 1930s as a Ukrainian, that he had met her sister and had no doubts about it. Our neighbour, Anastasia Stepanovna Dovbysh, witnessed that she had seen my mum's mother and she was definitely Ukrainian. E. G. Mikhailova, Mum's patient, signed this too. Our housekeeper Teresa who had lived with us for eight years, went to the investigator too. After talking to her, the investigator said that our housekeeper said Mum was Jewish, to which Mum replied, 'Do you know any housekeeper who would like her mistress of the house?'

On the fifth or sixth day the investigator didn't let us in his office, and we had to wait in the corridor. Mum cried bitterly; he walked a couple of times past us and then he said to wait until lunch. Mum said there was a hope. When everybody left for lunch he came up to us and said, 'Why do you keep coming here? I don't believe you. And I don't have time to investigate you. Go away, I won't be looking for you for two days. Go east.'

Mum said, 'You have all my things and all my documents.'

He thought then and said that we would receive our documents back at the registration office, but he couldn't get our things back – it was connected with the storage. And he signed the release form for the registration office.

When leaving, my mum said, 'Thank you, you don't believe me but you're wrong and we shall go west, to my mother.'

Mum didn't go back home. I stopped by and told Teresa we were leaving. We took some things that we kept at the Dovbysh flat, then we went to Mikhailova. She gave us something for the road too, and most importantly she gave us a letter to her mother in the town of Skvira so that she would welcome us.

We spent the night with my mum's friend, a doctor who lived in Gogolevskaya Street. At dawn her fourteen-year-old boy took us out beyond Stalinka, to the road that led towards Belaya Tserkov. We were fortunate, seeing a cart on the way, and we left the city limits fast.

And then we went by foot. We asked to spend the night at some poor village house.

Later, Mum said this was only the beginning. We didn't stay in Skvira for long. Mikhailova's mother could not comprehend why we had come to her. Next morning, Mum went to the local health administration and tried to get a job there. Unfortunately we met a person we knew and she reported us to the police. What could we do next? We fled.

We came to old Grandma Mikhailova. We stopped near the gate and saw policemen following us and standing at the end of the street. Mum ran into the house, grabbed our bag, and across the vegetable lots we came out to another street. Nature was helping us: it got dark and heavy snow started to fall. We entered some house to hide from the snow, and then asked the people there if we could spend the night. In the morning we went on. Where did we go? Mum decided to go towards Boguslav. Nobody as yet had checked our documents and we tried to stay away from the centres of the villages.

Once, on our way from one village to another, we met a woman. Mum asked her how far a certain village was. And suddenly they recognized each other. She was a doctor from Kiev, a little younger than my mum, and she was originally from Zvenigorodka, just like Mum. Her name was Anna. She was in the army, had served in a hospital, and was then taken a prisoner. Later, the women were released and nobody asked about their nationality. She already knew that she could not go to Kiev. Her family, her husband and son, had managed to get evacuated. Now we went along together, and it was more difficult because Anna looked very Jewish. She covered her face, spoke in whispers and was dressed in an old coat that she had traded for her uniform coat.

We went towards Boguslav, across Mironovka, to the village of Khokhitva. Our Kiev neighbours' grandma lived there. Before the war their father had been drafted, and a mother with a girl who was my age, left with their grandma, had been sent to this village. These were trustworthy people and that was why we went to their house and stayed there for three days. We cleaned up, had something to eat, but then had to leave. The grandma tried to ensure that nobody saw strangers in her house. She couldn't give us any advice, so she called in Uncle Sergey, her relative, to see what he would suggest. He told us we had to go to the village of Steblyovo: Jews were living there and maybe they would take us to live with them. Next morning he walked us far beyond the village.

Winter was approaching, and snow was everywhere. By evening we reached Steblyovo, and found the house where all the Jews were living together. These were poor, miserable and scared people. They were afraid of letting us in even for one night, but then they did. They told us that in Zvenigorodka had its own ghetto. In the morning we left for Zvenigorodka. There, we found out where the ghetto was and entered the first house we saw. The Gutnik family lived there.

The Zvenigorodka ghetto was not fenced. All Jews had been resettled in Proletarskaya Street and a few smaller streets that crossed it. All adults had to wear white armbands with six-pointed stars on them. The ghetto had its own council headed by Lazurik, the Kommandant. We stayed with the Gutnik family. Anna went to her relatives, and we had no one to go to.

We found out that a hundred Jews had been killed here, mostly men. Our grandma with her daughter (my aunt) and her Ukrainian son-in-law were killed too. Some Jews were murdered right in front of their houses, and their families saw it. There was no end to the torture, but nevertheless the majority was still alive. We had to ask Lazurik to be admitted to the ghetto, and Mum gave her watch to pay for this.

Lisa Prober, a dentist, welcomed us. There were two dentists in Zvenigorodka, Prober and Granovskaya; both were Jewish. That is why they were allowed to see patients in their homes. Even Germans came to Granovskaya. The winters were very severe that year and very cold, there was nothing to burn in stoves for heat, and we had nothing at all except the clothes we wore.

Many were getting ill in the ghetto. They were not allowed to go to the city clinic and we organized our own medical 'mobile clinic' where Mum saw her patients. It was hard to treat people with abscesses after a battering because there was no medication, or sterile materials such as bandages, gauze, cotton … We were going from house to house asking for old white sheets. We would cut them up into bandages, then boil and iron them.

Night raids by the police were terrorizing the ghetto residents. They would storm Jewish houses, rob and beat people.

One morning they called my mum to one family. It was a very poor family, and they had been the victims of a police raid the night before. A thin grey braid of hair was lying on the table, and the old woman had been battered and was in a very grave condition. During the night a policeman named Pritula (he was the most ruthless policeman) had stormed their house. There was nothing for him to take so he tore the hair off the old woman's head and beat her up badly.

Policemen didn't storm the dentist's flat because they knew that the local government officials came to be treated by her.

One woman in the ghetto fell ill with typhus, and this was a closely guarded secret. She lived alone, people gave her food through the window, and she died soon afterwards. People buried her quietly so that nobody would know. In spring, an old man named Chait died, and he was buried according to all Jewish funerary rituals.

Mum said that a holy man had died since he died of natural causes. At his funeral, my mum cried so bitterly and asked God about our salvation, and God heard her. In spring we moved into a separate room, in the house of the Dimarsky family.

One day old man Dimarsky developed hernia strangulation and he needed urgent surgery. The Jews from the ghetto were not admitted into the hospital so Mum decided to operate him at home. Surgeon Mamonov from the hospital gave her a set of surgical instruments. We prepared a room, washed a dining room table, and in the evening under the light of a kerosene lamp, Mum performed the surgery. By the end of the surgery, the surgeon secretly came across the backyards to help Mum. The surgery went fine, and the old man recovered.

Every day they would take teenage girls from the ghetto to the town to different jobs. And in early May a group of youngsters was sent to the village of Nemorozh to build a road.

On the night of 14/15 July Mum heard some noise and screams

outside, and pounding on neighbouring doors. She woke me up fast, we put on everything we had (I had a fur coat, and Mum had a fur jacket), and everything else we tied up into a little bundle. Somehow Mum hid the documents in the room, in her handbag.

And now they knocked on our door too. There was no way to escape. Germans, with dogs and policemen, were already guarding a column of people outside. We were pushed into this column. We were dressed; as for other people they varied: some wore nightgowns, some were dressed and some had no shoes on. People were taken out of their beds. Screams and laments sounded everywhere – adults and children cried, dogs barked, and policemen kept beating people. There was an eighty-year-old woman in a white gown and with long grey hair covered with blood who had a completely mad face and couldn't understand what was going on. The column was slowly marched along the street, which was filling up with more residents of the ghetto.

We were all moved into the yard of the Zvenigorodka prison. Mum kept saying, 'Is it all over now?'

That very same day Germans and police came to the yard and started putting us into columns two or three abreast. Policemen hurried people and whipped them. One elderly policeman raised his whip against Mum, and she caught his hand, and said, 'Don't you dare!'

He said, 'I haven't hit anyone yet, but I'm forced to.'

The column was sorted; young women, girls and boys were moved to one side of it. Children were pulled out of their mothers' arms, and mothers screamed. And the Nazis, with Koch, the Kommandant, stood and watched all this. Finally our turn came, and they wanted to pull me off my mum, pulling her away. Mum held my tight and came up to Koch. 'Please allow me to take my daughter with me, the girl is big enough and she will work, I'm a doctor,' she said in German looking straight into his eyes. 'You have a mother, too.'

And he said, 'You can take her.'

Thus, we both ended up in the column sent to work. I was the smallest and Mum said I had to tiptoe. The gates were open, and they marched us to the village of Nemorozh where the camp was.

During the march, the laments and cries were endless. Mum was trying to calm down one woman whose infant child had been taken away. Her name was Manya. (This woman survived all the horror, and came out of it alive. Her husband returned from the war. In 1961 we met with her in Zvenigorodka at the dedication of a memorial. She remembered my mum and myself well. She came together with her son and grandson and told her son that we saw with our own eyes how her month-old baby girl was taken away from her.)

Finally we were in the camp. It was located at the cattle farm. The yard was surrounded by a wooden fence. The prisoners worked on the construction of the motorway between Zvenigorodka and Lysenka, sleeping at night in the pigsty on straw mats. Anna got into the camp together with us; later she was transferred to another camp, and she died. There were many pretty and talented young girls in the camp, school and college students. Many of them sang well and even wrote a song in German. Together with adults, using a shovel, I worked on the construction of the road.

Mum worked as a doctor in the camp. The residents of the village learned that there was a doctor from Kiev in the camp. Sometimes in the evening they would come up to the policemen who guarded the camp and would ask for the doctor to be sent to a patient in the village, paying with home-brewed alcohol. Mum would always bring me back some food because they were only giving us some skilly.

Yozef Wassen, a German construction foreman, was supervising our work. He was an elderly man, and treated us pretty well. Half of the prisoners worked at one end of the village, while the other half worked at the other end. Some prisoners were transferred to another camp, in the village of Smelchintsy. The teams of policemen on guard would change every ten days. One team was relatively tolerable, while the other abused us to the utmost limits: they raped, beat and just tortured us.

People got ill in the camp. As a doctor, my mum could relieve one or two persons from work for a day or two. People were accounted for when going to work. A teenager boy got ill with typhoid (Mum diagnosed it), and they put him in an attic, in another building, in the stable. Nobody knew what was wrong with him, and even the police didn't know that an ill prisoner was staying there. People changed order so that the police wouldn't notice his absence. Eventually the boy got well (I don't remember his name now).

Some time in the middle of October we were resettled into the school building. We were so happy. A new German master was sent in, also a pretty decent, elderly man.

And then, on 2 November, rumours started circulating that the camp would be liquidated. On that day, from early morning, Mum was all filled with worry and anxiety (she had had a bad dream the night before). The morning was cold. I was continuously working with the group on the road towards Zvenigorodka. We came back into the camp for lunch and then returned back to work. But that day we were taken towards Lysenka. Mum asked a policeman to let me stay off work, and she took me to the distant house of a woman, to stay there and get warm (and when everybody was coming back, I was to come out and join the column of people returning to the camp). Mum returned to the camp. And suddenly she heard a lorry pull in and everybody who was in the camp (a cook, a cleaner and a water-carrier) was called to get in.

Mum realized what was happening. The police entered the school, and she hid behind the door, and when it became possible, she ran out and across the vegetable lots and reached the house I was in. She took me and we ran away, towards the river and away from the road, first we went into one house, then into another. A young woman lived there in the latter and Mum had treated her children. She hid us in the hallway and covered us with corn weeds. It turned out we were not alone there. A girl named Buzya Sigalova was already hiding there; she had fled straight from the work on the road once she saw the many police and Germans.

The woman was certainly afraid of keeping us in her house. She locked us in, and went into the village and when she returned she told us that many had escaped the killings and now they would be searching houses. We had to wait until darkness. Buzya started to ask my mum to please take her with us because she would die alone. Buzya had a typical Jewish face. Mum told her, 'We shall stay together.'

When it was completely dark, an elderly neighbour came. He had lost one leg, and he said his name was Sergey. He told us that we had to leave immediately. It was dangerous to walk on the road. If we went one way, there was a forest spread over many kilometres and on the other side there was a bridge that had a police patrol on it. But there was a way out – to swim across the river, or there was also a place where one could cross it on foot. And he showed us where this was. It was November and it was frosty. Buzya took off her clothes first, tied her clothes into a knot and started walking carrying it above her head. The water reached a little higher than her chest. She crossed the river. The local peasant knew well where that river could be crossed on foot. Mum undressed too, and so did I; then I took our knot of clothes in my hands and Mum put me up on her shoulders and we went into the river. The water reached Mum's throat. Thus, quietly, we crossed the river to the other side. The night was dark and cold. We quietly left the village, although dogs barked in the yards. We saw a pit outside the village and got into it. When dawn came, we found out where we were and went towards Zvenigorodka where Buzya knew some people who could give her something warm to wear, or some money. We had our coats with us all of the time.

Buzya's friends were scared and didn't let us into the house and advised us to hide in the pit where people were digging for clay. Only when it got dark did they bring us some food; a warm shawl, pants and more food were brought only the following evening. Thus we spent two nights in that pit. In the morning a woman came to get clay, together with her boy; she saw us but didn't turn us in.

Mum decided that from now on we had to tell everybody we were Russian. From then on Buzya would be called Olga (she used that name for the rest of her life; after the war she lived in Leningrad and then immigrated to Israel), and I would be called Zhenya.

And we went towards Uman. In the early 1930s, my mum used to work there and she had good friends there. We spent a few days in the house of a nurse named Polina. Mum asked her to get some documents for us. Polina's sister-in-law lived together with her; she had come from Chuguev in Kharkov oblast. She had many different papers and documents. One of these fitted us perfectly; we just changed a name a little, turning Grunevich into Prunevich. From now on my mum was Yekaterina Alexeyevna Prunevich, with two children, Olya and Zhenya. The legend was that our father, Nikolay Ivanovich, was a doctor who served in Chuguev, and we had come there when the war began. The older daughter looked like her father, and the younger like her mother. Now, there was much hunger and destruction in Chuguev, so we were going to move on anywhere, to find a job.

In Uman we received some clothes, got some food and were taken out into the road. And we went towards Vinnitsa. We covered sixteen kilometres during one day, and then asked to stay overnight in a poor house at the edge of the village of Oradovka.

It was cold in the evening but there was no snow, but in the morning it was white everywhere. The snow had fallen heavily overnight. The old woman advised us to go to the nearest village, Yagubets, only three kilometres away. There were no Germans there, or police, and the head of the village was a good man. There a *sovkhoz* had been preserved where we could work and, most important, the head of the village would accept strangers. Only by midday were we able to leave that old woman, and we went towards Yagubets. Days were short and we arrived there by the end of the day and immediately saw a well-off house, whose owner was standing by the gate. Mum asked them to let us in for the night. They put us to sleep on the top of the stove and told us to ask the head of the village to accept us into it. The following day Mum took me, leaving Olga in the house, and we went to the head.

The head of the village of Yagubets was indeed a very good man. He looked at my mum and me and said that now he wouldn't be checking our documents, but we had to go to the *sovkhoz* director so that he would hire Mum and then he would enter us into his registers too. We were walking towards the office of the *sovkhoz*, and saw a woman near the office who was a little older than my mum, and she started to ask who we were and where we were from. When she heard Russian speech and learned we were from Moscow (that was what we were telling people), she invited us into her house. She liked seeing and communicating with educated people.

It turned out that her daughter was working as a secretary in the *sovkhoz* office. She came home for lunch, and Mum asked her to make arrangements with the director. The paper that we had was enough to get Mum to work. This was the Shelestovsky family (we have stayed in touch with them throughout all the years, till now).

We rented a room from one old woman. Mum went to work, and Olya and I stayed at home. We told all those who were too curious that we had known the Shelestovskys' since before the war when they had lived near Moscow, and that was why we had come here. We were very close with that family but we never disclosed who we really were. They, of course, were suspicious, especially when they saw our Olga. Mum kept saying that Olga looked just like her father. In spring, Mum was very ill with pneumonia, and she even had to be put into the hospital in a village nearby.

One day, in summer, when we were walking home from the field, we saw a woman who was looking for Marina, her relative. And suddenly she told my mum, 'Maria Isaakovna, I know you.'

And Mum told her that she was mistaken.

Yet the woman persisted, 'No, I am not mistaken, I am a nurse, and I worked with you in Ladyzhenka, and I have assisted you many times during surgeries, I remember your face, your hands. This is your daughter, and I knew your husband.'

And Mum kept saying she was mistaken. We turned and walked away. Yet we didn't know what to do next. If we ran away – then where? We stopped by at the Shelestovskys', and Mum told them that a relative had come to stay with Marina, that she had seen them and she said that she knew them. Raissa, the Shelestovskys' daughter, calmed us down and promised that in the evening she would go to Marina and find out who the woman was. And she went there under the pretence of borrowing eggs, and decided to talk with the guest, 'So, it was you who picked on Katerina saying that you know her?'

And the woman kept saying, 'I am not saying she is Jewish, I only know that she is a doctor and I know her well.'

Raissa then said, 'You have come, and you will leave, and go with God, and I know her well too, from Moscow.'

She left and we stayed in Yagubets.

At that time we lived in an old bathhouse, in the room where the boilers stood, away from the village, near the pond. Winter was approaching quickly. Although our village was away from the Uman-Vinnitsa road, cars with Germans and carts with our people (from Novorossiysk) and Cossacks (from the Don) retreating with the Germans, started to go frequently across our village. All these people were very well dressed, they had loaded carts, with extra horses, complete families. So, these people would stay for a couple of days in the village and they were put up in free rooms in the bath-house. On one night, partisans came in, riding horses. Shooting and noise started, they came towards the bathhouse, and started taking something away from the Cossacks and shouted, 'Lie face down!'

We were also very scared; then Mum opened the door herself. One of the partisans said, 'Don't touch these people!'

After that experience we were resettled into a walk-through room, in a stable, near the road.

In another room, which was not walk-through, two sisters lived. They were strangers in this village, worked in the *sovkhoz*, and their names were Lena and Olya Ostrovsky. Mum told me quietly that they were Jewish (after liberation we knew it was really so). Then the rumours reached us that Kiev had already been liberated. Prisoners of war who worked for the Germans (taking cattle to the west) told us this news. By the end of the year we heard distant artillery, and somewhere violent battles took place. We were waiting for our army.

On one such day, Mum came and said that she had told the Shelestovskys who we in fact were. By then, I was grown up and very secretive, and started reproaching my mum for this because I was not able to trust anybody. And the Shelestovskys started to treat us even more gently and carefully.

In early March the skies above Uman became red with fire, and we clearly heard artillery shooting. And there was dead silence in our village. In the evening we would go out into the street and look into the skies. Once, suddenly, right above the village, a rocket flew up, and a few horse riders entered the village and then left it. In the morning of 9 March, our army entered the village.

The headquarters were located in the Shelestovskys' house. And my mum went to ask whether it was ever possible that our army would retreat again.

'This is the war, and nobody can give any guarantees,' was the answer.

And the following morning my mum took the decision to go to Kiev. For ten days we travelled towards Kiev. It was a very difficult road: travel-worn gravel roads, along which we could see broken machines and dead Germans. Then we rode in the rain on an open railway carriage, with the broken floor, and then in a cattle car together with our soldiers. But we endured everything and returned home.

NOTE

1. I interviewed Shelya Polishchuk in August 1944. Her interview was published in the collection entitled *In the Flame of the Shoah in the Ukraine: Testimonies of the Jewish Ghetto and Camp Prisoners and Members of the Partisan Movement* (Beit Lohamei haGhettaot, Israel, 1998), pp. 185–204. [Note by the editor.]

50. And they started killing people in one barrack after another[1]

Emma Polyakova (Chernaya) (b. 1936)

I was born in Kharkov, in 1936. When the war began, I was five years old and, together with my older brother, I was was sent to my grandma's in Nikolaev oblast. When we returned home, my parents started to get ready to leave. My father was ill then (he had a fractured sacrum). At work he was promised that all his family would be sent for evacuation but the train left a day before he was told, without us.

Soon the Germans came. All Jews were ordered to go to the barracks in Stankostroy. Our family joined all the rest and went to the barracks. In one of them, my mum found children of her schoolmate who had died on the way to the ghetto and her husband gave Mum her passport. A new acquaintance (his surname was Krichevsky) faked it carefully and she became Glafira Isayevna, a Russian (her name was Esther Isaakovna Seplyarskaya).

During the time that we lived at Stankostroy (in the ghetto) Mum went out to the city twice to get some food. When going back, she met a woman, who told her, 'If you want to get some things, go beyond Rogan; Jews were killed there.'

When Mum reached the barracks, as a proof of the woman's words, she saw two policemen who were dividing up the belongings of those killed. At that time it was prohibited to leave barracks, and those who left (even to use the toilet) were killed. They announced the 'relocation' to Poltava oblast, but in fact started killing people in one barrack after another. My parents calculated that our 'relocation' date was 2 January 1942.

Mum and Dad agreed that Mum would take the children (my brother and me) and leave for the village where my nanny lived. Mum already had her 'Russian' passport in which we were both listed. Mum also spoke German well (she taught it at school).

In the morning, she took a bucket as if she were going to get some water, and together with us she crossed the railway. She looked like a 'trader', and there were many of them in those days.

After our escape, Mum went with us to Kharkov, to Alexander Fedorovich Chumakov, the deputy director in School No. 82, with whom she had worked before the war. He helped her 'renew' her passport registration (he was connected with the underground). When we got it back, we went to the village of Semyonovka where Vera Romanovna Yakimenko, my nanny, lived. She already had two children. She helped us get a room at one house. Then, the head of the village allowed my mum to gather the remaining sunflowers off the field, and press oil from them. That was what saved us from starvation. Then they advised my mum to go to Lozovaya (then a village in Staroverovsky district, Kharkov oblast; now it is Kegichevsky district).

My mum met Efrosiniya Mossentseva, a very intelligent and kind woman. She helped us with the house, persuading her neighbour to let us a room, where nobody lived in winter. Mum worked in the field with all the other local women, as well as mending clothes for farmers. Thus, thanks to E. S. Mossentseva, we lived in the village until Kharkov was liberated, and we returned there in 1944.

My brother volunteered to the front, and returned home in 1946, a disabled veteran. He died in 1985, and my mum died on 12 February 1995.

NOTE

1. This originally appeared in Yu. M. Lyakhovizky, *The Holocaust Survivors: Survivors, Saviours, Collaborators. Testimonies, Facts and Documents* (Kharkhov/Jerusalem, 1996), pp. 81–2.

51. They gave us food once a day only

Philip Portyansky (B. 1925)

In 1941 I finished nine years of the Kamenka Secondary School No. 1. In June, together with my sister, who came on vacations from Kirovograd, we went to Revovka, to our parents' friends. They were busy with their farming, and we were helping them – I was looking after the colts and my sister was helping on the threshing floor.

When the war began we returned home. Our family was getting ready to be evacuated; my father was mobilized but at the regional executive council they refused to issue evacuation permits for our family. Thus, my mum, my sister and myself remained in Kamenka.

On 5 August in the afternoon, the Germans occupied Kamenka. Mass murders and robbing of Jews began immediately (not without the help of collaborators). At our house they broke down the door and took everything possible out into the street, and then Valentin Loga, with a group of other people like himself, took everything they looted away.

My uncle was among the first killed. Mum and my sister left for Revovka, and I went to the village of Rebedailovka, to my dad's friend. The family of Petr Fedorovich Bychok hid me well – they built a secret hiding place for me in the attic of their house. At my request, Petr Fedorovich took me during the night to Revovka, to Semyon Antonovich Barannik with whom my mum and sister lived. Fillip Ivanovich Olexenko, the headman of the village, and a relative of Semyon Antonovich, knew we were hiding with their family. His family (his wife and daughter) frequently brought us food (grain, oil, lard, etc.).

Mum, my sister and I went to work in the *kolkhoz*. Mum was reaping wheat with a sickle. (She was born into a country family. Her parents were originally from Revovka. My grandfather owned ten hectares of land and they processed everything themselves. My uncle was the first chairman of the communal farm. Even now, the dam there is called Volka's Dam).

My sister worked at the wheat mill and I, together with Onykiy

Chuchko, was taking grain from the field to the mill. When the Nazi, appeared, Chuchko would take me to his home and while we were going there would calm me and say, 'Don't be afraid, Filko, I will tell those bastards you are my son.'

There was no humiliation or abuse inflicted on us by the local population. Instead, they treated us with respect and compassion and were ready to give us any help that was needed.

Early in the morning, when Mum was going to work, the head-man of the village met her and said that we had to go to Kamenka and get registered there, and then we could return to Revovka and continue our work here.

In Kamenka, in the yard of the council, many Jews were gathered. Tziperko was the head of the council, and Shulika was his deputy. All Jews were registered but did not have permission to leave Kamenka. We all now had registration numbers. Mum's number was 215, my sister's was 216 and my number was 217. The numbers were supposed to be put on the front of our clothes, as well as the Star of David. Without this we were not supposed to appear in the yard of the council. After that all Jews were resettled, with fourteen to eighteen people sharing one house.

In the morning we went to a 'Jewish labour exchange'. Yosif Krasinsky was in charge of it and he was directing people to work. The working day lasted from seven in the morning till seven in the evening. Guards escorted us to and from work. We primarily dealt with cleaning streets and carrying bricks from burned-down warehouses and shops of the district consumers' union. Usually policemen named Orlyk, Piven, and Revyakov guarded us. Many died after being beaten by these policemen. Another monster of a policeman was someone named Nika, who rode a horse; he was Finnish. It is impossible to describe how he tortured people.

We were sent to work in the *kolkhoz* of the village of Yurchikha and also in the Pokrovsky *sovkhoz*.

In the village of Yurchikha an elderly woman, whom we didn't know, although she had known our parents, found us. Maria Ivanovna Dyshchinskaya (Grandma Zakharchikha) gave us a bottle of milk and a slice of bread. Starting that day, her children would come in turns in the morning and evening and bring us a bottle of milk, a slice of bread, seeds and apples. The village residents helped feed other Jews too. This [lack of food] was one of our major problems.

Once, working in the field, near the Komsomolsky forest, I saw a man who was walking towards us, limping. This was Dorofey Karpovich Dryga, my former school director. We talked, and he promised that, in time, he would take young people into his unit.

But this never happened. At the end of October they started selecting blacksmiths, tailors and hatters at our 'employment agency',
and they were transferred to a beet *sovkhoz*. Before that, the family
of Pukhovizky, who had many children, had already lived there
(they were called *lytvykhy*). And all remaining Jews were moved to
the camp that occupied the location of today's district hospital.
Police guarded the camp and Germans came to it very seldom.
(During all the time I was there, the chief of gendarmes came there
only once.)

Men were put into an almost dilapidated building. It was very
difficult to live there, especially at night: we slept on the weeds or
rotten straw, depending on where one could find a spot to lie down.
It is painful to recall everything else: the cold, hunger, lice, abscesses and different diseases that didn't let us rest day or night. We were
forced to go to work no matter how old or how ill we were. There
were many prisoners ill with tuberculosis and asthma, or with different mental and nervous disorders.

My cousin, Sonya Lvovna Portyanskaya, died in the camp. Her
body was taken out of the camp on a one-horse cart and nobody
knows where she was buried.

In the morning before work, and especially in the evening, after
it, policemen would storm the building making noise, swearing,
demanding a lot of valuables (silver and gold) – the poor people had
not possessed anything like that for long while now. They humiliated prisoners in any way possible.

During the winter the building was heated very poorly; many
people had frostbitten toes and fingers, and the wounds would
go rotten.

Not everybody would return to the camp in the evening, and
nobody knew what had happened to those people. People would be
punished severely if they started asking that question.

They gave us food once a day only. The food was cooked from
rotten vegetables (potatoes, beetroots, carrots), and we received 200
grams of pumpernickel bread a day, and not necessarily every day.

I cannot help but mention those people who risked their lives but
tried to help our family – Andrian Yulievich Schiring, Grandma
Schtadnykha, Petr Fedorovich Bychok, and his children, Evdokiya
Patievna Schkvorets, Semen Antonovich Barannik, and his wife.
Also, I would like to mention my schoolmate Petr Alexeyevich
Solomashenko, Genrikh Zinko, his mum Marina, and his stepfather.
This is not a complete list of the people who tried to relieve our
circumstances with whatever they could.

There was not a single chance for escape, and people were even
afraid of mentioning a word about it. At first I tried talking about it,

for which I paid in full – I was badly beaten by Itzya Raigorodsky. Yon Platkov tried to protect me, and he was beaten too. People (especially the elderly) were angry. After the midnight they would typically start fighting and reprimanding each other.

Andrian Yulievich Schiring, my father's friend, warned my mum that he was seeking ways for our liberation. Mikhail Nikiforovich Korolenko, whose brother worked with my father, served in camp security. He introduced Adrian Yulievich to his supervisors, Glagolyev and Shevchenko, who – together with him – developed a plan for our escape. We paid for this with cloth, a fur coat, boxcalf boots, two carpets, a sewing machine and many other things left with our friends to keep. Mum told Adrian Yulievich where we had left all this. The policemen took the three of us – my mum, sister and me – out into the road that led towards the village of Telepino and put us on a cart that took us beyond the beet *sovkhoz*. There we found a haystack, and spent the night. Then we left for Revovka, where we lived until the liberation of the village by the Red Army soldiers.

52. My war childhood[1]

Maya Pudalova (b. 1936)

My name is Maya Pinevna Sadovskaya (Pudalova) and I was born on 1 May 1936, in Ovruch in Zhitomir oblast. When the war began I was only five years old, whicht is why my memory can produce only individual episodes and impressions of my childhood. Unfortunately, my mum is already gone, and we used to frequently recall our trials and wanderings through the roads of the war together with her.

When Ovruch was already occupied, my mum and I left it on the last car that was leaving. My older brother put us on it. This was so unexpected that my brother didn't even allow Mum to go in the house and pack some things. But the car didn't manage to go far away, because we were bombed. Finally we came to a little hut where an old man with a dog lived. Mum and this old man spoke for a long time, I fell asleep and when I woke up, Mum was not there. I was crying and he tried to calm me down saying that Mum had gone out to look for a job. Later I found out that she went to search for a partisan unit. I lived with this old man for a very long time. He gave me pumpkin gruel and potatoes to eat. I only saw Mum a few times.

When I turned six years old, he gave me a small wooden cross on a thread that he had made himself. One day three Germans walked in and took him away.

I was hiding in the kennel and didn't show myself. Together with the dog, I waited for the old man for a long time, but he never came back. So I dressed and climbed under the covers to get warm, together with the dog.

That night Mum woke me up. She took me to the partisan unit. They gave me hot tea and soup.

I don't know how many days I spent in the unit, but one day my friend, Granddad Puzyr (Bubble), tied my arms to his legs, saying that he had to do so, and crawled away, pulling me with him. We crawled for a long time, and then we walked.

He took me to Uncle Mykola and Aunt Galya. Uncle Mykola worked in the Gestapo and sometimes he would bring prisoners home to would chop his wood.

One day, a prisoner looked at me and asked Uncle Mykola, 'What, are you hiding a Jew girl?'

Aunt Galya said, 'God, no, this is our youngest daughter!'

Soon afterwards Mum came after me. This was already in the autumn of 1942. First we went to Kiev, to Mum's relatives, but found out they had died in Babi Yar. Then we returned to Kharkov. We were cold and hungry. People were giving us whatever they could – someone would give old shoes, someone a coat, and someone a kerchief. We hid from the Germans continuously. Mum tried to go to big villages with many people. Thus we reached the town of Kalach, Voronezh oblast. I was extremely ill: my feet were swollen and I couldn't put on any shoes. Mum was also exhausted. There were kind people in Kalach, such as Aunt Zina with her son Seryozha and their ill grandfather who was bed-ridden and couldn't walk. They gave us shelter. Mum and Aunt Zina made some concoctions, treating the old man and me. Nobody among their neighbours knew we were living with them.

Nevertheless, the local headman of the village somehow found out about us. One late night he brought the police with him. Mum and I were locked in a dark closet for the night, under the threat of being killed together with our hosts. They sent a young Hungarian soldier to guard us. He felt sorry for us, and at night he let us out.

And again we were walking, not knowing where. And again we seldom had a slice of bread, and only one or two potatoes between us. Mum ate almost nothing, giving everything to me. She was afraid of getting into the Germans' hands most of all. When we reached Kharkov oblast. We stayed in one village, in an abandoned house, Mum worked in the field where they never asked for any documents.

Thus we survived until December 1943, when Mum found out our hometown of Ovruch was liberated. And again we set off on the road, but this time we were returning home. In March 1944 we were in Ovruch. Mum went to work. Schools were still closed. I started my schooling in September 1945 only, when I was nine years old. During the war years, my mum saved me and survived herself.

NOTE

1. This originally appeared in the *Jewish News* and as an Appendix to *The Voice of the Ukraine*, a special edition of the *Supreme Council of the Ukraine*, Nos 5–6 (Society for Jewish Culture of the Ukraine, 1999).

53. These people were a godsend to us

Petr Rabtsevich (b. 1923)

My name is Petr Ruvinovich Rabtsevich (Eruhim-Fischel Ruvinovich Rabinov), and I was born on 25 May 1923, in the town of Drogichin, Brest province (until 1939, this was Polish territory).

My father's name was Ruvin Shlemovich Rabinov (b. 1890); my mother's name was Polina Fischelevna Rabinova (b. 1892). I also had two sisters, Esther (b. 1914) and Riva (b. 1921), and three brothers, Lev (b. 1916), David (b. 1925) and Aron (b. 1927).

My parents were originally from Lyubeshov in Volyn. When the Germans retreated in 1916 they were resettled to Drogichin, where we lived until 1924.

In 1924, my father got a job on the estate of the landowner, Orda, in Mokraya Dubrava, Logishin district, Pinsk oblast, Brest province. My father was a cheese-maker.

All Jewish traditions were closely kept in our family, albeit we were the only Jewish family on the whole estate. The children went to a Polish school, but a teacher was hired to teach us Hebrew and Jewish culture.

My brother, Lyova, finished his schooling in Pinsk. By the time that David, Aron and I had grown up enough, the financial situation in the family worsened, and we could not go to study at the grammar school. My parents rented a room in the town of Logishin (five kilometres away from the estate). There, we went to a regular Polish school and continued studying Hebrew with the teacher. In Logishin, there were about 200 Jewish families, three synagogues, and two kosher butchers. Our parents spent all the holidays with us in Logishin.

In 1936, I finished school and entered Pinsk Jewish trade school. My parents rented a room in Pinsk, and David, Aron and myself moved there to study. I was studying at the college while my brothers went to a Jewish school. Our older sister Esther looked after us, and she was like a mother to us. Soon, Lyova was drafted into the Polish army, to the cavalry. In the army he was sent to study at the military nursing college as a medical attendant, from which he successfully graduated, and he served in the military as a paramedic.

My sister Riva lived with my parents in Mokraya Dubrava and helped them.

In 1938, Orda sold the estate to peasants and many families that worked on it were laid off, including my parents. In 1938 they moved to Pinsk and rented a flat at 10/10 Monyushko Street.

My father was unemployed, my mum began working as a seamstress, my sister, Riva, went to work as a shop assistant in the haberdashery on Koczusko Street, owned by Feldman, in the house of Schmitt. I studied in the technical school, but my parents didn't have the money to pay for my schooling. The board of trustees of the school relieved me from the tuition fee and during the vacations I had to work, helping the school manage their affairs.

In 1938 my sister, Esther, married Avraam Warshawsky.

In 1938, my brother, Lyova, got married and he worked at the plywood factory owned by Lurye.

We children lived with our own thoughts, attending clubs of Schomer-Olumi and Schomer-Atzer; we dreamed of building our own country. In the town of Pins, out of its 36,000 population, about 29,000 were Jewish.

On Saturdays, we would go to the big synagogue to listen to the cantor and to pray. We also went to the cinema. At that time, films were shown in Yiddish, such as *Tkiyaskaf, Derdybek, Mamele*. We dreamed of the future.

In 1938, after the *Anschluss* [union] of Austria and Czechoslovakia, Hitler demanded that Poland yield the 'Danzig Corridor', and it was clear that war was near. In March 1939 the first military mobilization was announced in Poland. My older brother Lyova was drafted. In the spring of 1939, I finished the technical school and started helping my father to guard the garden that he had rented.

My older sister was expecting a baby. My younger brothers, David and Aron, finished school. David was helping our brother-in-law to run his shop. Everybody was anxious and worried. In the city, Polish authorities were asking for financial support to buy defence equipment, in particular air raid systems. People started digging 'slits' in their vegetable gardens.

After the Ribbentrop–Molotov Pact had been signed, the German–Polish war began. In early September train carriages began arriving in Pinsk with wounded and injured. The hospital was in a Jesuit cathedral. My father and we children went to see if we could see our brother there.

Refugees started to flood into Pinsk too, especially Jews from the inner Polish regions.

On 17 September 1939, the Soviet army crossed the Polish–Soviet border, and on 20 September they entered Pinsk. The Polish authorities were set aside. Soon afterwards, all synagogues were closed, as well as Jewish school (public and private), and all these were transferred to the state authorities.

The Jewish population accepted the Soviet occupation better than the German because everybody had heard of their attitude towards Jews.

I began to work in the Western River Fleet, in the department of communications, as a communications mechanic.

My sister, Riva, went to work in the grocery shop, my younger brothers went to study in the Jewish school that had been opened on the premises of the grammar school.

My sister, Esther, gave birth to a daughter; yet we didn't know anything about our brother, Lyova. On the eve of 1940 he came home; he had from German captivity and walked all the way to Brest. He was detained for over a month by the Soviet border guards at the Brest fortress while they checked out his identity. Soon afterwards, his wife gave birth to a girl named Dina. After his return, he started working in the town hospital and entered the Pinsk Medical College.

The wealthier people of Pinsk were sent off to Siberia. My father envied them, saying they would survive while we would die here and that this was not the beginning of the war. We lived in this seemingly peaceful atmosphere until the Soviet–German war began. The last day when our family was together was on 22 June 1941. On that day, they called my brother Lyova to the military commissariat, Riva was called back to work, and so was I. Nobody knew what the following day would bring.

On the night of 23/24 June, panic began in the town, caused by the explosion of a gunpowder storage of the former 84th Polish Infantry Regiment. The town was lit up by the explosion, and the population fled across the bridge to the other bank of the Pina, towards David town. My brothers and I also left the town. On the third day we reached the former Soviet–Polish border, but the border guards didn't let us through since we didn't have passes. Our passports were not valid on the Soviet side, and we were turned back to Pinsk. Having returned to Pinsk, I started working again. (Our supervisors had left the town on a lorry on the night of the panic.) All power in the town was in the hands of the Kommandant of the Dnieper River Fleet.

The Germans came to Pinsk and their first objective was to annihilate all the Jewish population. First, they killed thirty Jewish men. Among them was a barber from Logishin; he fell down, and later

climbed out of the pit but a year later, in 1942, when entering the
ghetto, a policeman found a piece of bread on him, and shot him
dead on the spot.

On 9 August 1941, 10,000 men (aged from six to the very old)
very killed in Pinsk. My brothers David and Aron were killed on
that day. I survived because when the Germans entered our house
I was outside, in the outhouse. My father was also alive because he
was hiding in the attic. He was hiding because on 7 August there
had been an order from the Kommandant of Pinsk for all Jews who
didn't or couldn't work to report to the railway station to be sent to
work. On 8 August, a few hundred people showed up. They were
taken out of town and killed in a potato field. A few people survived
and returned to the town. The news of this murder spread fast and,
on 9 August, nobody showed up to the railway station. However, a
raid started throughout the town. On that day people were murdered in the forest near the village of Kozlyakovichi. On the very
same day, they announced the 'contribution', ordering people to
bring gold, silver and copper. If we failed to bring it, they would
start the second round of murders.

After the Germans occupied our town, they gave me the same
position of communications mechanic in the River Fleet. Malinovsky
was in charge of this department. He hired, beside me, three other
Jews: Botvinnik, Epshtein and Radkevich. They worked in the field,
and I was in the station. All four of us survived the killing on 9
August 1941.

In September 1941, the Pinsk magistrate exchanged the Soviet
passports of the Jewish population for a certificate [*ausweis*], yellow
in colour. Two sides of its cover bore the stamp, *Jude*.

Until 1 May 1942, the Jewish population had lived in their flats,
but we were now forbidden to walk along the pavements, talk to
non-Jews, or go to the marketplace.

On 1 May 1942, they marched us into a fenced ghetto that was
located on the perimeter of Zavalnaya, Logishinskaya, Gorky, and
Sovetskaya Streets. The Jewish cemetery was also a part of the
ghetto.

Our family of six (my parents, myself, my sister, Esther, with her
daughter, and Avraam, her husband) was accommodated in a six-
metre walk-through room. (Avraam had escaped from German
imprisonment in Czechoslovakia and in December 1941 he returned
home, to Pinsk.)

The conditions of life in the ghetto were terrifying. Those
who worked could get out of the ghetto and had some chance of
trading something for food, but it was forbidden to bring food into the
ghetto. If they found food on someone, that person would be killed

immediately. There were two water pumps in the ghetto, and we were allowed to leave our the houses, starting at seven in the morning, and everybody wanted to get drinking water. This was only possible early in the morning: if a person came to the pump a little earlier, he or she would be killed too. People in the ghetto ate anything that was growing from the earth, and many died from dysentery and dystrophy (especially children and old people).

Bread was delivered to the ghetto once a week only. Those who worked qualified for the ration of 200 grams, children for 120 grams, those who didn't work for eighty grams, and again the amount of the bread they were bringing was enough to give to 150 or 200 people only, and there was total of 28,000 people in the ghetto. The Jewish population of Pinsk in fact grew after the killings of 9 August at the expense of the incoming Jews who had run away from killings in smaller towns and villages surrounding Pinsk.

In May 1942, a young supervisor came to join the river transportation in Pinsk. This was a German, named Gunter Krull. Malinovsky, my supervisor, sent me to move the phone from one place to another within the room, because Krull had moved his desk in his office. Since I was Jewish, I had to wear a yellow circle on the left side of my chest and on my back. And since I was working, there was a stamp inside this circle, certifying that I worked in this particular organization. This was our ID. When I entered Krull's office he ordered me to take the circle off. I told him that this was my ID and I could not take it off because they would kill me without it. To this Krull replied that he could not see me so humiliated and that I was as human as he was. He told me to take off my coat and go in the office without those humiliating signs. After I did so, Krull started asking me about my family. I told him about the conditions in which we lived, that we received only fifty per cent of our wages, and that we were not allowed to go to the diner. Krull promised to help so that we would get food in the diner.

The following day, Malinovsky received a token for lunch at the diner for Botvinnik, Radkevich and me. Once a week a German soldier escorted us to the ghetto so that we could take some food into the ghetto. The police wouldn't search us if we were with a German soldier. This was thanks to Gunter Krull.

In August 1942, the wind of death started to blow hard around Pinsk. Rumours about the murder of the Jewish population started spreading fast. In the Pinsk ghetto we were waiting for our horrible end. This was clear to old and young. Krull told me he wanted to save my life. But he told me he didn't know at that moment how to do so. He told me to speak with my family at home.

He told me about his family, and that his father was a surgeon in

Berlin and so was his brother who served in the army now. He told me he helped two of his Jewish friends to leave Berlin and escape the horrible tragedy.

For a long time I couldn't summon up the courage to tell my parents that my boss wanted to save me. Krull used to say that if only he could, he would have saved all Jews from death, but this was beyond his abilities.

When, in September 1942, a junior officer, Friof, arrived from Kiev to Pinsk with a repair team aboard a steamboat, Krull sent me to fix the radio on the steamboat. I completed this assignment very quickly. Some time later Krull came aboard and started talking to Friof so that he would ask the chief of communications Shtoide to hire me for work in Kiev. Friof knew I was Jewish. Our organization was military. It was called the Second Field Division of Water Transportation, and it operated in the territory of the Dnieper–Bug canal, as well as the rivers of Pina, Pripyat and Dnieper with their inflows. Krull could send me to work in such places as Brest, Kobran or David town but he said those were very small towns, 'And the police could find you easily.' In Kiev, he said, 'You will blend and get lost among people.' Friof promised him to talk to Shtoide.

Krull started asking me whether I had told my family about his intention to save me. But I still couldn't get enough courage to tell my mother about it. It was horrible even to imagine that you would die, but perhaps I would survive. Then, having gathered all my courage, I told my mum. I asked her what she thought about it.

And she said, 'You know, when a man is drowning, he clings on to any straw. This straw has come to you, so grab it. If you survive, you will tell everyone about the horrors that we had to suffer and live through.' My mother gathered a few photographs of our family, two changes of underwear, a towel and a spoon. I took all this and hid at my workplace.

Every night this sort of action would lead to 300 hostages being taken in the ghetto. If any of those who had left for work did not return in the ghetto, their family and these hostages would be killed. That was why I couldn't and didn't want to leave Pinsk while my family was alive.

We marked *Rosh haShanah* and *Yom Kippur* in the ghetto (there was a synagogue in the ghetto, and these days nobody went to work). Old and young prayed alike because we knew it was our last holiday.

In order to be saved I had to be outside the ghetto during the night. Krull issued me a pass for night work. He explained this by saying that the power was supplied at night and I had to supervise the change of the batteries. My night shift lasted for about ten days.

On the night of 28/29 October, at about 5 a.m., I heard shots and the barking of dogs. The ghetto was not more than 800 metres away from my work. About fifteen or twenty minutes later, Krull came in and took me to his home. All the ten days that I worked at nights, every evening leaving the ghetto I would say farewells to my family for good.

From 29 October to 22 November, Krull had me stay with him, in his house where he lived and worked. On 22 November, a letter from Kiev came, from the Second Field Division of Water Transportation, so that I could be transferred to work there. Krull personally issued me a new certificate in the name of Petr Rabtsevich, thus changing my name and date of birth. He told me how to behave myself: to ride only in train carriages designated for Germans, and at the railway station to stay in the areas for the Germans. Having arrived in Kiev, I should find the organization by the signs and not ask anybody.

'Most importantly, stay away from any encounters with the police,' he said. 'From now on, your life is in your own hands.'

From his stories I knew that the Pinsk ghetto was liquidated on 29 October. Its residents were taken to the airfield of the village of Galevo, about five kilometres away from Pinsk, where they were shot. There were about 28,000 people in the ghetto. On that day I lost Polina Fischelevna Rabinova, my mother, Ruvin Shlemovich Rabinov, my father, Esther Ruvinovna Warshawsky, my sister, with Avraam Warshawsky, her husband, and Gita, their daughter, Chaya Rabinova, my brother Lyova's wife with their daughter Dina, as well as all their family and friends.

On 22 November 1942, in the evening Krull put me on a train heading towards Brest. I arrived in Kiev on 28 November. I spent the night at the station. Police tried to move me out of the area for Germans. I turned to the German gendarmes showing my ID and they allowed me to stay inside the hall.

When the curfew was over, I left the station and found the organization by following the signs. The Second Field Division was located at Bogdan Khmelnitzky Square, near Sophia Cathedral. A soldier on duty let me in, showed me to Shtoide's office and told me to go in and sit on the sofa to wait. I fell asleep immediately because I hadn't been able to sleep all the six nights on the way; I had been completely stressed out. At nine in the morning Shtoide woke me up and took me to the civil administration of the Division that was in Alexandrovskaya Street, on the Podol. Shtoide sent me to the personnel department, to a woman named Novitzkaya, to get documents ready for work. She started complaining, wondering how I had been sent from west to east to work, while they were sending people from east to west.

I told her that I was an employee and went wherever they told me. 'If you need further explanations, ask Shtoide.'

She then issued me with a new ID and instead of going to pick a work card at the labour exchange agency, she sent me to go and get it myself. The local clerks at the agency started to ask me the same question: why had I come from west to east? I turned to a German, who was their supervisor. I spoke German fluently, as well as Polish and Russian, with no accent. My appearance didn't show I was Jewish. The German ordered that I be issued a work card. (Without the card one wasn't allowed to be in the city, and every Saturday they would mark a week of completed work on it. And if, when checking the card, police didn't find a mark on it, a person would be arrested and sent to the transfer station to be sent to work in Germany.)

I was accommodated in the dormitory at 70 Verkhniy Val. I needed a passport to get registered there and I didn't have one. In Pinsk, Krull had foreseen this and told me that my ID contained a note saying that my passport was kept at my workplace in Pinsk, and that they would send it by mail upon a query from Kiev. In reality, my passport identifying me as Rabinov had been burned in the stove. I kept saying that my passport was in Pinsk, appealing to the note on my ID from Pinsk. They sent a query and received the answer from Krull that he had sent my passport by mail. A month later I received a document at work saying that my passport had been lost in the post from Pinsk to Kiev. Based on this document, and other papers signed by Krull, the Podol district division issued me a passport identifying me as Petr Romanovich Rabtsevich, a Russian.

In May 1943 I turned twenty years old. At my age I was now eligible for labour duty in Germany. I had to get physical at the agency, but as I am Jewish I could not get undressed – yet I had to go through the physical since without it I could no longer stay in Kiev. In the morning I went there and stayed there until 2 p.m. I saw many come up and say to the doctors that they were healthy and were ready voluntarily to go to work in Germany. I took a risk and also said that I was healthy and wanted to go voluntarily. They told me to show them my feet and arms, checked my eyes and immediately issued me papers to be sent to Germany. I didn't need anything else because my work for the Second Division relieved me from being sent to Germany.

While I lived in Kiev, throughout 1943, Krull was supportive. He sent me a package of matches via the junior officer, Friof. I could trade one box for half a loaf of bread. In 1943 Krull came to Kiev, and we saw each other from a distance, so that nobody would see us together.

In August 1943, under the pressure of the approaching Red Army, the Second Field Division evacuated promptly from Kiev. They offered to take me west with them. There was panic in the city and when I was going from the dormitory to work I got caught up in a raid. All of us who were captured by police and German patrolmen were sent to the station, to be shipped to Germany. Having stayed overnight at the railway station in the morning I turned to a German soldier and showing him my documents. I told him I was supposed to be evacuated with my organization. Later, they let me go. When I came to my former workplace, everybody was gone. Starting late August 1943, until the liberation day, together with other Kiev residents, I wandered from village to village around the city.

On 6 November 1943, Kiev was liberated. I returned to the city and started working again. Now it was the Dnieprovsky Military and Restoration Department of the River Transportation. When applying for this work I had to write my biography and fill in a questionnaire form. In my biography I described my whole life story and explained that, although my documents said I was Petr Romanovich Rabtsevich, I was in fact a Jew, named Fischel Ruvinovich Rabinov. I also wrote that I wanted to restore my real identity. When accepting me for work, the chief of the personnel, named Rodman, listened to my story carefully and told me that he felt really sorry for me but he had no authority to change my surname and advised me to go to the attorney's office or to the militia. I went to the law office of the river transportation immediately. They told me that if I changed my surname now this would mean that I wanted to hide my activities during the German occupation, and this could lead to my arrest. (Pinsk was still under German occupation.)

In November I was drafted into the army but my work at the transportation authority relieved me from active military duty. When being drafted, in their questionnaire I wrote that I spoke Russian, German, Polish and Yiddish. Having a release form, in December 1943 I turned to the military commissar with the request that he send me into the army. Having learned that I spoke Polish he decided to send me on a course of officer training for the Polish army. He warned me that I had to turn in my notice of the army draft at my work on the day I had to report to the recruitment station. I was supposed to report on 31 December, but on 27 December I fell ill with pneumonia. A month later, in January 1944, I came to the commissariat and they sent me for a physical. The results of the tests showed that the army didn't need such ill people and they issued exemptions for me, which were only revoked in 1956.

In 1944 Pinsk was liberated. I wrote a letter to friends of our family in the village of Kovnyatin, Pinsk district. My brother, Lyova, had sent a letter from the army to this village too. Thus, we found each other. He had served at the Second Byelorussian Front. I felt much relieved when I found him.

I was able to restore my surname only in 1956 because all Jewish records were lost, along with the rabbis who had kept them. By then, I was already married and had two children.

My sister, Riva Rabinova, served in the Soviet army throughout the war. She finished the war in Berlin. Now she lives in Pryluki, Chernigov oblast, in the Ukraine. She has two sons and four grandsons.

My brother, Lev Rabinov, finished the war in Port Arthur. In 1944 he married a girl from Moscow and moved there. He graduated from the medical institute, and then worked as a doctor in Balashikha, Moscow oblast, where he still lives with his daughter and her family.

All of my life I've been telling my children and grandchildren about my life and about their ancestors. I told them about the man who saved my life. Every year we go to Pinsk to the graves of our family.

I have tried for a long time to locate my saviour. In my first biography in 1943 I wrote about him. Official queries didn't bring any results and even the query through the German Embassy resulted in nothing.

In June 1996 the former prisoners from Warsaw and Krakow issued an invitation to a group of former Jewish ghetto and camp prisoners from Kiev. I was among the members of the group. The organization, called Maximilian-Kolbe-Werk, was this meeting's sponsor. Former young Polish prisoners met us in Warsaw, as well as the Müller family (Margret and Werner), the representatives of this organization. (They were German residents from the city of Cologne.) After we met each other, I asked the Müllers help me locate my saviour, or at least his relatives.

They listened to my story carefully. It was very difficult for me to talk to them since I hadn't spoken any German for over fifty-four years, and my speech was more Jewish now. Werner translated for Margret and she was writing it down. I showed them copies of the documents issued by Krull for me. They wrote down my story in full detail and took copies of my documents. I told them that maybe Krull lived in Berlin since he mentioned that his parents lived there. I told the Müllers that the Second Field Division of Water Transportation was a military organization and they had to try to search the German military archives. They promised to find Krull or his relatives.

On 14 November 1996, the Müllers called me from Cologne and told me that they had received a response to their query from the military archives. Krull had survived the war and died in 1979 at the age of sixty-two. Shtoide went missing during the war. Krull's wife, Christina and Yanina, their daughter, knew that during the war, in Pinsk, he had saved a Rabinov from death and they would like to meet me. Margret and Werner Müller sponsored my trip to Cologne. They sent invitations for my wife and me. After we received visas, they sent us round-trip aeroplane tickets. On 16 February 1997, they met us in Frankfurt-om-Main and took us by train to Cologne. In Cologne we stayed in their home, and they provided us with everything. We went to Dusseldorf, to Gunter Krull's grave, and visited his wife, Christina Krull. From her story I learned that the military archives had asked her, via the Dusseldorf police, whether she had heard the name of Rabinov. She confirmed that this was the name of a person saved by her husband.

Yanina, Krull's daughter, lives in Cologne. We met with her and I told her about the ghetto children who knew what was in store for them. She cried together with me. It was a pity that Gunter Krull died so young. He told his wife and daughter that I would be living in Kiev.

My family and I express our gratitude to the Müller family, who spent so much effort and provided the resources for me to meet the family of my saviour. These people were God sent.

In 1997 my survival story was entered into the Yad Vashem Institute of Memory and Courage of the Holocaust in Jerusalem. On January 1999 my German saviour, Gunter Krull, received the posthumous title of the 'Righteous among the Nations'.

54. I could draw the line

Lyubov Raigorodskaya (b. 1928)

My father was a binder and my mother a homemaker. I was the only child in our family.

In 1941 when the war started and the Germans came, my parents were killed. I survived accidentally. I was taken to our friends and I stayed there for three days. When I returned, I found out that in our small house, ten of our neighbours had been killed. I left and wandered through the Kamenka suburbs. Then, till the autumn, I lived with a Jewish family. But there were three Germans who tortured us in any way possible. And then one woman said that we had to leave for Zlatopol, it was more peaceful there. And so I did. The Zheleznyakov family took me to live with them (Efim, Dusya, his Ukrainian wife, and Nadya, their daughter). Efim worked as an engineer in the leather factory. I lived with them for a year. Then I was transferred to a camp along with other Jews.

The camp was located near the river; before the war a children's penitentiary had been there, which had a few houses. It was cold and hungry in the camp. When a lot of snow fell, we were forced to go and clear it away.

And then the *Aktions* started. One evening in spring, I heard screaming and ran towards the door. The policemen and Germans stood there. One of them pushed me and I fell down. A policeman was standing near each and every house. We were surrounded. Then they started grabbing people and throwing them on to a big lorry covered with a canopy. I found myself near the driver's cabin. Screams and moans were heard from everywhere. But I really didn't care. When the war began I was twelve years old but it seemed to me by then that I had lived a long life. Then I saw how people tore the cloth and somebody jumped out of the lorry. I wanted to get in front. There were many people and it was difficult to get to its running-board, but I succeeded. I put my foot on the edge and a girl named Rosa pushed me off the lorry. Thus she pushed sixteen people off. I fell to the asphalt and the lorry went on without stopping. They knew we could not go anywhere from the village.

And all those who were taken away in the lorry were killed the very same night on the steppe.

In the morning I came back: the workers still remained there. A week passed on, and on Sunday I heard screams again. I looked out of the window and saw a German and a policeman. We had our own policemen that escorted us to work – and he started shouting that they were taking only those who ran away from the lorry the last time. I decided to take a risk, opened a storage closet, saw a washing trough there and hid under it. They entered the house. The Germans stood so close to me that I could see their boots. Then they left. An hour later I came out of my hiding place and everybody cried when they saw me. My neighbours told me I had to leave; they gave me a warm jacket, shoes and there my wanderings began.

In one village I heard a story about those whom they took on Sunday: they were all killed at the police station.

I told everyone that I was an orphan and had come from an orphanage. I wandered from village to village. And then I got tired and decided to die together with all the other Jews. I came to Zvenigorodka, and then I went to the village of Nemorozh, not far away from Zvenigorodka. There was a real camp, with guards day and night; there was also an interpreter and the Kommandant. I spent about a month there. They took us to work – to construct the road that was going in the direction of Lysyanka. Some time later, people started saying that, soon, everybody would be killed. It was getting scarier. And one day while we were at work, lorries pulled up and Germans and policemen jumped out of them. I started to run. I was running wherever I could. I entered the village and suddenly I saw a policeman. He asked what I was doing there and I told him that I had come to beg for bread. He told me to return from where I had come, and went to get a bicycle. I looked around, and saw that there was a field nearby, so I ran there. I found a stack of hay, made a hole inside it and crawled inside. I spent three days there. And then people found me there. They told me that everybody in the camp was killed, including old people and children, and that they had thrown the interpreter from the bridge down on to the stones. I asked them what villages were nearby and they said Vodyanyki, and that the road to Berdychev was nearby too. I went away from the steppe, spending the night among some trees. In the morning I entered the first house I saw and begged for bread. They gave me a slice of the hot bread that had just been taken out of the oven. And again my ordeal continued.

I was walking from place to place; the snow started and I had no shoes and had hardly any clothes on. I remember how I came to one woman who made me some kind of bast[1] shoes and I wore them.

Once I came to the village of Panuzhintsy, Talnoye district. A woman with two children gave me shelter. She went to work and I had to look after her children. Once the winter was over, they called me to the village council, where they told me to go to Talnoye, to the police, and to get a permit for further residence in the village. I came home to my hostess and told her everything about myself. Her brother, a teacher, came and told me I had to go and I had to tell everybody that I was a refugee from Kramatorsk.

And again, I was on the road, cold and hungry, it was worse than being a dog. I frequently got into situations that are too scary to remember now. I remember a village near the forest. I entered one house and there was a policeman asleep and a boy sitting nearby. I got out and ran away to the forest. I wanted to meet partisans, I dreamed about this, but unfortunately it never happened. I even dreamed of getting to Germany, but I was afraid my true identity would be found out. But whatever happened, it was good to be alive.

Spring came. I got to a farmstead called Konstantinovka, where ther was a girl. I helped her dig and plant her vegetable garden. She worked as a cleaner in the village council. One day the village head-man saw me (his daughter was married to the chief of police) and asked who I was. The girl said I had to leave because it was no good that he had started asking about me.

And again I was on the road. This time it took me to the village of Nagornoye, Zhashkovsky district. I went into it (the village of Bashtechki was nearby). A woman gave me shelter, and I spent three days with her. And then she said that her cousin lived nearby, in Bashtechki, and that she needed a nanny. Then she told me how to find her cousin. I lived for about a year with that woman, being a nanny there. I also went to work instead of her, and took her cow out to graze. And then, our army came. Her husband was taken immediately.

And then there was the Korsun-Shevchenkovsky battle. The Germans reached our village and replaced the local authorities. This was terrible. One night, when our army had liberated us, we came out of the village. I had to carry a baby for nine kilometres, virtu-ally barefoot. We came to the village of Besidka, Stavishchansky dis-trict. There some people took my hostess, and a woman with a baby took me to stay with her. The soldiers stayed there for two and a half months, the bakery was operational, and I went there to sieve the flour. Then I got to another woman whose husband and two sons were at the front, while the youngest, eight year old, was at home. She was ill and I dug her fifty-hectares of the vegetable lot and went to work instead of her in the *kolkhoz*. Then I decided to go back home, hoping that maybe there was some relative who would return and remember me, but alas …

Refugees lived in our house, a family of nine people. I lived with them.

During 1945, I worked at the vegetable transition store. In 1946 I worked with some people – I washed floors, dug vegetable lots. And one day, Lyusya Ivanova, the head of the printing house, saw me. She remembered my father to be who had worked there. She suggested coming and studying to be a typesetter. It was 1947. I worked there for thirty years.

It was difficult; the pay was little. I had to get clothes, shoes. I also wanted to save some money because I started to develop health problems early. And all was in vain – I had neither health nor money. Everything was wasted. In 1957 I received disability based on occupational disease – lead poisoning. And my past also made itself felt.

I received a flat when I was fifty-seven years old. It was a flat shared with a neighbour: I lived in one room, and a paralysed woman in the other. Four years ago she died, and I moved into a one-room flat. I can draw the line here. I have everything now: a roof above my head, pension pay, diseases and loneliness. That's how my life has worked out.

NOTE

1. Bast is the inner bark of lime, or other fibrous flexible bark, used as fibre in matting or, in this instance, for shoes.

55. The shots sounded continuously, stopping innocent lives short

Leya Rog (b. 1928)

From the very first days of the occupation, we, Jews of the village of Melnitsa, were registered. We were not allowed to work, we received ninty grams of pumpernickel bread mixed with straw per person a day. Many Jews had their own houses built on the lots once purchased from Ukrainians. So these lots, near the houses, with all the harvest on them, were ordered by the Germans to be transferred to their former owners.

We lived within our four walls with 90 grams of bread a day, without the right to get out of the house to our own vegetable gardens. It was good that sometimes some of our neighbours would bring us some food, but secretly, so that nobody would see.

Thus we lived, starting on 1 July 1941, through to the middle of August 1942. During this time, Germans gathered men aged sixteen to a hundred twice, collecting and burning their documents, and taking the poor doomed people outside of the village and killing them.

In the middle of August 1942 all the Jews from Melnitsa and nearby villages were marched to Bozhichnaya Street where two synagogues were located. This was a place designated for the ghetto. We starved for two weeks, having no right to leave the neighbourhood of the ghetto and get a job in the fields or beg Ukrainians for some bread.

On 3 September 1942, at four o'clock in the morning, five Germans together with ninty-seven armed policemen and dogs – surrounded the ghetto, not letting anyone out. My younger sister Bella (she now lives in the Altay Krai) and I managed to get out of the ghetto through a vegetable garden and lie there on the ground till the night. While staying there we heard screaming women, the desperate prayers of old people and the blood-curdling crying of children who were being marched to the sand quarry at the south-western edge of Melnitsa. There, they were all killed. The shots sounded continuously, stopping innocent lives short.

During the night we got to the forest and then to the village of Chersk, Manevich district, to search for our mum's brother. But this was in vain. We accidentally met some man named Rafail (I don't know his surname), a former Communist Party member, who took us into the forest where the Jews who had survived t he slaughter in Tromovka were hiding. Together with them we went into another forest and spent the winter there hiding in huts built out of branches of fir trees and hay. We ate whatever we could find. In autumn we would steal potatoes from the field, in winter we would get potato peel from under the snow and boil it. Sometimes our men would go to villages and get cows previously owned by Jews from their new owners, butcher them and then we would have some meat and fat.

Once, after our return from the village where we went at night to beg for some bread, we found nobody in the camp – a tragedy had happened there. We returned to the village and waited for the partisans who took us with them; here we stayed until our liberation by the Red Army.

56. It is impossible to describe the whole period of living in the ghetto

Samuil Roitberg (b. 1932)

When the war started, together with my parents, a brother and two sisters, I lived in Mogilev-Podolsk, Vinnitsa oblast, at 7 Ermak Street, in our own house.

On the night of 3 July 1941, during a second bombing of the railway bridge that was near our house, a bomb hit the wall, and we were hardly able to get out of the house through the window. The house turned out to be completely ruined (later, the occupants levelled it to the ground), and I. Feldman, our neighbour, gave us shelter. In the morning of 3 July because we had no means to be evacuated, we moved to the village of Ozarintsy, twelve kilometres away from the city, and settled down in the house of my father's brother, P. G. Roitberg, hoping to wait until the bombings were over.

However, the situation at the front worsened drastically, and on the morning of 21 July 1941, German and Romanian divisions entered Ozarintsy. By midday all Jews, including old people, were forced out of their houses and were ordered to take their shoes off, and marched barefoot to the square. Guards and machine-guns were everywhere. We were told that soon we would be undressed and killed.

About one to two hours later we were all taken to the big synagogue and kept there, without water or food, until late evening. We were told that in order to save on bullets the occupiers had decided to burn us alive, along with the synagogue. It was so crowded that nobody could sit; everybody stood, holding the little children. Thus, my father stood, holding Basya, my younger sister in his arms. The physical suffering was worsened by July heat. The heartbreaking cries of children and women were heard all the time through the praying voices. Nobody asked for food – everybody was suffering from thirst, especially the children. They told us that there was no need to give us any water since very soon we would be burned alive. It is impossible to describe the reaction of the exhausted people. Though it may seem strange – no matter that everybody was attending to physical needs while standing – the memory pre-serves terrible thirst rather than the stench.

Standing next to me, my father, with my sister in his arms, prayed continuously and his strong cantor voice distracted people a bit, putting some hope in their hearts.

Late in the evening they started to let people out of the synagogue: we had to go through a corridor of soldiers and policemen, and each of them believed it their duty to hit us with a stick. My father was severely beaten, and Fuks, a seventy-five-year-old man, was pushed on to the ground in front of me, and they trod on him, and stomped on his feet and tore his grey hair from off his head and beard.

The police selected a big group (some forty people) of young black-haired men, including my older brother Yanya, who was fif-teen years old. My mum managed to pull him out of this death-con-demned group at the last minute. They were all killed the same night, but according to local people the earth above them was 'breathing' for a long time afterwards.

They started to cut the tattoo off the body of a sailor named Entin who was ill. The poor man died from the wounds.

One can write continuously about the numerous crimes of the occupiers. It is true, though, that with the course of time many things were forgotten, especially because the situation in the Soviet Union helped a lot. Thus I remember filling in my first questionnaire where I wrote that, in the period of July 1941 till March 1944, I was in the ghetto. They called me to the KGB and told me that I should not write 'in the Jewish ghetto', but instead, 'in the occupation', and they tore my first questionnaire into pieces and made me fill in a new one.

But I would like to return back to that horrible day. When we came back to our houses we saw that the windows and doors had been taken out and the houses were empty inside. The local marauders had taken all our belongings. Our group, twenty-two relatives and refugees from Mogilev-Podolsk and the villages near-by, entered a house standing near the main road along which the troops were moving continuously, and sat down on the floor. Nobody could even think about water or food, everybody was afraid of what violence would follow next either from the occupiers or the local police.

Once, the following happened. At night, one military man shone his flashlight inside and saw a book on the windowsill. This was *The Oppenheim Family* by L. Feuchtwanger. He shouted at us, 'Are you people crazy? You will be killed for this!' and cocking his gun he left.

We stood still but when he was far away, we began hissing and whispering at my brother and sister (we couldn't shout), asking who had brought this book in.

When day started to dawn, I quietly got out of the house and went to the 'ice-house' near my uncle's home. There I found a few churns with sour cream. I was only nine years old then, so with much difficulty I rolled one of them to the edge of the ice-house that was closest to the house, put it inside a small niche and covered its top with a straw. And I started bringing pieces of ice into the house for drinking (there was no water, and to get it you had to go out of town, and this was an offence punished with death. Though later we had to take risks …) Then we split them among the people in the house.

There were no dishes or plates, and only later after I got to the attic (the ladder had also been taken), I found a few old, small jars. I told my parents about the sour cream. They were absolutely against me bringing in the sour cream, but then an old typist over-heard our conversation and started to convince my parents that the sour cream was a gift from God for the twenty-two of us. Eventually, I was 'providing' everybody with the sour cream for a few days. This was the only food we had.

Some time later, an order of the Kommandant was posted every-where. I don't remember now every detail of it but I remember that violation of each article resulted in execution – either by being shot or being hanged. The articles covered wearing the Star of David, leaving the boundaries of the town, purchase of food, bringing water in, and so on. Of course, it is impossible to describe the whole period of living in the ghetto. But some moments, including nice ones, I remembered too well.

A few days later, a few military people stormed our house and started pointing their guns at us, threatening to kill us all. Then they took away my disabled father, who was fifty-six, his brother, my uncle Pinchas, and a seventy-year-old man, a typesetter. They were forced to push horse drawn carriages uphill, and they were beaten with sticks just as severely as the horses were. We understood that they would never come back again. I was running, following, stay-ing them away from the road, but when a shot came my way, I sat down and started crying. And then I fell asleep. Some time later (perhaps about half an hour to an hour) I opened my eyes, and … a true miracle! My dad and uncle were walking my way, holding up the old man. I ran home to say they were released, and then back towards them. I ran up, kissed them and heard the following con-versation.

'*Obe* [addressing my father], *wie der Got?* [Where is God?]' the old man said, 'Are you convinced now that there is no God?'

'Calm down, and never say that again,' replied my father, and went on, '*Der Ebershteir* [that was how he addressed God] helped us by sending an officer who reprimanded the soldiers torturing us and released us out of the seemingly desperate situation.' And he continued whispering a prayer.

The old man with tears in his eyes agreed that my father was right, and I remembered this for the rest of my life.

Or there is another episode that I remember. In 1942 the typhoid epidemic started. In Mogilev-Podolsk people were dying in their hundreds. In Ozarintsy at that time, a medical attendant named Stukalenko was in charge of the medical unit. People said that he was a veteran of the war of 1914–18 and had experience in treating typhus. He prepared some concoction and was giving it out to people. All the members of our family recovered, although my brother was so weak that he couldn't stand on his feet and he basically had to learn to walk anew.

However, I remember the feeling of continuous hunger most of all. This was a very unpleasant feeling. It went alongside the feeling of continuous fear and danger. It has been over fifty years now, yet it is still very difficult to forget it. But every time that it became absolutely unbearable we would find something and survive. Once we convinced the miller to allow us to clean the mill and I gathered all the mill dust that remained there – it was an incredible joy!

But the biggest joy of all would be on days when we got some work. Even if it carried a threat to our life, even if unbelievably hard, for small pay – we would be none the less happy. Thus, for instance, one day we were offered the job of carrying sacks with flour on our shoulder no matter the weather, from one till four in the morning. My father carried sacks weighing twenty-four kilograms each, my brother, twenty, my sister, sixteen, and I would carry a twelve-kilogram sack. We went in the group by fifteen or twenty people. We couldn't lag behind because it was dangerous and there was a huge risk of being robbed. We even attended to our physical needs along the way.

We would go to Mogilev-Podolsky down a steep hill with no pathways, we would stop by at our friends' every day, who would daily welcome us and give us some hot water. But if anybody had found out about that, they would have been killed together with us. I remembered the Kaplan family among those people, one of whose children, Abram, now lived in Mogilev-Podolsk too. The Kaplan family – parents, older son Vilya and twin brothers Abram and Lyova – were exceptionally decent people trying to help all those in need, although they were very needy themselves. Their father, named David, together with Vilya, made a device allowing nails to be manufactured and they worked days and nights, primarily at nights – all of their family – providing means for themselves and helping others. But Menikha, my mum's friend, gave especial help to us. She was very ill herself and yet she would find the opportunity to make herbal tea and cakes for us.

Dangers were waiting for us even when we didn't expect them. I don't remember exactly, but some time in the summer of 1942 or 1943 they suddenly ordered all Jews to report to the main square. Such checks were not rare. And suddenly they read out lists of young boys, among which we heard the name of Yankel Roitberg, my cousin. He was ill then. Soon the SS appeared and the group of young boys, including my cousin, was taken to the railway station. Soon we found out that they had been sent away to work in Tulchin. There was only one way out from there – once you were no longer able to work, you would be sent to the camp and that was the end. But then, about a month or two later, somebody knocked on the window at night. It was my cousin, who had managed to escape from there together with his former classmate, Srul Schtivelman. Wandering through forests they had met partisans and were very happy. But alas, even then the partisans had an order not to accept Jews into their units. And they had to return home and stay there in hiding until liberation day.

The most difficult days came in March 1944 when the occupants were retreating. During that cold season we had to hide in ravines or forests, or sometimes stay at our Ukrainian friends.

And we survived. Of course our father believed that this was the work of the Almighty. And how could he think differently? Under any circumstances he managed to gather *minyan* and celebrate religious holidays and he prayed continuously, as well as fasting. I don't think there was a single week when he didn't fast. But he was the only one who knew how to get Jews together for *Rosh haShanah* and *Yom Kippur*. I watched how he did it in 1942. A priest from a local church turned to him with a request to help determine dates for the Christian holidays. My father told him all he needed and the priest helped him with his only request – to talk to the village headman and allow Jews to pray during the whole day. He also helped with some food.

But those miracles happened but seldom. Thus, for instance, I will remember my birthday of 18 May 1943 for the rest of my days. I met a policeman while going to an underground flat where they baked bread. My attempts to run away from him with a twelve-kilogram sack of flour failed. The first thing he did was to knock out my teeth, from which I still suffer. But then he saw someone else and looked away – at that moment I fled with my load, and was happy to deliver it to its destination.

That is all I recall.

57. I remember those horrible days[1]

Mikhail Roitman (b. 1935)

I was born in 1935 in the village of Balabanovka, Oratovsky district, Vinnitsa oblast. My father, Yankel Batkilin, was a cooper and Rachel, my mother, was a housewife. We had a big family but during the famine of 1933, my two brothers died.

Before the war we had lived in a new house: my parents, my brother Senya, my sister Sonya, and me.

Semyon Yankelevich Batkilin, my older brother, born some time around 1922, worked and studied at that time, at first, in Zaporozhye, at Zaporozhstal, and later in Mariupol, at Azovstal. Our family last heard from him on the eve of the war. From then on, no matter where I searched for him, I received negative responses.

In 1941 our family moved to Monastyrishche, then of Vinnitsa oblast. Here we saw the war begin. Since my father was disabled (he had only one eye), he was not taken to the front. I remember well the aeroplane fight above Monastyrishche, when two German planes brought a Soviet plane down. I remember the retreat of the Soviet army across Monastyrishche. People would go out of their houses and give water, bread and home-grown tobacco to wounded and burned soldiers.

The artillery began shooting on the day of retreat. My father was away at work, my mum hid with me in the closet at our home. One of the shells hit the house, the ceiling fell down, and Mum was injured in her foot. My sister pulled us out of the ruins.

After the artillery attack the Germans entered Monastyrishche. The Kommandant's office was established, along with the police, and the headman of the village was appointed. In the mornings Jews were taken out to repair roads. And then my sister wrote the word 'typhus' on the entrance to our house.

My father decided to move our family to our home village of Balabanovka. The raids in the village began when the autumn came. A few lorries with Germans and police would come from the district. We would hide in the cellars, pits and vegetable lots, but not always successfully. During one such raid my father was killed, followed by my sister.

Our life was getting more dangerous, and we had to live with different people. My mother would sew clothes for a piece of bread.

In the autumn of 1942 my mother took me and went to the forest, to the partisans, to the farmstead of Bogdanovka. I remember that a Georgian, nicknamed Khomka, was in charge of the unit. In the Shabelyansky forest, nearby, there was a group led by 'Golden Zhora'.

My mother worked in the unit kitchen, did laundry and repaired clothes. I brought chopped wood into the kitchen. The guns that I had to clean were my toys. There were about ten houses at the farmstead, and their owners were partisans. And, as you can imagine, they kept Soviet authority throughout that time, and even on the holidays they would set up the Red Flag.

The Germans did not come to the place until 1944. One time a lost German wagon train encountered the detachment and there was a fight. Nizhnik, the political supervisor of the detachment, was severely wounded then.

There were many Jews in that unit. One of them, Vassily Semyonovich Schvets, later became the director of the Monastyrishche Food Factory. I also remember others who were called 'Lyovka and his sons'.

The members of the unit organized acts of diversion to the rear of the Germans.

One day, after a raid on the railway station, the arrested Vlasov soldiers were brought to the kitchen. My mother gave them food and I looked out of my place at the stove.

One of them said, 'Look, a Jew boy is there!'

And a partisan machine-gunner, a Russian man named Grishka, hit him with all his might.

I remember a partisan scout named Vanka Belobrov, whom I envied because he was grown up enough to fight the enemy openly.

This lasted till February or March 1944, until the first liberation of us by the Red Army. All partisans were immediately drafted to the front line. But one of the liberating officers didn't forget to reproach them with a common phrase in those days, 'You have been hiding here under your women's skirts while we were shedding our blood.'

Approximately two weeks later more trouble came. The German army occupied the territory where we lived for the second time.

The commander of the German division issued an order for all women, children and old people to be sent to the German rear. But, for this, one had to go through the German commission inspection and receive a German passport. My mum went to the commission and returned from there white-haired. And she was only forty-four years old then. She had her passport issued in the name of Mariya Bonkun.

At that time, the woman we stayed with left. She took a parcel to her husband across the front line to Tzybulev, and my mother had to look after her four children, with the oldest being only eleven years old. And now my mother, with five children had to go across the forest for about ten or fifteen kilometres to *sovkhoz* Onoratka. It was very difficult to walk through the forest. After the battle, there were dead soldiers and horses; many people were wounded and they asked for help. Broken carriages were everywhere.

We arrived at Onoratka and were accommodated there at the cattle farm. The Germans made my mother cook for the German soldiers. The kitchen was located in one of the barracks. She put us, the children, under the stove at the same barrack, and ordered us to stay quiet.

The very same day, a German officer entered the kitchen. He got undressed to his waist, and began shaving with a safety razor. Then he threw the razor under the stove, and leaned down to get it. He saw a child's hand and started calling us: 'Come, come.'

But we sat quiet and didn't get out. The German got dressed and left and then within ten minutes' time he returned and threw a package with five candies under the stove. Here we lost our patience and tried to get the package, but his calculations were precise. He brought his boot down on my hand and pulled me out. Then he started to look at me carefully. I had black curly hair. I don't know what the German thought but my carelessness caused a lot of worry for my mother. He let me go and took another package of candies from his pocket, threw it on the floor and left.

Two or three days later, under the sound of artillery, the Germans retreated. And in the morning the Red Army liberated us for the second time. Twenty to twenty-five people went back across the forest to the farmstead of Bogdanovka. There we met our hostess, who rushed towards us with tears in her eyes. The roof of her house was broken and my mother helped her cover it with straw, and a few days later, having thanked her for everything, we left for Balabanovka.

There, more trouble waited for us. The Germans had our wooden house pulled down and left only a pile of mud in its place. My mother asked Aunt Sonya to take us in. Aunt Sonya was married to my uncle. She had lost her husband and three children. She took us in.

That year I went to school using my surname, Batkilin.

In 1945, when the war was over, my mother moved with me to

Monastyrishche. There she met David Isaacovich Roitman, a war veteran, who had lost his wife and three children. He adopted me, and took us into his own village of Sarny, Monastyrishche district. That's how the war ended for me.

1. This originally appeared in *Hope* (1991), Vol. 1, the bulletin of the Regional Association of Jewish Organizations of Smaller Towns of the Ukraine.

58. And our life 'under German rule' began

Mikhail Rosenberg (b. 1933)

Many years have passed since the Great Patriotic War ended. These years have erased much out of our memory, but those horrible days can never be forgotten, even though I was only a child then – I was ten years old.

Our family lived in the village of Romanov, Dzerzhinsky district, Zhitomir oblast. There were four of us: my parents, my older sister and me. My father worked at the Jewish collective farm (*kolkhoz*).

When, in 1941, the war began, just like many other people we got ready to leave, got on a cart and set out on our way. But the Germans were already moving towards us, and they turned us back to the village. And our life 'under German rule' began.

I remember how they ordered all men to get together immediately with shovels. They were all taken outside the village and made dig a pit and then they were all killed – as we found out later. We waited for our father's return for a long time but he never came back. And the rumours spread across the village that 'all Jews had been killed'.

Some time later, the Germans started taking our flats away – and all Jews were put into one place. A policeman now lived in our house.

During the second *Aktion* they started to bring together women, children and old people. My mother and I managed to run away. Our Czech neighbours hid us in their attic. We stayed there for some time. It was impossible to get either water or food because the police were checking and watching everywhere. When things calmed down we returned to the flat, where there were Jews. Many people didn't want to take any risk and keep us with them – they would be executed for that. My sister lived with her friend.

In September 1941, shooting was again heard everywhere and people were anxious again. Children and old people started crying. They felt that something troubling was ahead, something horrible, and that it was their turn. Policemen broke down doors.

My mother held me tight and kept saying, 'If we die, then we shall die together so that you won't suffer.'

But I ran away, through the window into the garden, and escaped.

I didn't know where I should go. Noise, laments and shots sounded everywhere. But there were good people too (unfortunately, very few of those), who told me where to go and where there were no Germans yet.

Thus my lonely vagrant life began. I slept wherever I could find a spot, I ate whatever I could find in the field or if anybody gave me some food. When, some time later, I came back to Romanov, I found out that everybody had been killed that day, including my mother and sister. Only a few Jewish specialists were left to service the Germans. Everything calmed down and I stayed in Romanov, as I didn't have a place to go to. I lived with those Jews who were left alive.

And again the Germans gathered the remaining Jews in the building of the former military commissariat, out of the village. They took people out in groups and shot them dead. But, at that time, they decided to keep only a couple of specialists alive. And when one of them was named, I bravely stepped out alongside. Thus I was saved by a miracle. But I decided (and I was told the same by a Jew named Pekkerman) that I had to leave the village because they would get me nevertheless and kill me. He gave me something, some pieces of fur, some clothes to trade for food, and I left Romanov for good.

During my wanderings I became ill and had scabies and people kept away from me – I was very skinny and looked terrible. People were even reluctant to give me some water. Thus wandered for two years, being ill, cold and hungry, as the Red Army did not liberate our area. In 1943 I got to the front and became a 'son of the regiment'. I stayed at the front until 1945.

It is very difficult for me to recall those years and describe them.

Among those who survived the first killing, there was a little girl of about four years old, very beautiful. Her parents and all her family had been killed. She somehow grew very attached to me, and looked to me as if I were her own brother. Maybe I reminded her of someone in her family, or maybe it was because I shared food with her, which I got with so much difficulty by begging it from people.

As far as I remember, her name was Bronichka. She was very weak and small because of cold and hunger and I asked my parents' neighbour, Puto, a blacksmith, whom the Germans kept alive as a craftsman, to take her to live with them. And she lived with them for some time. And I was happy that she had food and was kept warm.

But this didn't last for long. The remaining specialists remained under close supervision by the police, and they would frequently get checked, each family. And when the second round of killing took place, she was taken away and shot. She was too small and weak to run away with me, sleep outdoors, in the streets, in haystacks or stables. I recall her frequently. The people back then were in so much grief, in so much shock, that each of them was thinking only about himself or herself and their own children. And I was alone already, having lost my parents and my sister. I felt so sorry for her. I cannot describe the feeling. She didn't have anyone to lean on, and there was nobody who could give her a hug or console her in that difficult time. She stood there silent. Although they were little, children realized the danger and didn't cry but stood silently as if under some spell.

Vel Pekkerman now lives in Israel. He was the only adult survivor. His family (his wife and three children) were killed.

59. This endless road to nowhere[1]

Sophia Rosenberg

When the war began we lived in Chernovtsy, in the very same house in which we live now. A day later we got evacuated. We hoped to return soon, but alas … a couple of days later our train was stopped, the road ahead was bombed and we couldn't go any further. Many people were killed. All people who were on our train walked off in different directions.

We walked for a day and a night, and the road seemed endless. People were exhausted. Many were lost along the way: those who could still keep going kept walking on. There were few people in the villages: everybody was either hiding or had gone away. The Nazis were approaching.

The first German tanks caught up with us in the village of Balin. They went by at high speed and didn't seem to notice us at all. By evening we reached Dunayevtsy.

At dawn we walked further, to Kamenets-Podolsky. Not staying there, we returned to Zhvanets, in the hope of reaching our home-town. But, again, alas … our hopes were all in vain. We found ourselves in the centre of the German occupation.

Soon all Jews were brought together, sent across the Dnieper to Khotin, and here the marches from village to village, and from town to town, began. New groups of Jews joined us at each location.

The road turned out to be very long – through Bessarabia and Moldavian villages. The guards changed at every location and we, exhausted, hungry and weak, were marched on and on, being tortured along the way. Some people left their little babies on the road in the hope that somebody would pick them up and save their lives, and many, unable to endure all this, died *en route*.

We were taken to Yedintsy. The horrors of this camp are impossible to describe. People were dying by their hundreds in the camp. There were people who could no longer walk, and they crawled.

One day they brought us all together and split us into two groups. Our group was taken to Transnistria, to Mogilev-Podolsky.

The horrors were so tremendous that they are impossible to describe. Everything was against us – God, people, and even nature. Autumn September days were filled with a continuous drizzle from early morning, and wind with wet snow in the afternoon. In the morning, hundreds of people remained in the field where they had spent the night. Those who got up were marched on.

We had only the clothes that we wore. My sister and I were still children. Our parents, Hersch and Polina Schechtman, were very energetic people with strong willpower. It was not easy to carry us on their backs, to encourage us, saying that this would be over soon. There was obviously no limit to parental love towards their children, or to their responsibility for them: they covered us with their bodies and hid us away from death.

I remember frequent raids in Mogilev, and marches to other camps. We were on different lists to be sent to other camps, to the Bug and to Pechera.

Nobody knew our destiny. It often happened that a minute or two would decide your life and your future.

In early spring of 1942, a few gendarmes and two Germans with trained German shepherd dogs surrounded the market-place bringing together all the Jews that happened to be there. I was among them – the only child. No matter how hard I tried to escape, I didn't succeed and they locked us in a cellar.

In the evening they took us out. Two women tried to run away and they were shot instantly. It became known that the group would be sent to Pechera. And indeed the following day at 2 p.m., they brought us all together and wrote complete lists of names. A Romanian officer, in the presence of four Germans soldiers who were supposed to transfer us, did this. Somebody called the Germans away. I used this moment – I was nine years old, and I managed to escape and run away – I didn't run, I literally flew away from that place. Near the gates of the ghetto through which we were supposed to be taken I saw my mum. She looked so miserable to me and shrunk with pain and crazy with the thought that she could not do anything to save her child. She waited to join us and to go with me, while my dad was to stay with my sister. Seeing Mum, I grabbed her hand and pulled her away, choking on my tears. I saw my father grow white within one day, and my sister looked different too.

In March 1944 the front line was approaching, and the German retreat began. The Germans were angry and were especially violent on their last day on this side of the Dniester. At night the bridges across the river were blown up and they never managed to murder so many people.

A week later we walked back home. But the road now didn't seem scary. There were many difficulties, we were exhausted and weak, and we were walking home along the same roads that we had taken to the camp.

Hope and joy filled us, the survivors, but there was a lot of pain too, and grief of our family and friends who were murdered, killed in the mud, who died because of starvation or impossible work.

I have managed to describe only a very insignificant part of my memories. You cannot put everything into words.

NOTE

1. This originally appeared in 'People Remain Human: Testimonies of Witnesses' *Bulletin*, issue 3, 1994, pp. 71–2.

60. The *Aktions* of mass slaughter against the Jewish population

Avram Rosengaft (b. 1938)

Before the war, our family included five people: Grigory Abramovich Rosengaft, my father, born in 1903; Maria Isayevna Rosengaft, my mother, born in 1900; my sister Shelya, born in 1929, my brother Yasha, born in 1934; and me. We lived in Nemirov, Vinnitsa oblast, the Ukraine.

During the very first days of war my father was mobilized and because I was ill with dysentery, we could not get evacuated.

The convoy of unarmed drafted soldiers, including my father, was bombed by the Germans near the village of Pogrebishche and surrounded by their paratroopers. At night the group of soldiers from Nemirov managed to escape from this encirclement and went on their way home. Most of them, including my father, succeeded.

In July 1941, the Germans entered Nemirov and immediately all the Jewish residents were driven out of their houses and put into the ghetto, completely isolated from the rest of the local population. Five or six families shared one flat in the ghetto. There was no communication with the outside world. Local residents were not allowed to come close to the ghetto fence. From the very first days, the starvation began. At first there were 8,000 or 10,000 people in the ghetto.

Every day, healthy and able people would be selected from the ghetto. They worked on the construction of the Nemirov–Gaisin road. The companies Fiks and Schtral were in charge of the technical supervision of construction. The workers were punished for every little mistake in their work; they were beaten with whips until they were barely alive. Nevertheless, the ghetto prisoners who worked on the road or unloading things were capable of getting some food from the local population and bringing it into the ghetto. Thus children and old people avoided death from starvation, while being locked in the ghetto for the whole day. I was three years old and weakened by dysentery and my seven-year-old brother looked after me. My twelve-year-old sister worked alongside the grown-up women. This lasted till

24 November 1941, when the first *Aktion* of mass slaughter of the Jewish population of the ghetto took place. A special unit of the SS, with help from the local policemen, drove people out of the ghetto between 6 a.m. and 6 p.m., and gathered them in the building of the former Palace of Culture. They took anybody; they made no distinction. The people were marched like a herd of cattle, hastened along by whips and beatings.

Near the palace, the prisoners were put on to the back of lorries and taken out of the town where huge trenches had been already dug out. They murdered people there. The *Aktion* was accompanied by inhuman cruelty. The young children had their heads smashed together and were thrown into the trenches. The wounded people were pushed there too, and dead people fell down on to them. The war prisoners were forced to cover the trenches with dirt. At exactly 6 p.m. they stopped bringing people to the trenches. The murder was over. Those of the ghetto prisoners who were alive were taken back from the palace into the ghetto. The trenches were overflowing with the bodies of the victims, who were barely covered with dirt. According to the stories of witnesses (the war prisoners who miraculously survived), the earth there continued to 'breathe' for another day.

Thus the first *Aktion* of the slaughter of the Jews of the Nemirov ghetto was over. Some six and a half thousand people died in this act of murder. Many families had been warned by the local population about the upcoming *Aktion* and had managed to run away from the ghetto before the *Aktion* started. Many, however, were publicly executed as a result of failed attempts to escape. Some families managed to save themselves by hiding in secret hiding places built inside the ghetto.

Our family (Mum, Dad, brother, sister, Aunt Sonya Dashevskaya, her husband, and Shura, their daughter of a year and a half, and Aunt Dora Guralnik) had also been warned and on the eve of the *Aktion* we fled under the cover of the darkness. We had to leave old people there (Grandma Hanna Guralnik, Grandpa David Dashevsky, and his wife Feiga). According to my dad's reminiscences, that night, at one of the gates of the ghetto, an elderly guard was on duty (one of the local guards) and he pretended not to see us fleeing. Vera Ivanovna Tunik, a friend of our family, warned us about the *Aktion*, and she gave us shelter on this fateful day.

But since our family was very big, and Vera Ivanovna couldn't accommodate all of us in her flat, we decided that my parents and Uncle Abram Dashevsky would leave for the Mukhovezky forest while everybody else stayed with the Tunik family. Her husband was at the front and she had three children of her own. She put us up into the attic of the shed. It was very cold and frosty that day. We had to spend the whole day in her attic.

During the day, at about 1 p.m., the older members of the family saw through the holes in the walls that the policemen had entered her yard, shouting, 'Give the Jews to us!' and went into the house.

At that time, everybody heard noise and saw commotion around the shed. This was Vera's eight-year-old son, who was running around the shed calling the chickens. By this they tried to distract the police's attention. We realized that after the search of the house they would come to the shed, and we were waiting for this moment in terror. My sister saw that they had come out of the house and were indeed walking towards the shed. At that very moment a neighbour walked in, who also served in the police, and he called the policemen. They started talking. Two were convinced that Jews were in the shed, but the man who just walked in suggested a bet for a large sum that there were no Jews in the shed. By some miracle he took the policemen away from the yard to his own house.

We stayed in the attic till night. Then, numb with cold, we were taken inside the house, where our hostess gave us something to eat and drink. The neighbour who had saved us told us that the *Aktion* was over and we had to return to the ghetto. Our aunts could not decide what to do with us, the youngest children. They agreed with a woman they knew, whose name was Ustya, that she would keep us until our parents were found. Two hours after the adults left, Ustya told my sister that she was afraid of keeping us in her home, and suggestedthat we leaveher house. My siste – having a younger (one-and-half-year-old) baby in her arms, with our seven-year-old brother and me of three years – decided to go back to the ghetto to our grandma. Everything was in ruins there. We couldn't find our grandparents. Later we learned that they had been killed. My sister took us and went outside. It got dark. One of the local police guards walked up to her and showed her in which house there were people. A family of a local tailor named Sirota was there. These people had saved themselves by hiding in a prepared 'secret chamber', dug in the centre of the room and covered with an old chest of drawers. They gave us warm water with a soaked biscuit. We spent the night on the floor.

On the morning of 26 November 1941, my sister took us out of this house and went towards our ruined home in hope that the adults had returned. Some time within the next few hours they indeed appeared. All this time our parents had been hiding with their friends, farmers in Zarudentsy (during the day, they hid in the forest, and at night in their home). And again we were all inside the Nemirov ghetto.

After the first *Aktion*, the slaughter of the Jews, the area of the ghetto was decreased by approximately a half. The guards became more severe. Those adults who remained alive were escorted daily to the road works. They would get some food there, while others were left on their own. The houses would not heat. Daily, some child would die. Children and adults who got ill were taken out of the ghetto and killed.

The only source of food was whatever our parents managed to bring in secretly from the road works. Thanks to our dad, who seemed to know many local residents of villages nearby, they would leave food products, clothes and shoes for him in designated places. That was how the children in our family survived. The Radionov and the Tunik families, as well as others, also helped us considerably.

By May–June 1942 the rumours began to spread in the ghetto that the *Aktions* of killing the Jews had been repeated in Vinnitsa, Bratslav and Ilyintzy. Dad foresaw this beforehand and, while going to the road works, he was preparing a shelter for us in villages nearby.

In June we left the camp, again assisted by the guard who let us out the first time. My father took us to the village of Ruban (twelve kilometres away from the ghetto) to his friend from before the war, Doctor Ossovsky. Notwithstanding the huge danger, he agreed to hide my mum, my brother and me in the attic of his shed. My father took my sister to another village, to Talageevka. He couldn't hide himself because he had to oversee the communication among the family members scattered throughout the oblast. Besides, somebody had to watch the developments and make the decisions. He went to the station of Karapina where he took part in the road works. Our aunts and uncle remained in the ghetto.

On 26 June 1942, the second *Aktion* of killing the ghetto Jews began. About 3,000 people were murdered this time. Only about 200 people were left (the most able and strong, and those who had good clothes and shoes). From the ghetto they were transferred to a specially established camp (for the construction of the Vinnitsa–Kiev road via Uman).

The Germans punished the population for their connection with Jews. The Ossovsky family noticed that their neighbours were watching them and suggested looking for another shelter for us. We stayed about half a month with them, and they treated us very well. Our father left Karapina, brought all of the family together, and took us across the forest to his home village of Dankovka (thirty kilometres away from Ruban). According to my father's stories, we walked only at night. During the day we would hide at homes of the farmers we knew. My father knew all the villages along our way. Everywhere he had some childhood friends or people he knew. Sometimes we would have to stay in the forest for a few days in a row. Our lives were continuously in danger. A few times local residents discovered us. Near the village of Dankovka (eight to ten kilometres further on), in the forest, we were found by local farmers, who turned us in to the local police. The police transferred us to the Pechera concentration camp. This was at the end of July 1942.

In the Pechera camp we met a few Nemirov families (the Mostovyes, the Aisenshteins, the Ostrovskys and others). The hard days in the labour camp began. My parents and sister had to work in the stone quarry, in a peat bog, etc. Again infections and death were everywhere. I was ill with typhus but this was kept secret from other prisoners and guards. People who died were thrown daily into the used quarries.

And again we were saved by the fact that local farmers knew my dad well. They started helping us immediately with whatever they could. They hid food in secret places, as well as clothes. Then would even bring herbal concoctions for me. Thanks to their support, we survived. In late March 1943 Dad's friends from the village of Dankovka helped us escape to Perepylychye, and from there Ivan Kozlov, a local resident and my dad's childhood friend, transferred us by boat across the Southern Bug to the territory occupied by the Romanians. We arrived at the Dzhurin ghetto where the conditions of life were not so severe. We stayed in Dzhurin until March 1944, when the Red Army liberated us.

And we got back home immediately. We were warmly welcomed back by our neighbours in Nemirov. We got our flat back, and people brought back our things, our clothes. My father was immediately mobilized to the front. Neither we nor our saviours received any help from the state. Stephania Assonovna Radionova (who lives in Nemirov, Vinnitsa oblast), and Valentina Tunik (who now lives in Kalinovka, Vinnitsa oblast) are the only ones who are still alive out of all our saviours.

There may be discrepancies in the dates of the events described here, primarily because my sister – who was only a child at that time – compiled the memories.

My sister and I are amazed that the town of Nemirov is not mentioned anywhere as a place of mass killings of Jews by the Germans. No fewer than 8,000 people were murdered there. After the war, five mass graves at the Nemirov Jewish cemetery were publicly exhumed. But these facts are not described anywhere and it is impossible to get hold of documents proving them.

61. My long ordeal

Mariam Sandal (Askes) (b. 1927)

My father was a clerk and my mum was a housewife, and I had a twelve-year-old brother, Izya Askes.

Both of my grandfathers were coopers. Nuta Yankelevich Askes and Abram Moiseevich Schafran, who lived in the village of Pyatki, were honest and decent people. My mum was originally from Pyatki. Nuta Yankelevich lived in Chudnov. Both grandpas were very religious. Grandpa Nuta used to go to the synagogue on the holidays and on Shabbat. When I was little, I remember how he once took me there. I remember our synagogue in Chudnov. It was destroyed in the early 1930s.

My parents were also religious and helped poor people a lot. My grandpa would let people of any nationality stay overnight in his place.

Later, when I was wandering throughout the place, when hiding in villages, I just had to mention that I was the 'cooper Askes' granddaughter', and people would open their doors to me. Some would give me bread, some would let me stay overnight, and some would shelter me in the cold winter of 1941–42.

In 1941, when I was fourteen and had finished eight years at school, the war began. We lived in Chudnov then. On 7 July the Germans entered the town. We hadn't been evacuated on time because my dad was an important clerk and his conscription had been postponed so that he would not be mobilized and have to leave, but when he was finally allowed to leave on 4 July it was only three or four days before the Germans took over Chudnov, and we didn't manage to leave.

When the Germans entered our village we hid immediately. A week later, on 15 July, it was announced that all Jews would be resettled into a separate quarter. The word 'ghetto' was not used then. We also moved to this quarter together with all the other Jews. We had to wear yellow stars on our left arm. There was no barbed wire, but police and German soldiers were everywhere.

When we moved to the ghetto, my grandpa was seventy-eight

years old. Once, he went outside the house and wanted to cross the street to see his daughter Chava. The minute he got out, two Germans captured him, and tore his beard off, beating him severely – they saw the yellow star on his arm. Grandpa was very ill afterwards, throughout all the time we lived in the ghetto, and he could never get better till the day of the killings.

My dad was taken to 'work' one day. In fact the men were taken to dig pits for a group of Jews from the village of Pyatki who were brought to be killed in the Chudnov Park. When all the Jews from Pyatki were killed, a few of the Chudnov men including my father were forced to cover bodies with a little earth, and then lie down in the pit alive. And they ordered those who were left to bury these men alive. The Germans and police were standing around, smiling and laughing. Then they ordered the buried men to get up and take turns with the others. Those who refused to do so were beaten with twisted wire. My dad was beaten badly; his lips and arms (near the shoulders) were torn so badly that he could hardly walk home. They hid in the park so as not to be killed and came home only in the evening. That was what 'the new order' was like.

We were not allowed to go out anywhere or to buy food. Our Ukrainian friends would have helped us. Somebody would have brought some food for us but the Germans wouldn't let them even approach our houses.

Thus we lived until 9 September 1941, the day of the first mass murder of Jews in Chudnov. Old and sick people, children and women were shot to relieve the Germans of the burden of feeding them. They also shot everyone they could get hold of. People were put on to lorries and taken out to be killed. Eight to nine hundred people were killed then. My old grandpa, seventy-eight-year-old Nuta Yankelevich Askes, was killed then, as well as my aunt, Chava Margulis. We barely managed to hide that day, and by some miracle or turn of fate we stayed alive that day – my parents, my brother and I.

Thus we continued to live in the ghetto, until 16 October 1941. Mum and I were not allowed to get out, and they didn't give us any food. People were starving, it was cold, and there was nothing to wear because we were not allowed to take our clothes from our homes. There was no water. Those who tried to get out to bring in some water were either beaten or shot.

On 16 October 1941, the second killing of the Chudnov Jews took place. We were hiding in the houses to which we had been moved in the ghetto. At dawn, the policemen and Germans came in and began pulling people out of cellars, attics and flats. My mum was put in one column with my brother, and my dad and I into another. But when we were taken out into the street, one woman recognized my mum and started shouting, 'Let this woman go, let her go! She is not Jewish!' (My mum was blonde with blue eyes and didn't look Jewish.)

Some policeman thought about it, and let them go. And my mum and brother went to that woman. My dad and I also quietly left the column, turned around, and stood behind an old house. It happened that the column made a turn and we stayed in that old house.

We went to the village of Vishenka. When we reached the bridge near a local distillery, three policemen stopped us. The policemen were both locals and outsiders unknown to the prisoners. We were away from Chudnov by then and my dad started pleading with them, 'Please, men, let us go, please.'

But they didn't. They took us back to a cinema theatre where people were going to be killed.

My dad wanted to hide me in a box. He begged me, 'My daughter, please, I will put stones here, cover you, they won't find you here.'

But I wouldn't agree. I told him, 'No, Dad. Whatever happens to you, will happen to me.'

But once we were outside I saw a policeman I knew: I had studied together with his girls. I ran up to him and asked him, 'Please, Uncle Voronyuk, you know me well, I am your girls' friend. Please let me out of here.'

And he told the other policemen to let me go. Then I said I was here with my dad, and they let my dad go too.

Then we went out into the street and ran towards our home but it was empty and looted. We went into the attic and hid there until darkness fell. When it got dark, a neighbour came and said that Mum was at her place. My dad made a decision that we had to leave. We told the woman who lived nearby that we would stop by to say goodbye. We did so. Mum and my brother were sitting on the Russian stove crying bitterly. And seeing them we also started to cry. I kissed Mum.

Dad and I ran away to Vilshanka. Some people were hiding us there. In the period of 16–22 October, it was quiet. There were no mass murders, only isolated instances. We didn't know what was to be my mum's destiny.

On 21 October, my dad said, 'Daughter, let's go and find out where your mum is. Seems to be quiet now, and they are no longer killing people.'

And we went to that same woman. Mum and my brother were still there. We decided to go to our shattered and looted house and spend the night there.

At five o'clock in the morning we heard screams and shots again. And again we saw Jews being taken to slaughter. The doors were flung open and policemen came in. My parents, my brother and I were again taken to the same cinema. We hid behind the backs of the others. We tried to delay the hard moment of farewell and the minute of death. However, nothing helped us. We were pushed on to a lorry and taken out to the park. There were old and dying people there. The disabled were screaming. There was horrendous noise and screaming. People were perplexed; they tore their hair. My mum, Genya Abramovna Askes-Schafran, was a very beautiful woman. And I saw her turn grey right in front of me when she saw her husband and children taken out to die. But it turned out that my mum and my brother were again put on to one lorry while my dad and I were left on another.

When we were brought into the park, we started to search for Mum and my brother but could not see them anywhere. They ordered us to undress before the pits: clothes were put on one side, and people were walking towards the pit on the other. They stood on a wooden board, were shot and fell into the pit. When they started to take us off the car, one old man died right on the spot. And they continued pulling us down: my dad was pulled to one side, and I was pulled to the other. While Dad was being taken out, and while they pulled out the old man's body, I lost sight of Dad and started calling him. I kept calling him as they pulled at me, as they ordered me to undress. I wanted to see him, but couldn't see him anywhere. I looked around and saw the same policeman who let us out from the park on 16 October. I didn't want to leave my family; I wanted to die with them. I ran up towards him and grabbed his legs, 'Uncle Voronyuk, please find my dad, please!'

But he replied, 'What? Will you search here? Go and save yourself!'

I told him I didn't want to stay alive and wanted to join my dad. He winked to another policeman and he pushed me with his gun into the bushes. The Jews were taken to be killed on the other side of this place.

He pushed me and said, 'Run for your life.'

And there was a road leading to a military division, and so I set off on it. I didn't want to, I didn't want to be alone without my parents but that was how it turned out.

I went to the division, and then to Stukalka. When it got dark, I went to Vilshanka. We had friends there and I stayed with them. Then, again, I wanted to return to Chudnov, but they asked me not to because they knew I would be killed. And I stayed. That was the beginning of my long ordeal.

It was winter of 1941, very cold and severe. I left my home dressed lightly because it was summer and then suffered the whole winter through. I didn't stay in Vilshanka for long. One woman hid me. Then there was Ivan Fedorovich Gorbik, my father's friend. He asked this woman to take me to her dug-out in Podolyantse and hide me. I stayed with her for some time. But I still couldn't grasp the thought that my parents were dead. And I left again.

I returned to Vilshanka, to the Czechs. And there the Germans also held pogroms. One woman we knew, Anna Prokish, came in and said, 'Manya [that's what I was called then], go away; the Germans will find you anyway and kill you here.'

She took me to the village of Korchinki, and from there I went to the village of Karvinovka where there lived people we had also known.

I went to five or six houses in Karvinovka during one evening alone. One lot of people said they were leaving now, others that they were scared. So I went from home to home until one girl let me in. She said, 'I know who you are. You are Manya Askes.'

I realized I couldn't stay here for long either.

Thus I wandered throughout the winter of 1941 and early 1942 from house to house. There were very good people, too, for instance, the Atamansky family. Genya Atamanskaya hid me and gave me clothes from time to time. During the day I stayed in the forest while at night she would ask me to come and stay with her, or spend the night in the shed if she had a stranger in, or in the cellar or attic.

There were also some good people in Karnilovka – the Mayevsky, the Druz and the Kushnir families. They would take bread out for me into the field, into the haystack where I stayed. They would have given me shelter but couldn't do it: they had young children who could tell people and police would come immediately and kill me together with them.

Also, the Petruk family (Gustya and Maxim) hid me during the winter in Pyatki, Chudnov district.

Many times I had to hide in the forest. It was cold and wet there. I was ill, coughed a lot and developed rheumatism. And people started to tell me to get out of this area because many people knew me too well. So I went away without really knowing where.

I went away in June 1942, with no warm clothes on. I realized that I might be easily recognized but nevertheless I set out on my way. I walked for five kilometres and entered the village of Maloselka, Berdychev district. I walked down to the river where I saw a woman doing her laundry and asked whether she knew someone who might be in a need of a shepherd or a babysitter. She asked me who I was and I told her I was from an orphanage that had been bombed. She realized who I really was because the children from the orphanage had something with them while only Jewish children were begging for food, with no clothes on, starving. And she told me to go to some people who were ill and confined to bed and could accept me. I went there. It was Lukyan Gavrilovich Samotyos, a brother of Tatiana Gavrilovna Samotyos-Kravchuk, who later kept hiding me in her house for almost a year and a half.

When I went to them they let me stay overnight and I spent two weeks with them. Then a German killing squad raided the village in search of grain and bread. And Lukyan Gavrilovich, together with his wife, was taken to the Gestapo, in Berdychev. I was out in the field at that time, and they didn't arrest me. I had nowhere to go.

But then his sister, Tatiana Gavrilovna, came and told me to go with her, though she didn't have any bread. She was a poor widow with an only son called Arseny, who was eleven or twelve years old. And she took me to her home.

She told me, 'Marusya, if I find a small piece of bread and give it to Arseny please don't be hurt at me – for he is my only child.'

And I told her I wouldn't be hurt. But she never ever did so. She split everything we had among herself, her son and me.

A German killing squad, together with the police, visited the village many times, forcing people to go to Germany. They hunted me. But Tatiana Gavrilovna hid me very well – in the cellar, in the attic, or in a mud pit. She would cover the place with boards and then with straw and a pile of manure. She knew who I really was because Abram Moiseevich Schafran, my grandpa, lived in the village of Pyatki (five kilometres away from Maloselka). She even guessed this by my looks, telling me that I must be a granddaughter of the Berdychev Cooper (that was his nickname). I nodded but never told her anything else because you could not tell the truth even to the most close friends and family – the Germans could make you confess under torture.

And there is another episode I remember. A man walked up to her, who was originally from Pyatki but lived in Maloselka and said, 'Tatiana, this girl that lives with you, she is not from an orphanage. She is the Berdychev Cooper's granddaughter, she is Jewish. You had better send her away because they will kill you together with her.'

She replied (and she told me this later), 'Ivan, you told me now, but if you say this anywhere again, I will personally come and burn your house down.'

And he saw that she was serious and never mentioned this to anybody else.

Tatiana Gavrilovna would cover my face with soot, covering me, putting a kerchief on my face – thus she hid me from the Germans. And thus I survived until the liberation on 6 January 44.

Throughout all of my life I have treated Tatiana Gavrilovna as my mother, and I respected her, and all my family considered her our mother. Together with her son she was my saviour. He used to bring me food when I was hidden in the pit, hid me too, and warned me when the killing squad was raiding the village.

That was how I survived.

Now, feeling indebted to those who were killed, I have completed a Book of Memory of the Chudnov Holocaust, with the names of all those killed during three *Aktions* in Chudnov. I wrote a book on how people were killed on 9 September 1941, and 16 and 22 October 1941. In all 809,000 Jews were murdered in Chudnov, all kind and honest people. I listed about 2,000 names from Chudnov. I wrote about the Holocaust in Pyatki, a small Jewish *shtetl* erased off the face of the earth – there were no Jews left there. I wrote about the Holocaust in the villages of Ivanopol and Yakushpol, in the Chudnov district, where there are no more Jews – and there is a list of the murdered. In the village of Malye Korovintsy, a few families were shot. In Novy Chudnov, Chudnov district, Jews were also murdered.

This is all written in my book; this has all been established from trustworthy sources and from district archives. There are photographs and names of people killed, and names of those who never returned from the front, as well as the names of the war veterans. They say that Jews never fought. Yet in Chudnov alone, we had seventy people return from the front.

62. They risked their own lives and the lives of their families

Irina Sapir-Sharinskay (b. 1929)

When the war began our family lived in Berdychev and included my father, Yakov Sapir, aged thirty-six, my mother, Manya, aged thirty-three, my sister Sarra, aged four and myself, eleven years of age. My father worked at the Fifth State Tanner Factory and my mum was a housewife.

On 7 July 1941, the Germans occupied our town. We had to find some means for living and V. L. Buiko found some work for my father as a tinsmith in a local theatre. During the occupation this man was the director of the theatre and he had known my father for a long time. He held himself guilty that we didn't manage to leave on time – when my father asked him whether he was getting evacuated, he said, 'Don't you remember 1918? They didn't hurt anyone.'

While my father worked in the theatre, I used to bring him his lunches. I didn't look Jewish; that's why I could go across the town easily. (Jews were forbidden to go to the centre of the town or to the market.)

One day a very tall, vicious-looking woman grabbed me by my hand but then she decided that she was mistaken. She could have got a reward for turning me in.

I was the main provider of food – I went to the stationed military units and the Germans would give me food, since they had plenty of it.

When there was no work at the theatre my father would go to Prokop Voloshin, the administrator of the theatre, to help him cover a shed. I went there too, and thus got to know all of his family: Aunt Lyuba and their three daughters – Olga, Valentina and Elena.

When the first raids on Jews began, they used to say that people were taken as though going to work. They were taking younger men and women who had no children. Some time later we found out what kind of work this was. My father was at his work, my mum was home, with us. When the raids began, she would send me out of the house and would remain home with my sister so that they would not take her away.

On 15 September, another raid was supposed to take place and we knew about it, having been warned by our non-Jewish friends. On the morning of 15 September I left the house as always and Mum stayed home with my sister. My father was in the cellar in our flat (he dug it out during the nights). When I got outside I met Donya, my friend, who was two years older than I was.

We used to live in Shirshov Street and a street parallel to it (now Russkaya) was quiet and empty; people would seldom go along it. So we went there but when we came out on to the street we found ourselves right in the middle of the inferno. The Jews were being marched along that street in a long column and local policemen escorted them. One of them told us to get into the column.

We said, 'Uncle policeman, we are only seven years old, we are young.'

And he replied that we had to be in the column even if we were seven months old, so we had to join everybody else. From Russkaya Street the column took a turn into Zhitomirskaya Street and went towards the Yatki (the name of a market before the war). On the right side of Zhitomirskaya Street there was a small alley with little old houses. When we approached that alley, Donya grabbed my hand and pulled me into it. We ran into one of the houses – completely looted by then. There were two rooms in it. We hid behind the doors. We sat on the floor and were afraid of making a move. During this time we heard people coming in, men and women, searching for Jews. But the house was abandoned and that saved us.

I don't remember how long we stayed there but it seemed to us to last for ever. Then we heard people in the street saying that the pogrom was over. We left the house but didn't know where to go. People were standing in the street and talking. From what they said we realized that the Jews had been taken to the Yatki and from there they would have been taken away and killed but now the Germans were letting them go. We went there. We saw a fence made out of barbed wire. People were there: the women, children and elderly were separated from the men.

Unimaginable noise and shouting sounded there; women and children were crying, 'Please take us, say that I am you wife, say that I am your child … '

It was something unthinkable. Later we found out that those men selected by the Germans would not be killed: they were professionals and had the right to take away their families. But it was hardly possible to find their relatives in this crowd of desperate and mad people.

I walked away, back to my home. I couldn't find my mother or sister and only my father was still in the cellar. I let him out. He told me that he heard Mum's final cry, 'Now, we are leaving!'

Mum was thirty-three years old, and my sister was only four. We lost them that day. Starting 15 September, my father and I were left alone.

On the following day, my father agreed with Buiko that I would go and spend the night in their home and during the day I would return home, to my father. He didn't go to work any more. That's how we lived till the second raid, in October. As always, I was going home in the morning, having heard nothing about the pogrom. I met Kazimir Zhuravsky, a friend of mine.

'Where are you going, Ira?'

'Home.'

'Don't go there, there is a pogrom.'

And I went back to the Buiko family. He lived with his wife Stasya and two children. Two days later, together with Aunt Stasya we went to my home. We didn't find my father, but the underground secret cellar was destroyed, and the house was completely empty – looted. My father was thirty-six.

I stayed for some time with Buiko, and then Aunt Stasya told me she was scared for her own children, and I had to leave. I wandered wherever I could, sleeping in ruined houses, sometimes on a threshold of somebody's flat; or sometimes some people would let me in, give some soup, or sometimes they would send me away.

I met many good people but everybody was afraid. Once I went to a family of a policeman and he called me inside (they would receive rewards for Jews they turned in). He put me to sleep into his own bed although his wife and children were in another room. I could not fall asleep that night. I don't know what stopped him, but he didn't hurt me. The second day I picked my moment and escaped.

Then I remembered that once my father had a friend in Ozadovka, I had visited him together with my dad. I remembered his name – Stepan Kovbasyuk – and went to him. I slept in a field in a haystack; it was cold and snowing. I tried to reach Ozadovka but couldn't because I didn't know the road. Finally, I came to the Kovbasyuk family. I lived in their home for some time, but in a village people knew each other too well, and they were frightened to keep me for long.

It was December and I returned to the Buiko family. Aunt Stasya went with me to the Kommandant's office and, telling them that I was her distant family, an orphan, she received a referral to the Dmitrov orphanage. Thus I got into the orphanage. People there were very kind and each of them tried to give us an extra piece of bread since we were hungry in the orphanage. In spring the children were let outside and we ate grass.

I was not the only Jewish girl in the orphanage. Somebody on the staff reported to the Germans that there were Jewish children in the orphanage. We were warned a day before they came. All older children ran away, and only the younger children stayed. They took children away, not really knowing who was Jewish – they were selecting curly, dark-haired children, following some signs known only to them. I lived with the old parents of our teacher, Lyubov Pavlovna Voloshchuk. A few days later, I returned to the orphanage because the Germans had returned the children. Later, before their retreat, they killed them all anyway.

In the summer of 1942, Tatiana Yarosh took me on as a nanny. She baptised me, being afraid of somebody reporting on her. But her neighbours turned out to be decent people. I lived with her until the autumn, and then I wanted to go and see Aunt Stasya. She worked in the theatre. There I met Lyubov Voloshina. All her family worked in the theatre. Aunt Lyuba offered to let me live with them and look after her grandson. (Later, I found out that when my father was taken with all the other Jews and was walking in the column he saw Aunt Lyuba and shouted, 'Save my daughter.') Thus in November 1942 I came to the Voloshin family. They turned out to be good people and treated me friendly and well. I helped around the house, and looked after their children. Near Novoselky they had a small house with a vegetable lot and I was there frequently while during the summer all their family worked on the lot. But most of the time the family lived on Dzerzhinsky Street.

One day Aunt Lyuba brought the news that somebody had reported me to the SD (Gestapo) and they were already coming after me. This was in the summer of 1943. They came after me a few times till the autumn but couldn't get me since I was no longer in the city flat. But then they learned about Novoselky. When a policeman came to find me we were all out digging potatoes.

'I have come to take the girl,' he said.

'I'm not letting her go anywhere,' Aunt Lyuba replied. 'I took her from the orphanage and I know she is not Jewish.'

But the policeman insisted. Then Aunt Lyuba and Olga said that they were not letting me go alone and would go with me. I don't know how these women weren't afraid of going with me to the SD, because they risked their lives and the lives of their family.

In the SD we were taken into an office of some officer. Beside him, there was an interpreter and a German woman. We spoke with the help of the interpreter: Aunt Lyuba and Olga were present, and I stood near the desk. The Germans were dealing with me and the interpreter spoke with the women. They looked at me from all angles but, as I said earlier, there was nothing in my face that would betray me as a Jew.

Before the policeman came, we had worked out a story that I was raised in an orphanage, that I never knew my parents or nationality, that I got the surname in the orphanage and the Voloshin family adopted me from the orphanage.

They looked at me. As I was wearing a neckerchief they made me take it off. The German woman liked my hair very much. She admired it, saying, 'A beautiful child, a very beautiful child.'

They let us go, believing I was not Jewish. Those two women did an impossible thing.

When the Germans were retreating, we all left for the village of Terekhovaya and waited there until our troops entered. The Germans tried to drive all the residents from the village in order to send them to Germany. We were hiding behind the village, in a ravine. Even then they wouldn't abandon me. I lived with them till February 1944. I don't have enough words to express all my gratitude to them.

It has been some sixty years since the days of the mass killings and the older I get the more frequently I recall those days. When I was young, I didn't want to think about them, it was so difficult. But all these years I have continuously dreamt about the war, and in these dreams I continue searching for my parents and my sister, and hiding.

63. It is impossible to describe the horror that reigned in the ghetto

Lydia Slepchuk (Goichman) (b. 1936)

I am returning from a fairground called 'life'. And recalling all the details of this fairground, I'm shuddering with pain and hurt. I ask God, and I ask people, 'Why?' Is it possible to call my existence a life? Why did I have to play such a tragic part in this fairground carnival? Perhaps an actor playing that part could expect many times his pay. But nobody has ever compensated the damage brought to my child's heart. To whom do I have to submit my claims? To the Nazis who took away my childhood, as well as my father, my joy, and my health? And the wheel of misfortune has kept rolling ever since. I cannot remember a single day in my life for which I could say, 'This day was normal.' I have been fighting my whole life for my place under the sun, and for the right to remain human. All of my life I've been persecuted, had it proved to me that I'm a second-class person.

When I was a child I dreamt of a piece of bread and of freedom. I dreamt of holding a real doll in my hands. But my dream was not meant to be. I grew old without a doll, without any toys. Later, when confined to bed, I dreamt of standing on my own two feet and breathing in fresh air.

And this was all of my life, filled with dreams only that were never destined to come true. What can a poor old woman dream of now? About the rest? And where could it be found? How can I have rest now among the ruins of my life? There is no future for me, and the present looks quite sombre …

My past began in the Jewish *shtetl* of Ternovka, in Vinnitchina, Dzhulinka (now Bershad) district. It was a colourful Jewish town with Jewish traditions and households. I remember old men with grey beards wearing black hats, and many children of different ages. This was an authentic Jewish town, with the Jewish school, Jewish council, with numerous workers, artisans and intelligentsia. I cannot give any numbers because I was only four or five years old then.

Almost at the very beginning of the war the Germans took over my Ternovka. Only a few had managed to get out because in its majority the population was poor, families with many children, while all the men had been mobilized for the war immediately. Where could my young mum go with three little children, each one smaller than the other? And those few thousand Jews that remained in Ternovka had even more children and were just as poor.

When our troops retreated, we were bombed terribly. Every time, Mum would grab us and run out into the street where we would hide under some bush.

The German motorcyclists entered the village with a roar, followed by columns of machinery and then by columns of the war prisoners, in rags, with bloodstained bandages. Women and children ran out of the houses and threw food into the column.

With the onset of the German rule, they established the Kommandant's office, and appointed the headman of the town and the police. Every day, somebody would be taken hostage and a 'contribution' (ransom) would be demanded. A few days after they entered Ternovka, they established the ghetto. Everybody from the peripheral areas of the town was moved to the centre.

Our house was located in the centre, and I remember well how, suddenly, a lot of people lived in it, each room shared by a few families. Young women were taken to the concentration camps. They wanted to take my mum too. We clung to her and cried and then Grandma started begging them because her daughter had three very young children. The policemen beat Mum badly, and took her teenage sister instead, and Grandma followed her daughter voluntarily.

I remember my grandma; she was small, thin, grey-haired and perhaps younger than I am now. She gave birth to many children. A few of her sons were fighting, and one of them was a military pilot and was killed near Leningrad.

I never saw my grandma again. This was in the spring of 1942.

The women who escaped from that camp told us that the Germans raped my young aunt, torturing her and she couldn't endure it and had gone insane, and then they shot her in front of my grandma, and Grandma charged at them and they shot her too. Ever since that, my mum and other young women hid in a so-called 'secret chamber' which Mum had prepared before the ghetto was established. The children and old people were left to sleep in the house. Every night pogroms would take place and people were taken away to the camps.

And, one day, old people with their grandchildren came to the secret chamber too, and only three of us were left in the house. Mum asked them what happened and they said that the Germans were now taking away everyone from the neighbouring houses. Mum asked why her children had been left and they said that these were just children and nobody would take them, but she demanded to be let out of the underground cellar, otherwise she would turn everybody in. They let her go. Mum grabbed us, sleepy, and dressed only in nightgowns, and ran back towards the secret chamber, literally throwing us down into it. There was no food there, moreover local Ukrainian teenagers had found the air outlet in the basement and closed it with stones, suspecting there were Jews hiding there but failing to find the entrance to the secret chamber. (The top of the entrance had been masterfully covered by Milya, a teenager, who hid himself in an attic among the logs that were kept there.)

On the fifth day in the secret chamber we began to suffocate, and we realized that we would die anyway – so we started to leave the basement for the attic. The house was looted and even the attic was searched. Milya was not discovered by some fortunate accident – one of the policemen went to attend to his physical needs near the logs, mumbled something against the Jews and went downstairs. Milya (Mikhail Aptekarev) survived the war; he now lives in Odessa.

While we were getting out, we were discovered. And again we rushed back into the basement but they started shooting and we had to leave. Mum begged them not to kill us, offering a ransom – she had buried some jewellery in the basement. This was the sixth day after the pogrom. We didn't know that everybody had been killed. Only specialists and a few members of their families were left alive.

When Mum gave up her jewellery they sent us into the ghetto, now downsized to a few houses near the marketplace. All the rooms in these houses were taken up by a lot of people. It was overcrowded, and Mum, with three children, got a place in the kitchen, above the Russian stove. And we lived there until the following pogrom. (The first pogrom took place 27 May 1942.)

It is impossible to describe the horror that reigned in the ghetto – the complete lack of hygiene, the cold (there was nothing with which to heat the houses) and the starvation, lice and typhus. People were dying, one after another. And raids, beatings and robbery were a constant hazard. Emil, a Gestapo officer, was the Kommandant and he was notorious for his extreme brutality. I remember all that horror well. I would definitely want to put it all down for the generations to come, but it would be a very long story.

I have to say that not everyone suffered under the German rule as Jews did. I remember sounds of music coming from our homes now taken over by Ukrainians and Poles (many Poles lived in Ternovka). Young people had fun with the Germans in the centre of the town, and many girls would gladly date the Germans;

weddings were celebrated. And in the meanwhile we were tortured and suffering from diseases and hunger.

In early March 1943, early in the morning, the ghetto was surrounded once again and people were taken out. But that day Mum woke up at dawn to clean the kitchen a bit, and saw this from the window. And, again, she grabbed her naked children and ran towards the basement. There were many people already in it. We heard shots through the windows. And again we stayed in the basement a long time, for about a week, with no food or water, with young children. People were going insane. And they started to leave there quietly. Mum also went out to see what was going on, telling us to sit and wait for her. We waited for a long time and then decided to get out too and find Mum, and then we suddenly saw her and she pushed us back into the basement. While she was outside, standing behind the corner of a house, she had seen Kommandant Emil catch a young woman, Shelya, a paramedic, with her little baby in her arms. He grabbed the baby and smashed its head against a tree, killing the child instantly; then he shot Shelya with his handgun.

I cannot tell you for sure how long we eventually stayed in that basement but, early one morning, everybody who was there decided to get out.

A girl named Fira, approximately of my age, sat down near us in the basement. Her parents were tailors and that morning they had gone to work and, seeing people fleeing from all the rooms, she ran away too, and came to the basement. When Mum walked out with her offspring, the girl followed us. Mum asked her to go with those who didn't have children but nobody wanted to take her, and may God forgive us, a long time later we knew that eventually nobody took her. After this pogrom only a few male specialists were left alive and she stayed with them, and then they were all killed.

And God led us further on. Mum was carrying our youngest brother in her arms. My older brother helped her carry him, and I was walking near them, barefoot and covered with rags. This was an early March morning, it was frosty and my feet were very cold and I began to cry. Then Mum threatened me that if I didn't stop crying she would drown me in the river along which we were passing. But the threat didn't help and Mum sat down to warm my feet with her hands. A local woman appeared near us and offered Mum to take a girl, that is, me, with her. Mum told me to go but I didn't want to. When Mum said that we would all be killed sooner or later, I said that it didn't matter, I wanted to be with them. And I didn't go. The woman brought old felt shoes for me, a piece of bread for each of us, as well as an egg for me. I still remember the taste of that bread – warm and fresh.

The sun rose. We got warm in a haystack and moved on. Mum was heading towards a nearby village where her father, a tanner, was at that time. Thus we met him halfway. He had heard about the pogrom and had gone to see what had happened to us. From his big family, after the first pogrom, we were the only ones left.

Grandpa took us to a farmstead where there were no Germans, hiding us in a pigsty, or ravines and forests, wherever it was possible. He brought us food and sometimes he stayed overnight with us, understanding how frightened my mum was alone.

Another big family lived in the farmstead. And somebody turned them in, and the killing squad took them out of the village and shot them all. (We heard the shots.)

Then things grew worse. We were not allowed to stay in the shed any more, and then our grandpa was turned in. He was taken to Dzhulinka and killed there. A farmer, whom he asked to pay for work done, had turned him in. My older brother was with Grandpa; Grandpa whispered to him to run for his life but he refused. Then Grandpa slapped him and ordered him to run. The policeman who escorted Grandpa looked away and pretended not to see this.

Thus our grandfather was gone, and it turned out to be much more difficult now. There was no food at all. Then winter came. Mum asked one local woman to let us live in her attic. My brother lived alone in some abandoned stables. In the evenings he would come over, Mum would move the haystacks and throw me down from the attic into the snow. Snow would hit my eyes, they would hurt and I had terrible headaches. I fell down on my knee and my brother pulled me by the hand to show me the way, I would crawl to the doors, knocking and asking for a piece of bread. Some people gave us bread, and some would set their dogs on us.

We were dying. And then Mum asked one woman to take me and hide me. For about three months this woman hid me in her closet, in the attic, in the chimney, and sometimes on the cold stove. I don't remember what I ate there. She didn't have anything to eat herself and she had two her own children. That woman wanted to take me to the church and baptise me, but I said no. Where did I get that? And now, an old woman, I cannot comprehend where that came from in a young, exhausted, uneducated, half-savage child? How can I explain this?

And thus we suffered until our liberators came. The first of our soldiers that saw me asked this woman, 'What illness does this girl have? She will die soon!'

But I didn't die then. But as a result I had this long serious illness from twelve to twenty, and I have had an unhappy difficult life, and a crippled and servile destiny.

64. I was left completely alone

Binah Tenneblat (b. 1928)

The town of Kamenets-Podolsky where I lived was divided by the Smotrich River into the Old Town and the New Town. In the early days of the war, the bridge connecting the banks was blown up and people had to walk across by going down a steep staircase and through the pillar stones.

In early July 1941, the Hungarians entered the town. On the first day of the occupation they shot 400 Jewish men in the Old Town. The Germans entered the town in late July. On 5 August, all Jews were forced into the Old Town. They were joined by a few thousand Jews who had been marched from Hungary. On 26 August the Hungarian Jews were taken out and shot.

On 28 August 1941, early in the morning, the Germans began to force people out of their houses and put them into columns. We were taken out of the town where five big pits had already been dug out. The Jews were brought together, and then *schutzmann* [police-men] encircled and guarded them until a German killing squad with machine-guns arrived. Then they began taking people to the edge of the pits and shooting them.

I lost my mum and dad in the crowd and was holding my brother, Bumchik, by the hand. He was nine years old. My uncle, Ersch Kaganovich, a plumber, had worked in a town hospital before the war. A part of the hospital had now been taken by the Kommandant's office and they needed him as a specialist. He received a paper permitting him and our family to survive. The paper was in German and that was why he didn't know he could have saved the family too. When he came to work on 28 August, he learned about the mass killings. An interpreter was sent to the field where people were being killed to get his family. Suddenly I heard the name Kaganovich called out and my aunt with her three children were taken aside. My brother and I followed them. My aunt warned me not to call her mum, but to say that I was not Jewish and had got into the column accidentally.

During the whole day we watched 13,000 people being taken to the pits and shot with machine-guns. I saw my father with three young children taken to the pit. When I saw my mum as they were going to take her to the pit I walked up to a German watching us and told him that my mum was not Jewish either. He helped me save her then.

Only 100–150 people were left alive after this bloody massacre. They were different specialists whose lives were spared so far by the Germans.

In early September all Jews left alive (many managed to hide) were gathered into the ghetto outside the town on the premises of a former military division (training battalion). I remember that a German officer named Bauer was appointed as the ghetto Kommandant.

In July 1942 a group of people living in the ghetto was shot and another group was transferred to another ghetto in the former Silicate Institute. Jews from all the small places surrounding Kamenets-Podolsky were brought there. We lived expecting death, in the most difficult conditions. We had to wear yellow Stars of David.

My uncle continued to work at the Kommandant's office. There he met a young Jewish man who had Romanian documents. He warned my uncle frequently about upcoming developments. On 29 October 1942, he told my uncle that a document had been sent from Rovno, in which it stated that the ghetto would be liquidated at night and everybody would be killed. And then my uncle persuaded his two daughters and me to stay overnight in the basement of the Kommandant's office. The following day he didn't come to work and we realized that something horrible must have happened. We couldn't stay in the basement of the Kommandant's office any longer so we left for the village where our family's friend lived. *En route* the *schutzmann* caught my cousins while I managed to escape.

We knew the headman of the village very well. Seeing me, he was scared but he didn't turn me in. However, he was equally afraid of letting me spend the night there. I spent the night in the forest and in the morning I returned to Kamenets-Podolsky. This equalled suicide, since everywhere there were announcements threatening death to those who hid Jews. I came out of the town, having walked through many villages, and by the time night fell I had reached the village of Slobidka-Rechtetzkaya. There I went to the village head and told him my story – that I was a refugee from Voronezh. I was taken into the family of nice people – Grigory Gumenyuk and his wife Dariya.

All the time, till liberation in April 1944, I had lived in fear of my identity being disclosed, but the wish of my mum for someone from our big family to survive came true.

When, after the liberation, the fear of death was not hanging over me, I felt all the pain for my innocent, murdered family with particular acuity. I was left completely alone, as all my closest family had died: my parents, my two brothers, two sisters, two of Mum's sisters with their families, two of Mum's brothers with their families, and my father's brother with his family.

Every year, on the date of their death, I go to Kamenets-Podolsky, sit next to their graves and cry over them bitterly.

65. Local people were trying to help prisoners

Boris Timoshenko (b. 1937)

My father, Nikolay Nikolayevich Timoshenko, a Ukrainian, was a native of the town of Polonnoe. In the 1930s, after graduation from Shepetovka agricultural college, he was sent to work to Turbovsky (now Lipovetzky) district, Vinnitsa oblast. Working there he met a very beautiful girl, my mother, Genya Markovna Druker, who was Jewish. They fell in love with each other and got married.

I was born in the village of Staraya Priluka in 1936 (according to my father's story), though my birth certificate has the date of 5 January 1937.

In 1938, having worked off the required period of time after his graduation, my father – together with his wife and son (that is, me) – went back to his parents in Polonnoe, to live there. In Polonnoe my father started working as a mechanic in a local transportation company and taught in the agricultural school while my mother worked as an accountant in a local dairy-processing factory.

Our family lived in the house of my father's parents. Beside my grandparents, Arkady, my father's younger brother, lived in the same house. He worked as the head of the renovation and construction unit at a local porcelain factory. He had been disabled since childhood and walked using a cane. In February 1939 my younger brother Anatoly was born.

In 1939 my father was drafted into the Red Army and we rarely saw him from that point – he took part in the liberation of Western Ukraine, and in 1940 he fought against Finland. Then in 1941–45 he took part in the war against Nazi Germany. After the victory over Germany as a part of our army he was sent to the Far East to fight Japan.

In the summer of 1941 Nazi Germany invaded the Ukraine. I cannot forget those days. Starting September 1941, we used to stand with my grandfather near our gates and lorry after lorry would pass by us slowly, with women, old people and children. People were crying. They were taking Jews from the city to be murdered.

There was no asphalt on the old Matrosov Street, and the cars would go slowly over the sandy surface. It was clear that every lorry was filled with people, and some women held babies in their arms, and on each of the cars there were two Germans with automatic guns. The lorries went by and soon in a forest nearby, just across the railway tracks, shots sounded and they were all killed.

After the mass killings of the Jews, the local Nazi administration organized a concentration camp/ghetto, together with a killing squad, near a granite quarry across from what is today a factory for decorative ceramics. Before the war the place had served as a Soviet concentration camp for 'public enemies'. Here, behind the barbed wire, the Germans, with their police collaborators, put professional and artisan Jews (shoemakers, watchmakers and so on) as well as other Jews found in the area after the first mass killings had taken place.

Somebody reported to the Germans that a Jewish woman with two children lived in my grandfather's house. So in the first days of December 1941 a cart with policemen drove up to our house and took my mother and us to the ghetto. When the policemen were putting us on to the cart, my grandfather tried to argue with them and begged them not to take us. But the policemen just beat him up badly with their gun butts.

Thus my mum, my young brother Anatoly and I were taken to the ghetto. The conditions of life there were terrifying – cold and hunger were common. As the ghetto became overcrowded, the 'extra' people were taken away and shot.

Local people were trying to help prisoners with whatever they could, throwing bread across the barbed wire, but this was extremely difficult – the Germans would start shooting with their machine-guns from the guard towers, and the policemen on guard would beat them with gun butts.

Even water was scarce after the Germans threw a woman down the only drinking-water well in the whole camp to scare us. After that the prisoners would bring water from the village while being escorted by the policemen. Children were always afraid of the Germans killing them, so we frequently hid under the bunks.

Sometimes our grandfather would manage to pass us a piece of bread via a policeman he knew; however, he would more frequently get battered for such attempts. Once he was so badly beaten that he lay ill for a long time, had fits and hallucinated that the policemen were beating him again.

My child's memory retains recollections about the day of our liberation from the camp. It was a June day in 1942. Two policemen pulled me and my brother from under the bunks and kept pulling us to the ghetto gate while we were screaming. Near the gate there was a carriage with horses, and nearby we could see our Uncle Arkady, my father's brother, with a group of policemen.

We heard orders and shouts from the police. Someone was ordering that a policeman named Kozyr be found urgently, and that Rogol be called.

A big policeman came out from an office near the gates and turning to the policemen that stood with uncle Arkady said, 'Mr Kommandant said we do not need these children and let him have them.'

Uncle Arkady put us on to the carriage and took us back to our grandparents' house. After our grandparents and Uncle Arkady had cleaned up me and my brother and changed our clothes, our neighbours stopped by. We had close and friendly relations with them – Stepan Cherny with his wife Varvara, Maria Mykhnyan, her sister Nadezhda Chalyuk, Marta Budnik and her husband Alexander. Together with our relatives they started to think how to save us, two little orphans. Everybody thought that we were still in danger from the Germans. After discussing everything, they decided to follow the suggestion of Alexander Ivanovich, Marta Budnik's husband.

And he suggested the following. He worked with the Germans as an engine driver in the Shepetovka depot. He had a flat in Shepetovka allocated by the depot. He almost never used it, as when he was done with his shift he would come back to Martha, his wife. So he suggested that a grown-up should live in his flat in Shepetovka and hide us there too. Our grandma, Stephanida Mikhailovna, our father's mother, agreed to go with us. It was a very courageous decision she took at that time.

The following day my brother and I went towards the railway and Grandma was near us. Grandma and Uncle Arkady took us to the freight train. A German soldier with a rifle was standing near the train. My uncle started talking to him about something, possibly explaining that this old woman with children needed to get to Shepetovka. The German objected, but when Grandma gave him a few eggs and a piece of lard he cheered up and waved his arm towards an empty car. My grandma, my brother and I climbed along the side of the car and jumped down inside. Soon afterwards the train got us into Shepetovka.

We went into the designated flat. Marta was waiting for us there and she told us how we should act – to stay in the room or on the terrace and, if the Germans or strangers appeared, to get down under the bed and not to move.

Thus we were hiding for a whole year. But after living in the ghetto, our life in a separate flat seemed just wonderful. In front of the house there was a separate lawn with blossoming flowers, Grandma put bouquets on the balcony where we played, and it was good, although sometimes we were cold and hungry.

Later we found out that the local policemen who guarded the ghetto learned that the Germans had received an order to liquidate the ghetto and some of the prisoners were supposed to be moved to Shepetovka and killed there. Some of the policemen were former classmates of our uncle and they had been friends before the war. Some of them told him how to save his brothers' children because otherwise they would be killed with all prisoners when the ghetto was liquidated. He took care to save us and he succeeded in it.

Many local people later told me how the last surviving ghetto prisoners were marched out to be killed. They were walking and crying, and our mum was among them. Local people were waving their farewells to them. They were all killed near Shepetovka.

66. The old and the weak were killed along the way

Naum Tkach (b. 1931)

When the Nazi Germans invaded the town of Shpikov, Shpikov (now Tulchin) district, Vinnitsa oblast, I was ten years old. I lived with my mother and my older sister, while my father and older brother were in the Red Army.

The Germans occupied Shpikov some me around July 1941. Their leading military divisions went by fast and didn't touch the Jews in this area. The Romanian army occupied the town in August. First they resettled all Jews into houses located along one of the secondary streets. Thus the Shpikov ghetto was established.

Notices marked the ghetto territory and it was forbidden to leave it under the threat of death. Later on, all Jews that lived in the villages of the Shpikov district were also resettled into the ghetto.

The Romanians announced the contribution to be paid by Jews – which would supposedly protect them – and were taking away jewellery and good clothes. We got food by trading clothes with local farmers. This was all done in secret so that Romanian soldiers and police wouldn't notice.

In early December 1941, all ghetto residents were gathered at the marketplace and under the escort of armed Romanians and local police they were marched to the village of Rogizna, about a dozen kilometres away from Shpikov. The old and weak were killed along the way.

In the village of Rogizna we were put into the building of a village club, which was surrounded by a big stone fence on the one side, and washed by the Southern Bug on the other. People sat down on the floors of the building and in its basements. The building was not heated. Here we lived until the summer of 1942 and then those who survived were conveyed to the concentration camp in Pechera.

The Pechera camp was located on the premises of a former TB sanatorium, which was also surrounded by a stone fence on the one side, and by the Southern Bug on the other. How was our life in this place? It was a nightmare! We lived in inhuman conditions: with cold, hunger and diseases, lack of hygiene. People were eaten alive by lice. In the morning people would get up, get out into the yard and shake the lice off. In winter the snow was carpeted with them. It was difficult to find a spot of clean snow. We were prohibited from getting drinking water from a well; we were only allowed to get it from the Bug or by melting the snow.

Policemen guarded the gates day and night. But we were destined to survive. I saw a family (a couple with a girl) who died before my eyes from starvation. I don't remember their surname now; they were my neighbours. Every day people would take dead bodies out of the building to a common grave.

It is scary to recall the killings of innocent people. Thus David and Rosa Bronshtein were killed. They wanted to escape from the Rogizna camp but police captured them, took them to the camp gates and shot them. A girl of five or six years old was left near the bodies of her killed parents. The girl survived and now she lives in Kharkov.

At night, when the policemen were drinking, the prisoners tried to get into the village to beg for food from local residents, or to go to the people they knew. Sometimes the village residents would throw food over the fence. A family of Natalka Oleinik was very helpful to my family. She lived with three children and was expecting another baby. Her husband was at the front and he died when liberating the Ukraine.

In spring on the camp territory there was not a single patch of grass; all the bushes had been gnawed.

Those grown-ups who were stronger were selected for agricultural work. A very few people survived in these horrible conditions.

The Red Army front divisions liberated us in March 1944.

67. The town was invaded by Germans: that was when it became scary

Faina Feld (b. 1929)

I was born in the town of Balta, on 29 September 1929, in a workers' family. My father worked in a printers as a mechanic and my mother was a housewife. Before the war our family had lived very well, and my parents loved me greatly. They wanted to provide me with a good education. I was taking music lessons and took part in all subject *olympiads*. We were supposed to move to Kiev in June but the war began. My father had an exemption from mobilization: he was dealing with the printers, hiding it from the Germans. He worked day and night for another month after the war began. But the town was bombed terribly and we decided to flee.

Mum had numerous relatives (grandparents, uncles and aunts), and so we found a carriage and put the children on it while grown-ups walked alongside. We suffered through much while fleeing. There was a terrible heatwave. We were walking towards the Bug, to the crossing, along the sand road. I got ill and we had to stop to bring me back to my senses. Later we hired a driver who would lead us to the river crossing. But we saw the Germans before we reached the crossing.

They were screaming, *'Zuruck, nach Hause!'* [Go back to your house].

We had to return to the town. *En route* it was mainly the Romanians who robbed us. The German units that had sent us back didn't belong to the SS. The winners humiliated people, raped women.

My father had a sister who did not live in the central part of the town, so we made our way to her, walking across the vegetable gardens. I remember that a ghetto was established very soon, on Kuznechnaya and Sinyanskaya Streets. The area was fenced off with barbed wire. Many people had to share one room. We were always hungry; there was nothing to eat. I don't know how my parents managed to find any food for us.

My father was a good professional, and the Germans certainly found this out. They had to restore a local power station and they found him – the town was small. They issued a pass for him, made him wear a six-pointed star (we all wore them, on the front and back of our clothes). There was a road designated for him to get out of the ghetto and go to the station to work. If he had taken another turn on this road, he would have been shot.

Mum tried to cook us something out of whatever my father received for his work. I remember the cold, and that we had nothing with which to heat the place. People were taking down trees, and all fences were removed to be burned.

The Germans took out all ghetto residents to work. Many would never come back. There were instances when people were just taken out – and that was about it. We have the Balta station, and very many people were killed there (a German had been killed and local people were killed in retaliation).

Temporarily our area was transferred to under Romanian supervision. They didn't organize mass killings the way the Germans did, but still abused us. Parapan, the chief of the police, beat people with a whip and took them out to work in winter, in the snow and frost.

When in 1944 our army was approaching, the Romanians left very rapidly. The Germans occupied the town and that's when it became scary – they were killing everyone. I remember one episode: there were many people living in the same house as we did. One old man was in bed. At that moment, the Germans stormed the house. The old man heard this and ran out on to the balcony and began calling for his wife. They of course followed him and killed him. Maybe the fact that they ran after him saved us – they didn't do anything to us.

They were killing the men first, and then raping the women. But people were trying to save their lives – they were digging pits in their houses, and hiding there.

I was running with food from my mum to my sister – we all were hiding in different places, and our niece was in yet another place. Once, when I was running from place to place, I literary stumbled over a man's body. I don't know what kind of state I was in, but I stepped over him and ran on, to my dad. And then the Germans came into the yard that I was entering with food. An old woman lived there and she immediately put me into her cellar. And the cellar was packed with people – they were standing tight, let alone sitting. The woman blocked the entrance to the cellar, putting a case with potatoes above it, and moved a wooden seat on top of that.

When you are underground and military boots go above your head, the noise they make stays in your ears. The Germans walked into the room, sat on the seat and started asking her where everybody was.

There were many dead bodies outside, and she said, 'Everybody is there, killed.'

They demanded something else from her, then hit her and she fell down. We heard it all.

They stayed for a little longer and then left. And we were still in the underground cellar. She was unconscious, and couldn't let us out. The lack of air was such that every inhalation was shorter than the previous one.

There was a young man who said, 'Let's move the lid.'

All the men tried to push it up. When we got out, she was unconscious but alive – and we brought her back to senses.

The gendarmes announced that on 28 March, we all had to gather near the leather plant, a theatre and a school. We all got ready, anxiouisly.

And at the dawn, one boy saw three men out of the window, and said, 'They are ours.'

They were dressed in felt cloaks, and we decided that perhaps they were the Vlasov's men. They would torture us too. But the boy said, 'No, I saw the stars!'

In our walk-through yard there was a little house where one woman's husband, son, daughter and daughter's fiancé had been shot a day before. Only she was left alive. She was out of her mind because of her terrible grief. All their bodies were still on the ground near the house. And a German weapon stood there – when retreating, the Germans left it. Our house was open to every wind – we could see out of it on three sides – our yard, the street and a part of another yard. And we saw how this old woman who had lost all of her family started hugging the soldiers. And then we realized they were indeed ours. (There had been instances when the Germans had staged such shows: people would run to welcome the 'Red Army soldiers', only to be shot later.)

Then we all ran outside into the yard, hungry, miserable, and looking terrible. Our soldiers came by. This was on 28 March 1944. Thus we were liberated.

Of course people started immediately to search for their families. Very many lives had been lost, way too many.

But Dad survived, staying in the pit where he had been hiding. The war went on. On 10 April Odessa was liberated. People worked with pleasure, my father went to work immediately, dug out all the machines and equipment they had hidden, and restored the printers and the power station.

On the day when we were liberated, and on the following day, the town was bombed heavily, killing so many more people!

There was another episode. A policeman was found (recognized by one of the soldiers) who had caused a lot of Jews to be killed in the town from where the soldier originally came. And here, in a small garden, gallows were set up; all the children came in, and witnessed the decision of the military field court to execute the traitor.

After the liberation everything was in ruins but the desire to study was immense. Lydia Moiseevna, our physics teacher, was generous hearted, and she agreed to teach me. Three years had passed by and I was fourteen now, too old for the fourth grade. There was another boy named Misha Teper. So together with our teacher, we crammed four years into two. After graduating from the eighth grade I entered a technical college in Odessa. The post-war years were very difficult.

In 1950 I got married: my husband was Jewish, a military officer and a war veteran. He studied in Kharkov in the Artillery College. After our marriage we lived in Moscow (where he studied) and I graduated from the college with honours and entered the Moscow Financial Institute. Then we had daughters.

There were two monuments set up at the site of the former ghetto – in the little garden and at the place of the mass killings.

68. New words entered our vocabulary: *Judeh*, ghetto, 'contribution', killing[1]

Grigory Ferman

From my childhood in the 1930s I remember hunger and a phrase, 'public enemy'.

In books we were always killing people – enemies. One Sunday my mum and I went to the market. In the centre of the town many people gathered around the public announcement speaker and then we knew that the war had begun.

No later than a month afterwards, the 'liberators' came – or that was what they called themselves on posters, and then new words entered our vocabulary: *Judeh*, ghetto, 'contribution', killing. If any order was not observed, executions followed, and Jews were to be blamed for everything. Those who used to be 'friends' to the family became their enemies, a dog-catcher became Mr Schutzmann, and the former teacher became a chief of the new administration.

And one order was followed by yet another order: not to walk on the pavements, and to walk in the road only; to wear a white armband, then changed for a yellow star on the chest. But then one wasn't enough and we had to have one more, this time on our back, so that we could be recognizsed from the front and from the back.

Then I learned what a 'sign of David' meant. We were not allowed to go out into the street until the designated time. We were sent to work; people were also sent to the cemetery to take o tombstones and use them in paving the road.

Mr Schutzmann selected beautiful girls to wash the floors in his house and sent people into the camps – Pechera and others. Nobody returned from there.

People were beaten at work, everybody abused them in any way possible, and we had no rights whatsoever.

I also worked – I sawed logs, took cows out to pasture, and was sent anywhere. The policemen from Western Ukraine were especially ruthless. When they arrived, the *Gebietskommisar* [territorial commissar] ordered the *Judenrat* [Jewish council] to provide them with clothes; there were other demands, too. There was a new command, to establish a ghetto. We had two of these – one for the professionals with their families and the other for everybody else. The ghettos were fenced off by barbed wire.

This lasted until August 1942. On the morning of 19 August we heard noise and shouts for everybody to go out into the marketplace. I didn't realize what it would lead to. They ordered the men to be separated from the women and children, and then ordered for everybody to be brought together again. Those who had gold or jewellery were ordered to hand it in.

Vinokur was standing not far from me, and he had gold sewn into his belt. I don't know how the Germans knew about it but I saw an officer with a whip order him to lie face down. He showed him with his whip how to lie down, then took his Browning out and shot Vinokur. His wife started screaming and they shot her, too. Both were put on to a cart and taken away.

Thus I witnessed the first killing, and realized what was expected us and how scary it was to go out into the marketplace.

An officer with a skull on his cap came and demanded us to be sent to the slaughter, but the *Gebietskommisar* let us go home.

A few days later I went into the other ghetto. It was a terrible sight: books were strewn around in the street, the houses were empty, it was empty everywhere and as people said, even the rats left the ghetto. Later I was told by Danilo Nechai, my father's friend who lived nearby, that all people were marched to a stadium and from there, they were sent to heaven.

On 15 October, less than in two months later, all Jews were brought out into the square again. This time my father hid us in the secret chamber together with our neighbour, locked the door and, together with our neighbour's husband, went to the square. They never returned. There were seven in the secret chamber: our neighbour with her two sons, my mother and the three of us. Nobody would come to let us out and we didn't know what had really happened to those who had left. Then my younger brother got out of the secret chamber and went to search for them. In the meanwhile we heard the policemen come into our attic, looking for people. They smashed the roof – we saw the light – but they didn't notice us. If they had only done it a bit to the right. I wouldn't be writing these recollections now. My brother came back and said that everybody had died and we had to go to the Romanian side, to the village of Balki, about one kilometre away. I call this road the way of life. The two Bonik brothers were the first to go and cross the border and they were killed near the river. My sister came out and she was sent across the river; not everybody was bad. When I came out I went to our neighbour Nechai and spent the night there. Knowing that children go to school from Bar to Balki, I walked in the morning through the first liquidated ghetto, gathered books and went on, across the gates which were a little way off, and went towards Balki. There I met my sister, and later my brother came and told us that when he was walking with our mother and neighbour, and they were walking a bit apart, local children started crying out, 'Here are the Jewish women!' And the policemen arrested them.

What was the Zhmerinka camp/ghetto like? Gorky Street fenced off by barbed wire; Urizky Street, which was parallel to it, was also fenced off with this wire. There were two exits or gates to the town. The main gate was used when we went out to work, and the second was opposite the gendarmes' office. There were streets and alleys inside the ghetto as well as its own police and every morning they would drive us out to work. The ghetto was a major supplier of the workforce to the Walter Schifler and Gleckler Company. I worked at this company, clearing the snow from the railway and the engines – this was my job while others were assigned different jobs. It was winter and it was cold, and I took a sack of used heating materials and, of course, the field gendarmes caught me. I got twenty-five lashes with a whip and couldn't work for three days afterwards.

The Zhmerinka ghetto was a small town in itself. There was a diner for lonely people who couldn't work, a shop and a bathhouse, a synagogue, a tannery, and even a theatre where the actors from Chernovtsy performed – including the famous Savila Pastor, who was like Sidi Tal. Even gendarmes came to the theatrical performances. *Papiryny Kinder* and other performance still ring in my ears.

Life was complicated. If the Germans didn't like something about our work, they beat us up, and local policemen would try to gain points with the Germans and add to our punishment. People were working, wearing out their shoes, and there were no soles, and then people started cutting off broken rubber hoses and using that instead of shoe soles. Once, going along Gorky Street towards the second gate, I saw a Romanian gendarme lead a young man into the ghetto, then take out his handgun and shoot him. The man's name was Goferman and he was also from Bar. He was killed for cutting off the rubber hose.

Then death caught up with all the Jews from Brailov. Moreover, the Germans demanded that all those who escaped from Brailov to Zhmerinka be turned in, otherwise the Zhmerinka Jews would be next.

In January 1944 the tank reconnaissance division stormed Zhmerinka; the Romanians fled but soon returned because the reconnaissance division didn't stay long. On 16 March Zhmerinka was liberated. Thus almost three years that I had spent in the ghetto were over.

My parents died in Bar, Vinnitsa oblast: my father, Abram Herschovich Ferman, and my mother, Ida Elevna Ferman.

NOTE

1. This originally appeared in 'People Remain Human: Testimonies of Witnesses', *Bulletin*, issue 3 (1994), pp. 42–4.

69. For two days the earth moved

Dora Fredkis (b. 1927)

We had a big family: five children. Our father was a shoemaker. In 1941, before the war, I completed seven grades.

In September 1942 the Germans entered our house and took all of us to a club. All other Jews were brought there too. But there were only a few Germans, mostly policemen, doing this work. Then the head of the village, named Koval, came and ordered all professional workers and artisans – shoemakers, tailors and glaziers – to step out. Together with my father we were taken to an old house where we stayed till the evening.

When we left, a lorry with Germans in it pulled up to the club. The doors were opened; two Germans stood at the door and ordered everyone to come out. Old and young men, and women with young children, came out. The children were pulled out of their mothers' arms and thrown into a pile. All old people were taken away to pits dug earlier and shot there. According to the stories of the witnesses, the children were thrown into a pile in the lorry like rubbish and also taken to the pits. There the Germans would grab them, shoot them and throw them down into the very same pit without checking whether they were alive or dead. For two days the earth moved and blood soaked the surface.

Eight our families were taken away to Novograd-Volynsky. Near the railway station there was a ghetto in which men and women were harnessed on to the carts instead of horses and they would bring water and hay for the horses. The children were hungry, naked and barefoot; those who could hide in the hay would run away to a village begging for bread or some other food. I got into the village that way too. I was young, fourteen years old, and worked ina vegetable garden, digging potatoes, or taking cows out to pasture. I did anything to earn some food. Thus I managed to survive.

70. My saviours

Boris Khandros (b. 1923)

I received a letter from Jerusalem. Dr Mordechai Paldiel, the Director
of the Righteous Among the Nations Department of Yad Vashem,
informed me that the honorary title of the 'Righteous Among the
Nations' was being bestowed on Khristina Burik and Tamara, her
daughter (No. 6704, posthumous), and Konstantin Ivanovich
Stukalenko (No. 6704a, posthumous). The title was given 'in recognition of the help rendered to Jewish people during the Second
World War'.

The letter also said that the saviours' names would be inscribed
on the Wall of Honour in Yad Vashem. It also stated that 'the copies
of the letter will be sent to those who were saved, to those who provided witness testimonies, and to other people in question'.

I am a 'person saved'. And I am also a 'person in question'. I'm
happy that the rightful honour has been given to those to whom I
owe my saving and my own life.

On 19 June 1941, we, the graduates of the Ozarintsy secondary
school who had grown up in that little village, or *shtetl*, received our
school graduation certificates. And then there was the war. A front
on the Dniester was kept for about a month. Mainly residents of the
district centre were being evacuated. I seemed to be the only Jew
from our *shtetl* who managed to leave the town not long before the
Germans came. I got surrounded. Heavily concussed, I came back
to my senses after a few days, and stayed in the attic of a village
teacher's house in Bukhovka (now Cherkassy oblast). Then I wandered across the occupied territory of the Ukraine, through little
places covered with the blood of recently held, first *Aktions*. In late
August in the evening I was approaching Ozarintsy from the side of
the Polish cemetery. And suddenly as if from the underground I
heard, 'Buzya, Buzya ...'

Thus I, the son of Khandros the teacher, was known in the village
and in the *shtetl*.

I thought I imagined hearing this or maybe that I was going

insane but then the corn moved … 'Don't be afraid, it's me, Tamara Burik.'

We had not known each other very well before the war. Tamara had finished school two years earlier, and worked as a teacher. It was her who told me about the two bloody Saturdays in the *shtetl*: 'Many have been killed, I don't know whether your father is alive.' She told me I couldn't return home now, and offered to allow me to live with them.

Thus I went into the Burik family's house (Khristina, her mother, and Ganna, her older sister). I was welcomed as if a relative. And here I lived in hiding for about a month. Later on I would find shelter in the house of the old woman during the raids, and food and human friendliness.

Vassil Burik, an older son of Khristina, also took much care in my case. He was a father of a big family (ten children). Galya, his daughter – Anna Vassilievna Melnichenko (for many years worked as a teacher and is now retired) – for all those years was the most important helper of her grandma Khristina, and her aunts. She would stay on guard near the house, warn about the dangers and bring food.

I heard about the new chief of Ozarintsy Hospital from Khristina Burik ('a good person', she said). In order to save our own family, young brothers and sisters, I had to leave the friendly house of the Burik family and meet Doctor Stukalenko. He probably had been aware of my 'adventures' and invited me to his place. His family (wife, son Seva and his daughter-in-law) all lived in the hospital. We talked about many things then. Then, before the epidemics, I made two more visits to Konstantin Ivanovich in the hospital, where I even had my own 'ward'. There during raids I was sure to find clean linen. Knowing well what threatened that family for hiding me, I tried not to abuse this opportunity.

K. I. Stukalenko had worked as a military paramedic in the border military divisions for many years. He was 'promoted' (in complete accordance with his merits) by my grateful compatriots, and he treated people very successfully for any disease. He came to Ozarintsy during the war. I learned from his wife about his arrest, imprisonment, and everything that he and his family had to go through in those difficult times. He himself didn't like to talk about it, considering the arrest 'an unfortunate incident'.

And now before I begin telling you the story of the human heroism of Dr Stukalenko in the terrible winter of 1942, I will cite another testimony. This is the testimony of Lyuba Katz-Lozover, who lives in the United States now:

I survived two bloody Saturdays in Ozarintsy – 19 and 26 July. I was sixteen years old then. The first was organized by the Germans, the other by the Romanians. Eleven of my relatives were killed on those two days. They were not shot. They were cut up. And this happened before my eyes, in the middle of the day, on the marketplace, in the centre of our *shtetl*. Arka Weinschtok was killed, Boris Khandros's uncle. They cut off the beard of Grandpa Fuks, too, he was Khandros's relative, and cut his eyes out. The Romanian killing squad came in, riding horses, and then left. I remember how they washed their hands in a big puddle of blood. After that massacre, my father Benyumin Geiselevich Katz, born in 1890, was the only one of twenty-eight people, who could breathe and was still alive. We took our father home and Dr Stukalenko came immediately. He examined my father and said, 'It is too late, he has lost much blood.' He could not save my father but he saved many others. I will never forget the kindness of this man.

So it was winter 1942. The front line was hundreds of kilometres away. Hunger, overcrowded houses and lice were all a problem in the Ozarintsy ghetto. Beside local Jewish prisoners, there were Jews deported from Bessarabia and Bukovina. The typhoid fever epidemic was taking away people's lives in packs. Our family was ill with it too, and we were all in a fever. In a small room there was my mum, Mina Borisovna, forty-two years old, my younger brother Bebik, aged fifteen, my brother Mark, sister Sopha, Grisha (Herschele), six months old, and I. My brother Bebik volunteered for the front on the second or third day following our liberation. He was gravely wounded in the head when storming the Oder, and died not long before the war was over. I still keep his death notice: 'Your son, Boris Naumovich Khandros, a corporal ... was wounded and died as a result of the wounds on 17 April 1945.' (This was not a mistake. My name is Borukh and my brother's name was Berl. In the school we were called Buzya and Bebik. In the army we were both named Boris.) In the ghetto I was the only provider. Without food and medical help we were all doomed.

One day, coming back to my senses, I saw Lyuba Katz near my bed and asked her to send a note to our doctor. He came immediately, and was coming almost daily for the following three weeks. When it got dark he would send his son over together with his wife, who was a nurse. They gave us shots, giving medicines that were invaluable at that time, brought bread, milk, sugar, and eggs. Endangering his own life, Konstantin Ivanovich and his family literally saved us all from death.

I recently visited my friend Yakov Roitberg, who has been my friend since the Ozarintsy ghetto, and who now lives in Chernigov. He is a famous mathematician, a PhD and a professor at the Chernigov Education Institute, a disabled war veteran. It turned out that when, in 1942, he was dying from typhoid and paratyphus, Dr Stukalenko visited and saved him too. A similar story was told by Riva Weisman-Portnaya in Haifa who, in autumn of 1941, was deported from Khotin. Together with her friend and hundreds of other people deported from Bessarabia and Bukovina, she was indebted to our doctors, 'Righteous Among the Righteous', for being saved. Who knows, and who could possibly now count, how many 'patients' like us he had?

Later there was 17 March 1944. On this day the retreating Germans killed a few Jews, our ghetto prisoners. I was shot at that day, too. I survived by a miracle; the bullet lodged a half centimetre away from my heart. And, again, risking his life, Konstantin Ivanovich answered the first call, and treated the wound.

It was dangerous to keep me, 'killed', in the hospital, so at night they transferred me to the village, to the house of a local tractor driver named Mykita Belous. Stukalenko kept coming day and night and did his very best to save me. This lasted until the Red Army came.

After my recovery, I went into the army. I finished the war on the Elb River in the cavalry reconnaissance of the 6th Guard Cavalry Division. I returned home and entered the university. The last time I saw my saviour was in the summer of 1946. I was told that soon afterwards he moved with his family to Chernovtsy oblast. From that time unfortunately we lost contact.

All my searches in recent years have unfortunately been unsuccessful. Only recently have I learned that in the 1950s Konstantin Ivanovich was seen in the town of Oknitsa (Moldavia) where he worked in a local hospital. Maybe reading these notes, his descendants will respond – son Seva (Vsevolod Konstantinovich Stukalenko), his wife, their children or grandchildren – all those who knew or met that wonderful man.

And what about the Burik family? On my every visit home I rushed to see my other mum. I have a photograph in which she is standing next to my mum, Mina Borisovna. Here is also Ganna, Tamara's older sister. I took this picture near Khristina's house in the 1960s. The old Burik woman was a rare expert in medicinal herbs and field plants. She was making different medical concoctions and gladly treated people, anyone who needed it. She preserved her clear mind and endless kindness till her very last day, almost till she was a hundred years old.

My 'sister' Tamara passed away very young (a case of whooping cough that developed very rapidly), back in the years of the occupation, in the summer of 1943. She had a son, born in 1942. I can't help but mention her motherly heroism. In the late autumn of 1941 Fedor Turovsky, son of a local teacher and Tamara's first and only love, returned to the neighbouring village of Borshchevtsy. They got married. The symptoms of this terrible diseases showed first when Tamara was two months pregnant. I told Konstantin Ivanovich about them, and he asked Tamara to come to the clinic. After detailed examination we stayed alone, and he asked me to tell Khristina, Vassily, her brother, and Ganna that it was possible to save Tamara's life only by aborting her pregnancy. The family council got together but she was adamant – 'What will come, will come' – and refused to have an abortion. She gave birth to her son in 1942 and died soon afterwards.

Volodya (Vladimir Fedorovich Turovsky), followed in his mother's footsteps and became a teacher too. Later he was a school principal, and then the chairman of the Subbotov village council for another ten years.

We met with him and really got to know each other well in August 1996, fifty years after I came to Khristina's house. We met as very close friends, as family. It was Volodya who send me a pre-war picture of his mother, and my 'sister' Tamara. He, Khristina's grandson and Tamara's son received the diplomas and medals for the 'Righteous Among the Nations' for Khristina Burik and her daughter Tamara, awarded by the Ambassador of the State of Israel, in my presence, in the Ukrainian House.

I have visited the welcoming home of the Turovskys many times since then. This summer Vladimir Fedorovich has become a grandfather himself. Galya's (Ganna Vassilievna Melnichenko-Burik) granddaughters are also grown up. Khristina Burik had a total of eleven grandchildren (all very good people) and twenty-two great grandchildren …

By saving one person, one life, you're saving the whole world … I really only ponder the deeper meaning of this ancient phrase now. I was not the only one saved by these people. Among other children, I was the oldest and the most experienced. As a result of my going into the ghetto, of my connections with the village residents, of my friendship with the Burik family, and with Dr Stukalenko, and of my night travels between Ozarintsy and the Mogilev-Podolsky ghetto ('a heavy burden bends down to earth'), we managed to pull my younger brothers – Grisha, who was less than a year old in 1941, and seven-year-old Mark, and my three-year-old sister Sarra-Sopha – out of despair and save them from starvation, epidemics and other grief.

I have two sons, Alexander and Vladimir, Mark has Boris and Tanya, Grisha has Sasha and Maxim and Sopha has Polina and Lilya. Now we have been grandparents ourselves for a long while.

And all of them now, living in the Ukraine, Israel, Germany, and those who are still on their way, not born yet, are also indebted for their birth and their lives to our saviours. Indeed, by saving one life, you're saving the whole world.

A nice surprise waited for me at home – a letter from Yad Vashem:

> Jerusalem, 31 August 31, 1998. Melnichenko Anna – Ukraine (no. 6704). The staff of the Righteous Among the Nations Department are happy to inform you that the special commission decided the award the honorary title of the Righteous Among the Nations to the above mentioned person. The medal and honorary diploma issued in the name of the saviour will be sent to the Embassy of the State of Israel in the Ukraine. Please get in touch with them to communicate the date of the ceremony. The name of the Righteous person will be inscribed on the Wall of Honour in Yad Vashem.

And so it happened. Ganna Melnichenko, Galya, the third in the Burik family, was awarded the honorary title.

71. Through absolute hell

Arkady Khassin (b. 1930)

I wrote these recollections long ago, soon after the Great Patriotic War was over. I was only fifteen years old then. Our family stayed in Odessa when it was occupied by the Nazis, and we had to go through all types of hell prepared for the Jews by the invaders.

Having miraculously survived I wrote these memoirs. They were kept for a long time by one Odessa publishing company, then by another, until they were returned to me with no explanations. I found explanations in the newspapers, though: the 'campaign against cosmopolitans of no origin' began then, as well as Stalin's anti-Semitic campaign, followed by the Case of the Doctors. And even after the death of Stalin, the years of rule of Khrushchev and Brezhnev were not encouraging for publications on 'Jewish topics'.

Now there are many publications like this. But the number of us, living witnesses of the mass murder of Jews in German concentration camps and ghettos, grows smaller with every year. And having found these memoirs in my archive some time ago, I have edited the style of my writing and would like to offer it to readers' attention. Nazism is still alive and one should never forget its crimes!

On the night of 14/15 October 1941, the last divisions of the Red Army protecting Odessa boarded ships and left for Sevastopol. Following an order from Moscow, although the Germans were advancing in the Crimea, Odessa was surrendered to the enemy.

But the Nazi army that was besieging the city entered the streets of Odessa only on the evening of 16 October. They were walking in and looking around like thieves, not believing that this fortress – which was blackened by fires, which had fought fiercely and was seemingly impregnable – had now been abandoned by its fighters.

The first occupier entered our yard the same evening of 16 October. He was a Romanian soldier. He indicated to the frightened women standing in the yard that he wanted to eat. One woman went into the house and brought out a few biscuits, another some soup in a saucepan. And a yard-keeper put a stool in front of him. He sat down, put his rifle down on the ground and started eating. Other neighbours went out into the yard too. I came forward to see the first enemy soldier better. When he emptied the saucepan, and licked his spoon, he suddenly said, '*Zhidan kaput*' [Jews, done for].

Everybody looked at each other. And the yard-keeper said, '*Zhidan?* That must mean Jews …'

Thus we were introduced to the occupiers …

The very same night the yard-keeper brought in 'guests' to our place. Expecting the worst, we didn't go to bed and sat up dressed. But the Romanians only searched for clothes in the wardrobe and left, taking warm clothes away with them.

We lived at 5 Krasny Alley. My father walked on crutches. Before the war he had had a car accident and had lost his leg. That was the reason why he decided not to leave the city. Thus we stayed on in besieged Odessa.

They didn't touch Jews in the first days of the occupation. And my father, together with Rosa, my older sister, used to go to *Privoz* to trade things from home for food.

On 22 October partisans blew up the Romanian headquarters on Engels Street. In retaliation for those killed, the Romanians started taking hostages from the streets. My father and sister got caught up in this pogrom too. But before they were taken down to some basement my father managed to give his watch to a Romanian corporal and this helped him and my sister to return home successfully. And on the morning of 23 October, not far away from our home, at Rosa Luxemburg Street I saw people hanged …

Two days later our turn came. Having returned from the market my father said that an order had been posted throughout the city ordering the Odessa Jews to report to a prison. Those who didn't obey the order would be executed.

My father was baking biscuits the whole night. My mother was filling backpacks. In the morning our neighbours came to say good bye. Cries and laments filled our flat. It was time to leave. My mother put our packs on our backs, and took hers; Father put his cigarette down and took up his crutches.

We were still in our flat when our yard-keeper started taking out our plates. And her husband opened our window (we lived on the ground floor) and started pulling our table through it. This was the first time I saw tears in my father's eyes. On his squeaky crutches he went on to the gate, and we followed him carrying heavy packs on our backs.

The prison was overcrowded. There was no room in the cells; we were put in the prison workshops. We lay down to sleep on a joiner's bench; cold wind blew through the broken windows. I immediately had a running nose. And everybody around me was coughing and sneezing.

At night I woke hearing loud voices. I opened my eyes and saw the Germans! They were standing near us trying to wake up my father. He sat up and took up his crutches. Seeing a handicapped man, the Germans went on. Soon we heard a blood-curdling scream. Somebody was pulled from our side and pushed out into the yard.

In the morning we learned that almost all men had been taken out of the prison. They were needed for manual labour at some German unit. And a week later a rumour spread that all men taken that night had been locked in the former gunpowder warehouses after the job was accomplished and burned alive. Now there is a memorial at that place, near Tolbukhin Square.

The days in the prison went by fairly quietly. In the mornings either my sister or I would go to the prison yard and stand in a queue to get water from the only tap with barely minimal water pressure. Mum brought a kettle from home, and while we were filling it up with water, my father would start a fire near the fence. Mum cooked some thin soups or *kasha* from whatever we managed to take from home in the very same kettle. But many people didn't have even such things and were cooking in army casks found on a rubbish pile.

But the nights were terrible! Drunk Romanians, lighting their way with torches, roamed the workshops in search of young girls. The latter would hide under the pieces of equipment and the Romanians pulled them out. Screams, weeping, and sometimes shots, filled the building with echoes throughout the night.

In mid-November we were suddenly released. The dreadful gates were opened and the Romanians started pushing us out shouting, '*La kassa!*' [Home!] Obviously the Romanian administration needed the prison for some more serious criminals.

We returned to Krasny Alley, but we saw a cross on the doors of our flat and an inscription, 'Here lives Olga Nekhlyudova, a Russian Orthodox Christian'. She was the yard-keeper's daughter. Seeing us she got confused and asked, 'Didn't they kill you?'

'Well,' my father replied, 'as you well can see they didn't.' And he stepped into the flat.

She left our flat but we didn't stay there for long. In December a new order was posted throughout the city now ordering the Odessa Jews to report to Slobodka, to go to the ghetto there.

And again, we started packing …

At the very beginning of Slobodka, right behind the railway bridge, there stood a huge building. It had housed the Water

Institute dormitory before the war. After the war and until now, it had been the staff and administration building of the Higher Navy School. And in the period of December 1941 till May 1942 this building was turned into the Jewish ghetto.

Even today the building is fenced off with the same fence, and near the same gates you can see a naval cadet on guard. But then these gates were guarded by Romanian soldiers. For a payment they would let residents of Slobodka into the territory of the ghetto and within days a real marketplace was humming days in the yard of our new prison. You could have a plate of soup, *vareniki* or pastries in exchange for the occupiers marks or for some clothes. The residents of Slobodka would bring this all on their sledges in pans covered with rags.

Our family was located in one room where there were about twenty people. My father managed to claim a table near the window and my sister and I slept on it. My parents slept on the floor. Later we started sleeping on the floor too, following the request of our mother to yield the table to a pregnant woman. One night something poured down on us. I heard moans and then some doleful squeaking. In the morning we knew that a boy had been born on our table.

And the winter that year was very severe. The frosts were down to thirty degrees below zero. And in these terrible frosts they started sending people out to work. Soon rumours began in the ghetto that all the Jews taken out of Slobodka were brought to the station of Berezovka from where the local policemen were taking them out to be killed. The villages of Mostovoye, Bogdanovka, Domanevka in Odessa oblast were named as places of mass slaughter.

On the day of the march the residents of Slobodka were not allowed into the ghetto. And when carts with people started pulling into the yard, laments and cries were heard from every room. Old women tore out their hair, old men called for God, and insane mothers were running around the floor trying to hide their children.

But nothing helped. Soldiers found them anywhere – in the attic, in the toilets, pulled out of the basement – and forced on to the carts all those found whom the Romanian administration had planned to be removed.

In January the ghetto was under the epidemic of typhus. The carts now were coming not only to pick up the living but also the dead. Almost daily piles of bodies were removed from the ghetto.

I fell ill with typhus too, followed by my sister and my mother. My father was taking care of us as much as he possibly could on his crutches. The Romanians didn't touch those who were ill – they were afraid of catching the disease. Ill people lived on the upper floor where the doctors from among the ghetto prisoners were in charge. I remember Professor Sriebner, Doctor Sushon, and doctor Turner. And also I remember 'Olya with the thermometer'. This was the nickname of one energetic woman who had the only thermometer in the whole ghetto. Not trusting it to anybody, she would take the temperature of the patients and write up the records for the doctors.

When we started to get better (in March), our father died. He died in April. His date of death is 17 April 1942.

We were taken from Slobodka in the last group. It was a bright sunny day. The tall gates behind us were closed, and the Odessa ghetto ended its existence.

Local boys who followed the carts were whistling and throwing stones at us. People on the pavements would stop and look at us. And we were going along a new sorrowful way, leaving behind one mass Jewish grave, in one of which there was my father.

We were taken to Berezovka in dirty freight carriages. The wheels made a terrible noise; starving children cried and old women wept. The cars were once used for transporting coal, and when in Berezovka the policemen opened up the carriages, we heard them laugh, 'Guys, these are not Jews! These are Negroes!'

While clearing the coal dust from ourselves, we looked at these people with terror. They had rifles behind their backs and whips in their hands. Obviously these were the same policemen who greeted winter convoys and took the people out to be killed. Having searched through our packs, the 'guys' took the clothes and things they liked the most and marched us on to Mostovoye.

As we were approaching the place, I was gripped by terror more and more. A young woman near me was pulling her little daughter behind. The girl cried and asked to be carried but her exhausted mother didn't have enough strength to carry her in her arms.

And then through her tears the girl said, 'My dear mum, please, carry me at least a little; they will kill us anyway now.'

The desperate woman held the girl tight. But then they told us to stop. The policemen went 'to eat'. And we sat down on the ground near the edge of the village and looked around like cornered animals.

A few boys were left to watch us. They were probably the policemen's sons: going to the village, the policemen left their whips to them. Cracking the whips, the boys looked at us sombrely as if saying, 'Just try to escape.' But where could we – miserable women, children and old men – go when put beyond the law?

Some two hours later the policemen returned and marched us on. Having passed by the village we walked slowly along the dusty road and expected to see a deep trench on the edge of which they would put us and start shooting any minute.

But Mostovoye was left far behind, and we kept on walking, and even the policemen were tired of hurrying us on with their whips and shouts. Only later did we find out that either according to the order of Doctor Alexyanu, the Transnistria Governors or according to the order of Michai, the King of Romania himself, the mass murders of Jews on Romanian-occupied territories were stopped by the summer of 1942. Those who survived were transferred to the concentration camps and used for different jobs. The Romanians called the entire left bank of the Dniester and Odessa oblast 'Transnistria'.

In order to accomplish this order we were marched with a police escort, not suspecting that many of us were doomed for another death – from hunger, disease and battering rather than a bullet.

A long way from Mostovoye we ended up near Domanevka, at the Semikhatka farmstead. We were escorted from here by the chief of local policemen, named Doroshenko, who was a huge man in a sweaty military uniform shirt and the cap with traces of where a Red Army star was once worn and could still be seen on it. He must have deserted his division when our army retreated. He had a whip in his hand. Having examined our pitiful ranks he swore and announced, 'Jews – I am your God!'

At the farmstead they put us to live in field trailers. At dawn we were marched to the fields to weed out the maize. This was a test; those who could work were later sent on to Domanevka or Karlovka, places nearby. Those who couldn't work were sent to Akhmechetka, which was the most terrible camp. In other camps of Odessa oblast those who worked were given at least some miserable ration of food; in Akhmechetka people were dying of starvation. Women with newborn and young babies, the disabled, and lonely old people were transferred there.

Together with my mother and sister we were sent to Karlovka. But there was another reason why I remembered the farmstead so well.

While back in Slobodka my mother had sewn two wedding rings into my suit. On the inner side of one of them there was an inscription that read 'To Sophochka from Yosif', and on the other ring, an inscription read, 'To Yosif from Sophochka'. And both had the date of their wedding. When I was searched in Berezovka, the policemen didn't find the rings. But when we came to Semikhatka, a few days later, we returned unexpectedly early from the field. (We usually would return to the farmstead when it was dark.) Doroshenko, with a few policemen, was waiting for us near the trailers. Having ordered us to sit down, he put a big aluminium bowl at his feet and commanded, 'All gold is to be turned in now. If I find it, I'll hang you!'

The threat worked and people began to get up, come towards

the bowl and put in jewellery – a ring, or a pair of earrings – whatever was saved from previous looting. But I didn't want to give the final keepsake of our father to the bandits. I sat behind everybody, and nobody paid attention to me. So I carefully cut the lining of my suit; took the rings and buried them under me. (The ground was soft because it had rained in the morning).

After the search I calmed my mother down, and ran towards the secret place once it got dark. But once I got the rings, I heard a vicious voice above me: 'Show me what you have there!' It was Doroshenko. In the darkness he had hidden behind the water barrel near the trailers and was watching us. He grabbed the rings, hit me with his whip and pulled me to a barn saying, 'I'll hang you in the morning!'

I screamed with pain and fear. My mother ran towards me. Seeing me in his arms, she fell down before him and started to beg him to let me go, while kissing his boots. Other women surround-many long tears and much begging, after my mother gave him all the money for things traded in Slobodka, he had mercy.

He pushed me to my mother, hitting me with his whip once again and said, 'Take your Jew.'

Thus I evaded the gallows.

And then there was Karlovka. While we were walking along the road, which was washed away with rain, the village residents standing in front of their houses watched us in silence. When we got out of the village we saw a girl who was pushing her cow with a stick. Having reached us she suddenly said, 'They march them and march them, but why? They are the same people as we are …'

I stopped and looked at the girl with surprise. But the escorting policeman pushed me with his rifle, commanding me to go on.

The concentration camp was located about three kilometres away from Karlovka, on the land of a former pig farm. In front of a former pigsty – and in which now we had to live – there was a piece of sports equipment known as a vaulting horse. As older camp residents explained to us, the policemen had brought it from a local school to use for the punishment of prisoners. For any fault a person would be tied to the vaulting horse and whipped severely.

On the very first day we listened to the address of a camp headman, Mr Abramovich, a Bessarabian Jew. The bottom line of his speech was that if we misbehaved, we would get to know the vaulting horse.

The Karlovka camp prisoners were constructing the road. We were also taken to the construction site. My mother was given a wheelbarrow, and my sister and I got shovels. We filled the cart with dirt and mother pushed it on the wooden tracks laid across the swampy area towards a mound on which the foundation for the motorway would rest.

It was mostly women and children who worked on the construction. Food was given once a day; usually it was some soup made from rotten potatoes. And when our cook, Madam Vanshtein, was bringing the soup, Mr Abramovich sat next to her on top of the cart. He watched the order in which the food was distributed. If any child tried to get ahead of the line or, even worse, asked for a second helping, Mr Abramovich used his stick.

At the end of the month we would receive our rations: two cups of dirty grain and the same amount of corn flour.

A dyslexic policeman named Stephan supervised at the construction site. His favourite expression was: 'Do you have a rear? Twenty-five!'

This meant that Stephan was ready to punish someone with twenty-five lashes, any time. If prisoners didn't push wheelbarrows fast enough, Stephan would ruthlessly beat their backs. He also carried out the vaulting horse punishments.

When it rained, the road works stopped. And like other children, my sister and I got out of the camp to go begging in the nearby villages of Ivanovka, Viktorovka and Novoselovka. This was dangerous. If the police caught us, Stephan would whip us to death on the vaulting horse. But hunger pushed us not only to humiliations but also to deadly danger.

There was a barrack in the Karlovka camp called 'the room of the naked'. Those who ruptured themselves during extremely hard labour were kept there, lying on the bunks, covered with dirty rags and dying of starvation. They didn't work, they were not supposed to get rations, some were supported by their working relatives. But those who were alone were doomed. Every morning a screeching cart driven by a couple of oxen would pull up to 'the room of the naked'. An old one-eyed man named Gerschman would get off it and shuffling with his bare feet would enter the barrack. Soon he would come out pulling a few dead bodies, putting them on to the cart and leaving. In the camp people didn't say, 'died', but instead, 'taken away by Gerschman'.

There was a woman in the 'room for the naked'. People called her 'the Muse'. In the evening she would recite poetry by Pushkin, Lermontov and Nekrasov to the 'naked', as well as stories by Chekhov and Zoshchenko. She recited them by heart and so artfully that when listening to her, residents of the barrack forgot their suffering. People from other barracks would come to listen to the Muse, too. And they would also bring her a potato or a piece of cornbread. Thus she survived. And she shared whatever she had with her neighbours on the other bunks. I don't know what she had done before the war, but her recitals saved the lives of many people.

In the winter of 1943 they brought Gypsies into the Karlovka concentration camp. And until our liberation we had one grief to share, and only death parted us.

In early March 1944 distant noise was heard in the camp. That was the approaching front. Suddenly, the police disappeared; Mr Abramovich started appearing less frequently. And soon enough the retreating Germans went on through Karlovka. They were walking along the road that we had built. And we hid in bushes and watched them.

These were different Germans from those I saw in the first days of the occupation of Odessa. Those had looked with contempt even at the Romanians; these were walking with their heads down, and many were in rags, just like us.

One evening a Gypsy woman ran into our barrack and cried, 'Hide! The Vlasov men are in Karlovka. If they know you are Jewish, they will shoot you all!' (There were bad stories told of the Vlasov men. People said that when retreating they burned down whole villages.)

For a few days we stayed in a deep ravine, behind the camp. And then I lost my patience and told my mother that I would go and see if our army was in Karlovka already. My mother just asked me to be careful.

My sister went along with me. Hardly had we made our way out of the ravine when we saw two horsemen. They had straps on their shoulders. We ran back but they saw us and shouted, 'Hey, children? Are there any Germans in the village?'

We stopped, and they rode up towards us. They had little red stars on their hats. These men were ours!

This happened on 28 March 1944.

72. From the frying pan into the fire[1]

Shmil Khlyap (b. 1929)

My father was a worker who had worked hard all of his life. My mother was a cultured woman but she had never had a real opportunity to get some education because her father, my grandpa, in the 1920s lost his right to vote. He had to restore this right in the coalmines of Donbass.

My parents are long gone, but I will preserve their memory for the rest of my days. They were honest and noble people ready to help others although our family had always been financially deprived. I'm grateful to my parents for teaching me to love our Jewish traditions, and I have observed them my whole life no matter where I have been. Unfortunately, in those years, it was absolutely impossible to get proper Jewish education.

I recall life in our little town with much warmth and nostalgic sadness. I will never forget its Jewish spirit and authenticity; when walking its streets you could hear Jewish speech and we called each other by our Jewish names.

And what kind of people lived there! They were hard-working people, extremely professional artisans in different fields: blacksmiths, carpenters, painters, joiners, tinsmiths, saddlers, thatchers and stove-setters … and this quiet and peaceful life was abruptly stopped by the war. The date of 22 June 1941 will for ever stay in our memory as some kind of borderline that divided our life into 'before' and 'after'.

On that wonderful summer day we could not even imagine what we would have to live through. It has been over half a century since the beginning of the war but everything that was kept in a child's memory has stayed with me for the rest of my life. I shall never forget those distressful days at the beginning of the war when children somehow instantly grew up and became serious. Children's play was no longer to be seen anywhere.

A few days after the beginning of the war we survived the first attack by enemy aeroplanes. That was how the war began for us.

With anxiety and worry we listened to the news on our radio, when a speaker announced that at such and such location our army was holding back the overwhelming enemy forces. In the meantime the front approached fast. I remember grown-ups saying that the Dniester would never be crossed.

Then the time came to get evacuated. We put our meagre possessions on to a lorry and left for Vapnyarka, the closest railway station. *En route* we became stuck in pouring rain; I got ill and had a fever, and we had to stop in the village of Komargorod, about eight to ten kilometres away from Vapnyarka. There were three of us in Komargorod – my mum, my younger sister and I. My father remained with his job (he was too old to be drafted), and my older brother was in the army. (He had entered a military school back in 1940.) Later, our grandpa joined us, having somehow come from Yampol. We never managed to get out of Komargorod. Vapnyarka was bombed badly. There were not enough trains for evacuation. At the same time we heard artillery booming continuously in the north west. It was painful to see our Red Army soldiers retreat; many of them were wounded.

One July morning (I can't give the date now, but I remember all events well and clearly) a terrible panic began. Mum dressed us quickly. I came out into the street; everything was moving. The army was moving in different directions, and I couldn't understand anything at all. I ran towards the tank crew members I had met (they were stationed in a garden not far from the house where we were staying), and my desire to leave with them was so great. However, an hour later, my mum picked me up, saying that we had to leave for somewhere – but nobody knew where exactly. This lasted approximately till noon, and then everything went quiet. It was an alarming silence.

By the end of the day two motorcyclists with machine-guns entered the main street of the village. They were the German military scouts. They looked around and then one of them turned around abruptly and left, perhaps to report on the situation. A few minutes later the German troops poured into the streets of the village. It was symbolic that they entered in the evening, and the night that lasted almost three years for us fell immediately.

The German army forward divisions didn't touch us. A day or two later, Romanian divisions, including killing gendarme squads, entered.

Their headquarters were located in the building of the former village council. At first gendarmes went through the Jewish homes searching for something, and taking everything they saw. Once they went to the house of a Jewish family from Bessarabia or

Moldavia that hadn't managed to get evacuated further, and killed them all. Then they gathered all the Jewish old men (young men were all at the front), including my grandpa and the owner of the house where we were staying, and took them all to the gendarme headquarters. They kept them there for the whole day, and then in the evening they put them in two rows – one faced the forest, the other the village.

Those who faced the forest were shot that night. The others were released in the morning but were ordered to report back to the gendarme headquarters in the evening. Among those who were shot was the owner of the house we stayed in, the kindest man imaginable and an honest and hard worker.

Our grandpa told Mum all this in the morning and said that we had to save ourselves. When he saw the approaching gendarmes, my grandpa, scared by the events of the previous night, managed to hide somewhere, and Mum took my hand and grabbed my sister and, as dressed as we were, we fled to Tomashpol.

Mum realized that we couldn't go along the main street, because the enemy troops were moving along it. We went across the vegetable lots and yards, not really knowing the way. When we were passing by some yard, a woman came out (I will always remember this). She was tall, thin, in a white head shawl and said, 'Oy, lady, don't go along the road, there are the Germans and Romanians on it.' And she showed us another path to take and remain unnoticed. She gave us some food, kissed my mum, and we went to Tomashpol.

In Tomashpol, as the saying goes, we went 'from the frying pan into the fire'. On that day they were killing local Jews. We didn't know this initially, but having got into some house packed with people we heard that the Jews were being captured right in the streets, pulled out of their homes and taken all to one place. There were different rumours but nobody could imagine that people were being gathered together in order to be killed.

At that moment two Romanians with rifles approached the house. Mostly women, children and old people were in the house, and the old men who survived Petlyura and Denikin. It was they who managed to take people out of the house calmly, without any panic, through the back door and hid us in the vegetable garden (we lay on the ground, among the potatoes and weeds) and in the garden, among the bushes.

When the Romanians broke down the door and entered the house, they didn't find anyone in it. For some reason they didn't go to look outside the house and left. I wanted to get out of the hiding place and see what was happening outside in the street but Mum would not let me go. However, carefully moving the bush branches I saw that the main street could be clearly observed from there. Soon afterwards I saw a huge column of Jews, mostly women, children and old people. Three Romanian soldiers and a German on a bicycle followed them. This was the last walk of a few hundreds of innocent people, since once they got out of the town, they were shot with machine-guns.

But we learned about this on the following day. At the end of the day people went away. And we began to look for a shelter to spend the night at.

At that time we met a woman with a girl in her arms and a boy Yasha, walking nearby (he was about my age; later he grew to become a Soviet army officer). The woman placed us in a room beneath the floor. In the morning we learned about the tragedy that could have happened to any of us, at any moment in time.

At night it was horrible and scary, and shots were heard all of the time. We kept thinking that now soldiers would come in, take us away and shoot us. In Tomashpol we learned what hunger was like for the first time ever. There was absolutely nothing to eat. We didn't have any clothes. Everything had been left in Komargorod since we left Tomashpol in a hurry. Thus we lived for some while. There was no hope that the situation would change in any way. Under such circumstances all the people from Yampol decided to return to their own homes in the hope that at home even walls could be helpful.

We set a date for our departure. Even a cart was found. Young children were put on it, as well as ill people, and we set off on the road with much risk. The journey went pretty smoothly and only near Yampol did encounter a cart with two elderly Germans on it; they didn't touch us.

Thus we returned to our hometown. I walked the distance of forty kilometres in one day – with not a single metre covered on the cart, exhausted by worry and hunger – when I was younger than twelve.

The police wouldn't let us go along the main street and we went along another, parallel street. And there, at a distance, I saw my dad who was standing still and was afraid of coming towards the refugees to find out the sad news that we had been killed (he hadn't heard anything from us).

As soon as I saw my dad, I ran towards him and we held each other tight. I felt tears running down his face. I will always remember this scene. Then my mum and sister came along and the joy of meeting was immense. But we couldn't get to our own home – we lived on the main street that was now beyond the limits of the ghetto.

The ghetto was established soon after the Romanians occupied the town. They designated a few streets that were immediately cordoned off with a tall fence made out of a few rows of barbed wire. There, the remaining Jews of our town had to live now.

Thus our long life in the ghetto began. It was a difficult and unbearable life. We were targets for humiliation and torture, and the children's labour was widely used. We all had to wear yellow six-pointed stars. Grown-ups had to work at the most difficult and exhausting jobs. The work was not paid, and the situation was extremely difficult. It was strictly prohibited to leave the ghetto without a special permit. There was an order issued announcing execution for leaving without a permit. Thus many were killed who tried to earn their living.

It was the autumn of 1941. We were naked and barefoot. Those things that had been left at home, in Yampol, were looted, and as I have mentioned above, we didn't manage to get anything from Komargorod. There was no way out of the situation and the winter was approaching fast. So my father made a decision to go to Komargorod and take our belongings back. This was a dangerous idea and my father risked his life. He agreed with one of his Ukrainian friends that he would wait for him on a cart at a designated spot. My father secretly got out of the ghetto and together with his friend went to Komargorod. They agreed that if they encountered any Germans or Romanians my father would go to one side, so as not to endanger the life of his friend. It is difficult to describe what we went through until our dad returned home. The road was relatively safe, and he brought some clothes back. It gave us a chance to change our old rags.

The occupiers never took pity on us, the children: they took us to different jobs, and systematically tortured us. This went on from day to day. One day, in late 1943, together with other boys and grown-ups, the Romanians took me to dig some trenches in the forest. We knew by then that first they would make you dig trenches and then they would shoot you.

The Romanian soldiers showed us where to dig and went away to drink vodka. After they had left, we decided not to dig anything. At the end of the day they returned drunk and seeing that we hadn't accomplished anything they began to beat us with gun butts. We scurried away and they chased us. I was beaten so badly that I couldn't get home without some help, and then had to stay in bed for over a month.

We lived in the constant fear of being killed. This could happen at any minute.

What gave us the strength to survive the humbling of human

dignity, to endure the tortures, and all other sufferings? The faith in the victory of our army did. We didn't lose this faith for a single second (the only doubt we had was whether we would survive till the moment they returned).

Somehow we managed to get all the news in the ghetto. We knew that the Germans couldn't occupy Moscow and that they had suffered a massive defeat near Stalingrad when our army advanced. Sometimes rumour had it that our army would come very soon and when it didn't happen we were extremely disappointed. We waited, hoped and believed – and this gave us the strength to endure all the suffering of the occupation.

And still, happy and bright day came on 17 March 1944, when at about 10 o'clock in the morning our tanks rolled into town.

I immediately jumped out of the basement where we had been hiding and ran towards our soldiers. They were still fighting – we could hear shots; our soldiers with machine-guns lay at the crossing of Komsomolskaya and Urizky Streets – and I fell down near them too. I saw and heard the officer commanding them to go on, and they ran to force the remaining Romanians out. Then I was next to our tanks and saw how our tanks destroyed a German car and a Romanian cart on the other bank of the Dniester. I saw our young soldiers still hot from the battle.

This was the joy of liberation, although we had to live through many raids by the German air force. The following day they began massive attacks, and many people, who had survived the occupation, were dying from the German bomb. Our house was also completely ruined. My father has never managed to restore it. But this was none the less our liberation. Again we became citizens of our country, with equal human rights.

Years and decades have passed. *'Mein shteitele Yampaly* [my shtetl Yampaly]' has ceased to exist. Every year I come to my hometown. I visit my father's grave (my mother is buried in Odessa). I walk along the streets of my former town and cannot recognize it. There are almost no Jews left; they left for different places. Many have returned to the historic homeland. The houses have been rebuilt, renovated, repainted, losing their former image … but my love for my hometown where my childhood and youth years took place will stay in my heart for ever.

And a few days later, ragged, dirty but happy, we were following the advancing Soviet Army to Odessa!

NOTE

1. This originally appeared in *A Bulletin from the Oblast*, Odessa.

73. One cannot forget those horrors[1]

Rachel Tselnik

In August 1941, my mum, brother and I were put into the Sokiryany ghetto, in the Chernovtsy oblast, where many Jews from Brichany, Lipkany, Khotin and Novoselitsy were dying of hunger, infectious diseases and lice. My little sister died there – she was born in the ghetto, completely mutilated, because *en route* to Sokiryany the local policemen kept beating my mum on her stomach.

Later we were transferred to the Ukraine, across the Dniester, to Vinnitsa oblast where half-naked, starving and swollen people who could barely move their feet were moved on several times from one place to another.

Old people, children and even young people were dying all the time and nobody had an opportunity to bury them: the dead people were left on the road, barely covered with rags.

I remember how we were transferred across the Dniester to Mogilev-Podolsky. Hundreds of people fell off the ferry into the river and nobody would save them. The Germans and police were doing their own jobs: taking passports, birth certificates and other documents from the Jews, laughing and telling them that they, the Jews, no longer needed those documents.

Somewhere around New Year's Eve we were brought into the village of Telelintsy (Vinnitsa oblast). Since the greater part of the column had died *en route* there were very few of us left. People in that village were kind; they took us and accommodated us in their houses, gave us food and warmed us up. Our family got into the house of a very good woman. Her name was Kseniya (she was lame), and she had a daughter named Gafiyka. In that village my mum knitted mittens and gloves, socks and jackets for the local people. They were supposed to donate these warm clothes to the German soldiers.

We had lived in Telelintsy until 1942. In April 1942 we were moved onwards, to the camp in Katzmasov, twenty kilometres away from Zhmerinka. We stayed in this camp until 1944, when the Soviet army liberated us.

The camp consisted of wooden barracks. During Stalin's rule, these barracks had served as a prison, and the Germans used it for the Jews brought from Central Europe in the cold winter of 1941. There were no stoves, or water in the camp, and there were big holes between the boards. The Jewish camp administration forbade leaving the camp. It was fenced in by barbed wire. People were dying from hunger, cold and the dirt – and they were buried only when there were enough dead bodies accumulated in the camp. The Jewish administration – Chaim of Khotin (the camp headman, I don't remember his surname now) and Kamenev, the chief of police, a murderer and a torturer, and two more policemen (I don't remember their surnames) – reported to the German and Romanian administration. Their chief would come frequently and the gendarmes would check people from the camp on the [*Appel*[1]] *platz* by calling their names. God forbid that somebody was missing with no valid excuse during this check. And there were numerous excuses: local people from villages nearby were taking camp prisoners for different jobs: to dig vegetable gardens, to cut wood, to do carpentry, to plaster walls, to sew clothes, to knit, and to repair shoes. People got a meal for their work, and if their hosts were rich, they would give some food for families in the camp. However, you had to give half of it to the camp headman and police, otherwise the following time they would not let you go to work.

It frequently happened that local nationalists stormed into the camp, raping girls, beating and robbing people (although there was nothing to rob – everything had been taken away from these people). People looked terrible; they were thin, looked like skeletons with skin, almost naked, dirty, with terrible oedemas. Many could no longer work.

I would like to note that we survived thanks to kind Ukrainian people – Sevastyan Kovalchuk and his family, Mariya Patychikha, Olga Asriyachka, Petro Belokon and many others.

It is impossible to forget the horrors of those days. Similarly, it is impossible to forget all the dear and loved ones that died then. Among those we lost there were: Uncle Shimon Meikler (buried in Voroshilovka), Uncle Blirya Barlam (in Polovtsy), Aunt Mariam Meikler (place of burial unknown); V. Korenblyum, Dad's brother, and his wife were killed; Aunt Molka and her husband died of starvation in Bolty, Uncle Dura Sadovnik, his daughters, Rosa and Chova, and son Moishe died somewhere and their burial place is unknown.

NOTE

1 This originally appeared in 'People Remain Human: Testimonies of Witnesses', *Bulletin*, issue 1 (1991), pp. 87–8.

74. We were afraid of dying from starvation

Raissa Tzerman (Barber) (b. 1925)

I was born into the family of a clerk. There were four children in our family: Mikhail Yakovlevich Baber, an older brother; Samuil Yakovlevich, a younger brother; and Rosa Yakovlevna, our sister.

Before the war I had completed eight years of schooling, including five years in the Jewish school.

When the war began, Mikhail was drafted into the army on 29 June 1941. We never heard from him; most likely his train was bombed.

My younger brother was in the hospital and my parents, Rosa (who was twenty-five) and I stayed in Rudnya. My dad was not drafted because of his age; and there was no evacuation organized in the town.

On 10 July, the town was bombed severely, and we had to spend the whole day in trenches. On 11 July we took our clothes – as much as we could – and headed towards Smolensk. We went together with our relatives. On our way we got into heavy rain and asked some people to let us in to get dry. They let us in but we left our passports there. When we went back we couldn't find our relatives – they had taken some other road.

But then the artillery started firing and we fell into German hands. This happened in July 1941, near Yartsevo. We lived there for a week. The division we were taken up by was good; the Germans gave us soup and bread. Then the division changed, and the new-comers wouldn't give us anything.

We were afraid of dying from starvation and decided to go back to our hometown, to Rudnya, in the hope that our house might be still there. When we returned we found that our house had burned down. We lived for some time with a Russian family; this lasted until the ghetto was established. A street was designated to become the ghetto and it was fenced off by barbed wire. Then we were resettled there, six to seven families sharing one flat. We slept on bunks. We had to wear yellow stars on the left side of our chests

following the order: 'All Jews of either sex must wear yellow markings eight to ten centimetres in diameter. Those Jews found with no
markings, will be shot. Signed: Korotchenko, Chief of Police.' He
was later shot by the Germans – people reported on him, saying he
was with the partisans.

We received 300 grams of bread per one working person a day,
and people worked at the oil refinery and on the road construction.

On 20 September 1941, a killing squad arrived. At that time we
were wearing white armbands. The killing squad protested saying
this was not enough, that one could hide the arm with the band on
it, and then the person was no longer '*Judeh*'.

That was why they gathered us all and began dividing us – to the
right and to the left. I got into a house where the Germans had put
up a bed. They made people lie on it face down and beat them with
sticks – two Germans from each side. They beat me so badly that I
fainted, but their shouts brought me back to my senses and I got up.
Then they ordered us to go to another house. We thought that they
would burn us alive now, but they didn't. Instead, they let us go out,
one by one, and a German would kick each person coming out.

Then, again, they brought us together to the square and a
German would ask, 'Who doesn't know why you have been beaten?'

Everybody was silent. Then they started shooting, and we had
wire under our feet. But they were only scaring us then, and
nobody was killed.

Then I ran into the house and hid under the bed. I stayed there
until the killing squad left. My body was covered with blue and red
stripes and I thought the wounds would never heal. I couldn't
move.

And my dad was shot that day with all the others who had been
taken out as though to go to work.

On 21 October 1941, the killing squad returned. The chairman of
the Jewish Council in the ghetto had warned us beforehand after he
returned from the Gestapo with new orders. That was why in the
morning (fortunately there was no German guard at the ghetto
gates) my sister and I went out of the ghetto, taking off our armbands. My sister went to one neighbour behind the wire, and I went
to hide with our other neighbour.

When we went back, when approaching Rudnyas we were told
that there was nowhere to go – the Germans had killed everybody.
Then we went towards Smolensk. A German wagon was on the
road, and one girl asked if we could be given a ride. The drivers said
'Yes' and I got up on the wagon.

This was October, the days were short and we arrived in darkness. I entered the house, and there were long tables, and the

Germans around them, laughing, *'Deutsch verstehen?'* [Do you understand German?].

But I couldn't admit that I did, since they would immediately recognize I was Jewish, yet they kept laughing, *'Nicht'* [nothing] in German.

Then one of them sat me down near a stove, poured me some coffee and gave me a piece of bread. Then the door opened, and another girl from our group entered the room. It turned out that there was a fork in the road, and she had been taken to some other place. Together with this girl we walked for other five weeks through the occupied territory towards Moscow.

From Smolensk we reached Roslavl where we asked to spend the night. One woman let us in. We were lying on the floor whenI heard her son come in. She told him, 'I let two girls in, and one looks Jewish' (that was my friend).

And he replied, 'Mum, why did you let them in? Today they gathered them all into barracks.'

We feared that he would turn us in the following day. But nobody arrested us in the morning.

We wanted to find out the name of the next village we'd see, and we told people that we were coming from the trenches, and thus we walked for five weeks – mostly in the day, till five o'clock in the afternoon. At five o'clock the curfew hour started and people were shot for its violation. We didn't enter bigger towns. When we were approaching Tula, we were given potatoes and bread. We asked a woman how to get to Tula, saying that we were originally from Tula. She pointed through the window saying, 'There, women are going to Tula to get bread.'

We followed them, but the Germans wouldn't allow them on the highway. Then they turned towards a burned village, and we followed them. In that village one of our soldiers stopped us. We were questioned and taken to the flat where girls from Kursk were already living. The following day we went to the town's Kommandant and told him our story. He said that they expected street fighting to begin within the following three days and that we had to be evacuated. The head of the evacuation station gave us permits and at night we left the place. We got nine kilograms of biscuits for the road.

We travelled for five weeks before we reached Kazakhstan. There, I first worked in a garden, and then entered a local veterinary college, graduated from it, and worked in the Crimea for seven years. Since 1951 I have lived in Kharkov.

75. Distant echo[1]

Vladimir Chepur

There is the ancient town of Pryluki at Chernigovshchina. For many years its home-grown tobacco was a symbol of the town. About a hundred years ago famous Jewish traders named Rabinovich and Fradkin founded a tobacco company there. Since then it has been a traditional law that almost one third of the factory's employees are to be Jewish. There were extraordinary experts among them. I remember Shaya Baikin, an old worker. He could determine the taste and quality of the tobacco himself before the results of the special tests returned from the factory lab.

Before the war, about a quarter of the Pryluki population was Jewish. They held leading positions in business, medicine and trade. But the majority of Jews worked in the local factories and plants.

When the terrible war began, the front line was approaching Pryluki fast. The majority of Jews in the town didn't have time to leave. Not all of them believed in the violence and cruelty of the Germans. I remember my father asked Chernin, a blacksmith and our neighbour, why he wasn't leaving. And Chernin said that during the civil war of 1918 the Germans hadn't hurt the Jewish population, and his sister had even had a romance with a German officer.

And finally the Germans occupied Pryluki. The Kommandant's first order was to make all the Jews register and wear white armbands with the yellow 'Star of David' on them. The Jews were forbidden to come to the marketplace in the centre of the town, near the cinema theatre. People were deprived of their sources of living. Then the Jews rushed to the fields to search for any potatoes left after the harvesting. And this was very dangerous too since policemen were everywhere. People were afraid of talking to their Jewish neighbours because the Germans punished them for that. In the cold and rain, the Jews were forced to do the most difficult jobs: they worked on road repair, cleared factory ruins, and dug ditches for cable connections.

One day, in autumn, when the first frosts set in, I was going back home from the marketplace. Not far from the bridge I saw a group of Jewish men who were pulling small aerial bombs from the bottom of the river. My neighbour, Chernin, was standing on the bank of the river, and was taking the bombs and putting them carefully on the ground. Then men, all in wet clothes, had to load the bombs into the trucks and the sappers took them out of town. Most likely the German fighter planes had tried to bomb the bridge during the fight but missed it. The bombs settled on to the soft river bottom and didn't explode.

It was difficult to find food in the occupied town for anybody, but the Jewish population were famished with hunger the worst. In November the frosts set in and they lasted till spring.

Metal small furnaces were now in almost every flat and house. Heat passed throughout their metal pipes. Our neighbour Kaspin, a tinmaker, started making the pipes but he couldn't sell them out in the market, and the local residents were afraid of coming to the place where a Jew lived. So farmers from other places who came on sleighs to the town market would trade pipes for grain, potatoes, or beans … but only a few could afford to do this …

It was difficult to get fuel. All those in our neighbourhood went out to the swamp to gather dry reeds and weeds. Together with them, Jewish families went to the ice (they were not prohibited from here). People wanted more than just to bring dry sticks into their homes, they wanted to freely communicate with their neighbours and to learn all the local news.

From 1 January 1942 all the Jewish population was transferred to the ghetto. It was established near the marketplace, in buildings that had housed two schools (Jewish and Ukrainian) before the war. The ghetto was fenced off with barbed wire. In the yards, the Germans posted special announcements in which the rules of life in the ghetto were posted. Jewish headmen from the council were responsible for order in ghetto.

The ghetto residents tried to survive in any way possible. They dug secret tunnels under the fence and went unnoticed into the streets of the town. This helped for some time. Before the war my parents had worked at the tobacco factory. Eva Bolotina, a young Jewish woman, had worked together with my mum. One cold winter day Mum went outside and saw a frozen woman covered in some rags. Mum could hardly recognize her friend, Eva Bolotina, in the stranger. My father told us to cover the windows with cloth, and my grandma got her a hot meal and tea. Eva told us about her sufferings in the ghetto. Mum put some hot boiled potatoes in her sack along with biscuits, a pack of tea and some home-grown tobacco the for men.

When leaving Eva cried bitterly and said through tears, 'Marusya, we all are going to die here.'

My mum and my grandma cried, and my father and I stood still. Eva never returned.

Soon afterwards we learned that the Kommandant had enhanced the ghetto security. Now children came to the rescue of its residents. Brave teenagers artfully conquered the barbed wire and got outside the ghetto. They didn't wear any armbands. They brought food back to the ghetto and with this they saved the lives of the ghetto residents. These courageous young people should be commemorated in a special memorial as national heroes.

On 20 May 1942, the worst happened. It was a wonderful spring day. Everything was blossoming all around, and the trouble came up unexpectedly. Neighbours spotted a black police wagon on the bridge. The car stopped near the Bugayov family home; they had a Jewish daughter-in-law named Dora. The young woman ran towards the river and jumped in, she wanted to drown herself. But they pulled her out, resuscitated her and took her into the car.

I quickly ran towards the ghetto to see what was happening there. A huge column of people was moving slowly from the ghetto to the street; there were four people abreast. A policeman rode on a horse ahead of the column and armed guards marched alongside the column. At first the residents of Pryluki thought that the Jews were being taken to the railway station to be sent to Poland, but the column moved past the railway's street, then towards the prison and on. Now the column was approaching me and I saw among the poor people our friend, Eva Bolotina, and Chernin, the blacksmith, and weak Dora Bugayova supported by two men. Senka Kaspin, a neighbour of my own age, saw me. Before the war we had played football together for the city school cup; now we looked at each other in terror.

The column went on towards the far end of the town. There was an open spot behind the prison and I was afraid of going further with the prisoners. A deep ravine lay behind a small wooden bridge.

Here my neighbours and compatriots went into eternity.

The terrible war was over long ago. But I still can see the last day of the Pryluki ghetto go before my eyes. And only in my old age, have I finally the chance of telling people about this horrible tragedy.

NOTE

1. This originally appeqared in the *Jewish News* and as an Appendix to *The Voice of the Ukraine*, a special edition of *The Supreme Council of the Ukraine*, No. 5 (Society for Jewish Culture of the Ukraine, 1999).

76. My brother left for the partisans

Raissa Schaikhet (Weinbrand) (b. 1930)

Before the war I had lived with my father, Zachar Yankelevich Weinbrand, born in 1885, two brother, and a sister in the village of Zamyslovichi, Olevsk district, Zhitomir oblast. My mother died in 1940.

During the occupation of our village, our family, together with all other Jewish families of Zamyslovichi, was taken out of the village to be killed, in November 1941.

When they told us to turn left we realized that they were taking us to the forest to kill us.

Then my father said quietly in Yiddish, 'Kinderlach ankleift' [Children, run!].

And we ran away, and our father followed us too. They started shooting their machine-guns but we ran further into the forest. But my father couldn't run fast, he was old and ill, and they killed him.

For some time we were hiding at different farmsteads and in nearby villages. But soon afterwards the Germans caught us and took to the town of Olevsk, to the local ghetto. We stayed there from November 1941 to February 1943. At the end of February 1943 the Germans, together with the police, took the ghetto prisoners outside the town to kill them. I managed to run away together with my sister and a brother, while our younger brother didn't, and he was shot.

After our second escape my older sister and I were hiding at different villages until Zhitomir oblast was liberated. My brother, Grigory Zacharovich Weinbrand, left for the partisans, and fought first in Zhitomir oblast and then in Western Ukraine. After liberation of Volyn oblast my brother was sent to work in the militia at Lutsk. He was an officer in the regular militia but for a long time he had to fight the German collaborators who survived the war and terrorizsed the local population. His service in the militia was not an easy one either, but he was promoted to colonel, retired, yet kept working till the end of his life. In 1995 he passed away following a grave illness.

In 1949 I came to my brother in Lutsk, and I have lived here ever since.

The war took away much of my health and I became a war invalid of the second category.

77. The Poles took me and saved my life

Mikhail Schafir (b. 1926)

When the Great Patriotic War began, on 22 June 1941, nobody managed to leave our village, and three days later – 25 June – the Germans occupied it.

When the first Germans entered the village, they got together about ten elderly Jews and marched them through the village, beating and humiliating them. Then they cut off their beards with meat knives, and shot them in the square. They would not let us bury them for a couple of days.

They gathered us together for different jobs; most frequently it was to mill grain that had been taken away from people. And once they made us bury the Red Army parachutists they had shot. Afterwards I was hired to grind the stones on the road construction site. We had a Polish supervisor who beat us all continually and constantly demanded some sort of payment.

Thus we survived till summer of 1942. We didn't have a separate ghetto because the village was small and the Germans were able to gather Jews for killing with the help of the Ukrainian police.

My father was born in a small village nearby and he had many friends among the local Ukrainians and Poles. We hid at these people's homes for some time. But then the Germans announced that if they found out that someone was hiding Jews, all their family would be killed. And we had to leave.

We spent some time out in a swamp, near the river, hiding in bushes, and waiting until the Germans stopped raiding the town. Then, all those who survived left their hiding places and some time later the Germans started gathering Jews and killing them again, aiming for our complete elimination.

Then we stayed at a farmstead with a Polish man, in a temporary shed that he had. On the night of 14 October 1942, these bandits broke into our place. I don't know how it happened but we began fighting them back. One of them began shooting and killed my father instantly. Then they took Mother outside, and killed her with two shots. Then they took my sister, and shot her, and then they searched for me. But I escaped: there was a lot of rubbish in the hut and in the darkness I hid behind the door and they didn't see me.

It was still dark when the bandits left. I got out of the hut and because I didn't know where to go, I hid in a small barn nearby.

In the morning, the village headman organized the looting of the dead. They took everything from them and I heard how he suggested taking all of their clothes and how their cold bodies were thrown on to a cart like logs. They were taken to be buried at the place where a local Jew had been shot a week before by the police.

Then I went to the Polish man with whom I had lived when my parents were alive.

In 1944, a Red Army unit that had been surrounded earlier was passing by this village and I joined them. Thus, I got into the active military division and served there until 1951. I took part in military actions; I was wounded and awarded with Orders of the Patriotic War of the first degree and the Glory of the third degree, as well as decorated for bravery. Now I am a war veteran and disabled of the second category.

78. I myself don't know how I survived

MOISEY SCHWARTZMAN (b. 1930)

On 10 July 1941, divisions from Nazi Germany occupied our town. A few days later, in an older part of the town (the 'Old Town'), a Jewish ghetto was established. The killings of Jews – at first separate instances, followed by mass slaughter – began almost immediately.

Our town is mournfully known as a place for mass killings of Jews brought from Hungary, Czechoslovakia and from other towns and villages of Khmelnitzky oblast. The local Jews confined in the ghetto were doomed for death. Only from time to time we would manage to trade some clothes for food. The farmers whom we had known before the war tried to bring us some food.

Our family included our parents, my older sister and my younger brother. I was eleven years old, and managed a few times to slip through the police security into town and bring some food for our family. But even such a life didn't last for long.

In late August, early in the morning, police woke us up and marched us all to the place of killings. This was a place outside the town. Today there are three monuments at that place, very modest ones.

My father was killed instantly, and my mum took us and managed to mingle with a group of families of those professionals selected for work. We were marched back to town and put in the building of the former Silicate Institute (now, the local Industrial College). From here we were taken to different jobs. We were not given any food; we were dressed poorly and had worn shoes. I remember how Mum made me a 'coat' from sackcloth and coloured it with elderberries.

Some time later, closer to winter, we were moved to the former German training barracks (before the war there had been a military union stationed there). My mum and older sister Fanya worked sewing clothes and doing embroidery. I tried to get out from there once in a while and bring some food back.

Thus we managed to survive winter and spring. By the time summer came, rumours of new killings started to spread. We decided to escape. The escape, during which my older sister Fanya was killed, took place in June. My mum, my three-year-old brother Arkady, and I got to the village of Beznoskovtsy (Abrikosovka), where Mum knew many people (we had lived for some time there before the war). We lived together for a few months but this was dangerous and Mum sent me to the village of Slobodka-Rykhtezkaya, about thirty kilometres away. She left my younger brother with a woman in Beznoskovtsy. He was forbidden to go outside the house, but one day when he was alone, he got out. A local policeman saw him. He took the child by the hand, took him out into the forest and killed him there.

Mum was hiding at the homestead of Danila Melnik, together with another Jewish man, in Slobodka-Rykhtezkaya. They were hiding in the hay store. But the police learned about it and came to arrest them. The Jewish man didn't want to fall into the hands of the police, so he cut his throat and died. Seeing the policemen approach the store, my mum covered her head tightly with a neckerchief, picked up a hoe in the yard and managed to leave through a vegetable garden and be saved. She managed to get herself a Ukrainian passport and she hid either in Kamenets-Podolsky or in the villages nearby.

Until liberation day I lived either in Slobodka-Rykhtezkaya or at a farmstead. I told people I was an orphan, that my name was Vasya Kovalevsky and that my parents had died during an air raid. I begged for food, I slept in hay and maize stacks. Occasionally a woman would let me in for a little while, out of pity. Once, I came to a woman's house by myself – I don't remember her; I was ill and had a high fever. But she didn't send me away; instead she put me in bed and kept me there. I myself don't know how I survived.

When Kamenets-Podolsky was liberated, we returned home.

79. I cried and asked God to help the German soldier

REVEKKA SCHWARTZMAN (b. 1921)

My name is Revekka Aronovna Schwartzman, and I am also known as Raissa Antonovna Kiseleva. I was born on 10 November 1921. On 19 September 1941 the Germans occupied Kiev. Being in occupied territory we lived in continuous worry. Horrible things happened but nothing could be done about it. Once I was walking along Shevchenko Boulevard carrying my little son, Vyacheslav, in my arms and I saw how a German officer hunted down a young Jewish man with his German Shepherd dog. The dog tore off pieces of flesh from the poor man. He fell down, fainted, and later he died. I also saw how German guards marched war prisoners down Brest-Litovsk highway. There were thousands of them, half-naked and barefoot, with shovels in their hands. There were Ukrainians, Russians and many Jews. There were marched towards the Lukyanovskoye cemetery. People threw pieces of bread to the worn-out, hungry prisoners, but those who dared pick them up were shot. Young boys who ran behind the prisoners said later that they had to dig a pit first, and after that the German soldiers shot them and pushed them into the very same pit. When people who stood on the highway learned about this, they cried, and we, a Jewish family, cried the worst of all – and were scared that this trouble would reach us.

And, finally, it was our turn. On 28 September an order was posted which said that all Jews of Kiev and surrounding area would have to report on Monday, 29 September, by 8 a.m. to the corner of Melnikov Street, taking our documents, money and valuables with us. We also had to take warm clothes with us. Killing was threatened for disobedience. The same order forbade the Ukrainians and Russians to loot Jewish flats; otherwise they would be killed too. On 29 September 1941, together with my son Slavik, who was fifteen months old then, and my sister Sonechka with her two children (Alik, aged two, and Nelya, aged three) I went to our parents, who lived at 17 Brest-Litovsk Highway. Polina, Dad's sister, with her husband Velvel and three children, also went there. We hadn't slept all night, cried and didn't know where they would take us.

And, suddenly, a German soldier ran into our flat. He had a rifle; he started shouting something at us and started pushing us out of the flat. Obviously someone had told him a Jewish family lived there. We went out into the yard. Our neighbours came up to us. They cried with us and said their goodbyes – we all grew up together, as did our children. Our neighbour, Aunt Pasha, with her daughters Lenochka, eleven, and Valya, sixteen, went to see us off. We all went along the Brest-Litovsk Highway, carrying younger children in our arms and crying. We turned into Kerosinnaya Street and finally reached Melnikov Street. Many people were walking alongside us. They pulled carts with their things, and pushed wheelchairs with paralysed relatives. The German killers were riding motorcycles with automatic guns in their arms and wearing chains with some eagles across their chests. They were laughing as we cried, not knowing our destination or fate. Thus we reached Babi Yar. There we saw a line of German soldiers who hurried people along. There was the rattle of machine-guns. Our neighbours said goodbye and left quickly, and the girls, Lenochka and Valechka, carried Slavik further but then they also said goodbye and left.

A German soldier looked at us. I had a small blond-haired child in my arms and he asked me, '*Judeh?*'

And I said 'Yes.'

And then he said, '*Zuruck, kaput scheine blonde kleine kind, zuruck!*' [Go back, you are done for, pretty blonde small child, go back].

And we realized, together with my sister, that he was telling us we had to flee. I hardly made it out of that crowd with Slavik, forgetting about our family. We found ourselves at the cemetery and hid in a crypt. The day of 29 September was hot but it was very cold inside the tomb. We sat there; I was breast-feeding my son, and he was quiet.

At dawn I went out on to the road and ran towards the station of Zhulyany, to the village of Kryukivshchina. There was a woman named Melaniya who lived with three boys, and Yarina with her daughter Manya. Before the war they had brought goats' milk to our home. They welcomed us and we spent two months there, living in their basement.

And then they read a poster at the station saying that those who hid the Jews would be killed together with them. They became frightened, and asked us to leave, giving me two pies and a bottle of milk for the road. And we went back to Kiev.

En route, I recalled that at 25 Pushkinskaya Street, Mum's friends named Radchenko lived, Anna Ivanovna and SavelyKlimentyevich.

They were religious people, and they had no children. I went to them with my child in my arms. I rang the doorbell, they opened it, and invited us in. They gave us food, and I asked them to take my child and I would turn myself in to the Germans and they would shoot me, because I had nowhere to go. They let us stay overnight. Anna Ivanovna spoke with people she knew and trusted well: Nechai, Luzanov and Tamara Oleksievich. They put us into the basement, took the child and baptised him in the Trinity church. Then they burned my passport, which read Revekka Aronovna Schwartzman, and got me a new one, with my husband's name in it – Kiseleva, changing my name into Raissa Antonovna, and stating my nationality as Ukrainian rather than Jewish.

I spent two years in this basement; they gave me food and helped me as much as they could. I was crying and asking God to help the German soldier who saved our lives in Babi Yar, so that he could live and his mother have him home alive and well.

Thus I lived until early November 1943 when Kiev was freed. Together with Slavik I went to Lvovskaya Street where my sister Sonechka used to live. Her mother-in-law told me that Sonechka had followed me and also fled Babi Yar with her two children. A couple of old people, the Boynov grandparents, wonderful Russian people, had been hiding her children Alik and Nelechka. But on New Year's Eve when Sonechka took the children out for fresh air, a German officer who was visiting her young neighbour saw her. He invited Sonechka to ring the New Year in with him. Sonechka said 'No' because she had two young children. However, the neighbour explained to the officer that Sonechka was Jewish. He didn't say a word, but in the morning he sent a gas wagon. Thus he took Sonechka, her two children and Mum away to Babi Yar.

I went to my old flat we had had before the war. But the house was in rubble and there was no place to live. Then I went to 17 Brest-Litovsk Highway, where my parents used to live.

I would like to thank the Russian and Ukrainian people – Nechai, Radchenko, Luzanov and Oleksievich. May they rest in peace – and I keep thanking them, as well as their children, Yulia Nechai and Elena Zvenyatskaya. It was thanks to them that we survived. A court restored my true name, thus Revekka Aronovna Schwartzman and Raissa Antonovna Kiseleva are one and the same person.

80. I thank all those people who helped us to survive

Tsilya Schport (Grabak) (b. 1928)

I am no longer a young person – I am seventy years old now. My life is almost over, but those horrible years keep haunting me, and in my dreams I frequently relive them over again.

My dad was a tailor at a factory, and my mum was a housewife. I was a student in the eighth form, in the town of Tulchin, in School No. 2 – since there was no secondary school in our village. My younger sister Clara had just finished her first year at school. Our grandma also lived in Kirpasovka.

Mum's sister, Riva, lived in the same village with her family. And when my parents left for Moscow, to visit Uncle David, my dad's brother, we stayed with our aunt. Expecting nothing bad, we stayed there waiting for our parents' return, yet we met them only in 1945.

Two days after the war was announced, the Germans bombed our railway station. The manager of the railway station and all his family were killed. The evacuation began.

My aunt's husband was mobilized at once and my aunt, having three children of her own, didn't go anywhere in the hope that my parents would return any day soon. Moreover, we were continually told that the Germans wouldn't come to our village.

But, literally three weeks later, the Germans entered our village, and a few days afterwards they issued an order for all Jews to be resettled in Tulchin.

Not expecting anything bad, we went to Tulchin, where my aunt rented a room at the edge of the town, with a Jewish family. One morning, the whole area of the Jewish town was surrounded. Nobody knew what had happened. But since we lived on the edge of the town we managed to get out into the road leading to our village through a ravine. There, together with Clara, we went to our parents' good friends, the Grabachki family, who lived at the edge of the village. My aunt, with her children, returned to her house, which had already been taken over by neighbours. My Clara was very ill; they rubbed her down, put her on a Russian stove and gave her milk. Not much later, as we fell asleep, the police knocked on the door. We didn't hide. So they seized us and took us into the building of the former village council. In the morning we had to cover twelve kilometres on foot escorted by a policeman on a horse; and he took us to a former Jewish school, which was already packed with people.

Nobody said anything about what would happen to us. I managed to talk a Romanian soldier into letting me go to our flat and bring us back some bare necessities. Here, in this school, we met our distant relative, Chopa Eikelis, who took us under her care.

Two days later, under police escort about two thousand of us were marched across fields into the unknown. Those who were slow were shot dead. And finally we came to Pechera, Shpikov district. There was a beautiful three-storeyed building, a former sanatorium of the air force. The River Bug flowed below it. A tall fence surrounded the building. We were not the first ones here. There were Jews from Bratslav, Shpikov and Nemirov. It was forbidden to leave the camp. We were put into a room on the third floor. Between thirty-five and forty people now shared a room where one person used to live and rest. It was possible to sit only. And at night it was impossible to lie down.

Everything that could possibly be traded was traded and used. The starvation began. Fima, Aunt Chopa's son, was the first to die. I even remember where he was buried. And then people began to die in their hundreds. The dead were thrown into a shed and later taken out. I will never forget how they shot one of our relatives. She climbed the fence and was offering to trade her dress for beets or potatoes. A policeman named Sabansky shot and hit her in the head. She fell down dead. And her children died here, in the camp, of starvation. By the way, when Pechera was liberated, our soldiers shot that traitor [Sabansky].

Two months later our Aunt Riva, with her children and our grandma, were caught and brought here too. By then the camp was joined by Jews marched from Chernovtsy and Moldavia. My cousin, Manya (Aunt Riva's older daughter), and I would jump over the fence at night and go to distant villages to beg. Everything that women in the villages could give us – potatoes or beets – was our salvation. Aunt Riva then cooked some soup on [top of hot] bricks, and we would share the few spoons among us. This would last for three days and then again – it was a case of getting out and begging.

I will never forget a case that shocked us all: a young woman, desperate from hunger and having heard that a dead woman had been taken to the shed, went there, cut her breast off and started eating it. Even the guards were shocked, let alone us. Some commission came to visit – I think it was the Red Cross, I don't remember exactly – yet nothing happened. People were killed slowly.

I can still see a young surgeon from Chernovtsy before my eyes. Everybody knew he was a doctor. He was dark-haired, very handsome. And here, having sold everything in order not to die, he walked around almost naked and kept asking for *'Ein lefn soupa'* [One spoon of soup].

He also died.

There were common graves in Pechera where 200–300 people were buried. But Pechera was in Romanian territory, and Jews still 'lived' here. On the other side of the Bug the Germans ruled. And in August 1942 they stormed the camp, getting everyone out into the square and selecting – old people and children went to one side, grown-ups to the other. And our grandma, my sister Clara and Aunt Riva's Clara were among those whom the Germans intended to shoot.

But they said that the Romanian Kommandant sent a telegram to Antonescu and when the first lorry with people on came up to the gates, it was stopped.

And we were taken to stone quarries near Nemirov. This was a German area. Lithuanians guarded us – and this says it all. We had to eat steamed millet and we had to work hard.

I don't know whether I can thank my lucky stars, but sometimes I believe I can. Residents of the nearby villages worked with us too. In the morning they would come, and in the evening they would go home. A veterinary doctor was among them. Unfortunately I don't remember his surname. We met and he asked where we had come from. It turned out that before the war he had worked in our village and he knew my parents well. And he decided to help us: to get documents showing that we were refugees, so that we could survive, if possible, all this repression. Thus we worked there until January 1943. A German engineer was in charge of constructions; he was very humane. When somebody became ill and didn't came to work he would keep this person in his trailer, far away from the barracks, so that the Gestapo wouldn't shoot them.

At that time I fell ill with the typhoid fever and I stayed there with no medical help. And then on 20 January or so, all Jews returned from work very upset. Two days before that, the local people had not been at work. And from them the prisoners knew that the local people had been made to dig pits for us. And when, the following day, the Kommandant and the construction supervisor waved their hands.

My aunt came running into the barrack and took us out as though for work, but in fact with the intention of escaping. And then we were in the quarry. Seizing the moment when the guard went into his hut to get warm, we ran off. The forest was near. But we could hardly move – fear made us numb. People were walking towards us. They showed us the quickest way to the Bug, the border of the German and Romanian areas. There had not been a chase so far and we ran for over twenty kilometres. And then we saw the Bug; it was flowing and wasn't coated with ice. Soon it would be three o'clock and the local people said that if the Germans saw anyone near the river, they shot them.

We saw some ice at one place and decided to walk over it. My aunt, with Mila, her daughter, stepped out first. Manya and I stood hugging each other and crying, in fear, expecting the Germans to shoot at us any minute now. But then we overcame our fear and ran across to the other side. We got into the forest, ran up along the pathway and came to the Jewish ghetto of Shpikov.

Of course we were given shelter. And in the morning the local people told us that the night we escaped, the Germans killed everyone. They put all the people into a column and shot every fifth person until they killed everybody.

Thus I escaped death twice.

We spent a week in Shpikov and went on to Pechera. There were the two Claras and Grandma left in the camp. By then our grandma had died and nobody knew when and where she was buried. And the two Claras were begging in villages, living in sheds – wherever people would let them. Those who also came begging found them. The girls didn't believe we were alive and back in Pechera. It is horrible to describe how they looked: covered in lice, itching, but … alive.

The desire to survive pushed us into taking risky and dangerous steps. Together with Manya we went by foot to our hometown. We went through ravines and fields, avoiding villages or meeting people. And in our village our friends supported us with food and even with money in case we had to bribe policemen or Romanians.

Such travels happened once every three months. That was how we survived, while younger children went to nearby villages.

When retreating, the Germans decided to kill us all. But then a partisan detachment guarded us.

It is hard to describe the feelings we had when seeing the first units of the Soviet army. Out of 6,000 (I could be mistaken) and perhaps more, only some 300 survived.

And we left for our homes. This was in March 1944. And then we received a letter from Nizhny Tagil, from Mum. She was asking whether people knew where her children had been buried. And Dad was at the front. And only by summer 1944 could Mum come, and Dad returned after the war; both were grateful to my aunt for saving their children.

Unfortunately, neither my parents nor my aunt are alive now. My cousins live in Israel, and my Clara and I live now in different countries: I live in the Ukraine, and she lives in Russia.

I couldn't help but go through the places of my wanderings and trials. I cannot describe my feelings when I came to Pechera. And when I showed how I was getting across the fence, and how and where I fled, my husband and my children couldn't believe me. And when I entered the building (it now houses the resort for war veterans), my feet started shaking and tears choked me. I was allowed to open the doors into one room. But I couldn't stay there for long: the feeling of fear and grief gripped me. It is difficult to write about it, and even more difficult to recall it all. But I am grateful to fate for my survival. Later I graduated from an institute, raised two sons and worked for forty-seven years in schools (I taught Russian language and literature). I tried to teach my students a feeling of love towards their homeland and internationalism, without hiding my past, and with pride that I was a daughter of the Jewish people.

I am grateful to the people who helped us survive during the days of the occupation. These are residents of Kirpasovka – Maria Bondarenko, Kharityna Storozhenko, Zoya Gaevskaya and Sophia Klimenko. They never closed their doors to us. My friend Zoya would lock me in her flat for the whole day and leave for work and nobody could have guessed that Jews were hiding next door to the Kommandant's office. Receiving all we needed, we left the village as unnoticed as we had come into it. I thank these people and will remember them for ever!

81. In Babi Yar I lost my mum and sister for ever

Ruvim Schtein (b. 1926)

I was born in January 1926, in the town of Kazatin, in the Vinnitsa oblast, into a big Jewish family. My grandpa died during the civil war; he had nine children (five sons and four daughters). My father, Yisrael Ruvimovich, together with my mother, Rachel Mikhailovna, moved to Kiev. During the famine in the Ukraine, in 1933 our family moved to Azerbaijan (to the town of Cuba, Khachmassky district) where my father raised cattle and sent them to Kiev.

In 1935 when we returned to the Ukraine, my father got ill (as a result of hard work during the civil war when he dug trenches in late autumn, standing in water waist-high). In April of 1938 he died. We were half-orphaned now, my sister, Maria, aged three, and I. My mum worked in a shoe factory and I went into the fourth form in School No. 122.

I learned what Fascism was like for the first time at a pioneer camp in Vorsel, where Spanish children spent their summer. I made friends with Pedro Gonzales, a Spanish boy. With tears in his eyes he was telling me about the fight of his people against Fascism. He would raise his tightly clenched fist above his head and shout, '*No passaran!*' [They won't pass!].

Then after seeing films about Germany (*The Swamp Soldiers, Professor Mamlock, The Oppenheim Family*, and others) I grew confident that Fascism was the worst enemy of humankind, and of the Jewish people in particular.

During my adolescence, I didn't waste my time in vain: I went into sports gymnastics at the Palace of Pioneers; during school summer break I took care of small tree saplings in 'The Green Trust' tree nursery. Before the war, in the summer of 1941, I had worked as a stamp operator at *Promgalkombinat* (I pressed metal buttons, stars and anchors for the military uniforms) and helped my mother to earn our living. I studied well at school, had many friends and even grown-ups respected me.

In June 1941 I finished seven years of my schooling, and a week later the war began.

In July 1941, the Germans dropped their parachutists above the Goloseevsky forest and the area where we lived became a front zone. On 19 September, the Germans entered Kiev.

On 25 September 1941, after blowing up buildings on the Kreshchatik and nearby streets, a state of emergency was announced in the city (curfew was extended), followed by arrests and other repressive measures. Two days later, on 29 September 1941, the Germans posted orders for the Jewish evacuation and the need for Jews to gather near the Lukyanovskoye cemetery. The order read:

All Jews of the city of Kiev and its environs must report on Monday, 29 September 1941 at 8 a.m. to the corner of Melnikov and Degtyarevskaya Streets (near the cemetery). They have to bring documents, money and valuables, as well as warm clothing, underwear etc. The Jews violating this order and found in another location will be shot. Those civilians who enter flats left by the Jews and take things out of them, will be shot.

I remember that bright and sunny autumn day of 1941 very well.

Look around yourself and see how much greenery, sun and fresh air are around. This was all around too, on the day that became the final day for all Jews in the city. The majority of them were families with many children and no resources to leave the city prior to the occupation, as well as the wives and children of those who had left for the front. There were so many elderly and respected people (Jewish families have always been big), and, in particular, there were many children!

The stream of people began early in the morning and went down Artem, Glubochitskaya, Melnikov and other streets. Like small brooks, the Jewish families made one big human river that stretched to Lukyanivskaya Square. Where was everybody going? Some people said that we would be sent to the ghetto, others that we would be put on trains and sent to Palestine. Almost nobody believed that we would be killed. Hope remained till the very last moment. Nobody wanted to believe that this was the last day of our lives, the last hour, the last minute. They would not dare kill women, children and old people, everybody said.

Like all the other Jews of Kiev, my family packed and set off on our way. Before we got out, I had heard a few people say that all Jews would be killed. I told Mum about it, but she wouldn't believe me. She didn't want to believe that they could kill so many innocent people – old people, children and women.

My family – my mother, thirty-eight; sister, six; and I, aged fifteen, believed in life and we did exactly the same as all the Jews of our city. We went towards death. With all our old belongings, documents and family photographs we entered that endless river of people walking down to the slaughter.

About 200–300 metres away from the cemetery, the stream of people stopped. Men dressed in brown shirts with swastikas on them, as well as field gendarmes, began forming columns and taking groups of people away, around one bend in the road and then around the other, beyond the cemetery. People who waited at this point couldn't see anything. Those who came to the final point would be gradually and ruthlessly humiliated: first our documents, things and valuables were taken away. Passports, photographs and documents were immediately thrown into the fire. The clothes were taken off women and thrown on to a big pile. Naked women, children and old people were put on to lorries with closed backs, and taken to Babi Yar.

It is impossible to describe what was going on at that spot – hysterics and terror, laments and despair, mothers' pleas to spare their children's lives. Many fainted.

At that place I lost my mum and sister for ever. They were taken away in a lorry, and I was pushed aside to the group of men, teenagers and old people who could walk. They gathered groups of 100–150 people and walked us down to Babi Yar on foot, with the guards escorting us.

From the very first steps along the way I began searching for any opportunity to escape out of this convoy. But how and when? We were escorted by the armed Germans along our way and when there was not more 250–300 metres to Babi Yar (we could already hear shots and screams), I slipped out of the group unnoticed. I rolled down into a ditch, crawled inside a sewer pipe under the road, and stayed there till darkness fell. When the groups became more infrequent, I crawled over to the other side of the road and reached the edge of the city by going across the old cemetery and vegetable gardens. Then, late at night, I reached our home. I stayed there a whole week, not leaving the place, and only when I heard someone trying to open the door from outside did I go out to the first floor's balcony, slide down a drainage pipe and run away. I would never return home after that.

While it was warm, I used to spend nights wherever possible (in ruins, sheds, and attics). But where would I go and what would I do? Then cold autumn began, and I had to search for a warm place and some food. I decided to go to my friends with whom I went to school – the Bobrovsky family (Maria Grigoryevna, mother; her sons, Nikolay, sixteen, and Mikhail, fourteen; and a six-year-old daughter, Olga; her oldest son, Georgy, was at the front). They

welcomed me and hid me in a cave dug our by their family in a
nearby hill that had served them as an air raid shelter. I lived with
them until November 1941. Not to endanger their lives any more I
decided to leave them and walk towards the front or find a partisan
detachment. But I didn't have any documents and gendarmes and
police checked these at every patrol checkpoint. Accidentally, in the
centre of the city, I met Yuri Lukich Tansky, who had been my classmate and whose father was the principal of the school we went to.
He got me a birth certificate out of the school's registrar, issued in
the name of Vladimir Sergeyevich Medvedenko, born in 1926, in
Kiev. But in order to go to the front I had to cross the Dnieper, and
there was a checkpoint on the bridge.

To get a pass, I had to work. I found some work at a loading
station, clearing the rubbish. I worked there for two weeks and
received an ID card [*Ausweis*] with the German seal on it. Now I
could cross the Dnieper; and so I went on, staying away from main
roads, from village to village, trying to reach my destination.

From November 1941 until March 1942 I crossed Kiev, Chernigov,
Orel, and Bryansk oblasts, over 600 kilometres. I spent nights in warm
houses, if people let me in, or in a haystack, or a cold sty (not everybody let me in, it was forbidden by the Kommandant's office). If I had
to stay in the village, I had to present my documents to the village
headman and police; and if they had carried out a religious or medical chek, then I would have been shot or hanged. The local people
had mercy on me and helped with whatever they could – with bread
or old shoes. Many invited me to stay and spend the winter months
with them, but it was dangerous while the front and the partisans
were near.

Once, in a bad blizzard, half-naked and weak, I froze in a deep
pile of snow. I woke up in the house of a local *kolkhoz* brigadier who
had picked me up in the blizzard, warmed me up, fed me and
healed my frostbitten body. A week later I worked as a stoker in the
kolkhoz of the village of Azarovka, Ponurov district, Bryansk oblast.

In March 1942 Agafiya Evdokimovna Martinets gave me shelter;
she was a mother of four girls aged two to eleven. Her husband was
at the front. She taught me to work in agriculture: to plough and
sow, to mow and work with wood, to lay roofing and make bast-
shoes, to process sheepskins and pasture horses, etc. Almost two
years of my life in the occupied territory passed in constant fear and
danger, and worry, not only for myself but also for my Aunt Agafiya
and her children. I think she guessed I was Jewish and using
somebody else's identity to hide from persecution by the police and
the Germans, who would occasionally visit the village in search of
runaway prisoners of war.

In August 1943 the military units of the Soviet army liberated Azarovka. I volunteered for the front, but I was not lucky. A special division of SMERSH sent me back into the village until the following draft of seventeen-year-olds.

In October 1943 I was drafted into the military and sent to the Bryansk Reserve Regiment, and then to the 5th Training Regiment. In summer of 1944 I took part in the battles for the liberation of the Baltic Republics. I was seriously wounded in the battle near the town of Tukumsa. Military nurses picked me up in a trench, and I woke up in a medical division where doctors removed shell fragments from my head. This happened on 25 February 1945. In May 1945 I was sent to the far east, to Vladivostok, to build a railway across the mountain pass to the Soviet harbour. In 1947 I was demobilized, and I went to Baku, where relatives of my mother lived. I worked at a local plant as a moulder and smelter of the fourth grade, and studied at the evening school for working youth.

In 1950 I entered the Azerbaijan Institute for Physical Culture and decided to dedicate my life to teaching and working with children. Later I got transferred to the Kiev Institute and from 1952 to April 1996 I worked as a teacher of physical culture. I worked for thirty-eight years in the very same school where I had studied before the war.

I was decorated with orders, medals and honorary diplomas for military and professional achievements.

Fifty-three years of work experience is more than just a figure. This was a difficult lifetime that needed to be lived with dignity, preserving a good name among your family and among your students. I have worked throughout all my life to the fullest, as they say, 'as if for another man, too'. Almost half a century has passed since the day of the terrible tragedy in Babi Yar, and all these years I've been haunted by nightmares that wake me up in cold sweat. But 'Nothing and nobody is forgotten.' Mikhail Dmitrievich Bobrovsky, whose family saved me during the war, was awarded the title of the 'Righteous Among the Nations'. I bow to and thank Agafiya Evdokimovna Martinets and her children, of Azarovka. I am for ever indebted to all those who saved me and helped me survive during the difficult war years.

82. This time was filled with great risk, fear and worry

Fira Schtemberg (Narodnitskaya) (b. 1933)

The train was taking us further away from our hometown of Korosten; my father had urgently come from Kiev to take my mum and me away. It was 1941, during the second month of the war.

My father, Isaac Moiseevich Narodnitsky, born in Kiev, after getting married worked in Korosten at a mechanical plant. My mother, Manya Davydovna Narodnitskaya, was born in 1907, in the village of Gorshchik, Korosten district. The village of Gorshchik was originally a German colony, but later many Poles, Jews and Ukrainians settled there too.

After an accident at the plant, in which a huge tub containing melted metal fell down on to my father's feet, he was ill for a long time and then he decided to move to Kiev and work there. In 1937 he found a job at a local plant as a cupola melter. In 1941, when the war began, he got a room at the plant's hall of residence, and immediately came to pick us up, since his plant was supposed to be evacuated.

We arrived in Kiev but the plant workers had already left. My father had a residence reservation at the plant: we got registered in Kiev at 26 Degtyarevskaya Street, in workers' barracks. In our room there were three families. From here my father left for the front and enlisted in a military commission for the Molotovsky district.

The Germans were approaching the city. The battle was fierce. All our neighbours moved to a two-storey building across the street, at 2a Ovruchskaya Street. This was a brick building and it didn't suffer as much during air raids as our wooden one. We also had to move there. The German planes were constantly over the city, bombing it. We slept fully dressed in order to have enough time to reach the boiler room. (There was a boiler room in the basement of our building where we used to hide.) The air raid sirens almost never ceased and before the end they didn't even have time to announce air raids, so continuous and frequent were they.

We carried around dry biscuits and bottled water with us all of the time: people said that bombed people had been sealed in their basements under rubble alive.

There were huge ravines near our house, on both sides of the road. Concrete pipes were laid under the pavement, through which the water ran. The road was not too wide. And in order to delay the Germans, broken tanks had been pulled over here to block the road. The residents dug a trench right through the yard of our house, with two exits. When the next air raid began, women and children hid in the boiler room and men in the trench.

Our troops were leaving the city. One tank pulled up to our house but could not go on because of the ruined tanks blocking the road. At that time, German planes flew by and, spotting a moving tank among the ruins, they began bombing it. One bomb hit the tank directly (this happened near our house) and the tower of the tank was blown off and thrown over a two-storey building, sending it down straight on to the trench where men were. We were shocked in the boiler room, the glass fell out of the windows, the power went out and it got dark. We rushed away from the windows and fell into a heap. The panic was terrible – we thought the house had crashed down on us. Only the air coming through the broken windows saved us. During the day men cleared the entrance to the boiler room and told us about the tragedy of the tank crew.

We stayed in the basement for the whole week, and then started to readjust ourselves to air and light. We shook as if drunk. After that tragedy we were afraid of going down into the boiler room – and we actually wouldn't have made it: the air raids became non-stop.

My parents registered me for school: I was eight then.

One day I came back from school and the door was locked and Mum was not home. She had gone to dig trenches at the edge of the city. I was pacing our corridor all night long, worried and weeping.

In the morning Tatiana Fedorovna Kravchenko, our neighbour came out; she used to work with my father. Seeing me, she asked me where my mum was. And I didn't know myself where Mum was. She took me to her flat, cleaned me, helped me change my clothes, gave me some food, and we began calling places to find out where my mum was. It turned out that an ambulance had taken her to the Oktyabrsky hospital, to the gynaecological department. She had been there until the Germans entered the city. When she came back home, I was happy because now I was together with my mum. Yet a violent and ruthless life lay ahead of us, filled with the daily fear of death.

In the morning the Germans were in Kiev.

My mum could sew very well. She began helping neighbours to mend their old clothes, and for this they would pay us with food. When the Germans issued an order for all Jews to report to Babi Yar, Tatiana Fedorovna stopped by and told my mum, 'The way you speak German and Polish, you have no right to go with your daughter and die. Tell everybody you're German. I will sign and confirm this.'

My mum replied, 'But we were registered here, and the documents had our nationality listed.'

And Tatiana Fedorovna said, 'I saw the registration clerk off myself. All the documents have been evacuated.'

Thus my mother and I didn't go to Babi Yar but stayed in our house.

Tatiana Fedorovna with her sister, Musya (she was a bit lame), moved to live in the centre of the city and took all our things with them, so that we wouldn't be robbed. One day, in early November 1941, my mother got up early and couldn't open the door – something was keeping it closed. When she finally managed to open it she saw our yard-keeper, Gritsenko. My mother asked him what he was doing here, and he said, pointing to the burning Kreshchatik: 'See what Jews do? And you can do this too! Go to Babi Yar or otherwise I'll report you to the Gestapo.'

Then my mum took me by the hand and we went to the Kommandant's office. There she showed her documents (where Narodnitskaya was changed for Verdetskaya, a Polish surname), and said that her house had burned down and there were no documents left except for this paper. Nobody listened to us and we didn't have any choice but to go to Babi Yar because we had no place to live.

My mother found a wheelbarrow; we loaded a few of our possessions on it and set off for Babi Yar. This was some time around mid-November at 5 a.m. On our way to Babi Yar, to Melnikov Street, a man who came out of one of the houses stopped us. He used to work with my father at the plant. He said, 'Narodnitskaya, where are you going? They kill people there; you have no right to get your child and yourself killed. Your husband will never forgive you!'

But my mother replied, 'What else can I do if our yard-keeper wants to report us to the Gestapo and we have no place to go?'

Then the man said, 'Come with me, and stay with me.' He tried to talk us into it, and persuade my mother, but she had made up her mind: we would be killed anyway, so why should we endanger somebody else?

We left our belongings at his place and went on to Babi Yar. There was a German soldier on duty who saw that nobody was escorting us and we had no clothes and things with us. But there were thieves there who started to pull our coats off, saying that we wouldn't need them any more. My mother began crying for help in German. The German soldier heard us, shot in the air and the thieves ran away.

We arrived there and lay down on the frozen ground. Professor Ryaboy, with his wife and a patient from the Kirrilovskaya (mental) hospital, lay down near us. The woman had seizures all of the time and kept screaming, 'My God, my God!' She had died by the evening.

Seeing my mother, the professor asked her, 'Why are you here? You speak German so well!'

And my mother said: 'You know, I have been struggling, but I have no more energy to go on.'

Then she suggested that the German soldier kill us so that we wouldn't suffer any more. It was very cold, and we were chilled to the bone. The guard said that he couldn't make any decision now without his supervisor and especially because he thought my mum was German. Thus we lay there till midnight. In the space of a day my mother turned from a young blossoming woman into an old ill lady. Her hair turned white, and worry and fear affected her health.

At midnight the German guard decided that his supervisor was not coming any time soon, and he let us leave.

There were local people too, mostly children and old people. One old woman told Mum: 'You're a saved person: you've left this inferno. Come and live with me.'

And Mum said, 'If I am destined to live on, I don't want to endanger anybody.'

This old woman, with other women and children, took us across the vegetable gardens right back to our house so that we wouldn't meet the patrol: it was during the curfew.

At morning the same people came over to our house at 2a Ovruchskaya Street and told Gritsenko, the yard-keeper, that we had been released from Babi Yar and they were witnesses. He left us alone after that. The following day we went and got our things that we had left with the man *en route* to Babi Yar. He told us to turn to him if we needed any help.

When cold weather set in, together with my mum, we moved back to the barracks with all our neighbours on Degtyarevskaya Street, since the house at 2a Ovruchskaya Street wasn't heated and there were small furnace stoves in the barracks. Many buildings were in ruins because of bomb explosions and shells, and small splinters could be picked up everywhere, while Andrey Alyansky, a keeper (whose real name was Kompaniets), guarded the boards and logs from the ruined barracks. He was a young man and pretended he was somewhat deaf – when people talked to him, he would always ask, 'Eh? Eh?' He noticed that my mother spoke German yet was afraid to get an extra splinter from the building.

Once, he stopped her and asked, 'Why aren't you getting any chopped wood?'

And she said, 'Well, you are in charge of it and I don't have the strength to drag wood and logs over.'

He asked her to give him a key for our shed, and since he was watching at night anyway, he could just as well bring over some wood for us. 'And could you please', he said then, 'listen to the Germans speaking and maybe if you hear something important, you will tell me.'

My mum was alarmed, wondering whether it was some sort of a trap or not.

He lived with his wife, Oksana, and daughter, Sonya, in a small house near the camp for prisoners of war. At night Oksana would secretly bake bread and give it to the prisoners, pushing it through the barbed wire.

Tobacco grew near our barracks. When it grew ripe I picked it, put it in a round basket, went down to a ravine, picked flowers and covered the tobacco with them. The ravine was located near the camp for POWs. It was fenced with many layers of barbed wire, and a very tall fence at that. A German soldier or a policeman with an automatic gun would continuously walk behind the fence. They wore armbands with swastikas on them. When the guard left for the other side, beyond a barrack, I would quickly throw the flowers away, call the prisoners and push the tobacco under the wire. They knew me by now, and every day would wait for a girl named Galochka Verdetskaya, who brought them tobacco as well as red tomatoes, which we grew in the ravine.

My mother once managed to talk to a prisoner named Misha near the barbed-wire fence and ask him whether anybody helped them at all. He said that Alyansky was helping them. From then on, my mother would tell Alyansky anything she heard from the Germans, and he would pass it on to his partisan contacts. She was the first to tell Alyansky that the Red Army had surrounded the Germans near Stalingrad. This news my mother also told Misha in secret.

A woman named Milya Filippovna Gerasimchuk lived in our barrack, and her husband worked as our district passport registrar during the occupation. He helped my mum to get a temporary ID issued Maya Davydovna Verdetskaya, and I was listed in it as Galina Ivanovna Verdetskaya. We used this document during in the name of the whole time of the occupation.

All this time was filled with great risk, fear and worry. A simple Russian woman named Marusya (unfortunately I don't remember her surname) lived with us in that barrack. She was a person of extraordinary kindness. She lived with us throughout all the time of the occupation, from the time the Germans entered Kiev till the city's liberation. Her husband was from the Ukraine and he had worked with my father at the plant. In 1941 he went to the front and she stayed behind with two little twins, Valya and Vitya. My mother got very close with her.

Marusya knew we were Jewish and kept warning my mother, 'Maria, you shouldn't go anywhere, people may recognize you. I'll go anywhere instead of you, and you stay and look after my babies.'

When she had to stop breastfeeding the babies, we looked after them for the whole week while she went to villages to trade clothes for food for the children. That lasted for a few months only. The children needed milk, and where could we get it? Valya was stronger, and she survived, while Vitya became ill and weak, and about half a year later he died from malnutrition. We were sharing every piece of bread, every potato with them, and lived like one family. Soon after Kiev was liberated from the Germans she received notification of the death of her husband and decided to leave for Russia. She would say to my mum, 'Maria, let's go together,' but Mum hoped that my father was alive and we'd get some news from him.

The Lapiny family also lived in our house – a couple with a daughter, Tanya, and her husband, a single daughter, Maria, and a son who was quite young. He was too young to be drafted into the Red Army but the Germans took him for slave labour in Germany. Somehow his parents learned how bad it really was for him there. Soon it was Tanya and Maria's turn to go. Maria disfigured her face and said that she was ill with skin tuberculosis, and she was not taken, and Tanya's husband went to serve in the police so that his wife wouldn't be taken away to Germany. He was the one who told us all the news and warned us when the Germans planned raids, and of many other things.

During that time we would spend whole days in the concrete pipes under the road. In October 1943 a few traitors wanted to turn us in to the Germans but our policeman warned us and we went into hiding in the pipes for the whole month. When things calmed down I resumed taking whatever I could to the prisoners.

One day, some time in late October 1943 Uncle Misha came up to me and told me, across the wire, that he wanted to speak to my mum. She came to the camp and he said that the Germans planned on moving the camp into such a place where they [the inmates] would say goodbye to their lives.

My mother asked him, 'What can a poor woman like myself do for you?'

And he said he had a sister here. He gave her the name of a woman who lived in Nagornaya Street, in a house with a terrace. I went there, knocked on a terrace window and a very pretty girl came out. I told her that Misha wanted to see her the following morning.

The following day the prisoners were taken out to dig potatoes near our barrack. Mum and I went out to our garden to dig potatoes too. The girl came over and began talking to us.

A German guard came up to us and asked her what she was doing here. The girl smiled nicely at him, and my mother said that the girl had come to have a dress made. The German left us alone, walked away and sat down on the barrack porch. Then Misha crawled through the grass to the girl and they spoke about something. I had to watch the guard to make sure he didn't approach them. I was picking up potatoes and watching, and when the German stood up, I said, 'Fritz is coming!' The girl talked to Misha for a long time, and then left.

Three days later the Germans organized a raid to catch all the prisoners who had escaped, including Misha. I don't know what happened to them next, but all the other prisoners were moved out in much haste because the Germans were retreating from Kiev.

Nadya Yakimenko, a young and very beautiful girl, lived in our barrack; she worked in a baking factory during the occupation. Her mother's surname was Moroz and I don't remember her first name now. Nadya was friends with a girl named Valya who lived near the Lukyanovskoye cemetery. Nadya's mother was taken to Germany but a policeman from our house let her out of the train as it was already moving and some time later she walked back home.

When the Germans retreated from the city, they would sweep everything off the face of earth, killing women and children so that not a single person would be left alive in Kiev.

Once Mum overheard the Germans talking, saying that they would be going to search for people at home. One said, 'There are people here – there is smoke coming out of the chimney, and here – there's a cat in their yard, and there where the windows are not broken.'

We had to leave the city as soon as possible, but where could we go? Then Tanya, the policeman's wife, offered to take us with them to Belichi, a Kiev suburb, and we agreed. We went there and spent about ten days with Tanya's in-laws. When the raids were over we returned home, but there was no food and we stayed hungry for a few days.

When our army came, we were barely alive: our continuous stay in damp pipes, and fear and worry had taken their toll on our health.

In November 1943 a special military division was located in our barrack, along with the field post 28855-K. Sadinin was the division commander (I don't remember his military title now), and there was a doctor named Zaytsev, as well as other officers whose names I don't know. Since the division was secret, all residents were asked to leave the building. They let us stay though, gave us food and some medical care, and brought us some clothes. Mum began working with them, making and repairing clothes and cooking, until June 1944 when the division left Kiev.

In July 1944 we again moved to live at 2a Ovruchskaya Street. We lived on the first floor, right above the entrance to the house. On the ground floor of the building an evening technical school was opened, with Skritzky, the principal. My mother went to work there on 31 August 1944, first as a seamstress and then as a linen-keeper.

The years of occupation affected my mum's health; the NKVD who interviewed and questioned Mum continuously in 1944–46 also took a toll. She fell ill, and doctors certified her disability as being of the second category.

There was no news on my father; most likely he thought we had died in Babi Yar. My mother wrote to the evacuation and archives units of the Central Military Department. On 9 October 1944 they answered that there were no data on him in their records either. The same answer was received from the Central Military Medical Department of the Red Army, on 22 July 1945. Only in late August 1945 did we receive notification of his death: he had died in May 1945. My mother gave this document to the state welfare service in order to receive some pension.

We were moved to a room in the plant-owned block of flats, notwithstanding the fact that my father had worked there before the war and died at the front.

During the war my mother met Raissa Yakovlevna Nassikan. She was Jewish, while her husband, Onufriy, was Ukrainian. Somebody reported this to the Gestapo and she was arrested and beaten up badly. They knocked out all her teeth, breaking her jaw and nose. Onufriy helped her escape from them and together with their daughter Alla and son Yasha they fled to Zhitomir. They returned only after Kiev was liberated. When we were thrown out into the street, Onufriy and Raissa took us to live with them at 4 Kagatnaya Street, Flat 42.

In December 1943 I started my schooling at the comprehensive School No. 61, Molotovsky district. They taught us in Ukrainian. The school was not heated and even ink froze in the ink-holder. There was only one furnace stove for the whole school and in the breaks between the lessons we would run there to warm up our ink.

In 1944 in the ravine near our house a religiously observant soldier from Western Ukraine who refused to take up weapons was executed.

After the war, Nikita Khrushchev called people to hold a city-wide *subbotnik* during which, in one day, tram lines were laid out throughout the whole of Molotovsky district. A line also went through Ovruchskaya Street. People dug out two ravines and filled them with dirt, as well as paving the road with the concrete pipes under which Mum and I hid during the occupation. The POW camp on the other side of our house was destroyed, and a five-storey building was built on top of the filled-in ravine. This was in the 1950s. Andrey Kompaniets (Alyansky), with his wife and daughter received a flat in that house.

In late 1946 my mum's brother came and took us back to Korosten; I have lived here ever since.

My mother searched for other relatives, kept sending inquiries to different organizations, but didn't find anyone. One of my father's brothers died at the front, and the other probably left for America. My father's name was Isaac. His perished brother's name was Zylyck, and the third brother's, Yosif. I don't know anything about the fate of Elik, his fourth brother. They all lived in Kiev, on the Podol.

Perhaps somebody who saved me, or our neighbours, or people who remember these events, will respond, because I don't remember them all. Maybe there are, somewhere, some relatives of Isaac Moiseevich Narodnitsky, born in 1908 in Kiev (Podol)?

For a long while I used to wake up in a cold sweat because of nightmares in which I still saw myself during the occupation or beneath falling bombs. In December 1952 I got seriously ill. The doctors diagnosed an acute form of rheumatism that perhaps resulted from long stays in damp concrete pipes. My legs were paralysed, then my heart went wrong. I stayed for half a year in bed and lived on injections, then I learned to walk anew. But my heart has continued to ache ever since: I developed a cardiac condition.

In 1953 I finished ten years of school but couldn't continue studying (my financial situation was very poor with only 240 Roubles for my monthly pension), and my disabled mother also required continuous care. I couldn't do any physically strenuous work, and in March 1954 I began working at the chemist's, sorting and packing medicines. When a long-distance course in pharmaceutics began at the Zaporozhye Medical College I enrolled in it. During the day I would work, and at night I would study. I graduated in 1958 and transferred to preparing medications, where I worked until 1974.

In 1960 I got married, and in 1961 I gave birth to a girl who died five days later; in 1963 I gave birth to a boy who was diagnosed with a heart condition when he was a child.

All this keeps reminding me of my horrible childhood. I have cried all of my life and in 1974 I felt I was losing my eyesight (I had an internal cataract) and I transferred into an over-the-counter department where I worked until 1986. In 1986 I had an operation on my eye, followed by urgent surgery on the other eye three months later. As a result of all this, and after three operationss I wear +14 lenses in my glasses and cannot cross streets without somebody's help. I had to work for a year and eleven months after my operations to qualify for retirement. The chemist's manager considered my situation and put me on a night shift (since I don't see well, and at night my husband and my son could help me). I have worked for thirty-five years and now the Chernobyl power plant disaster and the difficult material situation will just finish us off. I decided to describe my entire story because I won't last for long.

I would like to send my best wishes and regards to all people of goodwill who saved me and to whom I'm for ever indebted.

83. The last pogrom

Zinovy Schtivelman (b. 1936)

Since I was only five years old when the war began, my remembrances are intertwined with the remembrances and stories of my parents, who have already passed away.

Before the war we had lived in the town of Khmelnik, and we didn't leave it because of the illness of my parents and the absence of transportation.

When the Germans entered the town, local Jews were constrained from moving around, and eventually a ghetto was established (by January 1942). It was located in the area of the old militia building (on Shevchenko and Sholom-Aleichem Streets).

The Germans organized pogroms and we had to prepare ourselves accordingly in order to survive them. In the house where we lived (on the land of an old clothes-manufacturing factory) there was a room with sealed windows and doors, and with the entrance coming from the basement.

During the first pogrom, in March 1942, twenty-seven people were hiding in that room (children and grown-ups) during three days. At night we picked snow off the roof and melted it on the kerosene stove. And during the day the Germans and policemen went around knocking on the walls. There were a few infants with us. On one such occasion, one mother strangled her own crying baby to save the others.

Those who survived this pogrom were moved closer to the old militia building (where the occupiers' police force was stationed). Our new residence was on the land of today's regional hospital. (The old house was ruined and later demolished completely.)

The Germans organized a register of survivors. Each following roll-call didn't leave any chances for survival because these roll-calls resulted in grown-ups being taken away separately from the children. That was why people took their children with them. That was why our family went to the police all together during one such roll-call.

There was no hope of being saved and people began burning

rubber in order to die from asphyxiation rather than being killed on the edge of pits in the forest like the people who went before us.

However, perhaps luck was on our side and the Star of David marking our chests and backs shone down on us. On that day all the police's prisoners were released.

I remember the last pogrom. It was in March 1943.

There was a cellar in this new place where we lived. We began constructing a new shelter in it: we put a sofa above its entrance and made another entrance in its floor down to the cellar.

When the last pogrom was taking place everybody hid in the cellar. The ghetto ceased to exist after the pogrom. However, one old woman stayed in the house and in order not to give away the shelter, she got on to a Russian stove and hid herself behind a baking tray. The policemen couldn't find the shelter and left. At night the woman went downstairs and told us this. Unfortunately I don't remember her name.

We left the shelter at night. It was cold and frosty. The roof tiling was crumbling under our feet. I remember I was carried in someone's arms, since I had an abscess on my foot and couldn't walk. My parents stayed on at the camp for some time, they were saved because they were professionals.

My brother and I were sent away to our friends in the village of Verbivka. The name of the woman was T. Shelesta and we stayed with her for two weeks. Then we were put into a house near a local church where the joiner's workshop was. There, in the attic, we stayed for a whole month.

My parents escaped from the camp, and together with them we walked to Zhmerinka. It was the Romanian zone and they were not killing Jews but forcing them to provide slave labour. We stayed there until Khmelnik was liberated in March 1944.

When we returned home, we didn't find our house: it had been completely demolished.

84. Bullets were being fired at my back

Fanya Schubinskaya
(Sapozhnikova) (b. 1926)

I lived together with my parents and my sister in Zvenigorodka. Here, about thirty members of our numerous relatives lived as well.

When the Germans occupied the town, all the local Jews were immediately moved to one street, with a couple of families sharing each house. Policemen and German soldiers guarded the small street from all sides. We were not allowed to communicate with other residents of the town: the ghetto was established.

Daily we were marched out to do the most difficult and dirty work. The occupants beat us badly, often just in order to entertain themselves.

On the eve of 1 May elderly people, children, women with children, the sick and disabled were selected and taken out of the town. They were all shot in a local forest in 1942. There were over 2,000 people killed there, including my relatives.

Those who were able to work, including my mother (aged forty-one), my sister (twenty-one), and me (sixteen), were sent out from station to station under the escort of guards, with dogs, on to the village of Nemorogi, Zvenigorodka district, to work. (A highway was being constructed there and there was a stone quarry nearby.) We lived in a pigsty. On the eve of a holiday, 2 November 1942, when the road was almost complete, the camp prisoners were shot. Chance saved my life: I managed to escape. Bullets were being fired at my back, yet I ran down towards the river. There, in the bushes, I stayed until evening – a naked, cold, hungry and frightened girl, ill and with a high fever. I had galoshes on my feet and in November it began to snow. But there was nowhere to go and everybody had been killed.

When it got dark, I got into one house, walking across people's vegetable gardens. People let me in to spend the night, and in the morning, in a torn jacket and galoshes, and with a slice of bread, I left their home to try to save my life.

My face and a good knowledge of the Ukrainian language allowed me to cross fifty kilometres of distant villages and roads towards Bug district. I changed my surname, thought over details of the story behind my wandering, and finally, after many rejections, I was sheltered by Zinaida Overkovna Shchaslyva in Nova Greblya, Zhashkov district. May she rest in peace now – she died a few years ago, when she was over ninety years old. I spent that winter with her.

In spring I went to work in the fields, and in late April 1943, together with other girls of the village, I was taken away to work in Germany, at the farm of Kurt Schteinike. This was in the village of Gorslieben, province of Artern, near Weimar. I did everything around the house, out in the yard and out in the field (even around horses). The American army freed me and in November 1945 I was sent back to my homeland.

I didn't find anyone of my family or relatives in Zvenigorodka – everybody was killed. My father, who was missing, had never returned. And again I was alone. I worked. Soon afterwards I found my mum's sisters, who were in Dniepropetrovsk, and moved in with them. In 1947 I got married. I have two sons and grand-children. I worked for thirty years at the Dniepropetrovsk Radio Factory. For nineteen years I have been widowed. My health is bad, and all I went through has taken its toll on me. I try to take part now in some social work. My children and grandchildren bring me joy with their warm attitude towards me.

85. May my memory keep me from forgetting[1]

Naum Epelfeld (b. 1926)

On 5 July 1941, the town of Berdychev was beyond recognition. The streets were filled with retreating troops. Ragged columns of exhausted soldiers were passing by, and there was despair and confusion on their faces. Crowds of refugees followed the soldiers.

At our family council, Mum said that we had to leave immediately. The word 'evacuation' was not very common back then. My father was absolutely against it. He explained this by saying that he couldn't leave behind all that he had earned in life. The second reason he gave was that the Germans were an educated nation and he remembered well how, in 1914, they had always treated the Jews well.

Nevertheless, we managed to persuade my father to leave everything behind and leave for the east. However, by the time that this sensible decision was made, it was impossible to leave.

Some time around 6 July in the evening, we went to the station. We tried to get on military vans and lorries going along the way, but they would not pick us up. There was only one train at the station, with open carriages and no locomotive. There were many people who wished to leave. People began getting into the carriages and kept saying that the locomotive would be coming any time now, and that the train would leave for Kazatin.

At that moment, planes appeared over the station. These were German planes and they began bombing the station. Frightened people scattered everywhere.

We kept running with them. We reached a maternity home. Somebody said that they had a safe air raid shelter. And since everybody was expecting a new bombing, we all rushed down there.

Some time later, an official in the uniform of the *Osoaviakhim* visited the shelter along with an escort of many other officials. They calmed us down; moreover, they said that a few days later we would be able to return home safely.

People wanted to believe the best. They cheered up, somebody smiled, and somebody even told a joke. People were recalling with a smile how we had escaped from the station.

In the meantime, Berdychev was left without any authorities. Shops were looted. On 7 July there was total robbery and mayhem everywhere: doors were broken, locks taken off, and people stole everything they saw.

The last retreating columns of soldiers had gone. The NKVD staff burned papers in haste, changed into civilian clothes and fled. Even at that moment it was still possible to flee. I remember that a certain Likman, an administrator of the maternity home, harnessed a hospital horse, took a phaeton and left. He survived.

Everybody sensed that some horrible events were approaching. The night fell. The power went down. We sat in darkness, close to one another, and spoke in whispers.

Suddenly we heard some people breaking into the hospital building. We heard abrupt commands in a foreign language. I remember the sound of shattered glass and automatic guns shooting. It became clear what had just happened.

The Germans took Berdychev. Some time later two soldiers entered the basement where we stayed. They lit their way with torches and kept saying something, but we couldn't understand them. Then they started walking among people sitting on the floor and shining torches into their faces. Then they stopped near a girl and a woman, and ordered them to follow. They took them into an empty office and raped them. The girl's name was Gusta; she was our neighbours' daughter. Gusta Glozman was fourteen or fifteen years old. Soon she would be killed, together with her parents.

Thus the occupation began for me. It was the most horrible stage in my life.

The following morning there was heavy shooting everywhere. The Germans fired weapons of various calibres, guns and mortars. It was impossible to leave the shelter. At night the fighting got worse, shells burst somewhere near us. Frightened Germans were hiding in our basement without paying any attention to us. A day later the shooting started to gradually die away. We used this moment of silence, gathered all our meagre belongings with which we wanted to travel, and returned home.

When, after the days and nights of staying in the basement, we were back in the streets of Berdychev, the town seemed foreign and strange to me. Unknown sorts of motorcycles and cars were running along boulevards where the Berdychev public used to walk. There were young, strong men riding these cars, dressed in light-green uniforms, with rolled-up sleeves and open collars, talking happily and occasionally pointing their fingers at the rare civilians scurrying along the streets.

When we got home, we saw that the door had been forced open, and many things were missing. Nobody complained about the loss of even the most valuable possessions. We had not lived in our flat for a long time now anyway. Soon, a German official came over and ordered all Jews to leave the house. They planned on having a German bakery on the ground floor and obviously Jews were not allowed to live near a German facility. Thus we found ourselves out on the street. The Germans didn't allow us to take anything with us. We settled nearby.

It grew more distressing with every passing day. People said that a group of Jews had been shot, that a few dozen people had been taken away and nobody knew what had happened to them.

I remember an episode from the first days of the occupation. Somebody said that using Soviet currency we could buy potatoes and other food at the market. So together with my father we went to the market. As we were walking along we saw mostly soldiers in the streets and occasionally people in strange jockey-type caps wearing armbands and rifles on shoulder straps.

There were not many people at the market, just a few women selling some things. One was selling potatoes and people were already queued up near her. We stood there too.

Suddenly we heard commotion and screaming. It turned out that a seller didn't want to sell potatoes to a Jewish woman. The Jewish woman was screaming and complaining. At that moment, a tall old Jewish man with a grey beard and a thick walking cane in his hand walked up and wondered what was going on. Hearing the reason for the noise, he started scolding the saleswoman too. She saw a few policemen passing by – those men with white armbands – and called them. Without any deliberation, the policemen 'understood' the essence of the issue immediately, and began beating the Jewish woman.

The old man, who had walked away, returned, and saw they were beating the woman. I don't know where he got the energy, since he was a very old man, but he began energetically beating those men in caps. Soon, however, their shock passed and they began beating the old man with rifle butts. The Germans who were walking by tried at first to stop the police. One of the policemen was bleeding all over and the other had fallen down. The battered policemen explained that they were 'beating a Jew and not an old man'. Then the Germans caught up with the old Jewish man, who had walked away, and began beating him so badly that the poor man's body soon turned into a bag of bones. Only then did they leave him alone and walk away.

We also left the place, having bought nothing at the market. We walked in silence, depressed by what we had seen. We stood for a long time at the crossing, not being able to cross the street. The German cavalcade went down Zhitomirskaya Street. Hundreds of cars, lorries, armoured and all-terrain vehicles were coming along in an endless column. We stood there for a few hours unable to cross the street. This scene made us feel even worse.

From that point, we stopped going to the market. We got food from our neighbours. Daily I used to go to the abandoned vegetable gardens. I brought home cucumbers, which were now the main crop, and sometimes new potatoes. Together with my young sister Firochka we were spending most of our time at these abandoned lots. It was also relatively safe there. Neither the Germans nor the police were stopping by. Sometimes we would find a small garden. We climbed trees and ate green apples.

In August 1941, I don't remember the exact date now, there was an order posted everywhere which commanded 'all Jews of the town of Berdychev ... ' to resettle into the ghetto near Yatki by a designated date. From now on we were in the ghetto. We settled with my grandma's relatives. Their house stood near the bridge across the Gnilopyat River. We were extremely unfortunate with our new place of residence, as the police were right next door. We had to go through horrible hours on the very first night of our stay at the new place. At about two o'clock in the morning policemen broke into the house. They robbed, beat, tortured and humiliated us through to the morning. And this happened almost every night.

New orders were posted, now prohibiting Jews from going to the centre of the town, or from walking on the pavements. I don't remember all of them, but there were quite a few.

During one of the numerous raids, my father was taken away by the Germans. We were worried but he came back home by the evening, alive and not hurt. He told us that those arrested during the raid were taken to the building of the former Education Institute. They made people clean floors and wash windows, preparing the building for a German military hospital.

One of the German officers began asking about people's professions and backgrounds. Hearing that my father was an electrician, the officer ordered him to report the following day. My father tried to explain that he could not appear downtown but the officer would not listen to him. What was to be done? So in the morning my father went across the town to the hospital. And in the evening he returned with a loaf of bread! Besides the bread, he had been issued an ID card, in which it was stated in German and Ukrainian that

'Der Jude Epelfeld ...' and so on and so forth. This paper allowed my father to walk across the streets of the town in the morning. His work at the hospital relieved our starved existence somewhat.

Our life was a continuous nightmare. During the day we stayed inside the house, being afraid to go out. Every night, like clockwork, the policemen would break into the house. They beat, abused, and robbed (although in fact there was nothing left to rob any more, but this would make them even more angry and they acted like ruthless predators).

In those rare hours of calm when neither police nor Germans were storming our house we used to sit in our corner and talk about how our army would be back any day soon, or how somebody had heard artillery in the night ... we lived with this hope. By the way, these and similar rumours accompanied us throughout all our life during the occupation.

The most horrible day in my life was 15 September 1941. Please remember this date! On that day 20,500 Jews were killed in Berdychev – mostly old people, women and children. On a single day thousands of innocent people were murdered. It was the seventieth day of the occupation. It was from this date that the Fascists began mass executions of Jews in Europe. And they started with Berdychev, a town with a primarily Jewish population, where the majority hadn't left the town.

It all began at three o'clock in the morning. The police broke into the house. But instead of beating and robbing us the way they did every single night, they started taking us out into the street. They beat us with rifle butts, not allowing us to get dressed, and shouted at us. When we ran out we saw a street filled with people. The police beat them with guns, ramrods, sticks, trying to put them all into one column. But they didn't manage that well because the crowd had many old, weak people who could barely move, and many handicapped who were not able to move at all.

We could not grasp what was going on. Automatically, we moved along with the crowd of many thousands of people, instinctively protecting ourselves from being hit by a rifle butt or a stick.

Thus, accompanied by scolding, screams and shots, we were marched into the market square. There were many people accumulated there by then, and it is difficult to describe now what went on.

German soldiers in helmets were running through the crowd; they were armed and kept grabbing people and sorting them into two groups. My father and I were put into one while Mum, Grandma and Firochka were put into the other. We didn't see them. We don't know how it all happened. We were completely shocked and couldn't think clearly.

When we came back to our senses we saw that we were standing among a relatively small group of Jews, mostly men of middle age. The police surrounded us, and a few metres away a human river was flowing, hurried on by the rifle butts towards the lorries. The weak were thrown on to the trucks like as sacks. Lorries packed with people left while new ones were being loaded over and over again. And this lasted till late at night. Rumours started to spread that people were taken away to work. They would build airfields; they were the first to go, and when they returned, we would go instead.

In the evening we returned to the ghetto. The place where we lived had been completely looted. Feathers and down from torn pillows and mattresses were flying everywhere. They had probably been searched for gold. We didn't stay home at night and went to our neighbours.

They offered to let us stay in somebody's empty bed. I lay down together with my father; I closed my eyes, trying to fall asleep. And then I felt a lump in my throat and I started crying, with groans and screams, and I cried, 'Mamma, Mummy!'

Everybody in the flat woke up; people began to calm me down saying that everybody would be back soon. Finally I stopped crying but couldn't calm down for a long time. I fell asleep by the morning.

During the years of occupation I spent more than one sleepless night but when there was an opportunity to sleep I would gladly fall asleep, and not because I was tired. I would like to tell you that they woke us up at four o'clock in the morning, making us work for sixteen to eighteen hours a day. Of course, after such work you would fall into your bed from being tired. But fatigue was not such an important issue; most important, sleep alone could allow you to forget reality. It could let you return to your past. And another thing, if you survived till sleeping, through the evening, there was a chance you would survive till the morning. At night they wouldn't shoot people, as a rule, although there were exceptions to this rule as well. Drunken policemen with their emotions overflowing would break into our barracks at night, beating people almost to death and sometimes shooting them too.

In the morning, all residents of the emptied ghetto were up and around. They were looking out of the windows to see what was going on in the big wide world. And bad things were happening in the big wide world. Carts driven by farmers from nearby villages rolled down the streets of the ghetto; the men entered empty flats and took things out on to their carts. They were taking things they had left the night before.

The majority of people we met were feeling very hostile towards us, especially in the first years of the occupation. But I shall also speak of good people, of those who were helping us. I shall never forget those brave people. Yes, in those years it took a lot of courage to help a Jew. A person would be risking his or her life. But there were many that ignored the risk of being shot and helped us. People don't say enough about this, and it is wrong.

My father had to decide now where to put me. He decided to take me to the hospital as his assistant. Neither of us was sure that they would allow me to work, and supposed that they would throw me out. But very unexpectedly, not only did the local supervisors not throw me out but they understood the necessity of me being with my father. As far as I can tell, the chief officer of the hospital (or at least one of the chief officers) was a man with the title of *Oberleutnant* whom everybody would address as '*Herr Oberzahlmeister*' [Mr Chief Purser].

We felt that the situation was growing worse. Every day we lived in expectation of new incidents and new repression. And that day finally arrived. On the night of 30 October the story of 15 September repeated itself. But this time we were taken not to the marketplace but to the fortress of a former Carmelite cathedral. There we were all put into a big basement. All of the ghetto – or whatever was left of it, to be more precise – fitted in the basement. I was running around the basement trying to find some hidden passage to get out. The windows were all blocked with bars, the walls were many metres wide and the floor was made of cement. There was no exit. I saw many people I knew there, but everybody stood by himself or herself. Coming from above we could hear the shouts of policemen and rifle shots. I would like to note that on 15 September mainly the Germans carried out the *Aktion* with only a few policemen involved, while on 30 October the policemen handled everything.

Time went by, and the basement was filled with more and more people. At some point, the commotion at the door of the basement area increased, the door opened and we suddenly saw the hospital *Oberzahlmeister* on the steps. The policemen stood near him and kept saying something, but he ignored them and kept looking for someone in the basement. My father thought that perhaps the officer was searching for him. He moved towards the exit. And indeed once the German officer saw my dad he waved his hand, indicating for him to come upstairs. My father went towards the exit and I clung tight to my father and went along with him. A policeman jumped up and began pulling me away. My resistance wouldn't have been successful but for the *Oberzahlmeister*'s intervention. After he pulled us out of the basement, we all walked to the hospital. There he designated a room, in which he put a few more

Jews (tailors and barbers). He ordered us to work and live in this room. The Berdychev ghetto was liquidated. All those who were in the basement were shot dead.

A new stage in our life began. I don't know what our status was in the hospital – whether prisoners of war or crossed out from among the living. It was forbidden to leave the the hospital surroundings. During the day we worked in a hospital workshop, and at night we slept in the tailor's workshop, some on a table, some on chairs, and some on the floor. However, we didn't starve. It had been four months since the beginning of the war and a little less from the beginning of the occupation. On 22 June 1941 I was a small boy and in October 1941 I was already a grown man. Of course my father took care of me to some extent. He cared for me, but his opportunities were considerably limited. Under the circumstances, which I understood completely, I began developing new personal qualities, unknown to me earlier. I contacted people whom I had never known socially before the war; I hadn't even suspected that such people existed. I had to meet prisoners of war, and there were former criminals and pro-Fascists among them. Of course there were good people too. I was gradually adjusting and adapting to live in a society filled with my enemies. I learned to understand German well, and later I began speaking it fluently, and this helped me a lot. I learned to sense danger a few moments before it actually threatened me. I don't know how it all worked, but that was the way I lived. If not for those qualities, these notes would never have been written. The Germans began turning to me as an interpreter when they spoke to the prisoners of war.

It took only four months for me to develop an animal instinct for danger. My eyes and ears, and every cell in my body were on the alert from now for whether there was any danger ahead. I remember a lot from those days. Once, I was walking along the street. A car passed by, and when it was near me, somebody was watching me closely. From that moment on, everything happened in a few seconds. I jumped into the ruins of a house which – fortunately – were nearby. At the same moment I heard the screeching of brakes and heard someone running towards the ruins. I heard a throaty German voice. And again I was lucky. I saw a staircase leading down to a cellar, ran downstairs and hid in the cellar, which was dark as a sack. I sat quietly there and listened to the noises outside. When all became quiet I started to go out slowly and kept listening to the noises. I looked out and saw nobody. I am confident that under certain circumstances human beings are capable of developing qualities allowing them to foresee dangers before their onset.

Soon after the new year of 1942 began, *Unteroffizier* Iorick came to us in the evening and said that Knop, the chief of the SD, now knew about the Jews who lived in the hospital and it was very unlikely that the hospital administration would keep Jews on for any longer. And indeed very soon afterwards we were told to leave the hospital. They told us about this in the evening and didn't even let us spend the night.

So the question was, where to go? My father decided to go to a former spa and ask the attendant to let us spend a few nights in the boiler room. My father had known this man before the war and thought he was a decent and honest man. My father left and I remained, waiting for his return. It was very dark, and the curfew had started long ago.

Suddenly, I heard steps. I stopped and there was no place for me to hide. By that time the moon was up and it was fairly clear. In the light of the moon I could see a man who was walking towards me quickly. Having noticed me, the man stopped but then, seeing I was just a boy, he walked up. This was Victor, a man I knew very well. This was an amazing encounter. I began crying with joy at seeing him. Having calmed me down and listened to my story, Victor decided that to go and search for my father now would be a very dangerous thing and it would be better if I went with him. Where? 'To good people,' said Victor.

And we walked away. We came to Pashkovskaya Street and stopped not very far from my old, pre-war home. We knocked on the door. A small woman answered the door and invited us in. They knew Victor in that home. He told the woman about my situation and asked Zinaida Alexandrovna (that was her name) to let me stay at her home. She agreed immediately and I stayed with her family, which has become my own for as long as I live. Zinaida Alexandrovna Sivokhina lived with her daughter, Tanechka, and her mother. I was the fourth member of this family, and a very dangerous member at that. If I was found, the whole family was under the threat of being shot. A police office, the passport department, was located just a floor above. I never went outside during the day.

In the evenings, almost every night, we would go to our neighbours on the same floor. There, in a big room, young people, mostly former prisoners of war, would gather. They were dreaming up ways to get to the front and argued frequently.

But it the was spring of 1942. Almost daily the Germans were celebrating their victories. The sight of joyous Germans made us feel desperate. But our young men believed in our victory. Very few of them eventually survived – some were arrested by the police and were shot, and those who lived to see the liberation went to the front; none returned home alive.

On one of these days I was told that my father was living in a clinic. It turned out that Kovalenko, who was the head of the health care department in Berdychev at that time, met my father and offered to allow him to live in the yard of a municipal clinic. There was a stable in the yard of the clinic which had a small room added to it. My father was living in that room. During the day he stayed in the room and at nights he would fix their medical equipment. This was a condition of his stay there. Some time in May or June 1942, I moved to live with my father. It was impossible for me to live at Zinaida Alexandrovna's flat any longer: neighbours began prying into my identity and the raids from police became more frequent. One day I went to my father and, when I came back, I saw German cars in our yard. I was alarmed by that and didn't go to the flat but instead I hid in a neighbouring yard. Then I saw the Germans and policemen walking out of the flat. I waited for some while and then entered the flat. It turned out that while I was away, the SD and police came to the flat looking for something or somebody but didn't find anything and left. That was when we decided that I had to go and stay with my father.

Living in the yard of the clinic I had to hide, together with my father, during the day. We hid in the attic of the stable. We frequently spent nights there too.

A girl whose real name we didn't know often visited us. (At first she told us her name was Raya and later it turned out not to be her real name.) She spoke very little about herself but told us that she came to Berdychev having escaped from the prisoner of war camp. When she had got all the necessary documents she managed to find work as an interpreter in the gendarmes' office. She treated me with extraordinary care and tenderness, trying to save me from all possible trouble. I remember how angry she got when young men tried to use me to pass on information. She believed it could cost me my life. Soon afterwards she stopped visiting us. A few months later, when in the concentration camp, I heard that a Jewish girl had been caught and hanged in the camp when she was trying to put some powder into the food cooked for the gendarmes. When she was caught, it was found out that she was Jewish and had escaped from the prison. People said that before she died she had acted very bravely, and her final words were, 'Jews, don't let yourselves be killed; run away to the forests.'

The number of people we knew in the town grew smaller. Some were shot, some arrested, and yet some managed to leave Berdychev. We could not shop, go to the market, or walk in the streets. We were beyond the law. Anybody could kill us with no impunity. Moreover, such acts as killing a Jew or a Communist would even be rewarded. The people we knew tried to sustain our lives by bringing and sneaking in dry biscuits, a couple of potatoes or two or three carrots. Starvation was a torture for me, and we kept thinking how to get any food. And then we were told that the raids were getting more and more frequent and they were searching for Jews.

And one day we were discovered in our small room and taken to the SD. Zinchenko and Golub, from the SD, escorted us – we learned their names later. From this moment on a new period in our occupied lives began – life in prison, in a camp.

I often wonder how it happened that my father and I survived. The whole state machine was against us, with its powerful army, and a developed torture system including the Gestapo, SD, gendarmes, and finally local Ukrainian police. And we were weak and helpless, with no means for living; beyond the law, with all our basic human rights violated. But every time when all hope seemed to be gone and we were standing on the edge of the abyss, something would happen that changed the situation and we survived. This happened on 15 September and 30 October, and on numerous other occasions. And I keep asking myself one and the same question over and over again: what was this? Was it an accident? But it is known that any series of accidents is meaningful. What was the essence and meaning of this series? I know only one answer to this: there is some higher power that controls the world and our lives. But why did this power save me and what kind of merits do I have compared to those hundreds, thousands and millions of dead? This is another issue that needs to be pondered on and thought about over and over again.

Thus we were brought to the SD. They told us to stay near the wall and wait. Time passed by very slowly. Screams and shots were to be heard from across the street, in a yard where the SD basements were located. Then everything got quiet, and then again there were screams and shots. And we were standing and waiting. A passing officer told us that he would personally take us, in the morning, to the camp on the Lysa Mountain where they had decided to keep all Jews who remained alive.

The camp was located on the propertyy of a former military unit of the Red Army. We were put on the ground floor of a building where officers used to live. The first floor and a part of the ground-floor rooms were filled with the belongings of the camp's former residents. Our first job was to sort through these belongings. We had to sort children's clothes separately from men's and women's. After we completed this job, we were put to look after the cows from the SD's own farmstead. This was not a very difficult job and we received a litre of buttermilk daily. During that period the guards didn't touch us.

Gradually the camp was filled with new groups of Jews. Mostly these were Jews from villages where they had been hiding after having fled the town. There were young and old people, women and numerous children. The discipline became more rigid, and the number of guards grew. Now we were taken to do the most difficult jobs. For a few days I had to remove the hides from horses and then I was moved to work on road construction. I had to carry stones and sand. We worked from 5 a.m. till noon, then we had lunch and back again to slave labour until 6–7 p.m. We could sit down and take a break only if the guards left. There were mostly cruel and brutal people among the guards. They would beat us and force us do everything running. I remember how my partner could no longer endure the torture so he jumped in front of an on-coming car. Unfortunately, he didn't die but was only bruised. For this 'offence' the camp Kommandant, a former Soviet officer named Trotsky, ordered two policemen to beat him until he stopped moaning.

Every night drunken policemen stormed our barracks. They beat everybody they could get hold of with rifle butts, rubber batons and wooden sticks. They tortured us through to the morning and often they would take someone away with them and this person would never be seen again.

I worked on the road construction, then at the cattle farm, and finally I was sent to look after the horses. The job was not physically arduous but it was dangerous. Once they found scabs on the horses that I tended. I almost got shot because of this. Once Dzyuba, a camp policeman, saw that the horses went down to the water with shackles on their front legs (I hadn't taken them off a few horses). He grabbed me by my collar, took me to his hut where there were two more policemen and they began beating me all together. It hurt so badly that I even forgot to think they could kill me, got away from them, began running around the hut with them chasing me, and managed to run outside. Screaming loudly I ran towards the gates. Dzyuba pointed his gun at me – that was what my father told me – and who knows how the story would have ended if not for a phaeton rolling through the gates at the same time. There was some man named Pintz in the carriage, an SS *Unteroffizier*. He got out of the carriage and asked me what was going on. In my rage I told him that the police pigs had beaten me up. I said that and then stopped with fear since I had just called the policemen 'pigs'. His reaction was completely unexpected. Pintz started laughing (although nobody had ever seen him even smile) and told me to go back to work.

I was transferred to a smithy as the blacksmith's assistant but then was sent back again to tend to the horses. One day when I was driving the horses to one of the numerous ravines near the Lysa Mountain, I was called from above. I raised my eyes and saw a policeman and a German waving their hands at me. I went up to them quickly. The German asked me who I was and I said, '*Judeh*'.

Then he asked what I was doing here. I said I was ordered to [drive the horses]. Then the German started scolding the policeman that they were lacking workers in town while I was hanging around here. 'Tomorrow you must report to work in town,' he ordered.

At dawn on the following day we were taken to the town. When we returned, the barracks were empty. All those who had stayed in the camp – women, children and old people – had been killed. One more coincidence? The SS officer noticed me accidentally when I was driving horses down and decided this was way too easy a job for me, ordering to me to be sent to the town, to a harder job. And again I survived by accident. Because I could have taken horses into another place and then I would have not been sent to town, and I would have shared the fate of those who stayed in the camp.

Now – a few words about the camp itself. It was neither Auschwitz nor Dachau. There were no crematorium furnaces in the camp where they burned the dead. But the more 'discovered' Jews were brought to the camp, the more frequently they were slaughtered in groups of fifty to a hundred people each. Mostly these were women, children and old people. Men were left as the workforce. They were used at the most difficult jobs, and only a few in their area of expertise. They used to wake us up at four o'clock in the morning and give us breakfast – a mug of boiling water and a piece of bread. Then they would put us into a column and take us out to the town. There we worked until 6–7 p.m. and again we were walked back to the camp. There we received a bowl of soup, a piece of bread and a mug of hot water. After this lunch and dinner combined, we were locked in at the barrack for the night. At night the policemen – most often these were Dzyuba and Samborsky – came into the barrack and began beating people with rifle butts, sticks and rubber truncheons. Especially violent were their attacks on women and children. Sometimes they beat them till the victims dropped dead.

Some time around autumn, the Germans selected about ten Jews who had a construction background or professions in construction, including my father and me, and transferred us to the village of Semyonovka to build a house for an SS officer named Schweitzer. We were accommodated in a shed, and there was no guard. But we were warned that if somebody escaped, 100 Jews would be shot in the camp. This warning was more effective than any security. We rang in the New Year of 1943 in Semyonovka. I remember that the winter that year was very harsh. At nights, the water in our shed would freeze.

When the work was finished, the majority of the prisoners were taken away. Another three workers and I were left in Semyonovka. We prepared ourselves for the worst. They came after us, telling us to put our belongings on a sleigh, along with our shovels and spades, and told us to sit on the sleigh too. At the entrance to the town, near the town prison, the sleigh stopped. We were examined, ordered to pick up our possessions and were put into the third yard of the prison, in a long one-storey building.

There were many people in the cell. I was surrounded; people kept asking me where I was from, where they had caught me, as well as dozens of other questions. I didn't have the time to answer them all. And suddenly I saw my father. That was such a meeting! My father looked at me and tears were rolling down his face. He could not say a word. He looked at me and kept crying. And I couldn't think clearly at all. It seemed that they had taken us to be killed, but instead they had brought us into the prison. All this was very shocking to me, and I fainted.

Another digression from my narrative: my memory brings up more episodes and each of them could be enough to turn into a separate story or even a novel. I shall not tell you now about my escapes to the town. During the camp period of my life, when I was taken to work in Berdychev, I sometimes managed to get out in search of food. Each of these escapes could have cost me not only my life but also that of all the men who worked with me. I could not have afforded to be caught in the centre of the town because this meant death. But hunger pushed me to do dangerous things. Frequently I was saved by my basic instincts, developed during the months of the occupation. The fact that my knowledge of the town geography was excellent helped me a lot too. A potato or a carrot, or sometimes a couple of biscuits, were my reward for the risk. The latter was extreme luck. These things would dull the feeling of hunger for some time. But my escapes did not always go smoothly. There were times when I saw a policeman and then my quick running and good knowledge of the town helped.

In the Jewish prayer book *Siddur Tehillat Hashem*, there is a prayer – six things which you recall daily:

> Remember those events that you saw with your own eyes. And may they not be erased from your heart for as long as you

live; and tell your sons, and sons of your sons of what you saw on the day when you stood in the presence of G-d, your Lord, at the *chorev.*

This is what the prayer says. I believe in what is said, and that only historical memory and the knowledge of the past may help prevent new tragedies for my people. We have to remember this and I keep saying it over and over again. Because, otherwise, on that day, when our sons, our grandsons or ourselves forget those tragic years, that day will become the beginning of a new Jewish tragedy. Because, as it is said, 'Those who do not remember the past are condemned to relive it.'

I keep recalling my past and relive all of it again. And I have an endless feeling of guilt as regards those who went to the gas chambers or were shot. By remembering them, I may at least in part justify my miraculous salvation.

Of course it is by all means easier to forget. Why would I burden my soul with such a heavy load? Life is so short and there are so many daily petty troubles in this life.

But we must remember it all for the sake of our children and our grandchildren. I really hope that for the sake of my grandchildren, my sons do not lose the memory of those who died a terrible death at the hands of Fascist murderers on a daily basis. This is Esther, my mother, Hannah, my grandmother, and Firochka, my sister. They were killed on 15 September 41. Remember this date. It marked the first mass killing of Jews in Europe.

I can't believe that such words as 'debt' and 'memory' can have lost their meaning. Yet, even if not for the sake of the debt and memory, then for the sake of self-preservation we must remember and never forget what the fascists did to us.

Fortunately, there are people who understand the meaning of 'historical truth'. I'm for ver grateful to those who established, and work at, Yad Vashem; I'm in awe of Claude Lanzmann, who created a unique film awakening our memories.[2]

We were put into two cells. The doors of the cells faced a single hallway with a metal-sheathed door. The windows of our cell faced the wall that fenced the prison. The wall was fairly high and at the top of it there were layers of barbed wire. There was a deep trench at the base of the wall. All this made any ideas of escape almost impossible. I would like to say a few words about those who were imprisoned there. My memory has saved the surnames of a few people: Krashenny, a wonderful woodwork specialist in red wood; and Shklyar, a shoemaker. I remember Chaim Satanovsky, who was

short and thin, always optimistic, even in the scariest of times; Yasha
Roitman, from Yakushpol, a mechanic 'with golden hands', as people said. We were friends with him.

I would like to note that I didn't know exact dates or seasons. The
time was measured in days and nights and seasons as cold and hot.
Thus I know that, closer to spring, the majority of us were shot. One
day Ziebert, the prison director himself, entered our cells. He came
in with two of his assistants. Using a whip, from which he was
never parted, he began to personally move people from one cell into
the other. I was moved a few times from one cell to the other and
back. I was with my father, and then in the other cell where mostly
intelligentsia were gathered. But eventually he put me into the cell
where the professionals and workers were, including my father. We
were locked in. And we heard that people from the other cell were
taken out, and some time later we heard machine-gun shots. When,
the following day, our cell was opened we saw that the other was
empty. They were all shot dead in the prison yard, not far from our
cell.

Following this development our schedule changed. They began
taking us out to work. I started working with a blacksmith, at first as
an assistant and then as a mechanic. Sometimes I received 'private
orders' – to fix a bicycle or a lock. The Germans paid with a slice of
bread, real bread! This relieved my constant hunger, which tortured
me day and night. From the blacksmith's I was transferred to the
construction of an addition to the prison building, and from there as
a stoker in a prison bath, and then again back to the blacksmith',
where I worked till the end. The 'support staff' of the prison included policemen who mostly were patrolling, guarding and escorting
us. They would not interact with us a lot, yet sometimes the
Germans would leave for two to three days, probably for killing
squad expeditions, and then the police would brutally abuse us
while they were the bosses of the prison. They would beat and torture us.

It is not accurate to say that the Germans were killing Jews only.
Yes, in the first days of the occupation, the Germans were killing
Jews only. When there were no more Jews, they began killing prisoners of war, followed by non-Jews. Naturally, this caused mass
disruptions. At this point the Germans realized that they had made
a tactical mistake by killing all Jews instantly. They began arresting
Jews who had survived the first killings and putting them into one
place and before each mass murder of the local population they
would shoot five to ten Jews. The whole town knew about it: 'Jews
were killed again.' Hundreds and thousands of people of other
nationalities – Ukrainians, Russians and Poles – were 'quietly' killed

against this backdrop. Later this 'trick' stopped being a secret and everybody knew that if today the news of Jews being killed made the rounds, tomorrow it would be the turn of the Ukrainians.

I frequently speak about the police brutality. It may lead to the impression that the Germans treated us better. This is absolutely wrong. The Germans were just as brutal as, if not worse than the police, but they had their own system. The system meant that if you were put out to work, at that time most likely you would not be beaten, while the police beat us any time and anywhere: day, night, at work, after work.

The killings became more frequent with the onset of the typhoid epidemics in the prison. Each prisoner who was ill, or was suspected of being ill, was shot. I fell ill with typhus too. And I didn't die only because other prisoners did everything possible and impossible so that the Germans wouldn't know I was ill. Half conscious, I was taken to work; people kept watching so that nobody would catch me sitting or lying down at work. And yet somehow the Germans knew there were ill people in the cell. In the evening, after work, chief Ziebert entered the cell. He looked intently into the faces of the people and picked some six people who seemed to be ill. They were taken away immediately and we realized we would never see them again.

They would shoot not only gravely ill. I mentioned a wonderful man named Yasha Roitman who was among us. Unfortunately he developed an abscess on his shin. He bandaged it with a rag and asked the convoy policeman to let him stay in the cell as he had problems with walking. The policeman left him behind but obviously reported this. Yasha was taken out in the middle of the day. I shall never forget seeing him being taken away, walking past our smithy. He was dressed only in a shirt, barefoot. Passing by the blacksmith's doors, and as if guessing that we were watching him, he shouted in Yiddish, 'Stay alive, Jews, and don't forget me; remember, remember me … '

He said 'remember' a few times … I shall remember, Yasha, may you rest in peace, our dear friend and martyr, one of millions of genocide victims. I am writing this now, and tears fill up my eyes. I keep reliving those horrible minutes all over again.

The Germans began building a crematorium in the administrative part of the prison yard. Every day, from morning till night, hundreds of prisoners dug a big pit for the foundations of a future furnace. But Ziebert and Knop never managed to measure up to their colleagues in Auschwitz. It was 1943, and they had little time left.

At first, rumours circulated about the defeat of the Germans in one direction or another. Oh goodness! I cannot describe how strongly we wanted to believe that our army was winning and that the Germans were defeated. And finally we received the first 'news' from ours. One night, Berdychev was bombed by the Soviets. But they had so few bombs. Each of us dreamt of hundreds, thousands of bombs raining down on to the heads of the Germans. Nobody considered that the bombs did not discriminate between the Germans and non-Germans.

In the days left before their retreat, the Fascist murderers wanted, and tried, to kill as many people as possible. But it was then when our desire to survive was strongest. Earlier, during the endless months of occupation, amid daily killings, beatings and torture, hard labour and unbearable starvation, the instinct for life was the only driving force. Now we sensed it and wanted to survive – especially when seeing columns of police refugees with their families moving on to the west. And finally, a happy moment arrived! We saw endless columns of retreating German divisions following the police refugees. They were dirty, angry and thin. Where had their customary glamour gone, along with their white, wide smiles? They were nervous and scared, scattering the moment a plane was seen in the sky.

I remember the following episode. I was sent to the prison yard to do something and, at that time, a German officer from among those in the retreating columns entered the yard and began asking me where our supervisors were, as well as other questions. I told him. He looked carefully at me and asked me what I, a German, was doing in the prison. I told him I was Jewish.

'You have been extremely lucky to survive until now. Who let you go around alive? But we still have time to correct this mistake.' Thus, an officer, and a grown-up man told me, a teenager, without any viciousness and in a very friendly manner as if comforting me, that there was time left to correct this mistake and shoot me.

But hope lingered on in our hearts. My father believed in particular that God would bring us salvation. He talked about this continually. I began feeling the same and shared my father's faith.

The crowds of those fleeing grew thicker and more impressive. Finally the prison administration began preparing to flee too. They began burning papers, preparing boxes, and packing up all the loot.

One day in November 1943 we were taken out to work as always. But there was no work on that day. They seemed to have forgotten about us. The Germans were running around the prison yard, loading lorries, cars and carts; and closer to the evening an impressive column pulled out of the prison gates and left for the west. We stayed together and wondered what would happen to us next. It was then that two lorries and four cars pulled into the prison yard. They turned out to be an SS killing squad who had come to liquidate the prisoners. No matter that it was late in the evening; they began doing their job immediately: they took the prisoners out and shot them in the administrative part of the yard, in the huge pit dug out for the foundation of the crematorium. People were taken out in groups of fifteen or twenty prisoners each, every ten to fifteen minutes. And we were in the smithy waiting for our turn – though not just waiting but intently looking for a possible way to escape.

The evening came, and then it got dark. The machine-guns stopped shooting; the Germans most likely decided to postpone the liquidation until the following day. One of the Germans escorted us back to the cell, and locked us in. We were fervently looking for a way out, clearly realizing that otherwise we would be killed the following day. The most fantastic ideas were suggested.

And eventually we found the way out. The outside door was locked with a big latch, and a bolt fixing this lock was on our side. Taking advantage of the chance that this night there was no guard watching us closely, we unscrewed the bolt and pushed it out and the latch fell down. When the door opened, everybody rushed outside. There was a crowd and a lot of pushing when we tried to get out but it all happened in complete silence. Finally we were outside in the yard, running along the walls not knowing what to do next.

One man noticed that on the roof of the outhouse standing next to the wall there was either a ladder or a board that was long enough to reach the top of the fence. It turned out to be a door taken off the outhouse. It successfully served us as a ladder with the help of which we managed to climb the prison wall. Without any second thought we jumped down from this tall wall into the gutter. My father failed to jump well, sprained his ankle, and could not walk. But then we didn't walk but crawled out of the prison area. We crawled by the pit containing those who had been shot and I remember the screams of the wounded people who were still alive in that pit.

These screams hurried us up. We crawled, only guessing the direction towards the exit . Finally we reached the wire fence. We dug passages under the wire with our hands and set ourselves free. It was imperative to leave this area as soon as possible and to get as far as possible but my father could not move: his injured leg hurt badly. Unfortunately, I don't remember the surnames of the two other inmates who helped me to pull my father to the nearest forest. In the morning we saw that the few trees, which we had mistaken at night for the forest, could not cover us. Having made crutches from the tree branches with the help of which my father could move, we went on, heading anywhere in order not to stay in this 'forest' any longer. Thus we reached the farmstead of Alexandry.

A kind woman gave us shelter. Without asking us who we were, she gave us food, bandaged my father's leg, and put us down to sleep. It was the first night of being free – or of almost being free! (We still were in occupied territory and could not feel ourselves to be free.)

A few days later we started towards the east. We picked distant country roads and frequently went along forest pathways. We spent nights, and had food, in villages. The attitude towards us now was completely different compared to 1941.

For more safety we split into smaller groups. One evening we left the village of Skakovka, but having walked about five kilometres towards Chervonoye we got into a zone of heavy fire. Our artillery was firing as well as German sextuple mortars. It seemed that the earth and sky had changed their places. We crawled into a ravine and then ran forward, crying, to get out of the firing zone as quickly as possible.

When leaving the ravine, we were stopped by a patrol soldier. 'Halt, who is there?'

It was said in Russian. It is difficult, or rather impossible, to describe how we felt when we realized that we had been stopped by our Russian, Soviet soldier! I hugged him, kissing the soldier's sweaty and smoky coat, my tears flowing from my eyes; I could not speak. The soldier, who was scared by all this emotion,tried hard to push me, a crazy teenager, away from himself. He finally succeeded, but with much difficulty.

A feeling of constant, unbelievably good, happiness followed this. We spent some time in the military unit into whose territory we had entered. Then, together with this unit, we retreated under the temporary advance of the Germans. We got into Kiev.

When Berdychev was liberated in January 1944 we returned to our hometown.

NOTE

1. Recorded by S. Yelissavetsky, in *The Berdychev Tragedy: A Documentary Narrative* (Kiev, 1991), pp. 90–110.
2. *Shoah*, 1985.

86. Only some twenty people survived, including my brother, my sister, and me

Boris Yavorsky (b. 1927)

My father was a blacksmith and my mother was a tailor. I was the oldest child in the family. Beside me, my parents had a daughter named Itka (born 1928), and a son named Burekh (born1933). My grandma, Kheiva, my father's mother, lived with us too. We all lived in Zhornishche before the war.

When the war began, my father was mobilized to the army in late June 1941 (he was killed in 1943). At that time my mother was expecting a baby and in December 1941 she gave birth to a boy named Petya. Of course she couldn't go anywhere in her condition. Moreover, many Jews from Vinnitsa had come over to Zhornishche hoping that it would be much safer in a village: having a vegetable lot, one could count on having some food, and it was unlikely that a village would be bombed.

On 16 July 1941 the Germans occupied our village. Gordienko became the village headman, and Kosovenko was the chairman of the village council. After the war Gordienko was put on a trial and sentenced to fifteen years in prison, while partisans executed Kosovenko in February 1943. There were two policemen in the village (Lavrov was one of the two).

A month later a *Sonderkommando* arrived in the village. They caught thirteen Jewish residents including a thirteen-year-old boy (a refugee from Vinnitsa) and shot them all outside the village.

In September the Germans took all the Jews to the centre of our *shtetl* and established a ghetto there. All ghetto prisoners, including young children, were ordered to wear armbands with the Star of David (a blue star against a white background). The policemen, the village headman and the chairman of the council watched so that nobody could leave the ghetto territory. Daily a certain number of people were marched to work. The group in which I had to work was gathering the harvest and digging the soil with shovels for winter corn.

When my mother gave birth to a boy she insisted that, together with my younger brother, I went to our relatives in Ilyintzy: that is, scape from the ghetto. I was against it for a long time but had to listen to her. In January, together with my brother, I secretly left the ghetto and came to Ilyintzy to my mother's sister, who had three children. At that time there was a ghetto in Ilyintzy too. So from one ghetto we moved to another. I would go to work together with her two older sons. Sometimes, with her older son, Luzya Lekhtser, I would go to villages and repair shoes there just to get some food for the big family. (When my father was taken to the front and I became the major provider, a relative of mine had taught me how to repair shoes.)

During one such trip to the village of Varvarovka, a policeman caught Luzya and shot him near the village. This happened in April 1942.

About 500 people lived in the ghetto in Ilyintzy. Daily two or three hundred people were marched to work (mostly women and teenagers). In March they began taking a certain number of prisoners to dig pits near Ilyintzy. Every time they would pick five to ten people and kill them. On 10 April, after Luzya was shot, I took my brother and returned to Zhornishche.

We lived in the Zhornishche ghetto until 27 May 1942, when at night a big group of the armed Germans surrounded our village and all the ghetto residents were taken eight kilometres to Ilyintzy, where the pits had been dug. Everybody was killed there.

There were about 200 or 300 people in the ghetto, including local people and refugees from Vinnitsa. Only some twenty people survived, including my brother, my sister, and myself.

When the Germans surrounded our village we went up into the attic. The Germans took away our mother, grandma and our baby brother, thinking that there were no more people in the house. I was fifteen years old then, my sister thirteen, and my brother eight.

Beside us, the Govberg family of seven people were saved, and the Ulanovsky couple, but I don't remember the names of the rest.

When all the ghetto residents were taken away, we ran down to the village and went to the Vershigora family. They were our parents' friends. The woman's name was Pustynya, and she had a daughter named Paraska and a son named Andrey. Grandma Pustynya and her son died, and Paraska now lives in Zhornishche, Ilyintzy district.

I worked in villages, repairing shoes together with Andrey or my brother, and people with God in their hearts gave us food and warmed us. My sister took out cows to pasture and looked after babies. And when there was no work, we lived in the Vershigora house or in any other abandoned houses.

3: The following table shows the distribution of Jewish victims per month and per ion (in thousands) in 1943.*

on	I	II	III	IV	V	VI	VII	VIII	IX	X	XI	XII	Total
	10	4	5	11	13	26.5	2.3	1.5		2.5	4.5	0.2	80.5
itsa	1	0.5	1.3		0.7				0.1			0.8	4.4
o-Frankovsk	0.5	2.5				3.5	0.6	1.5					8.6
opol		2.5	1	11	3.5	22	5.5	0.4	0.1	0.1	0.3		46.4
y		0.5									0.5		
omir								0.1					
rkassy													
yn												1.5	1.5
essa										0.1	0.1		0.2
gions	11.5	10		7.3	22.5	17.2	52	3.5	3.5	0.2	2.7	4.9	2.5 143

* In 1943 Ukraine lost 143,000 Jews, in addition to around 145,000–150,000 victims unaccounted for. Approximately 10,000 were taken out of the Ukraine. Taken from A. I. Kruglov, *The Destruction of the Jewish Population of the Ukraine in 1941–44*, p. 93.

Wandering through villages we twice ended up in ghettos – once in Lipovtzy and the other time in Pechera – barely managing to escape from there. We spent some time there, about two to three weeks each, until we managed to escape.

Thus we lived until the village was liberated. After the liberation, we sold our family house and moved to Ilyintzy.

After the war, using the money raised by the Jewish community, a memorial monument was set up, dedicated to the victims of Fascism 1941–45.

Appendix

SUMMARIES

1. 1941: In the period of 22 June 1941–31 December 1941, that is, during 193 days of the occupation, the Germans and their collaborators killed over 450,000 Jews. Following is the distribution of victims per month and per region (in thousands).*

Region	June	July	August	September	October	November	December	Total
Lvov	> 1	11	> 0.2	≅ 1	0.47	2	3	18.7
Volyn	0.4	1.8	1.6	1.5	0.6			≅ 6
Rovno	0.5	0.8	3	2.5		> 15		22
Chernovtsy	0.1	> 8	0.5			1.7		10.5
Ternopol		≅ 9	0.15	0.5	1.5	0.6	1	12.5
Zhitomir		≅ 2	≅ 9	26.5	> 4.5	> 3		45
Khmelnitzky		1.8	32.5	1		0.6		35.2
Odessa		≅ 1	2.2	3.5	16	3	29	54.7
Vinnitsa		0.8	2.5	16	7	10	13	49.3
Ivano-Frankovsk		0.3	> 1		20	0.5	≅ 5.5	27.3
Kiev			1.5	39.5	7	> 1		49
Nikolaev			> 1	≅ 13		0.1		14
Cherkassy			0.5	3	> 6	1		10.5
Kirovograd			0.5	> 5	0.1	0.3		5.9
Kherson			0.25	> 13	> 2.5			16
Dniepropetrovsk			0.5	1	15.5	0.3	≅ 4	21.3
Poltava				0.5	5	4.5		10
Donetsk					≅ 9	0.3	1.5	10.8
Zaporozhye					≅ 2.2	1		3.2
Chernigov					0.53	0.7		1.3
Kharkov					0.3	0.1	1	1.4
Sumy						≅ 2		2
Crimea						1.3	22	23.3
23 regions	2	> 36	> 56	> 127	≅ 100	>50	80	450

* Taken from A. I. Kruglov, *The Destruction of the Jewish Population of the Ukraine in 1941–44: A Chronicle of Events* (Mogilev-Podolsky, 1997), p. 41.

Appendix

2. 1942: The death toll in the Ukraine, in 1942*

Region	I	II	III	IV	V	VI	VII	VIII	IX
Odessa	14.5	9	6	0.5		1.2			1
Vinnitsa	22	10	5	10	8.3	7		7	1.5
Kharkov	9.5	0.1	0.1			0.1			
Nikolaev	3.2		2.4						
Crimea	2.7	0.3	0.7	0.2	0.1	0.1	2.5		
Khmelnitzky	1			2	4	25	3.8	5	11	;
Zhitomir	0.6	0.2		0.5	2	0.2	0.7		
Donetsk	0.6	1.8	0.2	3.5					
Kirovograd	0.5	2.3	0.3		0.6				0.1
Lvov	0.5		13		2.2	3	8.5	68	24	11.!
Dniepropetrovsk	0.4		1		3.5		2		
Poltava	0.4			1.5	0.5				
Ivano-Frankovsk	0.4		4.5	15	7.5	2		4	25	10
Zaporozhye	0.6	1	3.7						
Cherkassy		0.5	0.1	2		1.5	1.4		
Chernigov	0.1				1.3				
Sumy		0.5							
Kherson		0.5	0.3						
Ternopol			0.7	1		1		26	17	12
Kiev	0.1	0.1	0.5						
Rovno				12			5	28	11	20
Volyn						11	7	39	30	4
Lugansk							0.2		0.5	1
23 regions	57.1	26.3	38.5	36.1	43.5	52	29.5	17.7	12.1	69.5	49.

* In 1942 in the Ukraine at least 726,000 Jews are known to have been killed, which there are around 750,000 victims who are unaccounted for. Out of t were taken out of the Ukraine and killed in gas chambers in the Belzec (Poland), including: 13,000 in March; 6,000 in April; 5,000 in June; 8,500 in in August; 54,000 in September; 29,000 in October; 25,000 in November; December.

Taken from A. I. Kruglov, *The Destruction of the Jewish Population of the Ukraine* p. 9.

390

3. 19
re

Regi

Lvo
Vin
Ivar
Ter
Sur
Zh
Ch
Vo
Oc
9 r

*

Appendix

4. 1941–44: The following table shows the distribution of Jewish victims in 1941–44 per year and per region.*

Region	1941	1942	1943	1944	Total
Lvov	18.7	164	80.5	3.5	266.5
Ternopol	12.5	66.7	46.4	0.5	126
Ivano-Frankovsk	27.3	73.5	8.6	0.2	109.5
Volyn	6	95	1.5		102.5
Rovno	22	76			98
Vinnitsa	49.3	76	4.4	0.4	130
Khmelnitsky	35.2	70.8	0.5		106.5
Odessa	54.7	32.2	0.2	0.4	87.5
Chernovtsy	10.5				
Zhitomir	45	4.2	0.6		49.8
Kiev	49	0.8			49.8
Nikolaev	14	5.6			19.6
Kherson	16	0.8			16.8
Cherkassy	10.5	6	0.5		17
Kirovograd	5.9	3.8			9.7
Dniepropetrovsk	21.3	7			28.3
Poltava	10	2.4			12.4
Donetsk	10.8	6			16.8
Zaporozhye	3.5	5.3			8.8
Chernigov	1.3	1.4			2.7
Kharkov	1.4	9.6			11
Sumy	2	0.5	0.5		3
Crimea	23.3	6.5			29.8
Lugansk		2.5			2.5
Subcarpathia				95	95
25 regions	450	716.5	143	100	Over 1,400

* Thus, at least 1,400,000 Jews were murdered in the Ukraine. With the addition of unaccounted-for victims, this comes to around 1.5 million Jews. The given number does not include Jews who died at the front and in POW camps, as well as Jews who were killed on Russian territory (primarily, the Northern Caucasus), to where they had been evacuated in 1941 and where they were taken over by the Germans in 1942. Considering all this, the total number of murdered Jews could be estimated at 1.6 million people. Taken from A. I. Kruglov, *The Destruction of the Jewish Population of the Ukraine in 1941–44*, p. 96.

5. 1944.*

By the beginning of 1944, the Jews were still primarily within the Romanian zone of the occupied area of the Ukraine ('Transnistria', Chernovtsy), as well as in the Subcarpathian Ukraine, which was then a part of Hungary. There were 65,000–70,000 Jews in 'Transnistria', mostly deported from other areas; 15,000 in Chernovtsy, and about 100,000 in the Subcarpathian Ukraine. In all, 405,000 Jews were under German government (about 1,500 in each of the camps in Drogobych and Borislav, a few hundreds each in Lvov, Tolstoye and the surrounding area of the Ternopol region, and a few dozens in Ivano-Frankovsk). In March, when the Germans took over Hungary, the Jews from the Subcarpathian regions came under their rule.

By the beginning of 1944 a total of 185,000–190,000 Jews were still living in the Ukraine.

In January–July 1944, approximately 1,300 Jews were killed and over 100,000 were deported to the concentration camps in Poland.

* Taken from A. I. Kruglov, *The Destruction of the Jewish Population of the Ukraine in 1941–44.* pp. 94–5.

Bibliography

Agmon, P., *Preserving the Memory. Some Peculiarities of Audio and Video Recordings of the Shoah Testimonies in the Ukraine*, a special edition of *The Information Bulletin of the Beit Lohamei haGhettaot – the Yizchak Katznelson Ghetto Fighters' House* (Kiev, 1996).

Agmon, P. and Zabarko, B., 'Trial by Holocaust', *Modern Times* (1996), Vol. 2.

Altman, I. *The Destiny of the Black Book: An Unknown Black Book: Testimonies of the Witnesses to the* Shoah *of the Soviet Jews (1941–1944)* (Jerusalem, Moscow, 1993.)

Arad, Y., *The Holocaust: Tragedy of the European Jewry (1933-1945): An Anthology of Articles* (Jerusalem, Yad Vashem, 1990).

——, (ed.), *The Destruction of the Soviet Jews in the Years of the German Occupation (1941–1944): A Collection of Documents and Materials* (Jerusalem: Yad Vashem, 1991).

Babi Yar: The Fiftieth Anniversary of the Tragedy on 29 September 1941 (Jerusalem The Aliyah Library, 1991).

Bauch, E. (ed.), *Babi Yar* (Bat-Yam: The Association of Communities of Immigrants from the USSR, 1981).

Budnik, D. and Kaper, Y., *Nothing Has Been Forgotten: Jewish Lives in Kiev* (Constanz, 1993).

Concise Jewish Encyclopaedia, Vols 1–8 (Jerusalem: Keter, 1976–96).

Deko, O. Keloishin, *The Story of the Shepetovka Ghetto* (Kiev, 1995).

Gefter, M., *The Echo of the Holocaust and the Russian Jewish Question* (Moscow, 1995).

Gorovsky, F. Ya., Khonigsman, Ya. S., Naiman, A. Ya. *et al.*, *The Jews of the Ukraine: A Brief History* Vol. 2 (Kiev, 1995).

Goshkis, D., *A Wound That Didn't Heal* (Slavuta, 1996).

Gritsak, Y., 'The Participation of the Ukrainians in Anti-Jewish Action During World War 2' (Lvov, 1996), Vol. 8.

Grossman, V., *The Ukraine without Jews: On Jewish Themes. Selected Works in Two Volumes* (Jerusalem: Aliyah Library, 1990).

Grossman V. and Erenburg, I. (eds), *The Black Book: On the Murderous Commonplace Slaughter of Jews by the German Occupiers in the Territories of the Soviet Union and in the Death Camps of Poland During the War, 1941–1945* (Jerusalem, 1980; Vilius, 1993).

The Group of Authors, Lyakhovitsky, Yu. (ed. in chief), *The Holocaust, The 'Jewish Question' and Modern-Day Ukrainian Society* (Kharkov, 1996).

Gutman, I. and Schatzker, Kh., *The Holocaust and Its Meaning* (Jerusalem: Aliyah Library, 1990).

In the Flame of the Shoah in the Ukraine: Testimonies of the Jewish Ghetto and Camp Prisoners and Members of the Partisan Movement (Tel Aviv/Kiev: Beit Lohamei haGhettaot, 1998).

Jewish Genocide in the Ukraine During the Occupation as Described in German Documentaries, 1941–1944 (Kharkov, 1995)

Khonigsman, Ya., *The Shoah of the Lvov Jewry* (Lvov, 1993).

——, *The Shoah of the Western Ukrainian Jewry: Eastern Galicia, Western Volyn, Bukovina, and Subcarpathia in 1933–1945* (Lvov, 1998).

Koval, M., 'The Nazi Genocide of the Jews and the Ukrainian Population (1941–1944)', *The Ukrainian Historical Journal* (1992), Vol. 2.

Kovba, Z., *Humanity in the Infernal Abyss: The Behaviour of the Local Population of*

Eastern Galitchina in the Years of the 'Final Solution' (Kiev, 1998).

Kruglov, A. I., *The Destruction of the Jewish Population in the Vinnitsa Region in 1941–1944* (Mogilev-Podolsky, 1997).

———, *The Destruction of the Jewish Population of the Ukraine in 1941–1944: A Chronicle of Events* (Mogilev-Podolsky, 1997).

Kuznetsov, A., *Babi Yar* (Kiev, 1990).

Lebedeva, V. P. and Sokolsky, P. P. (eds), *Tell Me, Drobitzky Yar: Essays, Memoirs., Documents, Poems* (Kharkov, 1991).

Levitas, F., *Ukrainian Jewry During the Years of World War II* (Kiev, 1997).

Levitas, I. M., *Heroes and Victims. Facts from the History of the Jewish People* (Kiev, 1997).

———, (ed.), *The Book of Memories: Babi Yar* (Kiev, 1999).

Lyakhovitsky, Yu., *The Disgraced Mezuzah (A Book of the Drobitzky Yar): Testimonies, Facts, and Documents about the Nazi Genocide of the Jewish Population of Kharkov During the Occupation, 1941–1942* (Kharkov, 1991).

———, *The Holocaust Survivors: Survivors, Saviours, Collaborators: Testimonies, Facts, and Documents* (Kharkov, 1996).

———, *The Yellow Book: Testimonies, Facts and Documents about the Nazi Genocide of the Jewish Population of Kharkov During the Occupation, 1941–1943* (Kharkov, 1994).

People Remain Human: Testimonies of the Prisoners of the German Ghettos and Camps. Vols 1–5 (Chernovtsy, 1991–96).

Podolsky, A., 'The Nazi Genocide Against the Ukrainian Jewry (1941–1944)'. The Summary of the Thesis for the Candidate of Historical Sciences Degree. Kiev, 1996.

Polishchuk, S., *The Baptismal on the Square: Notes of a Lawyer* (Odessa, 1995).

Popovich, M. 'The Jewish Genocide in the Ukraine', *Philosophical and Sociological Thought* (1994), Vols 5–6.

Schlaen, A., *Babi Yar* (Kiev, 1996).

Schulmeister, Yu., *Hitlerism in Jewish History* (Kiev, 1990).

Starodinsky, D., *The Odessa Ghetto: Testimonies* (Odessa, 1991).

Sushon, L., *Transnistria: Jews in the Inferno. The Black Book of the Holocaust in Northern Prichernomorye (Based on Memoirs and Documents)* (Odessa, 1998).

Suslensky, Ya., *True Heroes* (Kiev, 1993).

'The Lessons of the Holocaust and Modern-Day Russia. The Russian Library of the Holocaust: Materials the Round Table Discussion', International Symposium, Moscow, 6–8 April 1994, Moscow, 1995.

The Nazi Occupation of the Ukraine: A Collection of Documents and Materials (Kiev, 1963).

The Nuremberg Trial: A Collection of Materials, 8 Vols (Moscow: 'Yuridicheskaya Literatura', 1987–90.

The Soviet Ukraine During the Great Patriotic War, 1941–1945, 3 Vols (Kiev, 1988).

The Vinnitsa Region: The Shoah and the Resistance of the Jewish Ghetto and Camp Prisoners, Their Participation in the Partisan Movement and Underground (Tel Aviv and Kiev: Beit Lohamei HaGhettaot,1994).

Vanukevich, A., *The Holocaust in Poltavshchina* (Poltava, 1999).

Weiss, A., 'The Attitude of Certain Groups in the Ukrainian Nationalist Movement Towards Jews during World War II', *Bulletin of the Jewish University in Moscow* (1995), Vol. 2.

Yelissavetsky S., *The Berdychev Tragedy: A Documentary Narrative* (Kiev, 1991).

———, *Half a Century of Oblivion: Jews in the Resistance and Partisan Movement in the Ukraine (1941–1944)* (Kiev, 1998).

Yones E., *The Lvov Jews in the Years of World War II and the Holocaust of European Jewry, (1939–1944)* (Moscow, 1999).

Zabarkow, B., 'The Holocaust in Life and on Screen: The Lessons of the Twentieth Century', *Vsesvit* (1995), Vols 8–9.